INTRODUCTION TO
EXPERT SYSTEMS
SECOND EDITION

INTERNATIONAL COMPUTER SCIENCE SERIES

Consulting editors   **A D McGettrick**   University of Strathclyde

                       J van Leeuwen   University of Utrecht

SELECTED TITLES IN THE SERIES

POP–11 Programming for Artificial Intelligence   *A M Burton and N R Shadbolt*

Clausal Form Logic: An Introduction to the Logic of Computer Reasoning
  T Richards

Software Engineering (3rd Edn)   *I Sommerville*

High-Level Languages and their Compilers   *D Watson*

Programming in Ada (3rd Edn)   *J G P Barnes*

Elements of Functional Programming   *C Reade*

Interactive Computer Graphics: Functional, Procedural and Device-Level
  Methods   *P Burger and D Gillies*

Software Development with Modula-2   *D Budgen*

Common Lisp Programming for Artificial Intelligence   *T Hasemer and
  J Domingue*

Program Derivation: The Development of Programs from Specifications
  R G Dromey

Program Design with Modula-2   *S Eisenbach and C Sadler*

Object-Oriented Programming with Simula   *B Kirkerud*

Parallel Processing: Principles and Practice   *E V Krishnamurthy*

Real Time Systems and Their Programming Languages   *A Burns and A Wellings*

Programming for Artificial Intelligence: Methods, Tools and Applications
  W Kreutzer and B J McKenzie

FORTRAN 77 Programming: with an introduction to the Fortran 90
  standard (2nd Edn) *T M R Ellis*

The Programming Process: an introduction using VDM and Pascal
  J T Latham, V J Bush and I D Cottam

Prolog Programming for Artificial Intelligence (2nd Edn)   *I Bratko*

Principles of Expert Systems   *P Lucas and L van der Gaag*

Logic for Computer Science   *S Reeves and M Clarke*

Computer Architecture   *M De Blasi*

INTRODUCTION TO

EXPERT SYSTEMS

SECOND EDITION

PETER JACKSON

McDonnell Douglas Research Laboratories
Saint Louis, Missouri

ADDISON-WESLEY
PUBLISHING
COMPANY

Wokingham, England · Reading, Massachusetts · Menlo Park, California
New York · Don Mills, Ontario · Amsterdam · Bonn
Sydney · Singapore · Tokyo · Madrid · San Juan

Cover designed by Crayon Design of Henley-on-Thames and printed by The Riverside Printing Co. (Reading) Ltd.
Typeset by Columns Design and Production Services Limited, Reading
Printed in Great Britain by Richard Clay Ltd, Bungay, Suffolk

First edition published 1986.
Reprinted 1986 and 1988 (twice)
Second edition published 1990

British Library Cataloguing in Publication Data
Jackson, Peter
  Introduction to expert systems. — 2nd ed. — (International
  computer science series).
  1. Expert systems
  I. Title   II. Series
  006.33

  ISBN 0–201–17578–9

Library of Congress Cataloging-in-Publication Data
Jackson, Peter
    Introduction to expert systems / Peter Jackson. — 2nd ed.
      p.   cm. — (International computer science series)
    Includes bibliographical references (p.).
    ISBN 0–201–17578–9
    1. Expert systems (Computer science)   I. Title.   II. Series.
QA76.76.E95J33   1990
006.3′3—dc20   90–318
                                                    CIP

Preface

Since the publication of the first edition of *Introduction to Expert Systems* in 1986, the number of radically new developments in the field of expert systems has not been large; rather there has been a period of consolidation in our understanding of what expert systems can and cannot be expected to do. Also, as more courses on expert systems have been designed and taught, it seems to me that the subject matter is rather more integrated with the rest of the artificial intelligence and computer science curriculum than it was when I began teaching in 1983. I have tried to follow this trend towards consolidation and integration in this edition by imposing more structure on the overall text. This has been done by splitting it into six parts, and by grouping material into chapters which treat theoretical and practical concerns rather than individual systems.

Improvements in the second edition

In this, the second edition of *Introduction to Expert Systems*, I have tried

- to expand the first edition, in order to make it more accessible to readers with no previous background in artificial intelligence;
- to cover more ground and get a good balance between theory and practice;
- to revise and update those sections where the treatment now seems thin or dated;
- to introduce new material, some of which deals with more advanced topics; and
- to provide more pedagogical material, such as examples and exercises.

Course organization

As a guide to the course organizer and the general reader, I include a diagram which summarizes the main dependencies between chapters. An arrow from one chapter number to another indicates that Chapter *n* presumes a reasonable amount of familiarity with the material in Chapter *m*. This simple representation does not, of course, preclude the existence of other, less crucial dependencies.

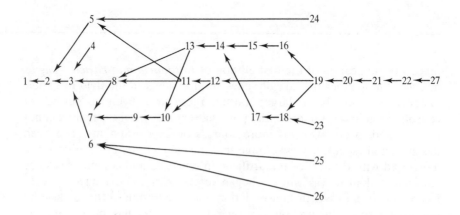

Figure 1 The interdependency of chapters

Structure and content

As a result of the changes listed, the book has now been divided into six parts to reflect the major subject areas covered.

Part I: Background in artificial intelligence

The contents of Part I are intended to ensure that the book is relatively self-contained. Although it is difficult to do justice to the artificial intelligence background in three chapters, the alternative is to do nothing at all. Students who have already covered this material should skip through Part I, reading only what looks new or interesting to them.

Chapter 1 serves to introduce some basic concepts of expert systems, such as *inference engine, knowledge base, knowledge elicitation*, and so on. However, it avoids technical detail as far as possible. It also attempts to avoid facile generalizations about expert systems technology: there are already enough of these in the popular literature.

Chapter 2 tries to give the inexperienced, but less than naïve, student a panoramic view of about thirty years of artificial intelligence research relevant to the theory and practice of expert systems. AI researchers are often berated for 'not delivering the goods', but I think that readers of this chapter ought to be impressed by what a small number of scientists have achieved over so short a period. Compared with the 2000 or so years that it took philosophers to improve on Aristotle's account of reasoning in terms of syllogisms, progress has been good.

Chapter 3 discusses two 'old faithful' expert systems, and argues that they can be seen as forming an essential link between the general-purpose problem solvers of the late 1960s and early 1970s and more modern approaches to complex problem solving. Many basic ideas about search, heuristics and constraints can be found in these early pieces of work; I wonder if we have learned all the lessons that they have to teach us. Readers who skip this chapter can always follow up on any back references from later chapters.

By the end of Part I, the reader should have a fairly good idea of the nature and scope of expert systems. The more theoretically inclined are encouraged to move on to Part II for some of the philosophical, formal and computational background. The more practically inclined can move directly to Part III, so long as they are willing either to skip over later sections involving mathematical logic and probability theory (especially in Chapters 11, 23, 24, 25 and 26), or to run occasional references back to this section.

Part II: Theoretical foundations

Part II covers a number of core topics in the theoretical foundations of expert systems: the interaction between *representation* and *control*, the basics of *formal logic*, and the problems and perils of reasoning under *uncertainty*. Students who have already done an introductory course in AI that touches on theoretical issues may wish to skip Chapter 4. Students with a strong mathematical background should feel entitled to skim Chapters 5 and 6, reading only that which is specific to AI applications. However, the issues raised in Chapter 4 are important; not least because a number of fundamental problems of representation and control in artificial intelligence remain unsolved. The trade off between expressive power and computational intractability is crucial, and it poses real challenges to expert system practitioners. Almost everything that we wish to do in AI can be shown to be computationally intractable in the general case. The question is how far programs can benefit from heuristics (generated by either man or machine) in providing acceptable solutions to hard problems. In recent years, researchers have been more scrupulous with respect to distinguishing the conditions under which various algorithms and heuristics can achieve results at moderate cost.

The background in logic and probability theory is really essential if expert systems practitioners are to avoid reinventing wheels (some of which may turn out not to be round). Formal systems do not address all the difficulties that one encounters in complex problem solving, but they do provide a basis for judging the correctness of less formal methods. Having a detailed understanding of the strengths and weaknesses of systems of logic and probability (as opposed to having opinions) is becoming an increasingly important prerequisite to doing good theoretical work in AI, and, in the long run, expert systems can only benefit from this increase in rigour.

Part III: Knowledge representation

I have noted that readers can skip Part II if they are impatient to get to the details of knowledge representation languages, such as production rules. In addition, some readers may wish to omit Chapter 7, either because they are already familiar with LISP, or because they are not interested in the programming side of AI.

Having to wait until Chapter 8 for a discussion of production rules may seem like a hardship (although they are covered to some degree in Chapter 3). However, some popular writers cover rule-based programming as if it had fallen from the heavens, with no regard to its mathematical origins, and with only the faintest inkling of its limitations. Chapter 8 takes a serious approach that emphasizes both the simplicity of the concept and the complexity of its realization. Similarly, associative nets, frames, and object-oriented programming are dealt with at a leisurely pace in Chapters 9 and 10, allowing a few highways and byways to be explored. The curious mixture of declarative and procedural knowledge found in some of these formalisms is very intriguing. We are still learning about the power and limitations of the object-oriented approach to implementing knowledge-based systems.

Chapter 11 is rather difficult because it deals with an area that is oriented more towards research than applications. I include it for completeness and because it is interesting. Readers who are not logicians and who skipped Chapter 5 should probably skip Chapter 11 too (although PROLOG programmers might wish to read it).

Comparing these different representation languages in Chapter 12 is hard, because they all do certain things well, and other things less well. It is a good exercise to take a simple problem and code it using different representation schemes, as recommended in one of the exercises. The results are usually illuminating and often surprising.

Part IV: Practical problem solving

The structure imposed on the chapters in this part emphasizes both the kinds of problem that are amenable to expert system solutions and the problem solving methods that need to be employed. In the first edition, the emphasis was more on knowledge representation schemes and the systems that exemplified them. In the early 1980s, expert systems were rather thinner on the ground that they are now, and the pros and cons of the different knowledge representation schemes was perhaps a hotter topic than it is today.

The new organization gives Part IV a more practical orientation than in the first edition, although the structure itself is theoretically motivated. The distinction between *classification* and *construction problems* seemed to be the best organizing principle for the comparison of the many different kinds of expert system that can now be found in the literature. This distinction appears to be very useful in explaining why certain representation schemes and control regimes work well when applied to some kinds of problem but not to others. However, I still look at a number of systems in a fair amount of detail. Some readers may have preferrd a shallower treatment of even more systems, but I feel quite strongly that (as in all forms of programming) it is detail that makes the difference between success and failure in expert systems applications, as well as between that which is interesting and that which is second rate. Too many accounts of actual expert systems resort to generalities that leave the reader wondering how the system really worked.

Part IV also places a far greater emphasis upon knowledge acquisition than did the first edition. In some cases, the work described is recent, and therefore the product of new research. However, in other cases, it is simply that the differentiation of problem-solving methods for classification and construction has clarified some of the knowledge acquisition issues. In particular, it now appears that automated knowledge elicitation should itself be knowledge based and that, in addition to knowledge of the domain of application, the elicitation program can benefit from knowledge the overall problem-solving method that the applications program will use. The implications of this insight for different kinds of problem-solving program are discussed in some detail in Chapters 15 and 18.

Part V: Software tools and architectures

This part of the book is intended as an expansion and update of the single chapter on *expert systems toolkits* in the first edition. The emphasis in Chapter 20 is on techniques and principles, rather than the details of current software packages. Such detailed information quickly becomes out of date, and software vendors can become quite petulant if you neglect to mention the latest features of their product. The new material focuses upon the practical aspects of using such tools: what kinds of facility they normally provide and how easy they are to use. In addition to discussing knowledge-engineering environments, there are extra chapters which discuss blackboard architectures and truth maintenance systems in some detail.

Another goal of Part V is to set the reader thinking about how theoretical insights into the organization and behaviour of expert systems might contribute towards the discovery and dissemination of methodologies for knowledge engineering. Ideally, such methodologies would maximize such practical desiderata as the productivity of programmers, the reliability of programs, the reusability of software modules, the ease of maintenance of expert systems, the ease with which they can be interfaced with other software, and so on. However, Chapter 21 provides evidence that many knowledge-engineering environments leave a good deal to be desired in these areas.

Chapter 22 suggests that some of the design issues raised by blackboard systems have methodological implications that impact upon AI programs in general. For example, it is useful to make a clear distinction between the problem solving *architecture*, the representational *framework* for solving for particular kinds of problem, and the *application* of the architecture to a particular problem by instantiating the framework. Chapter 23 describes a useful kind of adjunct to a knowledge based system, called a *truth maintenance system*, for keeping track of justifications in a dependency network.

Part VI: Advanced topics in expert systems

Part IV attempts to introduce the reader to some of the important research issues that will have an impact upon the expert systems of the future, and ends with a summary of the book and suggestions for further study. Rather than attempt panoramic surveys of these research areas, each chapter describes and discusses a small number of typical examples which are particularly relevant to expert systems applications. This selective approach may fail to cover the whole of the field, but it does ensure that readers see how the basic principles apply in particular case studies.

Chapter 24 covers a novel approach to fault finding, called *diagnosis from first principles*, which, unlike more heuristic approaches, uses a complete description of the device under diagnosis to generate minimal sets of faults that account for symptoms. Chapter 25 describes two mathematical approaches to *inexact reasoning* in hierarchical hypothesis spaces, and attempts to explain some of the criteria which have been put forward for comparing different methods for managing uncertainty. Chapter 26 provides a review of machine learning research, focusing on *induction*, that is, learning from examples. Much of the material in Chapter 24–26 may be too advanced for a short first course, and it is probably better to leave it out altogether rather than cover it in too much of a hurry.

Chapter 27 forms a summary of the whole book, picking out the dominant themes and providing pointers to the literature.

Acknowledgements

The publishers organized a substantial survey of users of the first edition to try to gauge what kind of revisions they would most like to see. I would like to thank everyone who took the trouble to respond. This feedback was extremely useful and I have attempted to incorporate very many of those suggestions. On the advice of such respondents I have also made a number of stylistic alterations, such as dropping words like 'baroque' and 'serendipitous', which caused some readers of the first edition lexical distress.

I hope that users of the first edition will not be disappointed by the second edition, and that teachers and students will enjoy reading it as much as I enjoyed researching and writing it.

Peter Jackson
St Louis,
January 1990

Contents

Part I

Background in Artificial Intelligence

1 What are Expert Systems?

Introduction

An *expert system* is a computer program that represents and reasons with knowledge of some specialist subject with a view to solving problems or giving advice.

Such a system may completely fulfil a function that normally requires human expertise, or it may play the role of an assistant to a human decision maker. The decision maker may be an expert in his or her own right, in which case the program may justify its existence by improving the decision maker's productivity. Alternatively, the human collaborator may be someone who is capable of attaining expert levels of performance given some technical assistance from the program.

Expert systems technology derives from the research discipline of *Artificial Intelligence* (AI): a branch of computer science concerned with the design and implementation of programs which are capable of emulating human cognitive skills such as problem solving, visual perception and language understanding. This technology has been successfully applied to a diverse range of domains, including organic chemistry, mineral exploration and internal medicine. Typical tasks for expert systems involve the interpretation of data (such as sonar signals), diagnosis of faults or diseases, structural analysis of complex objects (such as chemical compounds), configuration of complex objects (such as computer systems), and planning sequences of actions.

Although more conventional programs have been known to perform similar tasks in similar domains, I shall argue in the next section that expert systems are sufficiently different from such programs to form a distinct and identifiable class. There is no precise definition of an expert system that is guaranteed to satisfy everyone; hence the blandness of the definition given above. However, there are a number of features which are sufficiently important that an expert system should really exhibit all of them to some degree.

1.1   The characteristics of an expert system

An expert system can be distinguished from a more conventional applications program in that:

- It *simulates human reasoning* about a problem domain, rather than simulating the domain itself. This distinguishes expert systems from more familiar programs that involve mathematical modelling. This is not to say that the program is a faithful psychological model of the expert, merely that the focus is upon emulating an expert's problem-solving abilities; that is, performing the relevant tasks as well as, or better than, the expert.

- It performs reasoning over *representations of human knowledge*, in addition to doing numerical calculations or data retrieval. The knowledge in the program is normally expressed in some special-purpose language and kept separate from the code that performs the reasoning. These distinct program modules are referred to as the *knowledge base* and the *inference engine*, respectively.

- It solves problems by *heuristic or approximate methods* which, unlike algorithmic solutions, are not guaranteed to succeed. A heuristic is essentially a rule of thumb which encodes a piece of knowledge about how to solve problems in some domain. Such methods are approximate in the sense that they do not require perfect data and the solutions derived by the system may be proposed with varying degrees of certainty.

An expert system differs from other kinds of artificial intelligence program in that:

- It deals with subject matter of realistic complexity that normally requires a considerable amount of human expertise. Many AI programs are really research vehicles, and may therefore focus on abstract mathematical problems or simplified versions of real problems (sometimes called 'toy' problems) to gain insights or refine techniques. Expert systems, on the other hand, solve problems of genuine scientific or commercial interest.

- It must exhibit high performance in terms of speed and reliability in order to be a useful tool. AI research vehicles may not run very fast, and may well contain bugs: they are programs, not supported software. But an expert system must propose solutions in a reasonable time and be right most of the time – at least as often as a human expert.

- It must be capable of explaining and justifying solutions or recommendations to convince the user that its reasoning is in fact correct. Research programs are typically run only by their creators, or by other personnel in similar laboratories. An expert system will be run by a wider range of users, and should therefore be designed in such a way that its workings are rather more transparent.

The term *knowledge-based system* is sometimes used as a synonym for 'expert system' although, strictly speaking, the former is more general. A knowledge-based system is any system which performs a task by applying rules of thumb to a symbolic representation of knowledge, instead of employing more algorithmic or statistical methods. Thus a program capable of conversing about the weather would be a knowledge-based system even if that program did not embody any expertise in meteorology, but an expert system in the domain of meteorology ought to be able to provide us with weather forecasts.

In summary, expert systems encode the domain-dependent knowledge of everyday practitioners in some field, and use this knowledge to solve problems, instead of using comparatively domain-independent methods derived from computer science or mathematics. The process of constructing an expert system is often called *knowledge engineering*, and is considered to be 'applied artificial intelligence' (Feigenbaum, 1977). We shall develop the distinction between the knowledge engineering approach and more conventional computer sciences approaches to problem solving in Chapters 2 and 3.

1.2 Overview of the text

Part I is intended to introduce some basic concepts in expert systems. Chapter 2 contains a brief survey of those developments in artificial intelligence which created the intellectual climate in which expert systems research was conceived and conducted. Chapter 3 is also introductory in nature, in that it describes two early expert systems and explains why they were built that way and how they work.

Part II presents an introduction to some theoretical issues of *knowledge representation*: the rendering of human knowledge in a machine-manipulable form. It provides a general overview, which relates representational issues to issues in automated reasoning and general problem solving. Chapter 6 addresses the topic of uncertainty, where a problem solver is forced to represent and reason with vague concepts or incomplete information.

Part III covers the main *representation languages* for encoding domain-specific knowledge in programs in such a way that the knowledge can be applied to complex problems by a computer. We begin with an overview of symbolic computation in the LISP programming language, and proceed to explore special-purpose representation languages, such as OPS5 and FLAVORS. Chapter 12 compares and contrasts these different approaches, and argues that each has something to offer.

Part IV deals with the practical side of expert systems technology. We begin with the problem of *knowledge acquisition* – that is, how to elicit knowledge from a human expert and codify it – before representing it using the techniques described in Part III. Subsequent chapters consider a number of problem-solving paradigms, which have been found suitable for tasks such as diagnosis and design, and illustrate them with exemplars from the literature. These exemplars were chosen for peda-gogical reasons, rather than because they were necessarily the 'best' in the field. Nevertheless, they do include some success stories of expert systems research, and there are lessons to be learned from the ways in which these systems were designed and implemented.

Part V examines *software tools and architectures*. Chapters 20 and 21 take a critical look at the kinds of programming tool and programming environment typically provided for building expert systems. The other chapters describe two additional frameworks around which expert systems can be organized: *blackboard systems* and *truth maintenance systems*.

In Part VI, more advanced topics such as *diagnosis from first principles*, *reasoning under uncertainty*, and *knowledge acquisition by machine learning* are discussed at a somewhat higher level of abstraction. These topics are optional for a first course, but they serve to open out the field for research students. The final chapter contains a summary of the book, recommends some topics for further study, and discusses a few outstanding problems.

The rest of this chapter has the following plan. Four fundamental topics are identified which are intimately related to the theory and practice of expert systems development, and these are briefly discussed with a view to introducing some terminology and giving the reader an overview. The final section poses the question 'What is the state of the art?' and asks how far expert systems have come, and how far they still have to go.

1.3 Research topics in expert systems

Given that expert systems research has grown out of more general concerns in artificial intelligence, it is not surprising that it maintains strong intellectual links with related topics in its parent discipline. Some of these links are outlined in the following sections, with references to the general literature. There are also references to chapters of this book which have a bearing on the various topics.

1.3.1 Knowledge acquisition

Buchanan *et al.* (1983) define knowledge acquisition as:

> the transfer and transformation of potential problem-solving expertise from some knowledge source to a program.

As we shall see in Chapter 13, this transfer is usually accomplished by a series of lengthy and intensive interviews between a knowledge engineer, who is normally a computer specialist, and a domain expert who is able to articulate his expertise to some degree. It is estimated that this form of labour produces between 2 and 5 units of knowledge (rules of thumb) per day. This rather low output has led researchers to look upon knowledge acquisition as 'the bottleneck problem' of expert systems applications (Feigenbaum, 1977).

There are a number of reasons why productivity is typically so poor; here are some of them.

- Specialist fields have their own jargon, and it is often difficult for experts to communicate their knowledge in everyday language. Analysing the concepts behind the jargon is rarely straightforward, since these concepts need not admit of precise mathematical or logical definition. For example, a military strategist may speak of the 'aggressive posture' of a foreign power without being able to specify exactly what distinguishes such a posture from a non-threatening one.

- The facts and principles underlying many domains of interest cannot be characterized precisely in terms of a mathematical theory or a deterministic model whose properties are well understood.

Thus a financial expert may know that certain events cause the stock market to go up or down, but the exact mechanisms that mediate these effects, and the magnitude of the effects themselves, cannot be identified or predicted with certainty. Statistical models may enable us to make rather general, long-term predictions, but they do not normally sanction specific courses of action in the short term.

• Experts need to know more than the mere facts or principles of a domain in order to solve problems. For example, they usually know which kinds of information are relevant to which kinds of judgement, how reliable different information sources are, and how to make hard problems easier by splitting them into subproblems which can be solved more or less independently. Eliciting this kind of knowledge, which is normally based on personal experience rather than formal training, is much more difficult than eliciting either particular facts or general principles.

• Human expertise, even in a relatively narrow domain, is often set in a broader context that involves a good deal of commonsense knowledge about the everyday world. Consider legal experts involved in litigation. It is difficult to delineate the amount and nature of general knowledge needed to deal with an arbitrary case.

Dissatisfaction with the interview method has led some researchers to try to automate the process of knowledge acquisition. One area of research concerns *automated knowledge elicitation*, in which an expert's knowledge is transferred to a computer program as a side-effect of a man–machine dialogue (see Chapter 13 and other chapters in Part IV). Other researchers have looked to the subfield of AI known as *machine learning* for a solution to the bottleneck problem. The idea is that a computing system could perhaps learn to solve problems in much the same way that humans do, that is to say, by example (see Chapter 26).

1.3.2 Knowledge representation

Knowledge representation is a substantial subfield in its own right, on the borderline between AI and cognitive science. It is concerned with the way in which information might be stored in the human brain, and the (possibly analogous) ways in which large bodies of knowledge can be formally described for the purposes of *symbolic computation*. By 'formally described', I mean rendered in some unambiguous language or notation which has a well-defined *syntax* governing the form of expressions in the language, and a well-defined *semantics* which reveals the meaning of such expressions by virtue of their form (for more about syntax and semantics, see Chapters 4 and 5).

By 'symbolic computation', I mean non-numeric computations in which the symbols and symbol structures can be construed as standing for various concepts and relationships between them (see Chapters 4 and 7). AI researchers have expended a good deal of effort in constructing *representation languages*, that is, computer languages that are oriented towards organizing descriptions of objects and ideas, rather than stating sequences of instructions or storing simple data elements (see Chapters 8–11). The main criteria for assessing a representation of knowledge are logical adequacy, heuristic power and notational convenience.

Logical adequacy means that the representation should be capable of making all the distinctions that you want to make. For example, it is not possible to represent the idea that every drug has some undesirable side-effect unless you are able to distinguish between the designation of a particular drug and a particular side-effect (for example, aspirin aggravates ulcers) and the more general statement to the effect that:

> for any drug you care to name, there is an undesirable side-effect associated with it.

The latter requires some form of *quantification*, whereby variables range over such entities as drugs and side-effects (see Chapter 5).

Heuristic power means that, as well as having an expressive representation language, there must be some way of using representations so constructed and interpreted to solve problems. It is often the case that the more expressive the language, in terms of the number of semantic distinctions it can make, the more difficult it is to control the drawing of inferences during problem solving. Many of the formalisms that have found favour with practitioners may seem quite restricted in terms of their powers of expression when compared with English or even standard logic, yet they frequently gain in heuristic power as a consequence because it is relatively easy to bring the right knowledge to bear at the right time. Knowing which areas of knowledge are most relevant to which problems is one of the things that distinguishes the expert from the amateur, or the merely well-read.

Notational convenience is a virtue because most expert systems applications require the encoding of substantial amounts of knowledge, and this task will not be an enviable one if the conventions of the representation language are too complicated. The resulting expressions should be relatively easy to write and to read, and it should be possible to understand their meaning without knowing how the computer will actually interpret them. The term *declarative* is often used to describe code which is essentially descriptive and can therefore be understood without knowing what states a real or virtual machine will go through at execution time.

Several conventions for coding knowledge have been suggested, including *production rules* (Davis and King, 1977), *structured objects*

(Findler, 1979) and *predicate logic* (Kowalski, 1979). Most expert systems use one or more of these formalisms, and their pros and cons are still a source of controversy among theoreticians (although implementation is often a more pragmatic affair). The problems of knowledge representation form the subject matter of Part II; a number of proposed formalisms are critically reviewed in Part III; and a number of software tools for constructing such representations are described in Parts IV and V.

1.3.3   The application of knowledge

This subfield relates to the issues of *planning* and *control* in the field of problem solving. Expert systems design involves paying close attention to the details of how knowledge is accessed and applied during the search for a solution (see, for example, Davis, 1980a). Knowing what one knows, and knowing when and how to use it, seems to be an important part of expertise; this is usually termed *meta-knowledge*, that is, knowledge about knowledge.

Different strategies for bringing domain-specific knowledge to bear will generally have marked effects on the performance characteristics of programs. They determine the manner in which a program *searches* for a solution in some space of alternatives (see Chapters 2 and 3). It will not normally be the case that the data given to a knowledge-based program will be sufficient for the program to deduce exactly where it should look in this space.

For example, imagine that your car is difficult to start, and when running exhibits loss of power. These symptoms are not, in themselves, sufficient for you to decide whether you should look for a fault in the electrical system or the fuel system of your car, but your knowledge of cars might tell you that it is worth running some additional checks before calling a mechanic. Perhaps the mixture is wrong, so look at the exhaust smoke and the coating on the spark plugs. Maybe the distributor is faulty, so see if the cap is damaged in some way. These rather specific heuristics are not guaranteed to locate the fault, but with luck they may take you to the heart of the problem more quickly than running an exhaustive set of routine checks over the car's components.

Even if you are mystified by the symptoms of your sick vehicle, you probably know enough to perform global checks before very specific checks, for example, to see if there is a strong spark at the plugs (which would tend to rule out an electrical fault) before testing the battery for flatness. Even in the absence of specific heuristics, the more methodical your procedures, the greater the chance that you will find the fault quickly. The general heuristic that says 'test whole modules before testing their components' can be thought of as an aspect of control: a strategy for applying knowledge in some systematic way.

Most knowledge representation formalisms can be employed under a variety of control regimes, and expert systems researchers are continuing to experiment in this area. The systems reviewed in Part IV have been specially chosen to illustrate the many different ways in which the problem of control can be tackled. Each has something to offer the student of expert systems research and development.

1.3.4 Explaining solutions

The whole question of how to help a user to understand the structure and function of some complex piece of software relates to the comparatively new field of *human–computer interaction*, which is emerging from an intersection of AI, engineering, psychology and ergonomics (see, for example, papers in Sime and Coombs, 1983; Coombs, 1984). The contribution of expert systems researchers to date has been to place a high priority on the accountability of consultation programs, and to show how explanations of program behaviour can be systematically related to the chains of reasoning employed by such systems. Ongoing contributions include attempts to separate out the different kinds of knowledge implicit in expert performance, and attempts to make explicit and accessible the design decisions associated with the specification of consultation programs.

Explanations of expert system behaviour are important for a number of reasons:

- *Users* of the system need to satisfy themselves that the program's conclusions are basically correct for their particular case.
- *Knowledge engineers* needs some way to satisfy themselves that knowledge is being applied properly even as the prototype is being built.
- *Domain experts* need to see a trace of the way in which their knowledge is being applied in order to judge whether knowledge elicitation is proceeding successfully.
- *Programmers* who maintain, debug and extend knowledge-based programs must have some window on the program's behaviour above the level of the procedure call.
- *Managers* of expert system technology, who may end up being responsible for a program's decisions, need to satisfy themselves that a system's mode of reasoning is applicable to their domain.

The topic of explanations sometimes goes under the name of *transparency*, meaning the ease with which one can understand what the program is doing and why. It interacts with the issue of control, mentioned in the previous section, because the steps of reasoning exhibited by the program will depend on how it goes about its search for a solution. How best to manage the interaction between explanation and control is still a research question, which we address in Chapter 19.

Explanation is closely linked to the topic of *evaluation*, since it is by scrutinizing the outputs of a system and examining a trace of its reasoning that we decide whether or not that system is getting the right answer for the right reasons. Unless a system has a good explanation facility, an expert will be unable to assess its general performance or give advice as to how its performance could be improved. Evaluation is a difficult task that requires a certain level of commitment from both the expert and the computer scientist (see Chapters 3, 17 and 21).

The next section attempts an honest assessment of the scope of present expert systems technology.

1.4   What is the state of the art?

The main question that occurs to a potential consumer of this technology is 'Will it solve my problem?' and the answer is 'That depends'. The three most critical factors are the nature of the task, the availability of a certain kind of expertise, and the ability to analyse that task and that expertise in such a way that even a computer program, using rather limited forms of reasoning, can work out what has to be done. The following points cover most of the ground.

Someone (your expert) must

- be able to perform the task,
- know how they perform the task,
- be able to explain how they perform the task,
- have the time to explain how they perform the task,
- be motivated to cooperate in the enterprise.

These conditions will tend to rule out certain applications from the start. Weather prediction, for example, is not a task that anyone performs very well – not even the professionals. Speech recognition is a task that we all perform extremely well, but none of us (including linguists) have much idea how we do it. Even given a genuine expert with insight into his or her skills, your application depends crucially on that person's ability and willingness to explain those skills in detail. These conditions may not be met. Your expert may be too inarticulate or too busy to take part in the knowledge engineering enterprise. Experts are usually in demand, and they often prefer doing what they do best to talking about it. They may be jealous of their expertise, perhaps fearing that its mechanization will threaten their livelihoods.

Even if the above conditions are met, there may be features of the task that limit the extent that the skills can be mechanized, for example

- if the task involves complex *sensorimotor skills* beyond the scope of current technology in robotics and computer vision;
- if the task involves *commonsense reasoning* or arbitrary amounts of everyday knowledge.

Thus the production of a 'Robocop' is thankfully beyond the scope of present technology. An artificial law enforcement officer would require rather more in the way of scene analysis and hand–eye coordination than the present generation of robots if it were to patrol the streets of Detroit without either being destroyed or decimating the population. To be effective, it would also require an enormous amount of knowledge about the world: knowledge of objects and their properties, people and their motivations, physical causality and likely courses of events – the list appears to be endless. The fact is that we still have only the most rudimentary notions about how to impart this kind of commonsense, everyday knowledge to computers. So any task that is not sufficiently self-contained to be encapsulated in a finite set of particular facts and general rules is definitely beyond the start of the art.

The reader will have realized by now that many of the more interesting aspects of expert systems technology are inextricably tied up with ongoing research issues. However, there is a tendency in the commercial press to present as 'state of the art' many techniques which are imperfectly understood, and whose efficacy is far from being established. This places expert systems researchers in an embarrassing position for two reasons:

- They appear to be researching 'solved problems'.
- Their cautionary statements will appear negative and in conflict with the optimism of persons who wish to exploit new technology.

Undoubtedly there are those for whom the field of expert systems has all but engulfed the rest of artificial intelligence, insofar as expert systems seems to be its most commercially viable branch. However, it would be quite wrong to suppose either that expert systems would have developed in their present form without the nutrient context of artificial intelligence, or that it will continue to advance in the absence of input from its parent discipline. Thus, although I shall neglect other areas of artificial intelligence (such as vision, robotics and natural language processing) in the review of AI in Chapter 2, it is unquestionably the case that the expert systems applications of the future will draw upon the results of such research.

Bibliographical notes

Reviews of expert systems research can be found in Barr and Feigenbaum (1982), Hayes-Roth *et al.* (1983), Buchanan and Shortliffe (1984) and Waterman (1986). Applications of expert systems technology are described in Weiss and Kulikowski (1983), Klahr and Waterman (1986), Gale (1986) and Quinlan (1987). Business-oriented readers can consult Feigenbaum *et al.* (1988) for an up-to-date look at expert systems in industry.

STUDY SUGGESTIONS

1.1 (a) What are the features that distinguish an expert system from a more conventional applications program or a typical AI program?

(b) Can you think of a non-AI program that satisfies all of these features?

(c) What is the difference between an expert system and a knowledge-based system?

1.2 (a) Is a program that forecasts tomorrow's (say 16 June) weather by averaging the inches of rainfall, hours of sunshine and temperature of every 16 June occurring since the year 1900 an expert system or not?

(b) Is a program that forecasts summer weather in Southern California by printing out the sentence 'Tomorrow will be just like today' an expert system or not? Assume that it represents today's weather symbolically, is easy to extend or modify, performs well, and can explain its reasoning by printing out the sentence:

Daily variations in climatic conditions are unlikely at this time of year.

1.3 Why is knowledge acquisition such a bottleneck? What solutions have been proposed?

1.4 How far do you think that the following tasks are amenable to an expert systems solution? (Consider whether an expert system might perform part of the task. If the answer is yes, decide on the allocation of functions between person and machine.)

(a) Geological prospecting

(b) Planning a bank robbery

(c) Careers advising

(d) PhD supervision

(e) Creating an investment portfolio

Are any of these susceptible to more conventional computer science techniques?

1.5 Explain the notions of logical and heuristic adequacy as they relate to knowledge representation languages.

2 An Overview of Artificial Intelligence

Introduction

What is artificial intelligence? The following definition from Barr and Feigenbaum (1981) is representative of opinion in the field:

> Artificial Intelligence (AI) is the part of computer science concerned with designing intelligent computer systems, that is, systems that exhibit the characteristics we associate with intelligence in human behavior – understanding language, learning, reasoning, solving problems, and so on.

In other words, AI is concerned with programming computers to perform tasks that are presently done better by humans, because they involve such higher mental processes such as perceptual learning, memory organization and judgemental reasoning (Minsky, 1968). Thus, writing a program to perform complicated statistical calculations would not be seen as an artificial intelligence activity, while writing a program to design experiments to test hypotheses would. Most people are not very good at doing long calculations by hand, whereas computers excel at such tasks. On the other hand, devising good experiments to test hypotheses is a skill that the research scientist derives partly from training and partly from experience. Programming a computer to perform such a task would be entirely non-trivial.

There are differences of outlook and emphasis among researchers, however. Some incline towards the view that AI is a branch of engineering, since it is ultimately about building intelligent artefacts, such as robots (Nilsson, 1971). Others stress the link with cognitive science: a discipline which concerns itself with the study of human information processing, and sometimes uses computers to model or simulate such processing. Still other writers are interested in the overlap with problems of philosophy associated with knowledge and consciousness.

In the end, AI is about the emulation of human behaviour: the discovery of techniques that will allow us to design and program machines which simulate or extend our mental capabilities. It is therefore hardly surprising that the discipline should be closely related to a wide range of other academic subject areas such as computer science, psychology, philosophy, linguistics and engineering. The fact that AI crosses a number of traditional interdisciplinary boundaries sometimes causes friction, but is more often a source of inspiration and new ideas.

As an aid to the general reader, I will attempt to give a very brief overview of artificial intelligence research, insofar as it relates to the design and construction of expert systems. I will also try to explain in what way knowledge-based programming differs from both more conventional programming techniques and the general-purpose problem solving methods devised by the pioneers of AI research. For a more general introduction to AI, the reader is referred to textbooks cited in the Bibliographical notes at the end of the chapter.

2.1 The Classical Period: game playing and theorem proving

Artificial intelligence is scarcely younger than conventional computer science; the beginnings of AI can be seen in the first game-playing and puzzle-solving programs written shortly after World War II. Game-playing and puzzle-solving may seem somewhat remote from expert systems, and insufficiently serious to provide a theoretical basis for real applications. However, a rather basic notion about computer-based problem solving can be traced back to early attempts to program computers to perform such tasks.

2.1.1 State space search

The fundamental idea that came out of early research is called *state space search*, and it is essentially very simple. Many kinds of problem can be formulated in terms of three important ingredients:

- a *starting state*, such as the initial state of the chess board;
- a *termination test* for detecting final states or solutions to the problem, such as the simple rule for detecting checkmate in chess;
- a *set of operations* that can be applied to change the current state of the problem, such as the legal moves of chess.

One way of thinking of this conceptual space of states is as a graph in which the states are nodes and the operations are arcs. Such spaces can be generated as you go. For example, you could begin with the starting state of the chess board and make it the first node in the graph. Each of White's possible first moves would then be an arc connecting this node to a new state of the board. Each of Black's legal replies to each of these first moves could then be considered as operations which connect each of these new nodes to a changed state of the board, and so on.

The simplest form of state space search is *generate-and-test*, and the algorithm is easy to specify:

(1)   *Generate* a possible solution, in the form of a state in the search space, for example, a new board position as the result of a move.

(2)   *Test* to see if this state is actually a solution by seeing if it satisfies the conditions for success, such as checkmate.

(3)   If the current state is a solution, then quit, else go back to step 1.

There are two main variants of basic generate-and-test: *depth-first search* and *breadth-first search*. The difference between them lies in the order in which possible solutions are generated in step 1. The actual algorithms are given in Study suggestion 1.1; an informal description is given below. States are often referred to as *nodes*, because they can be considered as points in a connected graph. Generating the successors of a node in a graph structure is often called *expanding* the node.

At any given node, N, depth-first search considers the 'successors' of N, i.e. those states which result from applying operators to N, before considering 'siblings' of N (those states which were generated along with N, when applying operators to N's 'ancestor'). In breadth-first search, it is the other way round; N's siblings are checked out before expanding N, that is, before going on to N's successors. Thus, in breadth-first search, one searches layer by layer through successive levels of the search space, whereas in depth-first search one pursues a single path at a time, returning to N to pick another path only if the current path fails (see Figure 2.1).

Breadth-first search finds the shortest solution path, if there is one; algorithms with this property are called *admissible*. However, depth-first

Depth-first search

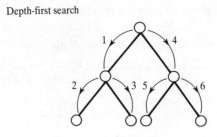

Breadth-first search

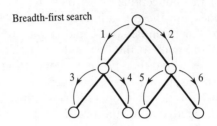

Figure 2.1 Exhaustive search strategies.

search gets there faster as long as it is guided in some way, that is, if it makes good decisions when choosing which path to pursue next. On the other hand, depth-first search may never terminate if the search space is infinite, even if a solution exists along some as yet unexplored path.

It is not hard to see how the number of nodes may grow exponentially at each stage, regardless of the order in which nodes are generated. This phenomenon is usually referred to as *combinatorial explosion*, and it poses insuperable problems to programs that attempt to play games like chess by 'brute force' enumeration of all the alternatives. Since human beings are slower than computers at such enumeration tasks, and much less reliable, one can safely assume that chess grand masters do not function in this way. Rather, they apply their experience, imagination and analytic skills to the selection of both overall strategies and winning moves. Such behaviour can reasonably be called 'intelligent'.

In addition to game playing, another principal concern of artificial intelligence that began in the 1950s was theorem proving. Roughly speaking, theorem proving involves showing that some statement in which we are interested follows logically from a set of special statements, the *axioms* (which are known or assumed to be true), and is therefore a *theorem*. As an example, suppose we have the two axioms 'If something can go wrong, it will' and 'My computer can go wrong', expressed as sentences in some formal language, such as the predicate calculus (see Chapter 5). Then we can derive a sentence representing 'My computer will go wrong' as a theorem, using only the inference rules of the calculus.

Thus 'My computer will go wrong' follows logically from the axioms, in the sense that it cannot be false if the axioms are true.

As is the case with chess, some of the concepts and techniques developed in the field of automatic theorem proving provided a starting point for students of general problem solving. Thus, knowledge relevant to the solution of some problem can be represented as a set of axioms, the *theory*, and problem solving can be viewed as the process of showing that the desired solution is a theorem. Unfortunately, the process of generating all the theorems that follow from some set of axioms is also combinatorially explosive, since one can add any theorems derived to the axioms and use the new set of statements to derive still more theorems. In other words, searching for a solution among the theorems generated is analogous to traversing a state space graph, and can be considered as such. Deriving solutions by theorem proving may involve computations which require more resources than can be provided by any conceivable computer (see the Bibliographical notes at the end of the chapter). Since human beings do not appear to be hampered in this way, it seems unlikely that they engage in formal reasoning of this kind when solving problems. Rather, they appear to intersperse valid steps of inference with plausible assumptions and likely hypotheses.

Nevertheless, at the present time, there is a resurgence of interest in the application of theorem-proving techniques to both general problem solving and expert systems. This is due to both an improved understanding of how to mechanize those techniques and a disillusionment (in certain circles) with methods based on less formal foundations. Accordingly, Chapter 5 gives the reader an introduction to techniques of automated reasoning relevant to expert systems research, Chapter 11 examines the workings of a number of problem solvers that adopt a theorem-proving approach, while Chapter 24 analyses logic-based approaches to diagnosis.

2.1.2 Heuristic search

Given that exhaustive search is not feasible for anything other than small search spaces, some means of guiding the search is required. A search that uses one or more items of domain-specific knowledge to traverse a state space graph is called a *heuristic search*. A heuristic is best thought of as a rule of thumb; it is not guaranteed to succeed, in the way that an algorithm or decision procedure is, but it is useful in the majority of cases.

A simple form of heuristic search is *hill climbing*. This involves giving the program an *evaluation function* which it can apply to the current state of the problem to obtain a rough estimate of how well things are going. For example, a simple evaluation function for a chess-playing program might involve a straightforward comparison of material between the two players. The program then seeks to maximize this function when it applies operators, such as the moves of chess. The algorithm for hill-climbing is given below (see also Study suggestion 2.3):

(1) Generate a possible solution as with step 1 of generate-and-test.
(2) From this point in the state space, apply rules that generate a new set of possible solutions; for example, the legal moves of chess that can be made from the current state.
(3) If any state in the newly derived set is a solution, then quit with success, else take the 'best' state from the set, make it the current state, and go back to step 2.

There are well-known problems with this approach, however. To begin with, your evaluation function may not be a faithful estimate of the 'goodness' of the current state of the problem. To pursue the chess example, I may have more pieces than you, but you may be in a better position. Simple estimates based on material advantage will not capture all the subtleties of the game. Furthermore, even if the evaluation function gives a good estimate, there are various states of play that can cause problems. For example, there may be no obvious next move, because they all appear to be equally good or bad. This is like being on a 'plateau' with no clear path towards the heights. Another problem is that of local maxima, which occurs when your evaluation function leads you to a peak position, from which the only way is down, while your goal is on some other, higher peak. Thus, I can take your queen, but in so doing lose the game.

The problem of local maxima arises because hill climbing makes an irrevocable decision at each choice point in the search space, based only on the 'local' information considered by the evaluation function. The algorithm will avoid this problem if the operators used to generate new states are *commutative*, that is, if applying an operator never hinders the application of other operators, or alters the state that results from changing the order of operators in a sequence of applications. However, not all problems can be represented by commutative operators, chess being an obvious case in point.

Another form of heuristic search, which does not rely on commutativity for completeness, is *best-first search*. As in hill climbing, we have an evaluation function that rates the nodes we encounter, but we select the next node for expansion from among *all* the nodes encountered so far, and not just from among the successors of the current node. The algorithm for best-first search is given in Study suggestion 2.4, but the general idea is that we must now keep track of all the nodes we have seen so far, and be prepared to 'take up where we left off' elsewhere if none of the successors of the current node looks promising. Best-first search improves on hill-climbing because it does not make irrevocable decision based on local information. However, it is computationally much more expensive, because of all the bookkeeping required to bear in mind nodes we have looked at but 'left behind' on unexplored paths through the search space.

Using the power of a computer to search for solutions, either exhaustively or guided by an evaluation function, is not always adequate for real applications. The search spaces associated with such tasks as understanding speech, configuring computing systems, and planning sequences of actions are too large to be traversed in a reasonable time unless constrained by more than 'local' knowledge. Many of these problems can be shown to be isomorphic with abstract problems that are known to be intractable, in the sense that the resources required to solve them are exponential in the size of the problem.

As we shall see, expert systems attempt to tackle the difficulties of search by explicitly representing *in detail* both the knowledge that experts possess about some domain and the strategies that they use to reason about what they know.

One can contrast the knowledge-based approach with the internal workings of commercially available chess machines. These devices know almost nothing about chess over and above a few 'book' openings, the legal moves, the rough value of the pieces, and the rule for checkmate. In particular, they have no overall plan for playing a given game. The chess machine I have at home beats me most of the time because I am a poor player (as well as being lazy), and because its hardware incorporates a very clever algorithm called *minimax* which is continually looking to maximize the machine's opportunities to take pieces and minimize mine. Occasionally, I manage to trade material for a superior position, in which case I usually go on to win.

Early attempts at game playing and theorem proving are well represented by the collection of papers in Feigenbaum and Feldman (1963). I tend to think of the period that begins with the publication of Shannon's (1950) paper on chess and ends with the publication of Feigenbaum and Feldman as the Classical Period of AI research. Among the most important discoveries of this period were the twin realizations that:

- problems of whatever kind could, in principle, be reduced to search problems so long as they were formalizable in terms of a start state, an end state, and a set of operations for traversing a state space; but

- the search had to be guided by some representation of knowledge about the domain of the problem.

In a minority of cases, it proved possible to restrict the application of knowledge to the use of an evaluation function which was able to use features of the problem local to the current state to give the program some idea of how well it was doing. However, in the majority of cases it was felt that something more was required, such as a global problem-solving strategy, or an explicit encoding of knowledge about the objects, properties and actions associated with the domain, or both.

2.2   The Romantic Period: computer understanding

The mid-1960s to the mid-1970s represents what I call the Romantic Period in artificial intelligence research. At this time, people were very concerned with making machines 'understand', by which they usually meant the understanding of natural language, especially stories and dialogue. Winograd's (1972) SHRDLU system was arguably the climax of this epoch: a program which was capable of understanding a quite substantial subset of English by representing and reasoning about a very restricted domain (a world consisting of children's toy blocks).

The program exhibited understanding by modifying its 'blocks-world' representation in response to commands, and by responding to questions about both the configuration of blocks and its 'actions' upon them. Thus it could answer questions like:

What is the colour of the block supporting the red pyramid?

and derive plans for obeying commands such as:

Place the blue pyramid on the green block.

SHRDLU was deemed to understand the sentences because it responded to them appropriately. The rationale for this view of understanding was called *procedural semantics*, the idea being that a program can be said to understand a query if it can answer the question correctly, and it can be said to understand a command if it can carry the command out. Needless to say, this is a rather operational view of understanding, that is, a view which explains understanding in terms of behaviour, rather than in terms of mental operations (see Chapter 4 for a further discussion).

Other researchers (Newell and Simon, 1972; Anderson, 1976) attempted to model human problem-solving behaviour on simple tasks, such as puzzles, word games and memory tests. The aim was to make the knowledge and strategy used by the program resemble the knowledge and strategy of the human subject as closely as possible. Empirical studies compared the performance of program and subject in an attempt to see how successful the simulation had been.

The fundamental problem was that there are no direct methods for showing that a human subject and an AI program do the same thing in the same way. Thus, indirect arguments have to be employed, such as showing that program and subject make the same kinds of errors when faced with hard problems or bad data, or showing that program and subject display similar profiles with respect to the time taken to solve different classes of problem. Simply showing that they get the same answer is obviously not enough, because there are a multitude of different strategies and encodings of knowledge that will solve the same problem.

Nevertheless, the new emphasis on knowledge representation proved to be extremely fruitful. Newell and Simon generated a kind of knowledge representation known as *production rules* (see Chapter 8), which has since become a mainstay of expert systems design and development. They also pioneered a technique known as *protocol analysis*, whereby human subjects were encouraged to think aloud as they solved problems, and such protocols were later analysed in an attempt to reveal the concepts and procedures employed. This approach can be seen as a precursor of some of the knowledge elicitation techniques that knowledge engineers use today. These psychological studies showed just how hard the knowledge representation problem was, but demonstrated that it could be addressed in a spirit of empirical inquiry, rather than philosophical debate.

In the Romantic Period, researchers explored a multitude of possibilities for encoding both particular facts and general principles about the world in such a way that they could be applied by a computer program in the course of its goal-directed reasoning. These involved using constructs of the following kind:

- *rules* of the form 'if these conditions hold, then apply this operator';
- various kinds of *network*, where nodes stood for concepts and arcs for relationships between them; and
- *logical formulas* for encoding facts and principles, including control information about when to draw what inferences.

Sometimes these constructs were used in combination. However, most of the programs produced at this time were essentially research vehicles. Few of them found their way into real applications.

Minsky (1968) contains a representative sample of papers from the first half of this period. All of them are interesting, but not all are convincing from the point of view of actual achievement. Nevertheless, many of the knowledge representation schemes that we currently take for granted were developed during this time. For example, Quillian's paper gave rise to *associative nets* (see Chapter 9): a graphical formalism for encoding facts and definitions. Without this decade of imaginative exploration, which had its share of spectacular failures, it is doubtful that expert systems would exhibit the variety of functions and structures that they do today.

A representative sample of papers from the latter half of this period can be found in Winston (1975); Minsky's paper on a knowledge representation formalism called *frames* is particularly worth reading. Also worth consulting are both volumes of Winston and Brown (1979), which summarize much of the work done at the Massachusetts Institute of Technology during the 1970s. They contain a number of important papers on such topics as natural language processing, computer vision and robotics, which will be neglected here.

The whole notion of 'computer understanding' is entirely problematic, of course. It is simply not clear under what conditions one would be prepared to assert that a machine understood anything. (Neither are the grounds for imputing human understanding particularly clear, for that matter.) However, even if one is unsure about what would constitute sufficient grounds for understanding, one can at least list some of the necessary grounds.

One is the ability to represent knowledge about the world, and reason using such representations. Expert systems exhibit this ability, insofar as they possess explicit representations of knowledge about some domain, and are capable of applying this knowledge to solve real problems. However, like the Winograd program, their outlook is strictly circumscribed; performance in terms of speed and reliability still tends to be an inverse function of the size of the domain.

Another sign of understanding is the ability to perceive equivalences or analogies between different representations of the same situations. Expert systems score badly here, since they expect their inputs to be in a certain form, namely one that corresponds to their stored knowledge. Any deviation from the patterns they expect tends to result in breakdown or unpredictable behaviour.

Finally, understanding implies an ability to learn in some non-trivial way, in some non-rote fashion that requires new information to be integrated with information already possessed, perhaps in a way that modifies both. Few expert systems have demonstrated this kind of facility, although some progress towards machine learning has been made in recent years (see Chapter 26). Also, progress has been made in the design of programs which elicit knowledge from experts via an interaction at the terminal and then compile that knowledge into an applications program (see Chapter 13).

Although expert systems fall short on some of these criteria, it is arguable (see Davis, 1989) that expert systems do not have to 'understand' a domain, in the way that a human understands it, in order to solve problems. A number of well-documented systems perform as well as human experts without exhibiting the kind of understanding that the Romantic Period was all about. As Davis points out, there is no necessary connection between the process of problem solving and the solution itself. In other words, all we require is that an expert system gets more or less the same answer as an expert, or helps an expert get the right answer. We do not demand that the system goes through the same steps of reasoning as a human, or organizes domain knowledge in exactly the same way.

2.3 The Modern Period: techniques and applications

What I shall call the Modern Period stretches from the latter half of the 1970s to the present day. It is characterized by an increasing self-consciousness and self-criticism, together with a greater orientation towards techniques and applications. The flirtation with psychological aspects of understanding is somehow less central than it was.

The disillusionment with general problem-solving methods, such as heuristic search, has continued apace. Researchers have realized that such methods overvalue the concept of 'general intelligence', traditionally favoured by psychologists, at the expense of the domain-specific ability that human experts possess. Such methods also undervalue simple common sense, particularly the ability of humans to avoid, identify and correct errors.

The conviction has grown that the heuristic power of a problem solver lies in the explicit representation of relevant knowledge that the program can access, and not in some sophisticated inference mechanism or some complicated evaluation function. Researchers have developed techniques for encoding human knowledge in modules which can be activated by patterns. These patterns may represent raw or processed data, problem states or partial problem solutions. Early attempts to simulate human problem solving (Newell and Simon, 1972) strove for uniformity in the encoding of knowledge and simplicity in the inference mechanism. Later attempts to apply the results of this research to expert systems have typically allowed themselves more variety.

It became clear that there were advantages attached to the strategy of representing human knowledge explicitly in pattern-directed modules, instead of encoding it into an algorithm that could be implemented using more conventional programming techniques:

- The process of rendering the knowledge explicit in a piecemeal fashion seemed to be more in tune with the way that experts store and apply their knowledge. In response to requests as to how they do their job, few experts will provide a well-articulated sequence of steps that is guaranteed to terminate with success in all situations. Rather, the knowledge that they possess has to be elicited by asking what they would do in typical cases, and then probing for the exceptions.

- This method of programming allows for fast prototyping and incremental system development. If the system designer and programmer have done their jobs properly, the resultant program should be easy to modify and extend, so that errors and gaps in the knowledge can be rectified without major adjustments to the existing code. If they have not done their jobs properly, changes to the knowledge may well have unpredictable effects, since there may be unplanned interactions between modules of knowledge.

- Practitioners realized that a program does not have to solve the whole problem, or even be right all of the time, in order to be useful. An expert system can function as an intelligent assistant, which enumerates alternatives in the search for a solution, and rules out some of the less promising ones. The system can leave the final judgement, and some of the intermediate strategic decisions, to the user and still be a useful tool. We shall see an example of just such a program in Chapter 3: the DENDRAL system for helping chemists discover the structure of an unknown compound.

The Modern Period has seen the development of a number of systems that can claim a high level of performance on non-trivial tasks, for example, the R1 system for configuring computer systems (see Chapter 17). A number of principles have emerged which distinguish such systems from both conventional programs and earlier work in AI (see Davis, 1982). The most important of these are considered below.

- As we saw in Chapter 1, the part of the program that contains the representation of domain-specific knowledge, the *knowledge base*, is generally separate from the part of the program that performs the reasoning, the *inference engine*. This means that one can make at least some changes to either module without necessarily having to alter the other. Thus one might be able to add more knowledge to the knowledge base, or tune the inference engine for better performance, without having to modify code elsewhere.

- Practitioners try to use as uniform a representation of knowledge as possible. This makes the knowledge easier to encode and understand, and helps to keep the inference engine simple. However, as we shall see in Part IV and beyond, uniformity can sometimes pose problems if different kinds of knowledge are forced into the same formalism. Thus there is a trade-off between simplicity and requisite variety in the representation.

- Unlike more conventional problem-solving programs, expert systems are expected to offer the user some kind of explanation as to how the conclusions were arrived at. Given a uniform knowledge representation and a simple inference engine, this usually involves presenting a trace of which modules of knowledge became active in which order. We shall see in Chapter 19 that such traces are often less informative than we would wish.

Present expert systems technology appears to work best in domains where there is a substantial body of empirical knowledge connecting situations to actions. A deeper representation of the domain, in terms of spatial, temporal or causal models, is often avoided, or deemed unnecessary (but see Chapter 24 for some recent research on diagnosis from first principles). Problems that require something closer to the 'computer understanding' researched in the Romantic Period tend to be passed by.

Nevertheless, the advent of expert systems has introduced a new rigour and realism into AI research. The R1 system mentioned above has been run on 500 000 cases since it came into commercial use: this program is not a prototype. We know that its problem-solving methods work, and we know that new methods will have to submit to similar testing. We also know that we have a lot to learn. AI has come a long way in the last 20 years, taking up the challenge of solving real problems. (It has also made progress on the chess front. In 1988, the program Hitech became the first to beat an international grand master. Twenty years ago, detractors of AI said that computers would *never* play even *master* level chess.)

One can see from this sketch that, surrounding the core of expert systems practice that has been built up over the last 15–20 years, there is a less stable and more speculative fringe of research topics which are at the heart of mainstream artificial intelligence. It's hard to tell at present whether more grandiose goals, such as computer understanding, have been abandoned, postponed or deemed somehow irrelevant to practical applications. This question need not concern us here, other than to note that any progress made on these fronts will extend the functionality of current expert systems.

The next chapter introduces two early expert systems, and gives a simplified account of how they worked. Although the systems are more than ten years old, they provide such good illustrations of the basic concepts that I make no apologies for using them here. Each can be seen as a bridge between earlier programs based on state space search and the evolution of a more knowledge-based approach.

Bibliographical notes

Rich (1983), Winston (1984) and Charniak and McDermott (1985) are all good introductory texts in AI. The various volumes of the *Handbook of Artificial Intelligence* (Barr and Feigenbaum, 1981, 1982; Cohen and Feigenbaum, 1982) are a good source of concise reference material, albeit somewhat out of date. For theoretical treatments of the relationship between human reason and artificial intelligence, the reader is referred to Simon (1976), Boden (1977) and Haugeland (1981).

The study of the tractability or intractability of computations is called *complexity theory*. For the uninitiated, it is necessary to know only that there are classes of problem whose solution requires resources which are an exponential function of the size of the particular problem. For example, the time taken to find a path through a maze increases exponentially with the number of branching paths. Similarly, the time taken to find a proof for a theorem of the propositional calculus is exponential in the number of variables. Such problems are intractable in general, and called *NP-hard*; the interested reader is referred to a standard text, such as Hopcroft and Ullman (1979) for further technical details and an explanation of the terminology. Problems that admit of polynomial time algorithms, on the other hand, are deemed tractable. For example, verifying a given path through a maze or checking a proof of some theorem is a tractable problem. Unhappily, most of the problems that interest us in artificial intelligence can be shown to be NP-hard; hence the importance of heuristic methods. A nice non-technical introduction to computational complexity can be found in Poundstone (1988, Chapter 9).

The early chapters of Nilsson (1980) provide an excellent introduction to topics in heuristic search. Pearl (1984) is also recommended for the more mathematically minded. Readers interested in the current state of computer understanding are recommended to consult Allen (1987) for a thorough account of recent research in natural language processing.

STUDY SUGGESTIONS

2.1 (a) Here is the algorithm for depth-first search. It is written in a functional notation which renders its recursive structure apparent. Thus dfs is a function of three arguments: goal, current and pending. goal is the object of the search, current is the current node (initially the start state), and pending is a list of nodes waiting to be expanded (initially empty). := indicates assignment, expand is a function that generates the successors of a node, and + is a function that appends two lists, for example:

(a b c) + (d e f) = (a b c d e f).

() is the empty list, while first and rest are functions which return the head of a list and the tail of a list respectively, for example:

```
first(a b c) = a
rest(a b c) = (b c).
```

Encode the following algorithm in the programming language of your choice:

```
dfs(goal, current, pending)
    if C = G, then success
    else pending:= expand(current) + pending;
        if pending = () then fail
        else dfs(goal, first(pending), rest(pending))
```

(b) Write a similar algorithm for breadth-first search, and implement it. It is necessary to change only one statement in the dfs function.

2.2   Consider the 'missionaries and cannibals' puzzle, shown in Figure 2.2. This puzzle can be stated as follows. There are three missionaries, three cannibals and

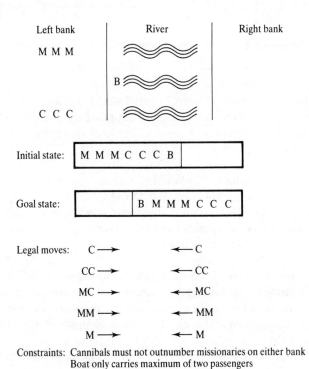

Figure 2.2   The missionaries and cannibals puzzle.

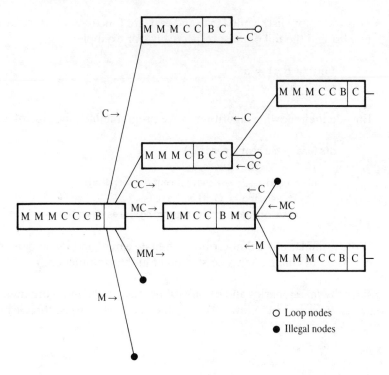

Figure 2.3   Developing the missionaries and cannibals search space.

a boat on the left bank of a river (initial state). To solve the puzzle, you must transport all six persons to the right bank using the boat (goal state). The boat carries only two persons at a time, and at least one person must bring the boat back. Thus the legal moves are:

C→   one cannibal from left to right
CC→   two cannibals from left to right
MC→   one missionary and one cannibal from left to right
MM→   two missionaries from left to right
M→   one missionary from left to right

plus the inverse moves from right to left. However, the following complication acts as a further constraint: if the cannibals ever outnumber the missionaries on either bank, then they will naturally devour them. A solution to this problem is therefore a sequence of moves which leads from the start state to the goal state without mishap.

It is possible to solve this problem by exhaustive generate-and-test, since the underlying search space is quite small. Figure 2.3 shows how the search space can be formed by the recursive application of applicable operators, with 'loop

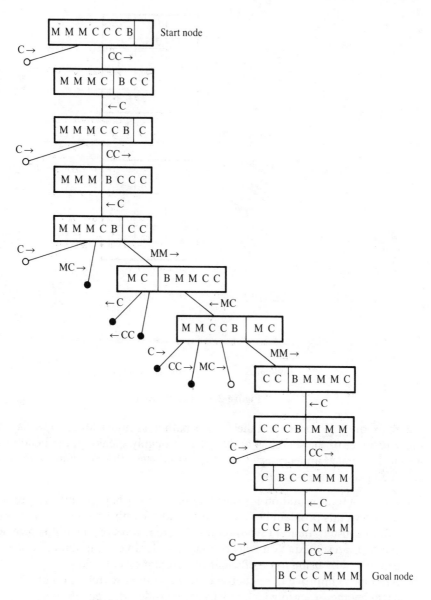

Figure 2.4 The complete search space as developed by depth-first search.

nodes' and 'illegal nodes' clearly marked. Loop nodes are nodes where the application of an operator leads back to an earlier state, while illegal nodes are nodes that fail the anthropophagic constraint. Clearly, the node expansion function, such as expand in the dfs algorithm, should not return such nodes.

Figure 2.4 shows the complete search space as developed by depth-first search, with moves being tried in the order in which they are listed above. The

2	8	3
1	6	4
7		5

Initial state: As above (say)

Goal state:

1	2	3
8		4
7	6	5

Legal moves: Move blank up
                                      down
                                      left
                                      right

Constraints: No diagonal moves

Figure 2.5 The 8-puzzle.

search expands 22 nodes, and the success path is 11 nodes long, so we say that the *penetrance* of the search is $11/22 = 0.5$. Roughly speaking, the penetrance tells us how much unnecessary work the search algorithm has managed to avoid, so a high penetrance is good.

(a) Choose a representation for the state of the river banks, and write programs that solve this problem by both depth- and breadth-first search. You might like to consult Amarel (1968) on the different ways in which this problem can be represented. You will see that considerable computational savings can be derived by using more efficient representations of states.

(b) Attempt to improve the penetrance of depth-first search in Figure 2.4 by changing the order in which moves are considered at each state.

(c) Generalize your program so that both the size of the boat and the number of missionaries/cannibals are now parameters rather than being fixed. If you experiment, you will find that these parameters cannot be varied independently, because some combinations render the problem insoluble, and increasing both parameters greatly increases the size of the search space.

2.3 Another classic problem is that posed by the 8-puzzle. In this puzzle, one can slide eight moveable tiles up, down, left and right in a 3×3 frame. The goal is to get from some arbitrary jumbled configuration to some order state (see Figure 2.5). Note that the specification of the legal moves can be greatly simplified if the movement of any tile is seen in terms of moving the blank, that is, the single empty space.

Unlike the missionaries and cannibals problem, the 8-puzzle is not soluble in reasonable time by exhaustive search methods. This is because the puzzle has 9! (over 300 000) possible states. Consequently, an evaluation function must be used to augment generate-and-test with hill climbing.

(a) Devise an evaluation function for this problem, and write a program which performs hill-climbing on the underlying search space. Possible evaluation functions for states include the number of tiles out of place and the sum of the Euclidean distance of each tile from its 'home' space.
(b) Which of the evaluation functions suggested above is the most sensitive? Can you devise a better guide for search?
(c) How does your program perform on the 15-puzzle? (This consists of 15 tiles arranged in a 4×4 frame. It has 16! (over 2^{13}) possible states.)

Note that the 8-puzzle is well discussed in Nilsson (1980, Chapter 1).

2.4 There is a well-known algorithm for best-first search, known as A* (pronounced 'A star'). The basic idea behind A* is that, for each node n that we develop, we compute the value of the function

$$f(n) = g(n) + h(n)$$

where $g(n)$ reflects the distance of n from the start node and $h(n)$ estimates the distance from n to the goal node. Thus a low value of $f(n)$ is 'good' (n is on a short path to the goal), while a high value is 'bad'. The idea is to use $f(n)$ to find the cheapest path from the start to the goal.

It turns out that if $h(n)$ is a lower bound on the *actual* distance to the goal (if $h(n)$ never overestimates the distance) the A* algorithm will always find an optimal path to the goal using $f(n)$ as its evaluation function. Algorithms with this property are called *admissible* (see Nilsson, 1982, Chapter 2 and Pearl, 1984, Chapter 2 for further discussions).

(a) Implement the following algorithm in your favourite programming language.

Notation
s is the start node
g is the goal node
OPEN is a list that holds unexpanded nodes
CLOSED is a list that holds expanded nodes

The A* Algorithm
1. OPEN := {s}.
2. If OPEN = { }, then halt. There is no path to the goal.
3. Remove a node n from OPEN for which $f(n) \leq f(m)$ for all other nodes m on OPEN, and place n on CLOSED.

4. Generate the successors of n, and give each successor a pointer back to n.
5. If g is among the successors of n,
   then halt and return the path derived by tracing pointers back from g to s.
6. For each successor n' of n do the following:
   (a) Compute $f(n')$.
   (b) If n' is not on OPEN or CLOSED,
       then add it to OPEN, assign $f(n')$ to n', and set a pointer back from n' to n.
   (c) If n' is already on OPEN or CLOSED,
       then compare new value of $f(n') = new$ with the old value $f(n') = old$.
       If $old < new$,
       then discard the new node.
       If $new < old$,
       then substitute the new node for the old in the list,
          moving the new node to OPEN if the old node was on CLOSED.

(b) Use the resulting program to solve the missionaries and cannibals puzzle and the 8-puzzle. (You will need an evaluation function for the missionaries and cannibals puzzle.)
(c) Finally, try the algorithm on the following cryptarithmetic puzzles (see explanation below):

	BEST		SEND		DONALD		CROSS
+	MADE	+	MORE	+	GERALD	+	ROADS
	MASER		MONEY		ROBERT		DANGER

Cryptarithmetic means coded arithmetic, where letters represent digits and words represent numbers. The problem is to find which digits must be substituted for the letters so that the sum is arithmetically correct. Such puzzles are discussed in many standard AI texts, (see, for example, Raphael 1976, Chapter 3).

You will need to decide how to represent the summands and their sum, what the possible 'moves' are (how you generate new nodes in the search space), and what are good heuristics for guiding the search.

3 The Early Years: DENDRAL and MYCIN

Introduction

In Chapter 2, we saw that researchers had, for the most part, become disillusioned with weak methods of problem solving, such as generate-and-test and hill climbing. Various technical problems were noted with the discovery and use of evaluation functions, and it was felt that such methods undervalued domain-specific knowledge and common sense, and overvalued the notion of general intelligence. It is unlikely that expert systems as a field of research would exist today, had these attempts to develop general-purpose problem-solving programs proved successful.

This chapter describes two early expert systems, each of which marks a somewhat different kind of departure from the 'general problem solving' tradition. DENDRAL can be seen as a stepping stone from older programs based on heuristic search to more recent systems involving an explicit representation of domain knowledge. The search for solutions is constrained by information supplied by the user, who plays an active role in guiding the program through the space of alternatives. MYCIN, on the other hand, is more like a theorem prover, in that it sets out to achieve a particular goal by splitting it into subgoals. It explores most of the search space, and then scores alternative solutions before ranking them.

In attempting to relate the theory and practice of artificial intelligence to the emerging technology of expert systems, it seems sensible to start with descriptions of systems which are well documented and well understood. A good deal of technical detail is suppressed at this stage, since the main aim is to give the reader an accurate impression of the design principles of the two systems. The chapter concludes with an attempt to evaluate the systems, and some preliminary comments on the problem of evaluation generally.

3.1 Heuristic search in DENDRAL

The DENDRAL project began at Stanford University in 1965, and was perhaps the first system to demonstrate that it was possible for a computer program to rival the performance of domain experts in a specialized field. The task was to determine the molecular structure of an unknown organic compound, and the method that the system used was a modified form of generate-and-test. To help the reader understand what the program does, it is first of all necessary to say a little about the domain, but the chemistry will be simplified and played down in favour of general principles.

3.1.1 Structure elucidation of organic compounds

Imagine that you are a chemist who has been presented with an unknown chemical compound. It is your job to find out the molecular structure of this compound, which involves determining which atoms are in the compound, and how they are connected together to form the molecule. Both the source of the compound and the procedures used to isolate it may give you some clues as to what kind of molecule to expect. Additional evidence can be gained by subjecting the compound to various tests. DENDRAL is concerned with the interpretation of data obtained from a laboratory device called a mass spectrometer, so this device needs to be explained.

A mass spectrometer works by bombarding the chemical sample with a beam of electrons, which causes the compound to fragment and its components to become rearranged. A molecule can be considered as a connected graph, in which case fragmentation corresponds to the breaking of edges in the graph, which stand for chemical bonds. Atom migrations correspond to the detachment of nodes from one subgraph and their attachment to another subgraph; these charged fragments are collected by mass to form a spectrum.

The problem is that any complex molecule can fragment in more than one way, because different bonds can be dissolved as a result of the bombardment, accompanied by different patterns of migration. The theory of mass spectrometry is therefore incomplete, in the following sense. We can

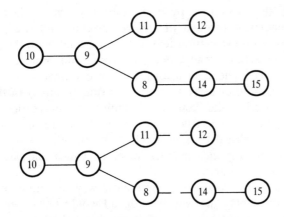

Figure 3.1 Fragmentation under electron bombardment.

make some predictions concerning which bonds in a given molecule are *likely* to break (and therefore contribute to peaks in the mass spectrum), but we are not always sure *exactly* how the molecule will fragment.

By analogy, if I sit on my sunglasses, one likely fragmentation path is that one or both of the lenses will fall out. If we now weigh the pieces (in order of size, say), we get a particular 'mass spectrum' of the mangled artefact. But it is always possible that the lenses will stay in and one or both of the 'legs' will break off from the frame. Weighing the pieces would now give us a different mass spectrum. Thus the theory of fractured sunglasses is incomplete in that, even if we know what the original object is, we can't predict what its post-accident profile will be.

Returning to the chemistry domain, Figure 3.1 represents a prediction to the effect that, if the substructure shown in the top half of the figure appears in a molecule, then the bonds between atoms 8 and 14, and between atoms 11 and 12, will break under the electron bombardment, as indicated by the three structures in the bottom half of the figure.

However, when you are working in the other direction, from peaks representing fragmentations to the original molecule, life is even more difficult. Think of the sunglasses again. Suppose all you are given is a mass profile that shows the masses of the pieces plotted in columns against the sizes of the pieces, and you are asked to determine the *make* of the fractured sunglasses. Thoughtfully, we provide you with a table that says, for any make of sunglasses in the world, what its overall mass is and what the masses of its lenses and legs are. The trouble is that some parts of some sunglasses may weigh the same as *different* parts of others, so you can't always tell whether the mass at a particular column is a lens or a leg.

Chemists are in a (somewhat) similar position. The best that they can hope for is to identify some of the compound's substructure, and then derive a set of *constraints* that the other subparts must satisfy. In other words, given that spectroscopy and other tests have allowed you to deduce the chemical formula of the compound, and the presence or absence of certain substructural features, you are left with the problem of discovering the actual arrangement of atoms and molecules in three-dimensional space. The conclusions you have drawn so far are called constraints because they serve to restrict or rule out many of the possible arrangements which could result in structural variants, called isomers.

The problem is not trivial. For example, there are about 10 000 isomers of the empirical formula $C_6H_{13}NO_2$. In other words, there are about 10 000 topologically distinct ways in which the atoms of the molecule might be arranged.

Given that you have some systematic way of enumerating all the possible arrangements, one way to proceed would be to generate them one after the other and then discard those that failed to satisfy the constraints. However, this would be very expensive in terms of computer resources. It is preferable to constrain the initial generation of candidates, and consider only a fraction of the possible arrangements.

The DENDRAL Planner is a program that can be used to assist with the process of deciding which constraints to impose. More specifically, it applies knowledge of spectral processes (how things break) to infer constraints from instrument data. There are two kinds of constraint: required and forbidden.

- *Required* constraints are based on the conclusions that we have already drawn, and the requirement that candidates exhibit the requisite features.
- *Forbidden* constraints rule out possibilities either because they fail to fit the data, or because the resultant structures would be chemically unstable.

These constraints can be supplied in various ways; for example, by giving the program a structural skeleton into which the atoms have to fit, or by supplying rules that say how you expect the compound to fragment. The program associates peaks in the spectrogram with fragments in this skeleton, and then handles the combinatorics of finding consistent ways of fitting the substructures into the skeleton. The output from the Planner is a list of incomplete structural hypotheses that have been developed as far as the data and fragmentation rules will allow.

3.1.2 CONGEN: a constrained generator

CONGEN is a DENDRAL program which constructs complete chemical structures by manipulating symbols that stand for atoms and molecules. It receives as its input a molecular formula, together with a set of constraints which serve to restrict the possible interconnections among atoms. Its output is a list of all possible ways of assembling the atoms into molecular structures, given the constraints imposed.

So CONGEN assists by allowing the chemist to specify various kinds of structural constraint and then generating an exhaustive and non-redundant list of complete structural hypotheses. The latter step employs a structure generation algorithm to determine all topologically unique ways of assembling a given set of atoms into molecular structures. This is an iterative process, during which the chemist can impose further constraints, suggested either by new evidence or by the hypotheses themselves.

A session begins with the definition of a molecular formula, such as $C_{15}H_{26}O$. Typically, the user also defines the following kinds of constraint upon structural hypotheses:

(1)   *Constraining structures*, or 'superatoms', that the compound must contain. Typical candidates for superatoms are chains or rings of carbon atoms with associated hydrogens, which are very common in organic compounds. CONGEN uses free valences to link such structures to other structures. (The *valency* of a structure is an index of its ability to combine with other structures. The notion is based on the theory that bonds between atoms are formed by their sharing electrons.)

(2)   *Other constraints* that the compound must satisfy. For example, one could specify that the hypotheses must contain a carbon ring of a certain size, or that particular superatoms are allowed only a certain number of internal bonds. Any such additional information will help to prune the hypothesis space.

Having done this, one can run the CONGEN program on the problem, and the structure generation algorithm will produce hypotheses consistent with both the specified superatoms and the constraints. Even so, CONGEN may generate hundreds of structures. Consequently, the user may wish to display some of them to see if important constraints have been left out.

DENDRAL also has programs to help the user rule out some hypotheses and order the others by using knowledge of mass spectrometry to make testable predictions about candidate molecules. Thus the program MSPRUNE eliminates candidates which are not worth considering because the fragmentations one would expect them to undergo are not found in the spectral data. MSRANK orders the remaining candidates according to the number of predicted peaks which appear in the data and the number of peaks not found. The scores for the presence and absence of these features are weighted according to the importance of the underlying spectral processes. This is basically a strategy of hypothesize-and-test. Initial data suggest some space of hypotheses, each of which predict the presence or absence of certain other data, and can be verified or eliminated as a consequence. (This problem-solving strategy is analysed in more detail in Chapter 16.)

After each iteration through the candidates, new substructures can be specified, and additional assertions about free valencies can be made. Such pieces of information enable the program to prune the list of candidate structures still further. This process is repeated until the chemist has succeeded in narrowing down the number of hypotheses, perhaps by running additional experiments on the compound to derive further constraints.

This section closes with part of a sample CONGEN interaction (see Figure 3.2) taken from Lindsay, *et al.* (1980, Chapter 4). It is interspersed with comments in italics; I have expanded on the comments given in the book referenced above. The dialogue itself is rendered in upper case, with bold face type distinguishing the user inputs from the outputs of the program. Dots (...) will indicate points in the dialogue where material is omitted.

WELCOME TO CONGEN, VERSION VI.

The user defines the empirical formula of the compound, $C_{12}H_{14}O$.
The goal of the session is to discover its molecular structure.

 # DEFINE MOLFORM C 12 H 14 O
MOLECULAR FORMULA DEFINED

The user knows that the compound contains a number of
substructures which are defined next.

 # DEFINE SUBSTRUCTURE Z

(NEW SUBSTRUCTURE)

The next three commands elaborate the substructure by forming a
five-membered ring, ...

>RING 5

... doubly bonding a carbon to an atom, ...

>LINK 1 1 1

...defining atom 6 to be an oxygen, ...

Figure 3.2   Part of a user dialogue with CONGEN.

>ATNAME 6 O

... and specifying the number of hydrogens associated with various atoms. The HRANGE command HRANGE a m n *states that atom* a *must have between* m *and* n *hydrogen neighbours. The arguments can be iterated, so that*

>HRANGE 2 1 1 3 1 2 4 1 2 5 2 2

indicates that atom 2 must have one hydrogen, atoms 3 and 4 must each have one or two hydrogens, and atom 5 must have two hydrogens.

The user can ask the system to draw and otherwise display substructures, before finishing a definition.

>DRAW NUMBERED

SUBSTRUCTURE Z (HRANGES NOT INDICATED)

$$6 = 1 - 5 - 4$$

$$2 - 3$$

Note that atom 6 is the oxygen defined earlier, which is doubly bounded to the carbon atom 1 to form a carbonyl group. Atoms 3 and 4 have free valencies for possible hydrogen neighbours.

>DONE
Z DEFINED

The user can also define disallowed structures, which are not *allowed to appear in the molecular structure.*

(...)

Eventually, the user is ready for CONGEN to generate candidate structures. The program queries the user regarding how

Figure 3.2 continued

substructures and constraints should guide candidate generation. Below, we see that the user insists on at least one occurrence of the previously defined substructure Z.

#GENERATE
SUPERATOM: **Z**
RANGE OF OCCURRENCES: **AT LEAST ONE**
(...)

The program prints out the 'collapsed' formula; that is, the formula incorporating user-defined substructures (or 'superatoms').

'COLLAPSED' FORMULA IS C 3 Z 1 V 2 H 9

The program also prompts the user for additional constraints. The first constraint prevents the superatom Z from bonding with itself, while the second stops ring 2 from having more than three double bonds.

CONSTRAINT: **LOOP Z NONE**
(..)
CONSTRAINT: **RING 2 EXACTLY 3**

(...)

18 STRUCTURES WERE GENERATED

The user can now ask for the candidates to be displayed. Future iterations of the program will consist of embedding more superatoms and applying more user-supplied constraints to narrow the space of alternatives.

Figure 3.2 continued

3.2 Subgoaling in MYCIN

This section concentrates on a particular medical expert system, MYCIN, giving a simplified account of its function, structure and run-time behaviour in some detail. The purpose is to illustrate certain ideas about representation and control, without having to resort to abstractions and generalities. As with the section on DENDRAL, a simplified account of the domain is essential to understanding why the program works as it does.

3.2.1 Treating blood infections

An 'antimicrobial agent' is any drug designed to kill bacteria or arrest their growth. Some agents are too toxic for therapeutic purposes, and there is no single agent effective against all bacteria. The selection of therapy for bacterial infection can be viewed as a four-part decision process:

- deciding if the patient has a significant infection;
- determining the (possible) organism(s) involved;
- selecting a set of drugs that might be appropriate;
- choosing the most appropriate drug or combination of drugs.

Samples taken from the site of infection are sent to a microbiology laboratory for culture – an attempt to grow organisms from the sample in a suitable medium. Early evidence of growth may allow a report of the morphological or staining characteristics of the organism. However, even if an organism is identified, the range of drugs it is sensitive to may be unknown or uncertain.

The purpose of MYCIN is to assist a physician who is not an expert in the field of antibiotics with the treatment of blood infections. Work on MYCIN began in 1972 as a collaboration between the medical and AI communities at Stanford. The most complete single account of this work is Shortliffe (1976).

There have been a number of extensions, revisions and abstractions of MYCIN since 1976, but the basic version has five components, as shown in Figure 3.3, where arrows show the basic pattern of information flow between the modules:

(1)   a *knowledge base*, which contains factual and judgemental knowledge about the domain;

(2)   a *dynamic patient database* containing information about a particular case;

(3)   a *consultation program*, which asks questions, draws conclusions and gives advice about a particular case based on the patient data and the static knowledge;

(4)   an *explanation program*, which answers questions and justifies this advice, using static knowledge and a trace of the program's execution;

(5)   a *knowledge acquisition program* for adding new rules and changing existing ones.

The system consisting of components 1–3 is the problem-solving part of MYCIN, which generates hypotheses with respect to the offending organ-

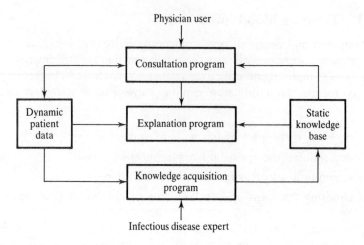

Figure 3.3 Organization of MYCIN (from Buchanan and Shortliffe, 1984).

isms, and makes therapy recommendations based on these hypotheses. We shall look at each of these components, emphasizing basic design principles rather than programming detail. The explanation system is discussed in Chapter 19, and the rule acquisition system is discussed in Chapter 13.

3.2.2 MYCIN's knowledge base

MYCIN's knowledge base is organized around a set of rules of the general form

> *if* condition₁ *and* ... *and* conditionₘ *hold*
> *then draw* conclusion₁ *and* ... *and* conclusionₙ

encoded as data structures of the LISP programming language (see Chapter 7 and Appendix A). It is important to realize that these *if...then* statements are *not* program statements of the LISP language. Rather they are declarations of knowledge which will be interpreted by the consultation program (which *is* a LISP program).

Figure 3.4 shows the English translation of a typical MYCIN rule for inferring the class of an organism. This translation is provided by the program itself. Because MYCIN's rules are just LISP data structures, they can be processed by the same primitive functions used to manipulate LISP data.

The rule says that, if an isolated organism appears rod-shaped, stains in a certain way, and grows in the presence of oxygen, it is highly likely to be an enterobacteriaceae. The 0.8 is called the *tally* of the rule,

IF: (1)   The stain of the organism is Gram negative, and
   (2)   The morphology of the organism is rod, and
   (3)   The aerobicity of the organism is aerobic
THEN: There is strongly suggestive evidence (0.8) that
         the class of the organism is Enterobacteriaceae

Figure 3.4 A MYCIN production rule.

which says how certain the conclusion is, given that the conditions are satisfied. Each rule of this kind can be thought of as encoding a piece of human knowledge whose applicability depends only on the context established by the conditions of the rule.

As we shall see, the conditions of a rule can also be satisfied with varying degrees of certainty, so the import of such rules is roughly as follows:

if condition$_1$ *holds with certainty* x_1 ... *and* condition$_m$ *holds with certainty* x_m *then draw* conclusion$_1$ *with certainty* y_1 *and* ... *and* conclusion$_n$ *with certainty* y_n

where the certainty associated with each conclusion is a function of the combined certainties of the conditions and the tally, which is meant to reflect our degree of confidence in the application of the rule.

In summary, a rule is a premise–action pair; such rules are sometimes called 'productions' for purely historical reasons (see Chapter 8). *Premises* are conjunctions of conditions, and their certainty is a function of the certainty of these conditions. *Conditions* are either propositions which evaluate to truth or falsehood with some degree of certainty, for example

the organism is rod-shaped

or disjunctions of such conditions. *Actions* are either *conclusions* to be drawn with some appropriate degree of certainty (such as the identity of some organism) or *instructions* to be carried out (such as compiling a list of therapies).

We will explore the details of how rules are interpreted and scheduled for application in the following sections, but first we must look at MYCIN's other structures for representing medical knowledge.

In addition to rules, the knowledge base also stores facts and

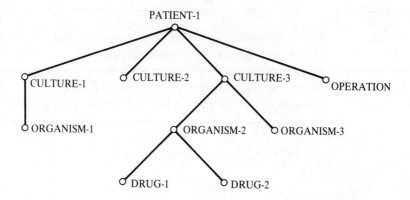

Figure 3.5 A typical MYCIN context tree (after Buchanan and Shortliffe, 1984).

definitions in various forms:

- simple lists, such as the list of all organisms known to the system;
- knowledge tables, which contain records of certain clinical parameters and the values they take under various circumstances, such as the morphology (structural shape) of every bacterium known to the system;
- a classification system for clinical parameters according to the context in which they apply, such as whether they are attributes of patients or organisms.

Much of the knowledge not contained in the rules resides in the properties associated with the 65 clinical parameters known to MYCIN. For example, shape is an attribute of organisms which can take on various values, such as 'rod' and 'coccus'. Parameters are also assigned properties by the system for its own purposes. The main ones either help to monitor the interaction with the user, or provide indexing which guides the application of rules.

Patient information is stored in a structure called the *context tree*, which serves to organize case data. Figure 3.5 shows a context tree representing a particular patient, PATIENT-1, with three associated cultures (samples, such as blood samples, from which organisms may be isolated) and a recent operative procedure that may need to be taken into account (perhaps because drugs were involved, or because the procedure involves particular risks of infection). Associated with cultures are organisms suggested by laboratory data, and associated with organisms are drugs that are effective against them.

Imagine that we have the following data stored in a kind of record structure associated with the node for ORGANISM-1:

GRAM = (GRAMNEG 1.0)
MORPH = (ROD .8) (COCCUS .2)
AIR = (AEROBIC .6)

with the following meaning:

- the Gram stain of ORGANISM-1 is definitely Gram negative;
- ORGANISM-1 has a rod morphology with certainty 0.8 and a coccus morphology with certainty 0.2;
- ORGANISM-1 is aerobic (grows in air) with certainty 0.6.

Suppose now that the rule of Figure 3.4 is applied. We want to compute the certainty that all three conditions of the rule

IF: (1)   the stain of the organism is Gram negative, and
    (2)   the morphology of the organism is rod, and
    (3)   the aerobicity of the organism is aerobic
THEN: there is strongly suggestive evidence (0.8) that
        the class of the organism is Enterobacteriaceae.

are satisfied by the data. The certainty of the individual conditions is 1.0, 0.8 and 0.6 respectively, and the certainty of their conjunction is taken to be the minimum of their individual certainties, hence 0.6.

(The idea behind taking the minimum is that we are confident in a conjunction of conditions only to the extent that we are confident in its least inspiring element. This is rather like saying that a chain is only as strong as its weakest link. By an inverse argument, we argue that our confidence in a disjunction of conditions is as strong as the strongest alternative, or, in other words, we take the maximum. This convention forms part of a style of inexact reasoning called *fuzzy logic*, which is discussed more thoroughly in Chapter 6.)

In this case, we draw the conclusion that the class of the organism is Enterobacteriaceae with a degree of certainty equal to

$$0.6 \times 0.8 = 0.48$$

The 0.6 represents our degree of certainty in the conjoined conditions, while the 0.8 stands for our degree of certainty in the rule application. These degrees of certainty are sometimes called *certainty factors* (CFs), and they fall in the range $[-1, +1]$. Thus, in the general case,

$$CF(action) = CF(premise) \times CF(rule)$$

The use of certainty factors is discussed in more detail in Chapter 6, where we broach the whole topic of how to represent uncertainty. It turns out that the CF model is not always in agreement with the theory of probability; in other words, it is not always correct from a mathematical point of view. However, the computation of certainty factors is much more tractable than the computation of the right probabilities, and the deviation does not appear to be very great in the MYCIN application.

3.2.3 MYCIN's control structure

MYCIN has a top-level goal rule which defines the whole task of the consultation system, which is paraphrased below:

> IF (1) there is an organism which requires therapy, and
> (2) consideration has been given to any other organisms re-quiring therapy
> THEN compile a list of possible therapies, and determine the best one in this list.

A consultation session follows a simple two-step procedure:

- Create the patient context as the top node in the context tree.
- Attempt to apply the goal rule to this patient context.

Applying the rule involves evaluating its premise, which involves finding out if there is indeed an organism which requires therapy. To find this out, MYCIN must first find out if there is indeed an organism present which is associated with a significant disease. This information can be obtained either from the user direct, or via some chain of inference based on symptoms and laboratory data provided by the user.

The consultation is essentially a search through a tree of goals. The top goal at the root of the tree is the action part of the goal rule; that is, the recommendation of a drug therapy. Subgoals further down the tree include determining the organism involved and seeing if it is significant. Many of these subgoals have subgoals of their own, such as finding out the stain properties and morphology of an organism. The leaves of the tree are fact goals, such as laboratory data, which cannot be deduced.

A special kind of structure, called an *AND/OR tree*, is very useful for representing the way in which goals can be expanded into subgoals by a program. The basic idea is that the root node of the tree represents the main goal, terminal nodes represent primitive actions that can be carried out, and non-terminal nodes represent subgoals that are susceptible to further analysis. Figure 3.6 shows an AND/OR tree for attaining the worthy goal of eating.

To eat, one must either earn money, borrow money, or steal food. To earn money, one can either find a job or write a book. To find a job,

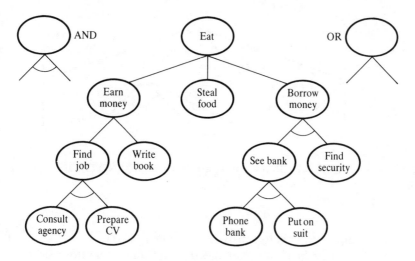

Figure 3.6 An AND/OR tree for eating.

one must consult an employment agency and prepare a curriculum vitae. (The 'steal food' subgoal is not expanded, for moral reasons.) To borrow money one must see one's bank and find some security to offer for the loan. To achieve the 'see bank' goal, one should make an appointment and put on a suit (since, to borrow money, you must look as if you do not really need it).

There is a simple correspondence between this kind of analysis and the analysis of rule sets. Consider this set of condition–action rules:

> if P and Q hold, then conclude R
> if S and T hold, then conclude R
> if U or V hold, then conclude P
> if W and X hold, then conclude S
> if Y holds, then conclude S
> if Z holds, then conclude T

We can represent this rule set in terms of a tree of goals, so long as we maintain the distinction between conjunctions and disjunctions of subgoals. Thus, in Figure 3.7, we draw an arc between the links connecting the nodes P and Q with the node R, to signify that both subgoals P and Q must be satisfied in order to satisfy the goal R. However, there is no arc between the links connecting U and V with P, because satisfying either U or V will satisfy P. Note that the links in the AND/OR tree represent rule applications. Thus the combined links between P and Q and R signify that P and Q implies R.

Thus one way of proceeding to satisfy R is to try to satisfy both P

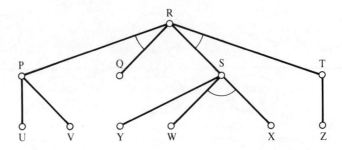

Figure 3.7 Representing a rule set as an AND/OR tree.

and Q; another way is to satisfy both S and T. Either U or V will satisfy P, while Q is a 'leaf' node of the tree and must therefore be satisfied without more ado, for example by data or by asking the user. The AND/OR tree can be thought of as a way of representing the *problem space* for R; that is, the way in which different operators can be applied to establish R as true.

This kind of control structure is called *backward chaining*, because the program reasons backward from what it wants to prove towards the facts that it needs, rather than reasoning forward from the facts that it possesses. Searching for a solution by backward chaining is generally more focused than searching by forward chaining, because one only considers potentially relevant facts (see Chapters 5 and 8 for further discussion).

In any event, it is easy to see that MYCIN's control structure is quite different from CONGEN's iterative loop, where each cycle of the computation is begun by a fresh initiative on the part of the user. MYCIN can ask the user for items of data as and when they are needed for the evaluation of a condition in the current rule, but does not enter into an extended dialogue with the user as CONGEN does. If the required information is not forthcoming, there may be rules which apply to the clinical parameter in question and which can be invoked in search of its value, but if there are no such rules the current rule application will fail.

This control structure is quite simple as AI programs go; there are only a few deviations from the exhaustive search methods described in Chapter 2:

(1)   The subgoal set up is always a generalized form of the original goal. So, if the subgoal is to prove the proposition that the identity of the organism is *Escherichia coli*, the subgoal actually set up is to determine the identity of the organism. This initiates an exhaustive search on a given topic, which collects all of the available evidence.

(2) Every rule relevant to the goal is used, unless one of them succeeds with certainty. This is because of the inexact character of many of the inferences drawn, necessitating the collection of evidence concerning more than one hypothesis. If the evidence about a hypothesis falls between -0.2 and $+0.2$, it is regarded as inconclusive, and the answer is treated as unknown. Otherwise, weights of evidence, X and Y, deriving from the application of different rules are combined using the following formula to yield the single certainty factor:

$$CF = \begin{cases} X + Y - XY & X, Y > 0 \\ X + Y + XY & X, Y < 0 \\ (X + Y)/(1 - \min(|X|, |Y|)) & \text{otherwise} \end{cases}$$

where $|X|$ denotes the absolute value of X. One can see what is happening on an intuitive basis. If the two pieces of evidence both confirm (or disconfirm) the hypothesis, confidence in the hypothesis goes up (or down). If the two pieces of evidence are in conflict, the denominator dampens the effect.

The selection of therapy takes place after this diagnostic process has run its course. It consists of two phases: selecting candidate drugs, and then choosing a preferred drug, or combination of drugs, from this list.

The special goal rule given above does not lead to a conclusion, but instigates actions, assuming that the conditions in the premise are satisfied. At this point, MYCIN's therapy rules for selecting drug treatments come into play; they contain sensitivity information for the organisms known to the system. A sample therapy rule is given in Figure 3.8.

The numbers associated with each drug are the probabilities that a *Pseudomonas* species will be sensitive to the indicated drug. The preferred drug is selected from the list according to criteria which attempt to screen for contraindications of the drug and minimize the number of

---

IF   the identity of the organism is *Pseudomonas*
THEN   I recommend therapy from among the following drugs:

1 – COLISTIN (0.98)
2 – POLYMYXIN (0.96)
3 – GENTAMICIN (0.96)
4 – CARBENICILLIN (0.65)
5 – SULFISOXAZOLE (0.64)

Figure 3.8   A MYCIN therapy rule.

drugs administered, in addition to maximizing sensitivity. The user can go on asking for alternative therapies until MYCIN runs out of options, so the pronouncements of the program are not definitive.

3.3 Evaluation of DENDRAL and MYCIN

There are many ways in which one might evaluate an expert system, but the most obvious one is in comparison with a human expert. In developing the system, expert and knowledge engineer typically work together on a set of critical examples until the program can solve them all. Evaluation then involves giving the system 'unseen' examples and seeing if its judgements agree with those of the expert.

However, this is an oversimplification in many ways. DENDRAL is really an assistant that tries to generate good hypotheses; it does not make definitive pronouncements. Thus the most relevant question is: Do chemists find DENDRAL a useful tool? In MYCIN's case, the situation is somewhat different. Here the program is attempting to mimic some of the judgemental reasoning of a human expert, and so comparison with the expert *is* relevant.

The issue of evaluation is developed further in Chapters 17 and 21.

3.3.1 Evaluating DENDRAL

The DENDRAL program runs on the SUMEX computing facility at Stanford University in California, and is available over the TYMNET computer network. It supports hundreds of international users every day, assisting in structure elucidation problems for such things as antibiotics and impurities in manufactured chemicals. When applied to published structure elucidation problems to check their accuracy and completeness, the program found a number of plausible alternatives to the published solutions.

At the beginning of the chapter, I described DENDRAL as a stepping stone between general-purpose problem-solving programs and more recent developments in expert systems, for two reasons:

- DENDRAL uses a weak method, generate-and-test, to traverse the search space of alternative structures, but, unlike earlier programs it takes advice from the human expert into account as it generates candidates for testing. Thus it is able to benefit from the real world knowledge of the chemist expressed as a set of constraints that candidate solutions must meet.

- DENDRAL has access to an explicit representation of knowledge, in the form of fragmentation rules, which augments the algorithmic base for enumerating graph structures. However, it does not have some of the more advanced features for controlling inference found in later systems such as MYCIN. Control over the program's iteration through the candidates remains in the hands of the user.

It is perhaps worth asking why DENDRAL is such a success story, and what lessons about the limitations of current expert systems technology can be learned from the project.

- DENDRAL sets out to be an expert's assistant, rather than a stand-alone expert in its own right. This enables the system designer to allocate functions between man and machine and draw on their different strengths, rather than exposing their respective weaknesses. Thus the heuristic search technique is constrained by the domain knowledge (and the 'hunches') of the human expert.

- The heuristic search program has an algorithmic base for the enumeration of chemical structures considered as planar graphs. Thus the generation phase of the 'plan, generate and test' strategy is founded on a procedure with proven mathematical properties. Furthermore, the implementation of this algorithm is both efficient and well understood.

- There is a language with a well defined syntax and semantics for representing and recursively elaborating chemical structures. In other words, there are rules for making new symbol structures out of old, and for interpreting the result. Thus it is known, for any combination of symbols, whether or not it describes a possible structure and what it actually means.

It would be going too far to say that these three features are either necessary or sufficient for a successful expert systems application. There are interesting and useful programs which do not meet all of the above criteria, and the possession of these features is no guarantee of a happy outcome to the knowledge engineering effort. Nevertheless, getting the right allocation of function between man and machine, availing oneself of existing algorithms, and using a representation language whose syntax and semantics are strictly specified are important points to bear in mind when setting out to apply artificial intelligence techniques to any real world problem.

3.3.2 Evaluating MYCIN

As early as 1974, an initial study using the current version of MYCIN produced encouraging results. A panel of five experts in the diagnosis of infectious diseases approved 72% of MYCIN's recommendations on 15 real

Ratings by 8 experts on 10 cases.
Perfect score = 80.

MYCIN	52	Actual therapy	46
Faculty-1	50	Faculty-4	44
Faculty-2	48	Resident	36
Infectious diseases fellow	48	Faculty-5	34
Faculty-3	46	Student	24

Unacceptable therapy = 0.
Equivalent or acceptable therapy = 1.

Figure 3.9 MYCIN's performance compared with those of human experts.

cases of bacterial infection. The main problem was not the accuracy of the diagnosis, but a lack of rules for judging the severity of the illness.

In 1979, more formal studies of an improved system showed that MYCIN's performance compared favourably with that of experts on patients with bacteraemia and meningitis. The program's final conclusions on ten real cases were compared with those of Stanford physicians, including the actual therapy administered. Eight other experts were then asked to rate the ten therapy recommendations on each of the cases and award a mark out of 80 for each set of recommendations, without knowing which, if any, came from a computer. The results are shown in Figure 3.9.

The differences between MYCIN's score and those of Stanford experts was not significant, but its score is as good as the experts and better than the non-expert physicians.

However, MYCIN was never used in hospital wards for a number of reasons, including:

● Its knowledge base is incomplete, since it does not cover anything like the full spectrum of infectious diseases.

● Running it would have required more computing power than most hospitals could afford at that time.

● Doctors do not relish typing at the terminal and require a much better user interface than that provided by MYCIN in 1976.

MYCIN was a research vehicle, and therefore did not set out to achieve practical application or commercial success. Nevertheless, descendants of

MYCIN have seen application in hospitals (see Chapter 19 on the PUFF system). Also, the success of the 'subgoaling' approach has not been confined to medical applications (see Chapter 13 on the SACON system).

3.3.3 Evaluating expert systems generally

Throughout, this text will deal with evaluation on a case-by-case basis. Expert systems, and their associated domains and tasks, are sufficiently diverse to resist generalization concerning the criteria for success. Nevertheless, we can identify a number of preconditions that are necessary for evaluation to be meaningful (see Hayes-Roth *et al.*, 1983, Chapter 8 for a discussion):

- There must be some *objective criteria* for success, otherwise we will never know whether or not the answer returned by a system is correct. In some domains, such as financial investment, there may be no criteria other than the consensual opinion of a panel of experts, or actually carrying out the advice of the system and seeing if it is proved right by events. The trouble with the former is that experts may disagree on precisely those cases where their opinion would be most helpful (the difficult cases); the trouble with the latter is that experimentation in the real world may be expensive or deleterious to health and safety.

- Proper *experimental procedures* must be followed. Rather than asking experts to rate a program's performance, it is better (as in the MYCIN study cited above) to run a 'blind' experiment, so that the raters do not know which solutions are generated by computer and which by humans. This design has the beneficial effect of both removing bias and imparting a real sense of how well a program performs with respect to the human competition.

- Evaluation should be done *painstakingly* or not at all. There is no point in attempting it with insufficient time or resources. It may take longer to test a knowledge-based program thoroughly than it did to design and implement it, so a certain level of commitment is essential.

Finally, the reader should bear in mind that expert systems may play very different roles in problem solving, which require rather different standards of performance. Some systems (like DENDRAL) function mostly as assistants, presenting the user with a range of possibilities. All we require of such systems is that they do not miss any solutions with respect to a given set of constraints, and that they get back to us in a finite time. Others (like MYCIN) generate whole solutions, which the user can accept or reject. Given that their recommendations are being monitored, such systems do not have to be 100% right all the time in order to be useful, but they should be capable of generating alternative solutions fairly briskly.

However, one can also conceive of systems which are entirely autonomous, in that they interact only with other systems, without human intervention. These programs had better get it right, and do so before changing conditions render their solutions obsolete; otherwise their mistakes had better be corrigible. They should also be robust in the face of *human* error, such as bad data inputs, which could form the basis of dangerous decisions.

Bibliographical notes

DENDRAL is well explained in Lindsay, *et al.* (1980). Readers with no previous knowledge of chemistry need not experience any difficulty in comprehending their account of the program. Apart from Shortliffe (1976), clear accounts of MYCIN can be found in Buchanan and Shortliffe (1984) and Clancey and Shortliffe (1984). The latter contains accounts of other, early forays into medical expert systems.

STUDY SUGGESTIONS

3.1 (After Nilsson, 1982, Chapter 1). Imagine that CONGEN is given the empirical formula C_5H_{12}, together with some spectrogram data, and asked what kinds of structure might be consistent with what we know about the compound. Suppose that the program replies with four structural candidates, as shown in Figure 3.10.

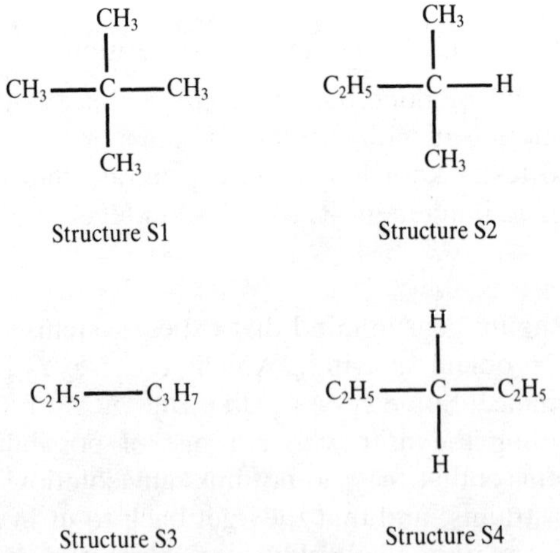

$$
\begin{array}{cc}
\underset{|}{CH_3} & \underset{|}{CH_3} \\
CH_3\!-\!\underset{|}{C}\!-\!CH_3 & C_2H_5\!-\!\underset{|}{C}\!-\!H \\
CH_3 & CH_3 \\
\text{Structure S1} & \text{Structure S2}
\end{array}
$$

$$
\begin{array}{cc}
 & \underset{|}{H} \\
C_2H_5\!-\!C_3H_7 & C_2H_5\!-\!\underset{|}{C}\!-\!C_2H_5 \\
 & H \\
\text{Structure S3} & \text{Structure S4}
\end{array}
$$

Figure 3.10 Candidate structures for C_5H_{12}.

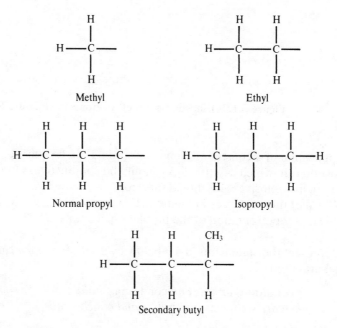

Figure 3.11 Possible arrangements of carbon and hydrogen atoms.

We can view the problem space for C_5H_{12} as a tree, where nodes in the tree represent candidate structures that are more or less filled out, and links represent the application of structure elucidation rules that propose further analysis of a structural skeleton. Thus, the root node of the tree would be C_5H_{12} itself, while its successor nodes would represent S1–S4. However, each of these successor nodes can be further developed, if we impose further constraints on candidate structures, based on a little knowledge of chemistry.

There are various ways that the atoms in a hydrocarbon molecule can be arranged. The fragments shown in Figure 3.11 represent some of the substructures (or 'superatoms') that might be present in the C_5H_{12} molecule. Note that carbon has a valency of four (four available bonds), while hydrogen's valency is 1.

Returning to CONGEN's four structural hypotheses, we can see that some of the structures could be further analysed. For example, S2 could be constrained to contain a methyl group, as in Figure 3.12, while S3 could be constrained to contain an isopropyl group.

(a) Continue the process of imposing constraints on the problem until you have all the structural hypotheses that can be generated by substituting substructures from Figure 3.11 into the skeletons of Figure 3.10.
(b) Draw an AND/OR tree of this hypothesis generation process in which nodes represent fully or partially developed hypotheses and links represent the

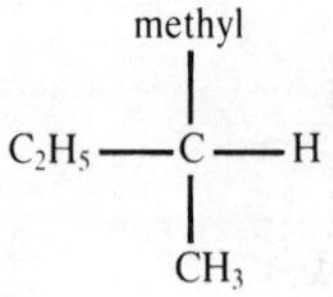

methyl

$$C_2H_5 \!-\!\! C \!-\! H$$

$$CH_3$$

Figure 3.12 Embedding a methyl group in structure S2.

application of a constraint. Some constraints can be consistently applied together, in which case the links should be conjunctive. Other constraints are mutually exclusive, and should therefore be disjunctive.

(c) Which of the structures in Figure 3.13 are possible, given your AND/OR tree as a representation of the problem space for C_5H_{12}?

3.2 (a) Represent the statements given below by a set of *if...then* rules of the general form

> *if* condition$_1$ *and* ... *and* condition$_m$ *hold*
> *then draw* conclusion$_1$ *and* ... *and* conclusion$_n$

Rules of the form

> *if* condition$_1$ *or* ... *or* condition$_m$ *hold*
> *then draw* conclusion$_1$ *and* ... *and* conclusion$_n$

have disjunctive conditions and should be split into more than one rule of the form

> *if* condition$_i$ *holds*
> *then draw* conclusion$_1$ *and* ... *and* conclusion$_n$

for each i, $1 \le i \le m$. Here are the statements.

The summit conference will be a success if Bush, Thatcher and Gorbachev attend and an agreement is signed.

Bush will attend if he can bring Barbara or the dogs, while Thatcher will attend so long as she can bring Dennis and Mitterand does not attend. Dennis will attend if refreshments are served, and Mitterand will not attend if the dogs are present. The dogs will attend so long as no-one talks politics.

An agreement will be signed so long as all three leaders are polite to each other. Bush will be polite to Thatcher so long as she is polite to him. Thatcher will be polite to Bush if Barbara comes to the meeting. Bush will be polite to Gorbachev if he pets the dogs. Thatcher will be polite to Gorbachev if she is in a good mood. Gorbachev will be polite to everybody so long as the dogs do not bite.

(b) Represent this rule set as an AND/OR tree. You may decide to convert this structure into an AND/OR *graph*, by eliminating duplicate nodes and redirecting their pointers.

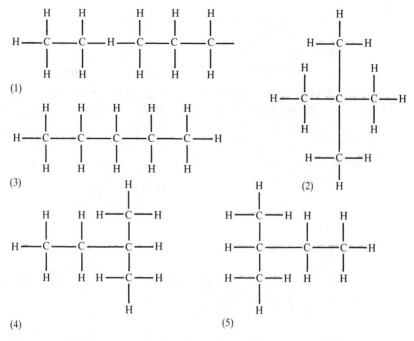

Figure 3.13   Putative structural arrangements for C_5H_{12}

3.3   Consider the following rule:

> IF: (1)   The stain of the organism is Gram positive, and
> (2)   The morphology of the organism is coccus, and
> (3)   The growth conformation of the organism is chains
> THEN: There is suggestive evidence (0.7) that
> the identity of the organism is *Streptococcus*

Suppose that the conditions of the rule are satisfied with the following degrees of certainty:

> Condition 1:   0.8
> Condition 2:   0.2
> Condition 3:   0.5.

What certainty will MYCIN associate with the conclusion that the identity of the organism is *Streptococcus*?

3.4   Consider the following pair of rules:

> IF: (1)   The site of the culture is blood, and
> (2)   The patient has ecthyma gangraenosum skin lesions
> THEN: There is suggestive evidence (0.6) that
> the identity of the organism is *Pseudomonas*

> IF: (1) The type of the infection is bacterial, and
>   (2) The patient has been seriously burned
> THEN: There is weakly suggestive evidence (0.4) that
>   the identity of the organism of *Pseudomonas*

Suppose that the conditions of the first rule are satisfied with certainties 0.8 and 0.9 respectively, while the conditions of the second rules are satisfied with certainties 0.2 and 0.3 respectively. According to MYCIN's evidence combination function, what certainty will be attributed to the conclusion that the identity of the organism is *Pseudomonas*?

Part II

Theoretical Foundations of Representation

4 Representation and Control

Introduction

In the field of expert systems, knowledge representation implies that we have some systematic way of codifying what an expert knows about some domain. However, it would be a mistake to suppose that representation is the same thing as encoding, in the sense of encryption. If one encodes a message by transposing its constituent symbols in some regular fashion, the resultant piece of code would not be a *representation* of the contents of the message from an artificial intelligence point of view, even if the code were machine readable and easy to store in the memory of the machine.

For one thing, the code would preserve any lexical or structural *ambiguity* of natural language inherent in the message. Thus the message 'Visiting aunts can be a nuisance' is just as ambiguous in its encrypted form as it is in English. Transcribing it into code does not alter the fact that it could mean either 'It is a nuisance having to visit one's aunt' or 'It is a nuisance having one's aunt to visit'.

Also, any communication of a technical nature always assumes some *prior knowledge* on the part of the addressee. Thus discourse on the subject of diagnosing digital circuitry assumes a knowledge of the basic principles governing electricity. Needless to say, a computer has no such prior knowledge, and so any representation of the technical expertise required for problem solving must be self-contained.

Finally, representation implies *organization*. A representation of knowledge should render that knowledge accessible and easy to apply via more or less natural mechanisms. Simply encoding knowledge in a machine readable form will not accomplish this. Relevant items of knowledge should be evoked by the circumstances in which they are most likely to be used. Thus a knowledge base should be extensively indexed and content-addressable, so that any program using it can control the way in which different pieces of knowledge are activated without having to know exactly how they are stored.

Of course, whatever notational system is used, ultimately a computer must be able to store and process the corresponding codes. It turns out that this is not a very constraining requirement, however. Many representational schemes that appear to be distinct can be shown to be formally equivalent – anything that can be expressed in one can be expressed in the other.

This chapter takes a look at representation from a certain level of generality. It begins by reviewing the place of representation in artificial intelligence theory, and by giving an extended example of how a simple language can be used to good effect. Then it considers the role of knowledge representation in expert systems, and discusses some of the problems that arise because of the imperfect state of knowledge under which even experts are usually forced to reason.

4.1 Representation and artificial intelligence

In an influential paper, McCarthy and Hayes (1969) argued that artificial intelligence researchers should be interested in artefacts that are 'equipped with a representation or model of the world'. In so doing, they were reacting against a behaviouristic or 'black-box' view of intelligence which I shall characterize by the slogan 'intelligence is as intelligence does'.

The black box view can be traced back to Turing's famous (1963) paper, in which he proposed what has become known as the 'Turing test' for intelligence. Roughly speaking, a computer would pass this test if a human observer could not distinguish its responses from those of a human subject in a blind experiment. The questions put to the two subjects could be on any subject whatsoever, from mathematical logic to favourite foods, and so on. An 'intelligent' computer program would therefore have to be clever enough to get some calculations wrong, and a good enough liar to convince you that it really did like beef stroganoff.

One can conceive of less exotic criteria for machine intelligence, of course, and these fall into two main groups: the behavioural and the epistemological. On the behavioural side, one could identify a certain class of problems, such as those normally requiring human intelligence for their solution, and then accord intelligence to programs that could solve them. The trouble with this approach is that it is not clear what that class of problems should be. On the epistemological side, one could emphasize our everyday abilities to identify objects, predict events, recognize the consequences of our actions, learn from experience, and so on. The trouble with this approach is that it appeals to entities that are available to us only via introspection, such as concepts, knowledge of facts, and so on. Who knows how these are actually represented in the human brain?

McCarthy and Hayes prefer the second approach, and argue that a system is intelligent if it has a model of the world that is adequate to the achievement of its goals. Such a definition of intelligence has two parts, which they call the *epistemological* and the *heuristic*. The epistemological part requires that the world be represented in such a way that solutions to problems can be shown to follow from the facts stored therein. The heuristic part is the mechanism that uses the representation of knowledge to draw inferences, make decisions and solve problems. The authors were most interested in the epistemological part, and posed such questions as 'In what kind of internal notation is the system's knowledge to be expressed?'.

Artificial intelligence researchers still ask themselves this question from time to time, although the answers are now thicker on the ground than they were in 1969. This chapter attempts to do no more than pose the question in an accessible way. I shall also try to show how the epistemological and the heuristic parts of a system interact, because this is where most of the problems arise.

4.2 Representation in STRIPS

Let us begin by trying to sharpen up our terminology. A *representation* has been defined as:

> a set of syntactic and semantic conventions that make it possible to describe things (Winston, 1984)

In artificial intelligence, 'things' normally means the state of some problem domain, such as the objects in that domain, their properties, and any relationships that hold between them.

The *syntax* of a representation specifies a set of rules for combining symbols to form expressions in the representation language. It should be possible to tell whether or not an expression is well formed; that is, whether or not it could have been generated by the rules. Only well-formed expressions are obliged to have a meaning.

A common syntax used in artificial intelligence is a *predicate–argument* construction of the form:

<sentence> ::= <predicate> (<argument>, ..., <argument>)

in which a k-place predicate is followed by k arguments. Thus at might be a two-place relation which takes as its first argument the name of some object and as its second argument the name of some place, such as a room, for example

```
at(robot, roomA).
```

The *semantics* of a representation specifies how expressions so constructed should be interpreted; that is, how meaning can be derived from form. This specification is usually done by assigning meanings to individual symbols, and then inducing an assignment to the more complex expressions (see Chapter 5). Thus, given meanings for the symbols at, robot and roomA, we say that at(robot, roomA) means that the robot is located in Room A (rather than Room A being located at the robot).

Now, problem solving typically involves reasoning about actions, as well as states of the world. As we saw in Chapter 2, problems can often be formulated in terms of an initial state, a goal state, and a set of operations that can be employed in an attempt to transform the initial state into the goal state. The question then arises as to how operations can be represented.

4.2.1 Operator tables and means–ends analysis

The STRIPS program (Fikes and Nilsson, 1971) demonstrates one approach to this representational problem (STRIPS stands for Stanford Research Institute Problem Solver). It was intended to solve the problem of plan formation in a robot designed to move objects about in a set of interconnected rooms. STRIPS was an influential program, and its basic representation for actions is still used in today's planning systems.

The current state of this world of rooms and objects was represented by a set of predicate argument expressions, the *world model*. Thus the set of formulas

$$W = \{at(robot, roomA), at(box1, roomB), at(box2, roomC)\}$$

would indicate that the robot was in Room A, and that there were two boxes, one in Room B and one in Room C.

Actions available to the robot took the form of operators upon the current world model which would add and delete certain facts. For example, executing the action

```
push(X, Y, Z)
    preconditions: at(robot, Y), at(X, Y)
    delete list:   at(robot, Y), at(X, Y)
    add list:      at(robot, Z), at(X, Z)
```

Figure 4.1 The push operation.

Move the robot from Room A to Room B

in world W would involve generating a new world model, W', from W by adding and deleting facts. at(robot, RoomA) would be deleted and at(robot, RoomB) would be added, to produce

$$W' = \{at(robot, roomB), at(box1, roomB), at(box2, roomC)\}$$

Note that this symbolic manipulation of W is in a sense distinct from whatever physical gyrations the robot would actually have to perform in order to get from Room A to Room B. As well as changing its external location, an intelligent robot must also update its internal representation of where it is. Of course, it is possible to run such a program without it being attached to a robot at all, in which case it is only performing 'imaginary' actions.

Permissible actions of this kind were encoded in *operator tables*, such as that shown in Figure 4.1. This shows an entry for the push operation, where push(X, Y, Z) denotes that object X is pushed from location Y to location Z (by the robot). The X, Y and Z are variables which range over objects, unlike roomA, roomB, roomC and robot, which are names of objects and hence refer to them directly. From a programming language point of view, X, Y and Z are like the formal parameters of a procedure definition which states that:

> to push any object from any place to any other place, if the following preconditions hold, then delete these formulas and add these formulas.

From a logical point of view, the operator table can be read as a formula which states that:

> for all X, Y and Z, X has been pushed from Y to Z if the robot and X were at Y and then changed to being at Z.

Goal statements were also represented as formulas, for example:

at(box1, roomA), at(box2, roomB)

The STRIPS program consisted of many procedures that did various jobs, for example:

- maintaining a list of goals,
- selecting a goal to work on next,
- searching for operators that are applicable to the current goal,
- matching the goal against formulas in the add list, and
- setting up preconditions as subgoals.

Essentially, STRIPS performed a state space search of the kind described in Chapter 2, and its output was a *plan*; that is, a sequence of actions that would achieve the goals. The main difference was that, instead of using generate-and-test, it used another weak method, known as *means–ends analysis*.

Think of what generate-and-test would mean in the present context. The program would simply apply all the operators that it could to the current state and then see if the current goal is achieved. But that would be madness, because the number of things that the robot could do in any given world state is very large indeed, and most of them would do nothing towards the achievement of a given goal. After only a few operations, the state space would be enormous and would continue to grow exponentially with each new operation applied. A more focused approach to the problem is essential.

The basic idea behind means–ends analysis is that each operation applied should reduce the difference between the current state and the goal state. This requires that there be some measure of the 'distance' between the current state and the goal. Such a measure is rather like an evaluation function. If the current goal is at(box1, roomA) and the box is in Room B, then moving the robot from Room A to Room C will do nothing towards achieving it, but moving the robot from Room A to Room B does reduce the distance between the current state and the goal, because the robot is now in a position to push the box from Room B to Room A. In a sense, the robot is reasoning backwards from the goal to subgoals that must be achieved on the way to achieving the main goal. We have already met this kind of behaviour in MYCIN (see Chapter 3).

The way that a STRIPS style program actually works is to read in a list of goals, such as

at(box1, roomA), at(box2, roomB)

and then match the goals one at a time against the add lists of the operators. Thus at(box1, roomA) matches at(X, Z) in the add list of push(X,

Y, Z). Pattern matching will be discussed in more detail in Chapters 5 and 8, but for now it is easy to see that there is a *substitution* of values for variables

{X/box1, Z/roomA}

which renders at(box1, roomA) and at(X, Z) identical.

The program then sets up the preconditions as subgoals in two steps:

(1) *Instantiate* the preconditions by applying the substitution {X/box1, Z/roomA} derived from matching at(box1, roomA) with at(X, Z) to get

at(robot, Y), at(box1, Y)

(2) *Find* the formula in the world model that represents the current position of the box, at(box1, roomB), and match it against at(box1, Y) to derive the substitution {Y/roomB}, which is then applied to the part-instantiated preconditions to derive the subgoals

at(robot, roomB), at(box1, roomB)

The first precondition now gives a desired location for the robot; the second precondition is trivially satisfied, that is, already true.

Given that the operator tables, the world model and the goals were all represented in the same predicate–argument syntax, the program could easily determine which actions were applicable in the achievement of a given goal by a process of pattern matching and table look-up. One virtue of the operator table representation is that it is easy to tell, for any given goal, which operators will be effective in achieving it. All you have to do is look in the add lists of the operators for formulas that match the current goal. It is also easy to see what the preconditions of the operators are, and subgoals can be derived from them by a process of matching and instantiation. So once an operation has been selected for application, its preconditions can be added to the list of goals. Subgoals may themselves be achievable by other operators, and the process of goal reduction should bottom out with operations that have no preconditions or preconditions that are trivially satisfied.

4.2.2 Assessment of STRIPS representation and control

Things would not be so simple if the current state of the world was represented by a typed array (in which cells stood for locations and entries in the cells stood for objects, say). The array representation would be more space efficient, but it would not permit the kinds of matching operation described above. One could, of course, express goals and operations in a compatible array-oriented language, but then several things would have been lost:

- Operators would now be array manipulation procedures that were less easy to read, write and debug than the operator tables.

- The program would be less easy to modify or develop. Suppose more locations are added or the connectivity between rooms is altered. The array access procedures will probably need to be modified by hand, because array dimensions will have changed. In STRIPS, one would only have to change the world model. The operators could stay the same, because they deal with goals at a certain level of generality, and are therefore insulated from the details of how world states are stored.

- Suppose that, in addition to being able to reference specific boxes in goal statements, you want to have non-specific goals like 'bring *any* three boxes to Room A'. The array-oriented procedures will have to be modified substantially to achieve this extension. In a predicate–argument representation, non-specific goals can be represented by goal statements containing variables, such as

    at(X, roomA), at(Y, roomA), at(Z, roomA)

    and one can use pattern matching to look for suitable boxes to bring.

However, one would have to be careful that achieving at(X, roomA) didn't cause the other goals to appear satisfied. The program must somehow be told that the bindings for X, Y and Z should be distinct. The trouble with this style of programming is that you had better say exactly what you mean!

STRIPS is interesting because it introduces a number of fundamental ideas in the artificial intelligence approach to problem solving:

- Problem solving is mostly search, and there is usually more than one way in which a search can be conducted, even in quite simple-looking problems.

- Having a uniform representation can facilitate search, in that it is then easier to see what operations are applicable and what the effects of applying them will be, and it is easier to write programs that reason about how to search.

- As we saw in Chapter 3, goals can often best be achieved by a process of problem reduction, in which we reason backwards from what we want to achieve to simpler subgoals until we reach goals that are trivial, in the sense that they can be accomplished by simple actions.

In general, a representation language, such as the predicate–argument language used by STRIPS, requires an *interpreter*; that is, a program capable of recognizing formulas in the language, such as push(box1, roomB, roomA), and realizing their meaning in terms of procedures that must be carried out. Thus the meaning of push(box1, roomB, roomA), as far as the interpreter is concerned, lies in the achievement of the preconditions

at(robot, roomB), at(box1, roomB)

and the enactment of the add and delete postconditions, adding

at(robot, roomA), at(box1, roomA)

and deleting

at(robot, roomB), at(box1, roomB)

This approach to interpretation is sometimes called *procedural semantics*, because all the program knows about what a formula means is what actions it must carry out to make the formula true.

As we noted in Chapter 2, this is not a very rich view of meaning, and it does not take us very far down the road to computer understanding. While this is undoubtedly true, procedural semantics does at least have something to say about the vital link between thought and action. There is no point in a robot having a deep understanding of life, the universe and everything if it is not capable of translating that understanding into actions that achieve its goals.

The trouble with STRIPS is not that its understanding of formulas is shallow, but that its search strategy is still not adequate for the sensible solution of anything other than the simplest planning problems. Thus a 'bring n boxes' problem such as the one described above is not amenable to simple means–ends analysis if we want to generate a solution efficiently. Neither can STRIPS cope well with problems where the world model has to become more disordered (further from the goal state) than it already is before the goal state can be approached. This is another example of the inherent limitations of using an evaluation function, and it points to a shortcoming in the heuristic part of STRIPS, not the epistemological part. The leading (and so far unanswered) question in the domain of planning is whether or not providing a robot with more knowledge about the world can generate acceptable solutions to computationally intractable problems using bounded resources.

4.3 Knowledge representation and expert systems

The reader may be wondering what expert systems can bring to bear on problems that are known to require exponential resources for their solution. The short answer is 'knowledge', although it is an answer that poses a few questions of its own. The rest of this section attempts a somewhat longer answer. In essence, the argument will go like this. Most of the problems for which we have depressing complexity results are purely formal problems, involving such tasks as satisfiability of formulas and graph traversal. But real-world tasks are rarely just formal problems. A real travelling salesman has all kinds of extra knowledge about the towns he needs to visit and the routes that he might use. The difficulty is that this knowledge is hard to formalize, being derived from experience rather than mathematical theory. The challenge of expert systems is to use such knowledge to solve hard problems in the majority of cases, even if the underlying formal problems are known to be intractable in the worst case.

4.3.1 Procedural versus declarative knowledge

In this discussion, it is useful to maintain a distinction between the *domain* of an expert system and the *task* that the system is called upon to perform. Within a given domain, such as internal medicine, an expert system could perform a variety of tasks, such as computing plausible diagnoses, generating treatment plans, or monitoring a patient's recovery. By the same token, similar tasks may turn up in different domains, such as medical diagnosis, fault-finding in electronic circuits, or automatic debugging of programs.

Knowledge about domains often has a strong declarative component; that is, it is knowing *that* something is the case. Such knowlege is generally a matter of knowing facts or laws or terminology peculiar to the subject matter. Knowledge about tasks, on the other hand, is often more procedural in character; that is, it is knowing *how* to do something. Such knowledge is not normally a matter of being certain of facts or laws, but of being able to exercise good judgement in the achievement of goals.

There has been some controversy in the literature concerning the relative ease and naturalness of *declarative* descriptions of knowledge versus more *procedural* or algorithmic descriptions (see, for example Winograd, 1975). Declarative representations of knowledge are rather more flexible than procedural ones, in that they can be put to a number of different uses, while procedural representations are usually crafted for a particular purpose, which makes them less flexible but more efficient. It is worth exploring this distinction in a little more detail.

On the one hand, there are times when knowledge is easiest to absorb and apply when represented as a sequence of steps. Think about recipes in cookery books which tell you exactly what to do and in what order. These are algorithmic representations in which much of the reasoning about what to do when has been suppressed in the interests of clarity and simplicity. So long as you have all the ingredients and utensils exactly as listed, following the algorithm is more or less guaranteed to give good results. It is only if you are lacking certain resources that you might have to think about how to prepare the meal from first principles, considering what needs to be ready before what, or improvising if ingredients or utensils are missing.

On the other hand, there are times when it is better to be given a description of the end-product and allowed some latitude about how to achieve it. Suppose you are given a list of errands, and a list of constraints that partially determine the order in which the errands should be done. The constraints constitute declarative knowledge about how some errands depend on others, but they do not dictate a single optimal order in which the errands should be done. This will usually operate to your advantage, because you can adapt your plan to changing conditions, such as weather or traffic, about which you are knowledgeable. In the cookery example, it is assumed that there are few intervening conditions, and so the follower of the recipe is relieved of the task of solving the constraints.

Of course, if there is no known algorithm that will solve a given class of problems in an acceptable time (or, worse still, we can show that such an algorithm cannot exist), then heuristic methods are the best that we can do. In this situation, any knowledge that we can bring to bear about the generalities of the domain and the specifics of the case is potentially useful. The trick is to obtain this knowledge and then represent it in such a way that even a computer can apply it.

4.3.2   Heuristics and complexity

In Chapter 2, we noted that pioneers of expert systems research were quick to realize that giving a program a lot of domain-specific facts and rules at different levels of abstraction, and then applying rather simple rules of inference, was more beneficial than giving it a few general laws of the domain together with a general-purpose algorithm for goal-directed reasoning. Experts tend to work from first principles only when confronted with an unusual case, or an especially difficult one. Much of the time, experience enables them to 'home in' on the important aspects of the problem, and derive a solution in a relatively small number of steps.

We also noted that one way in which expert systems differ from more conventional programs is that they are generally programmed to use heuristics of various kinds to find a solution with a minimum of search. These short cuts mean that expert systems, like human experts, rarely derive their results from first principles. As a result, the chains of reasoning involved are usually both short and highly focused. Unfortunately, unlike the human expert, current expert systems are not able to revert to first principles if a problem does not succumb to heuristic means (but see Chapter 24 for an account of some relevant research).

The use of heuristics also means that an expert system's reasoning will not always be *sound*; that is, it will not always consist of a chain of reliable deductions. Certain pieces of evidence crucial to drawing a definite conclusion may be missing, in which case the system must proceed on the assumption that the evidence will ultimately support the conclusion (or qualify the conclusion in some way). Also a system's reasoning may not be *complete*, in that another chain of reasoning might have found a solution that the system missed (see Chapter 5 for more formal definitions of soundness and completeness.)

Thus, in addition to deciding *how to structure* the knowledge in an expert system's knowledge base, a knowledge engineer must also decide *how to use* that knowledge to derive conclusions. The design of the inference engine will usually determine both when representations of knowledge are applied and how their application is controlled. For example, at any given point in a computation, there may be more than one piece of knowledge that appears to be applicable. Furthermore, it may not be consistent to apply both of them. Thus our errand planner may have a heuristic that says

do errands that are close together first

and another that says

avoid going downtown during heavy traffic.

If the errands that are close together are also downtown, and plan execution is scheduled to begin during the rush hour, these two pieces of knowledge give contradictory advice. It is normally the job of the inference engine to resolve conflicts of this kind.

Heuristic reasoning may seem rather slipshod, in that two heuristics can contradict each other in some circumstances, and neither may be guaranteed to work. The problem is that for the majority of tasks requiring human experience and expertise, either there are no algorithmic solutions known, or it is known that the problem is computationally intractable, in that any algorithmic solution will consume resources that increase as an exponential function of the size of the problem. The mass spectrometry interpretation problem we met in Chapter 3 is an example of the former, while our errand problem is an example of the latter.

Thus it is the importance of domain-specific knowledge and the primacy of task-specific heuristics that have shaped the knowledge representation schemes which we shall explore in Part III and beyond.

However, the rest of Part II will be spent examining some of the formal foundations of these schemes in disciplines such as mathematical logic and probability theory. In particular, we shall explore to what extent AI researchers are able to avail themselves of existing results in these areas, and to what extent new results are required.

Bibliographical notes

It is worth reading McCarthy and Hayes (1969) in the original to get the flavour of the debate, although it is probably unnecessary for readers to understand all the technical proposals in that paper. STRIPS planners are well discussed in Nilsson (1980). See Genesereth and Nilsson (1987, Chapters 11 and 12) for additional background on state-space search and planning problems.

STUDY SUGGESTIONS

4.1   Imagine that a robot arm hovering over a tray of toy blocks can move a block, B, from one location, L, to another, M, using the operator table given in Figure 4.2. on(B, L) means that B is resting directly on L. L may be another block or the tray itself. Only one block can rest on another block, but by convention any number of blocks can rest upon the tray. clear(L) means that there is nothing on L.

(a) Represent the scene in Figure 4.3 using symbolic descriptions of this kind.
(b) The goal is to have the blocks stacked into a tower, with the blue block on the red block and the red block on the green block resting on the tray; that is, to have the database representing the world contain the following formulas:

   on(green, tray), on(red, green), on(blue, red)

   Describe a plan for achieving this goal.
(c) Show how the database is modified as the plan is executed by the robot's operator table.

```
move(B, L, M)
      preconditions: on(B, L), clear(B), clear(M)
      delete list:    on(B, L), clear(M)
      add list:       on(B, M), clear(L), clear(tray)
```

Figure 4.2   An operator table for move.

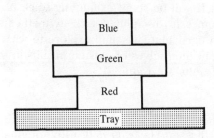

Figure 4.3 A blocks world problem.

(d) Why do we need to add the formula `clear(tray)` after every application of `move`?

(e) Can you use the operator table for `move` to achieve negative goals, for example to achieve the goal that the green block is not on the red block?

4.2 Figure 4.4 is a (very) approximate map of Edinburgh watering places, and Table 4.1 shows the (even more) approximate walking distances between them in minutes.

(a) Use the A* program you wrote in Exercise 2.4 to search for the shortest tour of all nine establishments that begins and ends at Proctor's.

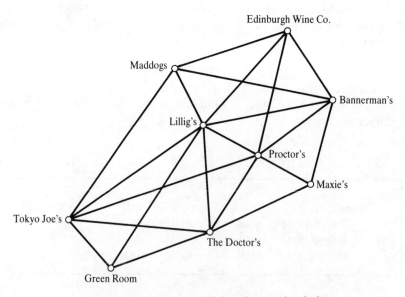

Figure 4.4 Map of Edinburgh watering holes.

Table 4.1   Distances between Edinburgh watering holes.

		1	2	3	4	5	6	7	8	9
1	Edinburgh Wine Co.	0								
2	Maddogs	5	0							
3	Lillig's	11	6	0						
4	Bannerman's	9	7	4	0					
5	Proctor's	15	10	6	5	0				
6	The Doctor's	30	25	10	12	4	0			
7	Maxie's	23	20	15	11	7	8	0		
8	Green Room	38	29	19	32	16	13	10	0	
9	Tokyo Joe's	36	27	21	24	15	12	18	3	0

(b) Repeat the search using the following pieces of additional knowledge:

- All establishments north of Proctor's are downhill, and should therefore be visited first, to avoid returning uphill on the last leg (or rather on *your* last legs).

- Half way through the tour (at the fifth stop), you must eat, which means that this stop must be at Maddogs or Maxie's.

5 Automated Reasoning

Introduction

Mathematical logic is a *formal language*; one can say, for any sequence of symbols, whether or not it conforms to the rules for constructing expressions of the language (*formulas*). Formal languages are usually contrasted with natural languages, such as French and English, where grammatical rules are imprecise. In saying that a logic is a *calculus* with syntactic rules of deduction, one is saying (roughly speaking) that the inferences sanctioned depend solely on the external form of expressions in the language, and not on any extraneous ideas or intuitions.

Automated reasoning refers to the behaviour of any computer program which draws inferences in a law-like way. (Thus a program which effectively tossed a coin to decide on whether one formula followed from a set of other formulas would not be deemed an automated reasoner.) However, much of the literature is actually given over to automated *deduction*, because that is what we understand best.

5.1 Normal forms

In automated reasoning, one often aims for maximum uniformity and standardization in the representation of formulas, avoiding the full syntactic variety of the propositional and predicate calculi, with its range of connectives (such as 'and', 'or', 'implies') and quantifiers ('all' and 'some'). The main syntactic schemes employed are *conjunctive normal form* (CNF), full *clausal form*, and the *Horn clause* subset of the clausal form. We shall see that these representations simplify the inference procedure considerably – but first let us look at the elements of the propositional and predicate calculi.

5.1.1 Propositional calculus

Propositional calculus is the logic of unanalysed propositions in which *propositional constants* can be thought of as standing for particular simple expressions, like 'Socrates is a man' and 'Socrates is mortal'. I shall use lower case letters in the range p, q, r, ... (possibly with subscripts) as propositional constants. These constants are sometimes called atomic formulas, or *atoms*.

The following are all the syntactic rules you need for constructing well-formed formulas (*wffs*) of the propositional calculus. In these rules, Greek lower case letters such as ψ and ϕ are *propositional variables*, and stand not for particular atomic expressions, but for any simple or compound proposition. Propositional constants like p and q are part of the propositional *language* that we use when we apply the *calculus* of propositional variables to actual problems.

> (S.ψ) if ψ is atomic, then ψ is a wff
> (S.$\neg$) if ψ is a wff, then so is $\neg\psi$
> (S.$\vee$) if ψ and ϕ are wffs, then so is $(\psi \vee \phi)$

$\neg\psi$ is read as 'not ψ', and $(\psi \vee \phi)$ is read as the disjunction 'ψ or ϕ (or both)'. We can introduce the other logical constants, $\wedge$ (conjunction), $\supset$ (implication, or the conditional), $\equiv$ (equivalence, or the biconditional), as abbreviations:

> $(\psi \wedge \phi)$, read as 'ψ and ϕ', is defined as $\neg(\neg\psi \vee \neg\phi)$
> $(\psi \supset \phi)$, read as 'ψ implies ϕ', is defined as $(\neg\psi \vee \phi)$
> $(\psi \equiv \phi)$, read as 'ψ is equivalent to ϕ', is defined as
> $\quad (\psi \supset \phi) \wedge (\phi \supset \psi)$

In the CNF of the propositonal calculus, conditionals and bi-conditionals are eliminated in favour of disjunction and negation, by expanding their abbreviations. Then negation is driven in, so that it governs only atomic formulas (propositions containing no logical operators), using the following equivalences (known as De Morgan's laws):

$\neg(\psi \wedge \phi)$ becomes $(\neg\psi \vee \neg\phi)$
$\neg(\psi \vee \phi)$ becomes $(\neg\psi \wedge \neg\phi)$
$\neg\neg\psi$ becomes ψ

Finally, disjunction is distributed over conjunction using the following equivalence:

$$(\zeta \vee (\psi \wedge \phi)) \text{ becomes } ((\zeta \vee \psi) \wedge (\zeta \vee \phi))$$

It is customary to reduce the nesting of parentheses by making $\wedge$ and $\vee$ operators of variable *arity* (allowing occurrences of them to govern any number of operands) using the following equivalences. Both the disjunction sign and the conjunction sign can now be dropped without ambiguity, and the resulting expression treated as an implicit conjunction of disjunctions. An example will make this clear.

$\neg(p \vee q) \supset (\neg p \wedge \neg q)$
$\neg\neg(p \vee q) \vee (\neg p \wedge \neg q)$ eliminating $\supset$
$(p \vee q) \vee (\neg p \wedge \neg q)$ driving $\neg$ in
$(\neg p \vee (p \vee q)) \wedge (\neg q \vee (p \vee q))$ distributing $\wedge$ over $\vee$
$\{\{\neg p, p, q\}, \{\neg q, p, q\}\}$ dropping $\wedge$ and $\vee$

Expressions within inner brackets are either atomic formulas (*atoms*) or negated atomic formulas. Such expressions are called *literals*, and from a logical point of view their order is immaterial, hence the use of the curly brackets from set theory. Literals in the same clause are implicitly disjoined, while clauses within outer brackets are implicitly conjoined.

Clausal form is very similar to CNF, except that the positive and negative literals in each disjunction tend to be grouped together on different sides of an arrow and the negation symbols are dropped. Thus

$$\{\{\neg p, p, q\}, \{\neg q, p, q\}\}$$

from the above example would become the two clauses

$p, q \leftarrow p$
$p, q \leftarrow q$

where positive literals go to the left of the arrow, and negative literals go to the right. Most people agree that this is more readable (for humans) than CNF. A little thought will convince you that

$$\leftarrow p$$

is equivalent to $\neg p$, and that

$$p \leftarrow$$

is equivalent to plain p.

More precisely, a clause is an expression of the form

$$p_1, \ldots, p_m \leftarrow q_1, \ldots, q_n$$

where $p_1, \ldots, p_m \leftarrow q_1, \ldots, q_n$ are atomic formulas, with $m \geq 0$ and $n \geq 0$. The $p_1, \ldots, p_m$ are the disjoined conclusions of the clause, while the $q_1, \ldots, q_n$ are the conjoined *conclusions*.

5.1.2 The predicate calculus

The propositional calculus has its limitations, however. You cannot deal properly with general statements of the form 'All men are mortal'. Of course, you can let a propositional constant, like p, stand for such a statement, and you can let q stand for 'Socrates is a man', but you can't derive 'Socrates is mortal' from $(p \wedge q)$.

To do this, you need to analyse propositions into *predicates* and *arguments*, *quantifiers* and *variables of quantification* (rather as we did in the STRIPS example of Chapter 4). Predicate logic provides syntactic rules for performing this analysis, semantic rules which interpret expressions so formed, and a proof theory which allows us to derive valid formulas using syntactic rules of deduction. Predicates stand for properties, like 'being a man', and relationships, like 'being taller than'.

Arguments can be:

(1)   individual constants, like *plato*;

(2)   function–argument compositions, like *AUTHOR-OF*(*republic*), which stand for entities in some universe of objects that we are interested in;

(3)   individual variables of quantification which range over such a universe.

Special operators called *quantifiers* are used to bind such variables and delimit their scope. The standard quantifiers are the universal, $\forall$, and the existential, $\exists$, which can be read as 'all' and 'some' respectively.

Here are the syntactic rules of the first-order predicate calculus:

(S.α)   Any constant symbol or variable is a term
and if Γ_k is a k-place function symbol
and $\alpha_1, \ldots, \alpha_k$ are terms
then $\Gamma_k(\alpha_1, \ldots, \alpha_k)$ is a term

(S.Ψ)   If Ψ_k is a k-place predicate symbol
and $\alpha_1, ..., \alpha_k$ are terms
then $\Psi_k(\alpha_1, ..., \alpha_k)$ is a wff

(S.¬)   and (S.∨) from the propositional calculus

(S.∀)   If ψ is a wff and χ is a variable, then $(\forall\chi)\psi$ is a wff

As before, we use variables like Ψ (to stand for arbitrary predicates), Γ (to stand for arbitrary functions), α (to stand for arbitrary terms) and χ to stand for arbitrary variables). Actual names, function symbols and predicates, like *plato*, *AUTHOR-OF*, and *PHILOSOPHER*, are elements of a *first-order language*; that is, an application or instantiation of the calculus.

We can introduce the existential quantifier, $\exists$, as an abbreviation in terms of the universal quantifier, $\forall$:

$$(\exists\chi)\psi \text{ is defined as } \neg(\forall\psi)\neg\psi$$

The expression $(\exists X)(PHILOSOPHER(X))$ is read as the sentence 'Something is a philosopher', while the expression $(\forall X)$ $(PHILOSOPHER(X))$ is read as 'Everything is a philosopher'. The expression $PHILOSOPHER(X)$ is well formed, but it is not a sentence, because the occurrence of the variable X is unbound by any quantifier. Formulas in which all occurrences of all variables are bound are called *closed formulas*.

As in the propositional calculus, predicate calculus expressions can be put into normal form, although we need to extend the rules of syntactic transformation. The sequence of rule applications is now as follows. For any expression:

(1)   Eliminate biconditionals and then conditionals.

(2)   Drive negation in, using De Morgan's laws and the equivalence between $(\exists\chi)\psi$ and $\neg(\forall\chi)\neg\psi$ (and hence between $(\forall\chi)\psi$ and $\neg(\exists\chi)\neg\psi$).

(3)   Standardize variables apart. For example, in

$$(\exists X)(PHILOSOPHER(X)) \ \& \ (\exists X)(ATHLETE(X))$$

it is sensible to give variables bound in the scope of different occurrences of quantifiers different names. Otherwise, when the quantifiers are eliminated, logically distinct variables might end up with the same name. Then, in the above example, one might end up deriving

$$(\exists X)(PHILOSOPHER(X) \ \& \ ATHLETE(X))$$

which does not follow from the original formula.

(4) Eliminate existential quantifiers. Existential variables that occur outside the scope of any universal quantifier can be replaced by arbitrary names (called Skolem constants), while existential variables that occur inside the scope of one or more universal quantifiers must be replaced by Skolem functions, whose arguments are the universally bound variables within whose scope the existential occurs. A Skolem function is just an arbitrary function name that says 'the value of this variable is some function of the values assigned to the universal variables in whose scope it lies'.

(5) Convert to prenex form. The remaining quantifiers (all of them universal) should now be moved to the 'front' of the expression, so that we have a list of universally quantified variables followed by a 'matrix' in which no quantifiers occur.

(6) Distribute disjunction over conjunction.

(7) Drop the universal quantifiers. All free variables are now implicitly universally quantified variables. The existentials are either constants or functions of universal variables.

(8) Drop the conjunction signs, as before, leaving a set of clauses.

(9) Rename variables again, so that the same variable does not appear in different clauses.

We can now convert to clausal form, with positive literals on the left of the arrow, and negative literals on the right. If a clause of the form

$$p_1, \ldots, p_m \leftarrow q_1, \ldots, q_n$$

contains variables $x_1, \ldots, x_k$, then the correct interpretation is

> for all $x_1, \ldots, x_k$
> p_1 or ... or p_m is true
> if q_1 and ... and q_n are true

If $n = 0$ (if there are no conditions specified) the correct interpretation is an unconditional statement to the effect that

> for all $x_1, \ldots, x_k$
> p_1 or ... or p_m is true

If $m = 0$ (if there are no conclusions specified) the correct interpretation is the following denial:

> for all $x_1, \ldots, x_k$
> it is not the case that q_1 and ... and q_n are true

If $m = n = 0$, then we have the empty clause, whose correct interpretation is always falsity.

Thus, in the predicate–argument language of the last chapter, the clause

$$AT(X, roomA) \leftarrow AT(X, box1)$$

would be interpreted as

for all X, X is at Room A if X is at box1

the clause

$$\leftarrow AT(X, box1)$$

would be interpreted as

for all X, X is not at box1

and the clause

$$AT(X, roomA) \leftarrow$$

would be interpreted as

for all X, X is at Room A

The *Horn clause subset* of first-order logic is just like the full clausal form of logic, except that one atom at most is allowed in the conclusion. Thus the Horn clause equivalent of a rule will have the general form

$$p \leftarrow q_1, ..., q_n$$

Write this as

$$p :- q_1, ..., q_n.$$

(not forgetting the full stop at the end) and you have a clause in the syntax of the PROLOG language for logic programming, with the intended interpretation:

for all values of variables occurring in the clause
p is true if $q_1, ..., q_n$ are true

Thus ':–' can be read as 'if' and commas can be read as 'and'.

PROLOG is an unusual language in which programs consist mostly of logical formulas, and running a program consists mainly of a form of theorem proving. A clause of the form $p :- q_1, ..., q_n$ can be viewed as a procedure. Such a procedure is invoked when a literal successfully unifies with p, which is called the *head* of the clause. Invocation of such a procedure causes the $q_1, ..., q_n$ to be instantiated with the unifier and set up as subgoals. Thus unification serves the function of parameter passing in more conventional languages.

For example, consider the following PROLOG clauses:

```
on(a, b).
on(b, c).
above(X, Y) :- on(X, Y).
above(X, Y) :- on(Z, Y), above (X, Z).
```

Imagine that a and b are blocks in a blocks world. The first two clauses state that a is on b and b is on c. The third clause states that X is above Y if X is on Y. The fourth clause states that X is above Y if there is some other block Z on top of Y, and X is above Z. It is clear that we ought to be able to derive the goal above(a, c) from this set of clauses. We shall see exactly how in Section 5.2, but the derivation involves invoking the two procedures for above, and using the two on clauses to terminate the proof.

5.2   The resolution principle

PROLOG employs the 'problem-solving interpretation of Horn clauses' described in, for example, Kowalski (1979, pp. 88–9). The fundamental theorem-proving method that PROLOG relies on is called *resolution refutation*, and is fully described in Robinson (1979). This section attempts to impart no more than the basic ideas and the rationale behind the method.

It was mentioned earlier that we simplify the syntax of calculi so that we can reduce the number of inference rules that we need to prove theorems. Instead of the dozen or more rules found in most methods for doing proofs by hand, automatic theorem provers for clausal forms typically use only a *single* rule of inference: the *resolution principle*, first described by Robinson (1965).

Consider the following example from the propositional calculus. From now on, I shall use upper case letters in the range $P, Q, R, ...$ to denote particular clauses, using ψ, ϕ and ζ (possibly with subscripts) for propositional variables, as before.

If ψ and ϕ are any two clauses which have been transformed into CNF, and

Inference rule	Usual form	CNF
Modus ponens	$\dfrac{\psi \supset \phi,\ \psi}{\phi}$	$\dfrac{\{\neg\psi, \phi\},\ \{\psi\}}{\{\phi\}}$
Modus tollens	$\dfrac{\psi \supset \phi,\ \neg\phi}{\neg\psi}$	$\dfrac{\{\neg\psi, \phi\},\ \{\neg\phi\}}{\{\neg\psi\}}$
Chaining	$\dfrac{\psi \supset \phi,\ \phi \supset \zeta}{\psi \supset \zeta}$	$\dfrac{\{\neg\psi, \phi\},\ \{\neg\phi, \zeta\}}{\{\neg\psi, \zeta\}}$
Merging	$\dfrac{\psi \supset \phi,\ \neg\psi \supset \phi}{\phi}$	$\dfrac{\{\psi, \phi\},\ \{\neg\psi, \phi\}}{\{\phi\}}$
Reductio	$\dfrac{\psi,\ \neg\psi}{\perp}$	$\dfrac{\{\neg\psi\}\ \{\psi\}}{\{\,\}}$

Figure 5.1 The generality of resolution.

$\psi = \{\psi_1, \ldots, \psi_i, \ldots, \psi_m\}$ and
$\phi = \{\phi_1, \ldots, \phi_j, \ldots, \phi_n\}$ and
$\psi_i = \neg\phi_j$ for $1 \le i \le m,\ 1 \le j \le n$

then a new clause, ζ, can be derived from the union of ψ' and ϕ' where

$$\psi' = \psi - \{\psi_i\} \quad \text{and} \quad \phi' = \phi - \{\phi_j\}$$

$\zeta = \psi' \cup \phi'$ is the *resolvent* of the resolution step, and ψ and ϕ are its *parent clauses*. We sometimes say that ψ and ϕ 'clash' on the pair of *complementary literals*, ψ_i and ϕ_j.

Resolution is very powerful because it subsumes many other inference rules, as can be seen if we express more conventional rules in CNF.

In Figure 5.1, the left-hand column gives the name of the inference rule, the middle column shows how it commonly appears in logic texts, with expressions above the line being premise schemas, while the expression below the line is the conclusion schema. The right-hand column shows the rules with their premises and conclusions in clausal form. You can see from this column that each of the five rules cited above is just an instance of resolution!

Note in the rule *reductio* that a contradiction, normally denoted by $\perp$, gives the empty clause, $\{\,\}$, signifying that the premises are inconsistent. Considered as a 'state description' of some world, we say that the premises are *unsatisfiable* – roughly speaking, there can be no such world. The significance of this will become apparent shortly.

For the moment, suffice it to say that the theorem prover at the heart of many AI programs, and AI programming languages such as PROLOG, is a *resolution refutation system*. To prove that p follows from some state description (or *theory*) T, you assume $\neg p$ and then attempt to derive a contradiction from its conjunction with T. If you succeed in doing this, you are justified in asserting p; otherwise you are not.

Resolution in the predicate calculus requires more machinery than this because of the presence of variables. The basic pattern-matching operation in resolution theorem proving is called *unification* (see Nilsson, 1980 for details of the algorithm). When matching complementary literals, we look for a substitution of terms for variables that makes two expressions identical.

For example,

RUNS-FASTER-THAN(X, zeno)

and

RUNS-FASTER-THAN(tortoise, Y)

have the following substitution that renders them identical: {*X/tortoise, Y/zeno*}. This substitution is called a *unifier*. We want the most general such substitution; roughly speaking, the one that binds as few variables as possible. A unifier is a *most general unifier* if and only if any other unifier can be derived from it by composition with a further substitution. We rename all variables before unification as a further precaution against logically distinct variables ending up with the same name.

Clauses that contain no variables, often called *ground clauses*, can be resolved as before. To resolve two non-ground clauses, you must first find a unifier for the complementary literals, then do the clash and then instantiate the resolvent with the unifier. For example,

{*BEATS-IN-FOOTRACE(X, zeno)*,
    ¬*YOUNGER-THAN(X, zeno)*}

and

{¬*BEATS-IN-FOOTRACE(tortoise, Y)*, ¬*PHILOSOPHER(Y)*}

have unifier $v = $ {*X/tortoise, Y/zeno*}, and generate the resolvent

{¬*PHILOSOPHER(zeno)*, ¬*YOUNGER-THAN(tortoise, zeno)*}

Thus, if Zeno is beaten by everyone younger than him, and the tortoise cannot beat a philosopher, we can safely conclude that, if Zeno is a philosopher, the tortoise is not younger than him.

5.3 Proof search in resolution systems

Resolution is a rule of inference that allows you to derive new wffs from old. However, the logistic system described so far does not tell you how to do proofs. This section explores the strategic aspects of theorem proving.

5.3.1 Forward and backward reasoning

Let p represent 'Socrates is a man' and q represent 'Socrates is mortal'. Let our theory be

$$T = \{\{\neg p, q\}, \{p\}\}.$$

Thus we hold that if Socrates is a man implies that Socrates is mortal, and that Socrates is a man. $\{q\}$ is derivable from T in a single step of resolution equivalent to *modus ponens*.

$\{\neg p, q\}$ and $\{p\}$ clash on the pair of complementary literals p and $\neg p$, and $\{q\}$ is the resolvent. Thus T *logically implies* q, written $T \vdash q$. We are therefore entitled to add $\{q\}$ to T to derive the theory $T' = \{\{\neg p, q\}, \{p\}, \{q\}\}$.

Many proofs will require more than one inference step, of course. For example, let T be

$$\{\{\neg p, q\}, \{\neg q, \neg r\}, \{p\}\}$$

where p and q are as before and r represents 'Socrates is a god'. If we want to show that $T \vdash \neg r$, we require two steps of resolution:

$$\frac{\{\neg p, q\}, \{p\}}{\{q\}}$$

$$\frac{\{\neg q, \neg r\}, \{q\}}{\{\neg r\}}$$

Note that in the first step we used two clauses from the original set T, but that in the second step we used a resolvent $\{q\}$ that we had added to T, to complete the proof. Note also that we could have done the proof a different way:

$$\frac{\{\neg p, q\}, \{\neg q, \neg r\}}{\{\neg p, \neg r\}}$$

$$\frac{\{\neg p, \neg r\}, \{p\}}{\{\neg r\}}$$

which results in a different resolvent being added to T. A number of problems arise in connection with this.

- If T is very large to begin with, it is conceivable that there might be many ways to derive a particular formula that in which we are interested (our *goal*). Obviously, we would prefer the shorter proofs, if we can obtain them without too much search.
- T may support all kinds of inferences which have nothing to do with the proof of our goal. Yet how can we know in advance which inferences will lead to the goal?
- The whole process has a built-in potential for combinatorial explosion. T grows with each inference step, giving us more and more options. Some of these options may lead to circularity.

The pattern of reasoning we have followed so far is usually referred to as *forward reasoning*. That is to say, you start from what you know and reason in the direction of what you are trying to prove (you hope). One way of tackling some of the problems listed above is to reason backwards from the goal towards the evidence you need.

5.3.2 Resolution refutation

Suppose you want to derive $\{q\}$ from some set of clauses

$$T = \{..., \{\neg p, q\}, ...\}$$

It seems sensible to comb the set looking for clauses that have q as a literal, and then try to resolve the other literals away (if there are any). However $\{q\}$ does not clash with, for example, $\{\neg p, q\}$, since the pair of literals q and q are not complementary.

If q is a goal, then *resolution refutation* works by adding the *negation* of the goal to T, and then trying to show that $T' = T \cup \{\neg q\}$ is inconsistent. Assuming that T was consistent in the first place, if T' is inconsistent, it must be because $T \vdash q$. (If T is not consistent, q is a trivial consequence of T.)

Let us consider this in more detail. First we negate the goal to derive $\{\neg q\}$, and then we attempt to resolve $\{\neg q\}$ with another clause in T'. There are only three possibilities.

- Either there is no clause containing q in T, in which case the proof fails.

- T contains $\{q\}$, in which case the proof is immediate, since from $\{\neg q\}$ and $\{q\}$ we can derive the empty clause $\{\}$, signifying contradiction.

- T contains a clause $\{..., q, ...\}$ that resolves with $\{\neg q\}$ to generate $\{...\}$, which contains one or more literals, all of which need to be resolved away if we are to demonstrate the contradiction.

These remaining literals can be thought of as *subgoals* that need to be solved if we are to solve our main goal. This is clearly a *backward reasoning* strategy; as such it resembles subgoaling in MYCIN (see Chapter 3).

As an example, let T be $\{\{\neg p, q\}, \{\neg q, \neg r\}, \{p\}\}$ as before. If we want to show that $T \vdash \neg r$, then we negate $\neg r$ to derive our goal statement $\{r\}$, and then add this to T. The search for a contradiction proceeds as follows:

$$\frac{\{\neg q, \neg r\}, \{r\}}{\{\neg q\}}$$

$$\frac{\{\neg p, q\}, \{\neg q\}}{\{\neg p\}}$$

$$\frac{\{\neg p\}, \{p\}}{\{\}}$$

This method of proving theorems is called *resolution refutation* because it uses the resolution rule of inference, but adopts a refutation strategy. The use of resolution in backward reasoning is characteristic of the *modus tollens* of natural deduction systems, just as its use in forward reasoning is characteristic of *modus ponens* (see Figure 5.1).

To return to our earlier PROLOG example, Figure 5.2 shows a resolution refutation proof of above(a, c), laid out as a *proof tree*. By convention, we draw the tree upside down, and each branch of the tree connects two 'parent' clauses containing complementary literals with a clause that is generated from them by a single step of resolution. We write all goals on the right hand side of a :–, since they are implicitly negated (refer back to Section 5.1.2 if this seems mysterious). Goals are listed on the left of the tree, while clauses from the database are listed on the right.

The root of the tree is the empty clause, signifying that our proof search has been successful. Adding the negative clause :– above(a, c) to our theory results in an inconsistency. Therefore, we are entitled to conclude that above(a, c) is a logical consequence of the theory.

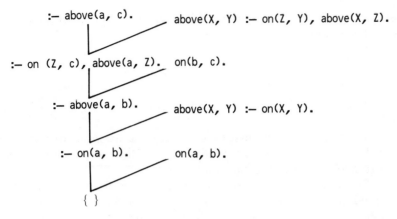

Figure 5.2 A PROLOG-style proof tree.

The main advantage of resolution refutation is that reasoning backward from what you are trying to prove serves to focus the search for a solution, since inferences drawn are at least potentially relevant to the goal. Also, seeing the production of resolvents as the generation of subgoals is intuitively satisfying. However, it does not solve all the problems noted above. For example, it doesn't guarantee that you will find shorter proofs rather than longer ones. Neither does it abolish the combinatorial explosion inherent in the proof-generation process discussed in Chapter 2, although the 'attention-focusing' effect of goal-directed reasoning obviously prevents totally irrelevant inferences from being generated and added to the set of clauses.

It is worth pointing out that failing to prove a proposition p is not the same thing as proving $\neg p$. Refutation strategies tend to obscure this distinction because, once you have negated p, it will no longer generate a contradiction by resolving with $\neg p$, assuming that $\neg p$ is in the database or is a consequence of it. This problem does not arise with forward-reasoning strategies, where it is possible in principle to discover that the database logically implies $\neg p$ and conclude that p is false. Consequently, there are some problems with representing negation in logic programming languages like PROLOG. However, we shall see in Chapter 11 that simple mechanisms will suffice for most practical purposes, if used carefully.

Another important issue with regard to proof procedures and theorem proving strategies is that of *completeness*. A procedure is complete if and only if it is capable of finding a proof whenever one exists. It turns out that resolution is complete for the Horn clause subset of clausal logic, but it is not complete for the full clausal form, unless it is augmented by a technique called *factoring*. Roughly speaking, factoring allows us to recognize that two clauses are inconsistent because they have instances which can be seen to be in direct contradiction after the removal of duplicate literals.

For example, the clauses

$$p(a), p(X) \leftarrow$$

$$\leftarrow p(Y), P(Z)$$

are inconsistent, since the first says that either a has p or everything has p, while the second says that nothing has p. However, resolution alone will not allow us to derive the empty clause.

Factoring allows us to recognize that $p(a)$ and $p(X)$ can be collapsed into a single literal $p(a)$ via a process of unification with substitution $\{X/a\}$, while $p(Y)$ and $p(Z)$ can also be collapsed into $p(W)$, since $p(Y)$ and $p(Z)$ unify after variable renaming. This gives us the new set of clauses

$$p(a), p(X) \leftarrow$$

$$\leftarrow p(Y), p(Z)$$

$$p(a) \leftarrow$$

$$\leftarrow p(W)$$

from which the empty clause *can* be derived. It turns out that the technique is not needed very often, but it is necessary for completeness; see Section 5.4 for another sense of the term *complete*.

5.3.3 Theorem-proving strategies

We saw in the last section that additional strategies are required to help resolution refutation deal with combinatorial explosion. Here is a brief survey of some of the main methods, together with their advantages and disadvantages. None of these is guaranteed to be effective in the general case, but each has something to recommend it.

- *Breadth-first search*. Compute all the first-level resolvents, then all second-level resolvents, and so on. This strategy will ultimately find the shortest proof; however, it is grossly inefficient.
- *Set of support strategy*. At least one parent of every resolvent must be a descendant of the goal. This strategy is guaranteed to find a proof if one exists, and is usually better than breadth-first search. It is particularly effective if the 'forward' search space is very bushy.
- *Unit preference strategy*. Use unit clauses as parents whenever possible. They generate resolvents with fewer literals, and

therefore help the search to converge on the empty clause. However, using only unit clauses is not a *complete* strategy, in the sense that not all proofs can be found in this way.

- *Linear input form.* Every resolvent has a parent in the base set. This strategy is not complete for the full clausal form of logic, but it *is* complete for the Horn clause subset. Because of its simplicity and efficiency, it is the strategy used by PROLOG.

A major focus of interest in applications of automated reasoning and logic programming is the control of deduction. One approach is to hard-code into one's theorem prover domain-specific heuristics, which make decisions concerning which particular clauses to try first, and which literals one should try to resolve away first. Another approach is to attempt to reason about control using logic itself; that is, to have a relatively domain-free meta-theory of how one ought to search. The latter approach, called *meta-level inference*, is discussed further in Chapter 11.

5.4 Some formal properties of logistic systems

In this section, we show that logical languages have some nice mathematical properties, and that they also have some undesirable computational properties. This will help motivate the consideration of other representation languages in Part III. After all, why would we look any further than well-understood systems of formal logic as a vehicle for representation and reasoning unless there were compelling reasons to investigate alternatives?

5.4.1 The good news: soundness and completeness

The meaning of expressions in a formal language is as strictly defined as their form. In fact, the two are closely correlated. Unlike more haphazard notational systems, logic is precise about the conditions under which expressions are deemed to be true or false.

For example, the statement $(p \lor q)$ means that 'p is true or q is true' – no more and no less. The meaning of $\lor$ is therefore completely given by the *truth table* in Figure 5.3, which signifies that for any propositions ψ and ϕ, $(\psi \lor \phi)$ is true only if ψ is true or ϕ is true, otherwise it is false.

Figure 5.3 shows that the value of $(p \lor q)$ depends on the values we assign to p and to q; that is, whether we consider them to be true or not. An assignment of truth values to propositional variables is called an *interpretation*. More formally, an interpretation, V, is a function from the

ψ	∨	φ
1	1	1
1	1	0
0	1	1
0	0	0

Figure 5.3 The truth table for disjunction.

set of all atomic propositions to the set of truth values $\{1, 0\}$.

Given an interpretation for the atoms, the interpretation of compound propositions, V^*, is now fixed by the following semantic rules

$(T.\psi)$ If ψ is an atom, then $V^*(\psi) = V(\psi)$

$(T.\neg)$ If ψ is $\neg\phi$, then $V^*(\psi) = 1$ if $V^*(\phi) = 0$, else $V^*(\phi) = 1$

$(T.\vee)$ If ψ is $(\phi \vee \zeta)$, then $V^*(\psi) = 1$ if $V^*(\phi) = 1$ or $V^*(\zeta) = 1$ else $V^*(\psi) = 0$

If you find this hard to understand, compare $(T.\vee)$ with the truth table for $\vee$. These are just two ways of saying the same thing.

An interpretation which renders a proposition true is said to be *a model of* that proposition. However, there are certain propositions whose truth does not depend on an assignment to the atomic propositions. These propositions are true under *all* interpretations, in other words, every interpretation is a model of the proposition. Such propositions are called *tautologies*, and are said to be *valid*. If all interpretations of a theory T are models of ψ, then we say that T *entails* ψ, written $T \vDash \psi$.

The propositional calculus has some nice properties, which I shall state here in terms of the consequences of some theory T.

- *Soundness.* If $T \vdash p$ then $T \vDash p$.
- *Completeness.* If $T \vDash p$, then $T \vdash p$.
- *Decidability.* For any p, there is an effective procedure for showing whether $T \vdash p$ or not.

Soundness means that our inference procedure will never lead us from true premises to false conclusions; in other words, we will draw *only* valid inferences. Completeness means that our inference procedure is capable of generating *all* the valid inferences that can be drawn from a set of premises. These are the minimum properties that we like logistic systems to have, because they guarantee that our reasoning in them will be 'correct'.

Decidability means that we can always show, one way or another, whether or not a proposition follows from a theory. This is also a highly desirable property, especially from a computational point of view. However, as we shall see in the next section, this turns out to be a much stronger requirement than it appears.

5.4.2 The bad news: intractability and undecidability

Correctness is not the only property that we need to consider in automated reasoning. Just as important is tractability; that is, the complexity of proof search.

Although there is an effective procedure for the decision problem in the propositional calculus, this problem can be shown to be intractable in general, because in the worst case it is exponential in the number of propositional constants involved. However, the predicate calculus is not even decidable, so long as we have predicates of arity greater than one. The details of this result are well beyond the scope of this text, but its immediate consequences are two-fold:

- No proof procedure for the predicate calculus is guaranteed to terminate if we try to show that an arbitrary formula follows from a theory. If the formula *does* follow, the procedure *will* ultimately terminate with success; but, if it does not, the procedure may *never* terminate. By reason of this asymmetry, predicate logic is *semi-decidable*.

- In the general case, it is impossible to show that an arbitrary predicate calculus theory is consistent, *even in principle*. This astonishing result was proved by Godel in 1931, and it has had tremendous repercussions throughout the fields of logic and mathematics. For example, it can be shown that any formalization of arithmetic (for example, Peano's axioms) will be either incomplete or inconsistent, and any proof of consistency must resort to principles extraneous to the theory.

Godel's result bears directly on the use of logic as a basis for representing knowledge. If we wish to formalize expertise in some complex domain using the full expressive power of predicate logic, we will have to live with the fact that it may be impossible to demonstrate that our formalization is consistent, and that some of our deductions based on this representation of knowledge may never terminate. This is a rather sobering thought. We are already used to the idea that certain computations will always take too long on even the most powerful machines, and that heuristics will be required to cut the cost. But Godel's result says that certain computations *cannot* be carried out, even in infinite time and using infinite resources. In such cases, heuristic methods are our *only* resort, and these will usually compromise either soundness or completeness or both.

Bibliographical notes

A clear technical introduction to the proof theory of mathematical logic can be found in Andrews (1986). Serious readers are also recommended to consult Quine (1979), which is the revised edition of his 1940 classic *Mathematical Logic*. For a thorough introduction to automated reasoning, it is still hard to improve on Robinson (1979). A gentler introduction, with an emphasis on artificial intelligence, is Genesereth and Nilsson (1987, Chapters 1–5). In addition, Hayes and Michie (1984) provide an accessible discussion of mathematical logic in the context of AI.

STUDY SUGGESTIONS

5.1 Draw truth tables for the propositional connectives ∧ and ⊃. Refer back to the truth table for ∨ shown in Figure 5.3 and the definitions of these connectives in terms of ∨ given in Section 5.1.1.

5.2 Translate the following statements into predicate logic:

(a) Every student uses some computer, and at least one computer is used by every student. (Use only the predicates *STUDENT*, *COMPUTER* and *USES*.)

(b) Every year, some male students fail every exam, but every female student passes some exam. (Use only the predicates *STUDENT*, *MALE*, *FEMALE*, *PASSES*, *EXAM*, *YEAR*.)

(c) Every man loves some woman who loves another man. (Use only the predicates *MAN*, *WOMAN*, *LOVES* and =.)

(d) No two philosophers have the same favourite book. (Use only the predicates *PHILOSOPHER*, *BOOK*, *LIKES* and =.)

5.3 Put the sentences of Exercise 5.2 into clausal form.

5.4 How worthwhile is it to translate the following quotations into predicate logic? Identify the difficulties involved in representing the author's intention in each case.

(a) No man is an island. (John Donne)

(b) The man who lives everywhere lives nowhere. (Tacitus)

(c) The past is another country; they do things differently there. (L.P. Hartley)

(d) A man of the highest virtue does not keep to virtue, and that is why he has virtue. (Lao Tzu)

5.5   Consider the clausal formula

shaves(X, X), shaves(barber, X) ←

which says that one shaves oneself or the barber shaves one.

(a) Show that

shaves(barber, barber) ←

follows from this formula using backward reasoning.
(b) Demonstrate the same result by forward reasoning.
(c) What do you understand by the following clause in this context?

← shaves(Y, Y), shaves(barber, Y)

(d) Show that the following clauses are inconsistent by using them to derive the empty clause.

shaves(X, X), shaves(barber, X) ←

← shaves(Y, Y), shaves(barber, Y)

5.6   Here is a simple fault-finding problem.

If an engine misfires and the spark at the plugs is intermittent, then the ignition leads are loose or the battery leads are loose. My engine misfires. The spark at my plugs is intermittent. My ignition leads are not loose.

(a) Translate these sentences into formulas of predicate logic.
(b) Put the formulas into conjunctive normal form.
(c) Show that 'My battery leads are loose' follows as a logical consequence of the set of sentences using forward reasoning. Then repeat the process using backward reasoning.

6 Representing Uncertainty

Introduction

Unlike game playing, puzzle solving and theorem proving, many applications often require a problem solver to reason with imperfect information. This chapter introduces a number of basic ideas to do with the measurement of uncertainty and methods of inexact reasoning: themes which recur later, especially Chapters 16 and 25. Here the emphasis will be on the representation of uncertainty and the reason why AI researchers have deemed it necessary to experiment with different formalisms.

6.1 Sources of uncertainty

There are many different sources of uncertainty in problem solving, but most of them can be attributed to either *imperfect domain knowledge* or *imperfect case data*.

Thus, the theory of the domain may be *incomplete* (as was the theory of mass spectrometry on which DENDRAL was based) or even *erroneous* (as may be the case in some areas of medicine). Incomplete domain theories may use concepts which are not precisely defined; consider the concept of schizophrenia in the diagnosis of mental illness. Incompleteness necessitates the employment of rules of thumb which (unlike scientific laws) may not always give the correct result, even on simple cases. Having incomplete knowledge also means that the effects of actions are not always predictable; for example, therapies using new drugs frequently have unexpected outcomes. Finally, even if the domain theory is complete, an expert may find it profitable to employ heuristic methods in preference to exact methods, because of the inherent complexity of the domain. Thus fault repair of electronic devices by swapping boards until the device works is often preferable to exhaustive circuit analysis in search of the actual fault.

In addition to problems with the domain theory, case data may be *imprecise* or *unreliable*. Sensors have only finite resolving power and less than 100% reliability; reports may be ambiguous or inaccurate; evidence may be missing or in conflict. We say that data is *partial* when answers to relevant questions are not available. Even when answers are available in principle, they may not be available in practice. Thus, although it may be possible to gain additional information about a patient by means of surgery or expensive tests, considerations of cost and risk rule out such procedures in all but extreme cases. We say that data is *approximate* when answers are available but these are of variable precision; for example, it may be possible to second guess some costly or high-risk procedures with more acceptable methods that give less accurate results. Finally, even if complete and exact data are available in principle, the situation may render exact methods inappropriate. Thus, the decision about whether or not to shut down an ailing nuclear power station should not always wait on a full analysis of all the facts.

In summary, experts employ inexact methods for the following reasons:

- Exact methods are *not known*.
- Exact methods are known but are *impractical*, because of lack of data or problems with collecting the data (cost and risk), or difficulties with processing the data within the time constraints set by the problem (where there is danger to life).

There is broad agreement among artificial intelligence researchers that inexact methods are important in many expert systems applications; however, there is very little agreement concerning what form these methods should take. Until recently, opinion tended to follow McCarthy and Hayes (1969), who felt that probability theory was epistemologically inadequate to the task of representing uncertainty. They argued that:

- It is not altogether clear how to deal with the interaction of probabilities with quantifiers.
- The assignment of probabilities to events requires information that is not normally available.

The twin convictions that probability theory had little to say about inherently imprecise notions, such as the quantifiers 'most' and 'few', and that the application of probability theory required 'too many numbers' led to the exploration of alternative formalisms, such as *fuzzy logic* and *belief functions*, for many expert systems applications (although those in favour of the probability approach have staged a rather effective counterattack in recent years, reclaiming some of the ground that had been lost). Fuzzy logic is described later in this chapter, while the theory of belief functions (also called the Dempster–Shafer theory of evidence) is outlined in Chapter 25. In Chapters 16 and 22, we shall also explore approaches to uncertainty that use domain-specific knowledge to compute the impact of evidence on hypotheses instead of using a domain-free calculus.

6.2   Expert systems and probability theory

This section looks more closely at some of the problems involved in taking a probabilistic approach to the management of uncertainty. It begins with a brief elementary account of conditional probability, and considers why probabilistic approaches have not been very attractive to expert systems researchers. Then it explains the certainty factors approach of MYCIN (mentioned in Chapter 3) in a little more detail, and compares its results with those of probability theory.

6.2.1   Conditional probability

The *conditional probability* of d given s is simply the probability that d occurs if s occurs; for example, the probability that a patient really is suffering from disease d if he or she complains only of symptom s.

In traditional probability theory, the conditional probability of d given s is computed using the following formula:

$$p(d \mid s) = \frac{p(d \wedge s)}{p(s)} \tag{6.1}$$

Thus conditional probability is defined in terms of joint events; it is the ratio between the probability of the joint occurrence of d and s and the probability of s. Now

$$p(d \wedge s) = p(s \mid d)p(d)$$

and if we divide both sides by $p(s)$ and substitute using Formula 6.1, we derive the simplest form of *Bayes' rule* – sometimes called the inversion formula, because it defines $p(d \mid s)$ in terms of $p(s \mid d)$.

$$p(d \mid s) = \frac{p(s \mid d)p(d)}{p(s)} \tag{6.2}$$

$p(d)$ is the *prior probability* of d; that is, the probability prior to the discovery of s. $p(d \mid s)$ is the *posterior probability*; that is, the probability once we have discovered s.

For the purposes of knowledge-based systems, Formula 6.2 is much more useful than Formula 6.1, as we shall see.

Given that a patient has a disturbing symptom, such as chest pain, one would like to know the probability of this being due to something potentially serious, such as myocardial infarction (heart attack) or acute pericarditis (inflammation of the chest cavity), or something less serious, such as indigestion. However, to calculate the probability

$p(myocardial\ infarction \mid chest\ pain)$

using Formula 6.1, one would need to know (or estimate) how many people in the world were suffering from the disease, how many complained of the symptom, and how many were both suffering from the disease and complaining of the symptom. Such information is usually unavailable, particularly for

$p(myocardial\ infarction \wedge chest\ pain)$.

Thus the definition is not much use at it stands, because the practising clinician will not have the data that this form of reasoning requires.

The difficulty of obtaining these numbers has caused many AI writers and researchers to dismiss probabilistic approaches to uncertainty (see Charniak and McDermott, 1985, Chapter 8). In this dismissal, they have been unwittingly aided and abetted by much of the literature on probability, which gives the impression that:

- Probability is about *long-run relative frequencies* of events, and so the numbers needed to model inexact reasoning must be derived from empirical investigation, such as medical records.

- What one really needs is a *joint distribution function*; that is, a function which assigns probabilities to every elementary event or state of affairs that one might be interested in.

However, there is a growing body of opinion in AI (Pearl, 1982; Cheeseman, 1985) that these fundamental assumptions are questionable from the point of view of practical applications. Firstly, we can work with probability estimates rather than empirically determined ones. Doctors may not know, or be able to calculate, what proportion of chest pain patients have had heart attacks, but they will have some consistent notion of how many heart attack patients have chest pain, and therefore be able to give an estimate of

$$P(\text{chest pain} \mid \text{myocardial infarction})$$

This way of looking at probability is sometimes called *subjectivist*, because it involves human judgement, unlike the objectivist view implicit in the emphasis on long-run frequency. Given a reasonable estimate of $P(s \mid d)$, for symptom s and disease d, one can then use Bayes' rule to calculate $P(d \mid s)$. Medical statistics should enable an estimate of $P(d)$, while a doctor's own records could provide an estimate of $P(s)$.

The computation of $P(d \mid s)$ is not too problematic in the single symptom case, when we are reasoning about some set of diseases, D, and some set of symptoms, S, and limiting ourselves to calculating, for each disease in D, the conditional probability that a patient is suffering from D given that he or she complains of a single symptom in S. Nevertheless, given m diseases in D and n symptoms in S, we require $mn + m + n$ probabilities. This will not be a small number for a reasonable set of diagnostic categories, such as the 2000 or more that clinicians actually use, and the wide range of signs and symptoms that people present with.

The situation becomes considerably more complicated if one attempts to take more than one symptom into account when performing the diagnosis.

The more general form of Bayes' rule,

$$p(d \mid s_1 \wedge \ldots \wedge s_k) = \frac{p(s_1 \wedge \ldots \wedge s_k \mid d)p(d)}{p(s_1 \wedge \ldots \wedge s_k)} \tag{6.3}$$

requires $(mn)^k + m + n^k$ probabilities, which is a very large number for even modest values of k. These probabilities are required because, to compute $p(s_1 \wedge \ldots \wedge s_k)$ in the general case, we must compute

$$p(s_1 \mid s_2 \wedge \ldots \wedge s_k)p(s_2 \mid s_3 \wedge \ldots \wedge s_k)\ldots p(s_k)$$

However, a simplification is possible if you can assume that certain symptoms are *independent* of each other; that is, if, for any pair of symptoms, s_i and s_j,

$$p(s_i) = p(s_i \mid s_j)$$

because then it follows that

$$p(s_i \wedge s_j) = p(s_i)p(s_j)$$

If all the symptoms are independent, Formula 6.3 does not require that the expert supply any more probabilities than in the single symptom scenario.

Even where this is not the case, we can sometimes assume *conditional independence*; that is, that a pair of symptoms, s_i and s_j, are independent once we have some additional evidence or background knowledge, E, so that

$$p(s_i \mid s_j, E) = p(s_i \mid E)$$

For example, if my car has a flat tyre and the lights do not work, I am safe in assuming that these symptoms are independent, because there are no direct or indirect causal connections between them. On the other hand, if my car will not start and the lights do not work, I would be foolish to assume that these symptoms are independent, as there are common faults, such as a flat battery, that would cause them both.

6.2.2   Certainty factors

If we return to MYCIN's use of certainty factors (CFs), previously outlined in Chapter 3, we are now in a position to see how its treatment of uncertainty deviates from probability theory.

In a perfect world, one would like to be able to calculate $p(d_i \mid E)$, where d_i is the ith diagnostic category and E is all the evidence you need, using only conditional probabilities $p(d_i \mid s_j)$, where s_j is the jth clinical observation. We have seen that Bayes' rule provides a convenient means of doing this only if:

- all the $p(s_j \mid d_i)$ are available; and
- independence assumptions make the computation of the joint probabilities of symptom sets feasible.

The alternative explored by MYCIN was to use a rule-based approach, in which statements that link evidence to hypotheses are expressed as decision criteria, along the lines of:

> IF: the patient has signs and symptoms $s_1 \wedge \ldots \wedge s_k$, and
>   certain other conditions $t_1 \wedge \ldots \wedge t_m$ hold
> THEN: conclude that the patient has disease d_i, with certainty x

x is a certainty factor in the range $[-1, 1]$. $x = 1$ means that the conclusion is certain to be true if the conditions are completely satisfied, while $x = -1$ means that the conclusion is certain to be false under the same conditions. Otherwise, a positive value for x denotes that the conditions constitute suggestive evidence for the conclusion d_i, while a negative value denotes that the conditions are evidence against d_i.

The idea was to use production rules of this kind in an attempt to approximate the calculation of $p(d_i \mid s_1 \wedge \ldots \wedge s_k)$, and provide a scheme for accumulating evidence that reflected the reasoning process of an expert. As we saw in Chapter 3, the application of such a rule results in the association of a degree of certainty with the conclusion, given by

$$CF(d_i, s_1 \wedge \ldots \wedge s_k \wedge t_1 \wedge \ldots \wedge t_m)$$
$$= x \times \min(CF(s_1), \ldots, CF(s_k), CF(t_1), \ldots, CF(t_m))$$

The extra conditions $t_1 \wedge \ldots \wedge t_m$ represent background knowledge that serves to constrain the application of the rule. It is often the case that such conditions evaluate to truth or falsity, so that their CF equals $+1$ or -1, so that only the signs and symptoms contribute to a non-trivial CF for the conclusion.

Buchanan and Shortliffe (1984, Chapter 11) argue that a rigorous application of Bayes' rule would not have produced accurate probabilities in any case, because the conditional probabilities used would have been subjective. As we have already seen, this is the primary argument used by AI people against the employment of Bayesian inference. However, it assumes an objective interpretation of probabilities – that the 'right' numbers are out there somewhere, but we cannot get at them and therefore there is no point in applying Bayesian methods. In some ways, this is a curious argument, because any knowledge-engineering enterprise is surely seeking to represent an expert's knowledge of the world (imperfect though it may be), rather than create a veridical model of the world. Also, from a theoretical point of view, it seems more sensible to apply a mathematically correct formalism to (albeit imperfect) data than a formalism that is mathematically incorrect, since this can only compound any problems with the data.

However, as Pearl (1988, p. 5) points out, there is a striking difference between the rule-based approach and that of probability theory which conveys an enormous practical advantage to Shortliffe's method. The computation of the certainty associated with a conclusion is entirely *modular* – we don't need to consider any information that is not contained in the rule. Thus we do not care about the certainties of any other propositions, or how the current certainties of the conditions of the rule were derived.

This property is often assumed in expert systems, even though it does not often hold in general. In practice, it would mean that rule premises had to be logically independent for all rules dealing with a particular parameter. With respect to MYCIN, Shortliffe advised that dependent pieces of evidence should be grouped into single rather than multiple rules (see Buchanan and Shortliffe, 1984, p. 229).

Statements of conditional probability are not modular in this sense. Thus the statement

$$p(B \mid A) = x$$

does not santion the inference $p(B) = x$ in the presence of A unless A is *the only thing we know*. If, in addition to A, we acquire extra knowledge E, then we need to compute $p(B \mid A, E)$ before we can say anything about $p(B)$. This degree of context-sensitivity forms the basis of a very powerful inference mechanism but, as we have already discovered in Chapter 5, inferential power usually means computational cost.

6.2.3 Certainty factors versus conditional probabilities

Adams (1976) showed that the CF associated with a hypothesis by MYCIN does not correspond to the probability of the hypothesis given the evidence, if you adopt a simple probability model based on Bayes' rule. This may not sound too bad, as CFs are used only to rank hypotheses. However, Adams also showed that it is possible for two hypotheses to be ranked in reverse order to their respective probabilities by the use of certainty factors; it is worth looking at this in a bit more detail.

The expert's subjective probability that hypothesis h is correct, $p(h)$, can be taken to reflect the expert's degree of belief in h at a given time. If we now complicate matters, by adding fresh supporting evidence e, such that $p(h \mid e) > p(h)$, then the increase in the expert's degree of belief in d is given by:

$$\text{MB}(h, e) = \frac{p(h \mid e) - p(h)}{1 - p(h)}$$

where MB stands for Measure of Belief.

If, on the other hand, e constitutes evidence against h, such that $P(h \mid e) < P(h)$, then the increase in the expert's degree of disbelief is given by:

$$\text{MD}(h, e) = \frac{p(h) - p(h \mid e)}{p(h)}$$

where MD stands for Measure of Disbelief.

However, as Adams points out, degrees of belief in a hypothesis derived from the consideration of different pieces of evidence cannot be chosen independently. If some piece of evidence is an absolute diagnostic indicator for a particular illness (for example, if all patients with symptom s_1 have disease d_i) then no other piece of evidence has any diagnostic value. In other words, if there are two pieces of evidence, s_1 and s_2, and

$$p(d_i \mid s_1) = p(d_i \mid s_1 \wedge s_2) = 1$$

then

$$p(d_i \mid s_2) = p(d_i)$$

Adams also criticizes the treatment of conjoined hypotheses. The MYCIN model assumes that our belief in a joint hypothesis $d_1 \wedge d_2$ is as great as our belief in the weakest hypothesis, while our degree of disbelief should be as great as that associated with the strongest hypothesis. But this treatment makes strong assumptions regarding the independence of d_1 and d_2. Suppose d_1 and d_2 are not independent, but mutually exclusive alternatives. Then $p(d_1 \wedge d_2 \mid e) = 0$, for any evidence e, regardless of our degree of belief (or disbelief) in d_1 or d_2.

Buchanan and Shortliffe (1984, p. 249) describe the certainty factor as an artefact for combining degrees of belief and disbelief into a single number. It is simply the difference between the measures of belief and disbelief, according to the formula

$$\mathrm{CF}(h, e_a \wedge e_f) = \mathrm{MB}(h, e_f) - \mathrm{MD}(h, e_a)$$

where e_f is the evidence for h and e_a is the evidence against h. However, this is not equivalent to the computation of the conditional probability of h given $e_a \wedge e_f$ that one would derive from Bayes' rule:

$$p(h \mid e_a \wedge e_f) = \frac{p(e_a \wedge e_f \mid h)p(h)}{p(e_a \wedge e_f)}$$

Thus, although changes in belief brought about by rule applications can be related to subjective probabilities in a fairly direct way, the certainty factor is a composite number. Its main uses are:

- to guide the program in its reasoning;
- to cause the current goal to be deemed unpromising and pruned from the search space if its CF falls in the range $[+0.2, -0.2]$;
- to rank hypotheses after all the evidence has been considered.

However, Adams shows that in some circumstances this ranking will depart from that produced by the application of probability theory. The example that he gives is the following.

Let d_1 and d_2 be two hypotheses, and let e be a body of evidence that tends to confirm both of them. Let the prior probabilities be such that

$$p(d_1) \geq p(d_2) \quad \text{and} \quad p(d_1 \mid e) > p(d_2 \mid e)$$

In other words, d_1 has a higher subjective probability than d_2 to begin with, and this superiority remains after the consideration of the evidence. Under these circumstances, it is possible that $CF(d_1, e) < CF(d_2, e)$.
Suppose that

$$p(d_1) = 0.8$$
$$p(d_2) = 0.2$$
$$p(d_1 \mid e) = 0.9$$
$$p(d_2 \mid e) = 0.8$$

Then the increase in belief in d_1 is given by

$$\frac{0.9 - 0.8}{0.2} = 0.5$$

while the increase in belief in d_2 is given by

$$\frac{0.8 - 0.2}{0.8} = 0.75$$

so $CF(d_1, e) < CF(d_2, e)$ even though $p(d_1 \mid e) > p(d_2 \mid e)$.
Adams describes this as an 'undesirable feature' of certainty factors. To avoid it, all prior probabilities would have to be equal; one can easily see that the effect in the above example is caused by the fact that the evidence favoured d_2, even though d_1 triumphed in the end, because of a superior prior probability. However, such an equality would be at variance with the way in which diagnosticians reason, given the widely differing frequencies of occurrence associated with different diseases, and hence the widely different subjective probabilities that a diagnostician would provide for them.
The chaining of rules in MYCIN also causes some theoretical problems. The combination functions employed appear to be based on the assumption that if some evidence, e, implies an intermediate hypothesis, h, with probability $p(h \mid e)$, and h implies a final diagnostic category, d, with probability $p(d \mid h)$, then

$$p(d \mid e) = p(d \mid h)p(h \mid e)$$

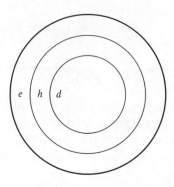

Figure 6.1   Populations validating $p(d \mid e) = p(d \mid h)p(h \mid e)$.

This transitive relation across chains of reasoning seems acceptable at first sight, but it is not true in general, because the populations associated with these categories have to be nested in the manner of Figure 6.1 for this inference to be valid.

Adams concludes that the empirical success of MYCIN, and other systems that use the same combination functions, may be due to the fact that the chains of reasoning are short and the hypotheses involved are simple. He argues that these shortcomings in MYCIN illustrate the difficulty of creating a useful and internally consistent system of inexact reasoning that is not simply a subset of probability theory. Thus the careful comparison of such systems with the standard theory can be beneficial in showing exactly where the differences and possible difficulties lie, as we shall see in Chapter 25.

More recent criticisms of MYCIN (Horvitz and Heckerman, 1986) have centred on the use of certainty factors as measures of change in belief, when they were actually elicited from experts as degrees of absolute belief. In attaching CFs to rules, experts responded to the question 'On a scale of 1 to 10, how much certainty do you affix to this conclusion?' But the evidence combination function employed by MYCIN treats CFs as belief updates, and this results in values which are inconsistent with Bayes' theorem.

6.3   Vagueness and possibility

Apart from certainty factors, there are a number of other alternatives to probability theory in the literature, notably fuzzy logic and the Dempster–Shafer theory of evidence. We shall deal with Dempster–

Shafer theory in Chapter 25, which delves further into some of the theoretical issues. This section reviews fuzzy logic to see why it has often been preferred to probability theory for expert systems applications.

6.3.1 Fuzzy sets

The knowledge that an expert uses in interpreting some signal, or perceiving a symptom as a manifestation of a particular disorder, is usually based on relationships between classes of data and classes of hypothesis, rather than individual data and hypotheses. Most forms of problem solving involve some kind of data classification: signals, symptoms and the like are seen as instances of more general categories. However, such categories may not be sharply defined. Thus class membership may be difficult to assess; a datum may exhibit some of the properties of the class but not others, or may exhibit properties only to a certain degree. *Fuzzy set theory* is a formalism for reasoning about such phenomena, and it forms the basis of both *fuzzy logic* and *possibility theory*.

Classical set theory is based on two-valued logic. Expressions of the form $a \in A$, where a is a constant denoting an individual and A denotes a set of individuals, are either true or false. Since the advent of fuzzy sets, classical sets are sometimes called *crisp*. The crispness of set theory poses a problem when we deal with concepts that are not sharply defined.

Consider the concept denoted by the word 'fast' as applied to an automobile. Given the vagueness of the concept, how do we characterize the set of fast cars? In set theory, we can describe a set A either by enumeration (listing the members of A) or by providing a characteristic function, f, such that for any X in the universe of discourse,

$$f(X) = \textit{true} \text{ if and only if } X \in A$$

Thus we could characterize the set of cars capable of more than 150 mph by the function

$$GT150(X) = \begin{cases} \textit{true} \text{ if } CAR(X) \text{ and } \textit{TOP-SPEED}(X) > 150 \\ \textit{false} \text{ otherwise} \end{cases}$$

The set so defined is often written as

$$\{X \in CAR \mid \textit{TOP-SPEED}(X) > 150\}$$

that is, those members of the set CAR such that their top speed is over 150 mph.

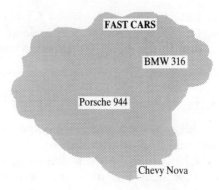

Figure 6.2 A pictorial view of the set of fast cars.

But what of the set of fast cars? Intuitively, the situation is more like that depicted in Figure 6.2, where the boundaries of the set are unclear, and membership appears to be graded in some way. Rather than being an all-or-none member of the set, individual cars appear to be more or less typical of the associated concept.

One way round the problem might be to provide an operational definition of 'fast' for practical purposes by introducing an artificial boundary to the set, such as every car with a top speed of over 150 mph is fast, and all other cars are not in the set. However, as well as violating our intuitions, such rigid definitions might have a detrimental effect on our ability to act. If it is my ambition to own a fast car but I am presented with a limited choice, a car that will do 140 is still a better proposition than one that will only do 100.

Elements of a fuzzy set are members of that set *to a degree*. A fuzzy set is therefore a function, f, from an appropriate domain to the interval $[0, 1]$, where $f(X) = 0$ denotes that X is not a member of the set, $f(X) = 1$ denotes that X is definitely a member, and all other values denote degrees of membership. In the car example, we need a function from the domain of top speeds; thus we might have $f_{FAST}(80) = 0$, $f_{FAST}(180) = 1$, and some histogram of monotonically increasing values between the two, constructed over intervals of 5 or 10 mph. Thus the set of fast cars could be characterized by the function

$$f_{FAST\text{-}CAR}(X) = f_{FAST}(TOP\text{-}SPEED(X))$$

from the domain of cars, yielding a set of ordered pairs of the form (*make, degree*), for example:

$$FAST\text{-}CAR = \{(Porsche\text{-}944, 0.9), (BMW\text{-}316, 0.5),$$
$$(Chevy\text{-}Nova, 0.1)\}$$

6.3.2 Fuzzy logic

Just as classical set theory is governed by a two-valued logic, fuzzy set theory can be related to a many-valued logic in which propositions such as *FAST-CAR(Porsche-944)* have a value which is a real number between 0 and 1. The question then arises as to how to compute the truth values of compound statements involving vague concepts, such as

$\quad\neg FAST\text{-}CAR(Chevrolet\text{-}Nova)$

In the case of negation, if *F* is a fuzzy predicate, then

$\quad\neg F(X) = 1 - F(X)$

by analogy with probability theory. However, in its treatment of conjunction and disjunction, fuzzy logic departs from probability theory in significant ways. Consider the sentence

$\quad$ Porsche 944 is a fast, pretentious car.

In classical logic, the proposition

$\quad FAST\text{-}CAR(Porsche\text{-}944) \wedge PRETENTIOUS\text{-}CAR(Porsche\text{-}944)$

is true if and only if both conjuncts are true. In fuzzy logic, the convention is that if *F* and *G* are fuzzy predicates, then

$\quad f_{(F \wedge G)}(X) = \min(f_F(X), f_G(X))$

as we saw in Chapter 3, when computing the certainty of conjunctions of conditions for MYCIN's production rules.

$\quad$ Thus if

$\quad FAST\text{-}CAR(Porsche\text{-}944) = 0.9$

$\quad PRETENTIOUS\text{-}CAR(Porsche\text{-}944) = 0.7$

then

$\quad FAST\text{-}CAR(Porsche\text{-}944) \wedge PRETENTIOUS\text{-}CAR(Porsche\text{-}944)$
$\quad\quad = 0.7$

But consider the statement

$\quad FAST\text{-}CAR(Porsche\text{-}944) \wedge \neg FAST\text{-}CAR(Porsche\text{-}944)$

The probability of this statement is 0, since

$$p(\textit{FAST-CAR}(\textit{Porsche-944}) \mid \neg \textit{FAST-CAR}(\textit{Porsche-944})) = 0$$

but it is easy to see that in fuzzy logic its value is 0.1. What does this mean? Fuzzy logicians would regard this as representing the Porsche's degree of membership in the fuzzy set of medium-performance cars, which are both fast and not fast to some degree.

The main difference between the two approaches is that a probability is normally regarded as an approximation to something more precise. There is a 50% chance that a fair coin will come down heads, but the coin, when tossed, will come down 100% heads or 100% tails. In the 'fast car' example, the intended meaning of

$$\textit{FAST-CAR}(\textit{Porsche-944}) = 0.9$$

is not that a Porsche really is 100% fast or 100% not fast but that we are only 90% sure that it is fast. The uncertainty is inherent in the vagueness of the concept. Thus it seems reasonable to suppose that there remains a degree to which it is not fast; for example, it is slow by comparison with a Formula 1 racing car.

Fuzzy logic deals with disjunction by taking the maximum value of the disjuncts; thus

$$f_{(F \lor G)}(X) = \max(f_F(X), f_G(X))$$

for fuzzy categories F and G. This is similarly in contrast with probability theory, where

$$p(A \lor B) = p(A) + p(B) - p(A \land B)$$

Consider the following propositions and their values in fuzzy logic with reference to the fuzzy set *FAST-CAR*, given above.

$$\textit{FAST-CAR}(\textit{Porsche-944}) \lor \neg \textit{FAST-CAR}(\textit{Porsche-944}) = 0.9$$

$$\textit{FAST-CAR}(\textit{BMW-316}) \lor \neg \textit{FAST-CAR}(\textit{BMW-316}) = 0.5$$

$$\textit{FAST-CAR}(\textit{Chevrolet-Nova}) \lor \neg \textit{FAST-CAR}(\textit{Chevrolet-Nova})$$
$$= 0.9$$

In probability theory, the value of each of these propositions would be 1. Fuzzy logicians would explain that the high values accorded to Porsche and Chevrolet are due to the fact that their degree of membership in the fuzzy set *FAST-CAR* is extreme. The fuzzy concept 'fast or not fast' therefore applies to them, whereas the more medium performance *BMW* is neither one thing nor the other, and therefore gets a lower value.

The max and min operators are commutative, associative and mutually distributive. Like the operators of standard logic, they obey the principle of *compositionality*; the values of compound expressions are computed from the values of their component expressions and nothing else. This is in contrast with the laws of probability, where conditional probabilities must be taken into account when computing conjunction and disjunction.

6.3.3 Possibility theory

Fuzzy logic deals with situations where the question that we pose and the relevant knowledge that we possess both contain vague concepts. However, vagueness is not the only source of uncertainty. Sometimes we are simply unsure of the facts. If I say: 'It is possible that John is in Paris', there is nothing vague about the concepts of John and Paris. The uncertainty is about whether or not John really is in Paris.

Possibility theory is a species of fuzzy logic for dealing with precise questions on the basis of imprecise knowledge. Here we shall content ourselves with no more than a brief introduction. The best way to proceed is by example.

Suppose that an urn contains 10 balls, but all we know is that several of them are red. What is the probability of drawing a red ball at random?

Now we cannot compute an answer directly from the knowledge that several balls are red. Nevertheless, for each value, x, of $p(RED)$ in the range $[0, 1]$, we can compute the possibility that $p(RED) = x$, as follows.

Firstly, we define 'several' as a fuzzy set:

$$f_{SEVERAL} = \{(3, 0.2), (4, 0.6), (5, 1.0), (6, 1.0), (7, 0.6), (8, 0.3)\}$$

For example, $(3, 0.2) \in f_{SEVERAL}$ denotes that 3 out of 10 barely qualifies as several out of 10, while $(5, 1), (6, 1) \in f_{SEVERAL}$ denotes that 5 and 6 out of 10 are excellent candidates for 'severalhood'. Note that neither 1 nor 10 is not a member of the fuzzy set, since 'several' normally implies 'more than one' and 'not all'. Fuzzy sets whose domains are numbers are called *fuzzy numbers*. f_{FEW} and f_{MOST} could be defined as fuzzy numbers in an analogous way.

The possibility distribution for $p(RED)$ is now given by

$$f_{p(RED)} = SEVERAL/10$$

which evaluates to

$$\{(0.3, 0.2), (0.4, 0.6), (0.5, 1.0), (0.6, 1.0), (0.7, 0.6), (0.8, 0.3)\}$$

where $(0.3, 0.2) \in f_{p(RED)}$ denotes that there is a 20% chance that $p(RED) = 0.3$. We can regard $f_{p(RED)}$ as a *fuzzy probability*.

Given that almost anything can be the domain of function, it is natural to think about fuzzy truth values. We frequently talk of statements being 'very true' or 'partly true', in addition to plain 'true'. Thus one can imagine a fuzzy set

$$f_{TRUE}: [0, 1] \rightarrow [0, 1]$$

where both the domain and range of the function f_{TRUE} are the possible truth values of fuzzy logic. Hence we could have

$$TRUE(FAST\text{-}CAR(Porsche\text{-}944)) = 1$$

even though $FAST\text{-}CAR(Porsche\text{-}944) = 0.9$, so long as $(0.9, 1.0) \in f_{TRUE}$. This would mean that we take any proposition with a value of 0.9 as being true, or 'true enough'. Thus we are sure that a Porsche is a fast car, even though there are faster cars on the market.

6.4 Uncertainty in AI systems

The great advantage of fuzzy logic for expert systems appears to be the compositionality of its logical operators.

We have seen that, given a MYCIN-style rule of the form

> IF: the patient has signs and symptoms $s_1 \wedge \ldots \wedge s_k$, and certain other conditions $t_1 \wedge \ldots \wedge t_m$ hold
>
> THEN: conclude that the patient has disease d_i, with certainty x

the evaluation the conjoined conditions $s_1 \wedge \ldots \wedge s_k$ according to the axioms of probability theory involves the computation of

$$p(s_1 \mid s_2 \wedge \ldots \wedge s_k)P(s_2 \mid s_3 \wedge \ldots \wedge s_k)\ldots p(s_k)$$

thus requiring $k - 1$ probabilities over and above those required for the s_i, in the worst case.

We have also seen that MYCIN interprets conjunction as a fuzzy operator, computing $\min(s_1 \wedge \ldots \wedge s_k)$, and that this can lead to results that run counter to probability theory. What should we conclude from this? There is little or no consensus in the literature, although probability theory has recently gained ground, for a number of reasons.

- People are becoming more willing to use subjective probabilities, and even second-order probabilities (probability statements about probability statements, which estimate the chance that a probability statement is objectively accurate). The latter have been advocated as an alternative to fuzzy probabilities by Cheeseman (1986), although the approach is probably less intuitive from a knowledge-engineering point of view.

- Empirical studies comparing different methods for handling uncertainty commonly used in AI have discovered further examples of error, in which methods based on fuzzy logic perform less reliably worse than Bayesian approaches (see Wise and Henrion, 1986). Surprisingly few such studies have been performed, however.

- AI researchers have rediscovered theoretical work which shows that any consistent system of plausible reasoning that attaches real numbers to propositions *must* obey the axioms of probability theory (see Chapter 25). Heckerman (1986) has proposed a correction of the certainty factor model based on this observation.

- New research on the implementation and application of Bayesian techniques (Pearl, 1988) has led to a better understanding of how problems associated with dependencies might be circumvented. Nevertheless, computational problems remain if we allow arbitrary associations between causes and effects, such as multiple links.

It is worth pointing out that human beings do not appear to be reliable Bayesian reasoners. The research of Kahneman and Tversky (1972) showed that people are apt to discount prior odds and accord more weight to recently presented evidence. Other research suggests that people are over-confident in their judgements (see papers in Kahneman *et al.* 1982).

Part of the charm of fuzzy logic is that it seems at first sight to be grounded in our use of language. Thus terms such as 'fast', 'few', 'true' are given an interpretation that seems to be in accordance with our everyday intuitions. However, it is by no means clear that the inference rules defined over such interpretations are appropriate for arbitrary expert systems applications. After all, our everyday use of language need not be bound by strict mathematical constraints, while higher standards of formality and precision may be required for some problem-solving applications.

We shall return to these topics later in the book (in particular, in Part VI). The present chapter provides no more than a basic grounding in the concept of uncertainty and uncovers a few theoretical problems. Nevertheless, the reader can see, even from this brief review, that we still have a way to go before we understand all the issues involved in choosing a representation for uncertainty.

Bibliographical notes

Part 4 of Buchanan and Shortliffe (1984) contains a coherent account of MYCIN's certainty factors and why they were preferred to alternative treatments. It also reproduces Adams' critical paper. Pearl (1988) provides an intriguing account of how to apply Bayesian decision theory to problems that require reasoning under uncertainty. Mamdani and Gaines (1981) is a book of papers that seek to apply fuzzy logic to substantive problems. Sanford (1987) contains an easy to read but interesting review of psychological research into probabilistic judgements.

STUDY SUGGESTIONS

6.1 Suppose that the probability that an engine will fail on a three-engined aircraft is 0.01. What is the probability that all three engines will fail, if the failure of each of the three engines is independent of the failure of the other two engines?

6.2 What is the probability that all three engines in Exercise 6.1 will fail, if the independence assumption does not hold, but we have the following conditional probabilities?

$p(engine1\ fails \mid engine2\ fails\ or\ engine3\ fails) = 0.4$
$p(engine2\ fails \mid engine1\ fails\ or\ engine3\ fails) = 0.3$
$p(engine3\ fails \mid engine1\ fails\ or\ engine2\ fails) = 0.2$

$p(engine1\ fails \mid engine2\ fails\ and\ engine3\ fails) = 0.9$
$p(engine2\ fails \mid engine1\ fails\ and\ engine3\ fails) = 0.8$
$p(engine3\ fails \mid engine1\ fails\ and\ engine2\ fails) = 0.7$

6.3 Given that $p(three\ engines\ fail \mid sabotage) = 0.9$, and the probability of any one engine failing is 0.01 as before, use the probabilities in Exercise 6.2 to compute the probability that the airplane was sabotaged if all three of its engines fail.

6.4 Suppose that 'few' is defined as the fuzzy set:

$$f_{FEW} = \{(3,\ 0.8),\ (4,\ 0.7),\ (5,\ 0.6),\ (6,\ 0.5),\ (7,\ 0.4),\ (8,\ 0.3)\}$$

If an urn contains 15 balls, but all we know is that few of them are blue, what is the probability of drawing a blue ball at random?

6.5 Suppose that 'abnormal marks out of ten' is defined as the fuzzy set:

$$f_{ABNORMAL} = \{(0, 1.0), (1, 0.9), (2, 0.7), (3, 0.5), (4. 0.3), (5, 0.1)$$
$$(6, 0.1) (7, 0.3) (8, 0.5) (9, 0.9), (10, 0.9)\}$$

and 'high marks out of ten' is defined as the fuzzy set

$$f_{HIGH} = \{(0, 0), (1, 0), (2, 0), (3, 0.1), (4, 0.2), (5, 0.3)$$
$$(6, 0.4) (7, 0.6) (8, 0.7) (9, 0.8), (10, 1.0)\}$$

Derive the composite function 'abnormally high marks out of ten'.

Part III

Knowledge Representation Formalisms

7 Symbolic Computation

Introduction

Before discussing specialized languages for knowledge representation, it is worth spending some time on the more general topic of artificial intelligence programming languages.

This chapter has three aims. Firstly, it attempts to explain why artificial intelligence research requires particular kinds of programming languages, and discusses ways in which these languages differ from more mainstream languages for scientific computing and data processing. Secondly, it attempts to introduce the beginning student to the central concepts of LISP: the main programming language of artificial intelligence. The idea is not to turn the reader into a LISP programmer, but to explain why LISP is the way it is and why AI programmers still use it after more than 20 years. Finally, it attempts to explain that LISP lacks many of the features that we require for knowledge representation, although such features can be implemented in LISP.

An introduction to COMMON LISP for programmers is provided in Appendix A.

7.1 Symbolic representation

The notion of a *symbol* is so pervasive in the current theory and practice of artificial intelligence that its importance is easily overlooked. It is this notion that forms the crucial link between artificial intelligence and formal systems of logic and mathematics. In the simplest possible terms, a symbol is something that stands for something else. This 'something else' is usually called the *designation* of the symbol. It is the thing that the symbol refers to or represents. The designation may be a physical object or it may be a concept, but the symbol itself is physical. Thus an occurrence of the numeral 7 is a symbol; it stands for the number 7, which is a concept.

Originally, it was thought that computers were only for processing numbers; the popular view of computers is still that of a 'number cruncher'. Although all programs and data in a computer are encoded in binary numbers, computers routinely manipulate symbols representing machine instructions and symbolic addresses; such symbols in an assembly program stand for sequences of binary numbers that mean something in machine code. The association between these symbols and their values is usually maintained in a symbol table.

The idea behind symbolic computation is that we want to allow symbols to stand for anything at all. Programming languages based on this paradigm provide a number of primitive data structures for associating symbols with other symbols, as well as primitive operations for manipulating symbols and their associated structures. A programmer must then specify:

(1) *syntactic rules* for forming symbol structures out of symbols, in such a way that the resulting structures have a meaning that is a function of their constituents;

(2) *transformation rules* which turn symbol structures into other symbol structures.

Typically a symbolic program takes as its input one or more symbol structures, representing the initial state of some problem, and returns as its output a symbol structure, representing a terminal state or solution, that is both well formed in terms of the syntactic rules and has been derived by the application of legal transformations. *Programs in such languages are themselves symbol structures.* Thus there is no reason why some programs cannot treat other programs as data, and it turns out that this uniformity in the representation of data and programs is particularly useful in the context of artificial intelligence.

7.2 Physical symbol systems

We have already encountered examples of symbol systems in the propositional and predicate calculi of Chapter 5. There we specified notions of well-formedness and theoremhood in terms of syntactic rules and inference rules, respectively. However, these are not *physical* symbol systems, unless they are realized in some physical device. Thus, that part of my brain that (thinks it) understands propositional and predicate logic can be considered as a physical symbol system. A logic textbook is not a physical symbol system, because it is unable to perform symbolic operations, such as transformations on physical symbol structures.

Newell (1982) describes a physical symbol system as a machine with the following components, located in some environment:

- a *memory* containing symbol structures, which can vary in number and content over time;
- a set of *operators* for manipulating symbol structures, such as reading, writing, copying;
- a *control* for the continual interpretation of whatever symbol structure is currently active, or being attended to;
- an *input* from its environment via receptors, and an *output* to that environment via some motor component.

A *program* in a physical symbol system is just a symbol structure that is interpreted or *evaluated* in some manner that is a function of its constituent symbols and its symbolic input. The primitive programs correspond to operators for manipulating symbol structures; more complex programs describe processes composed of these operators. Control is able to tell the difference between data and programs, even though both are just symbol structures; the former are just returned, while the latter must be interpreted.

A physical symbol system resembles a general-purpose computer equipped with symbol processing software. We know that stored program computers are universal machines (roughly speaking, they can simulate the operation of any other machine), and therefore capable in principle of computing all general recursive functions (roughly, all functions computable by any machine). It is the apparent power of these physical realizations of symbol systems that has encouraged researchers to suppose that such systems are capable of intelligence.

The *physical symbol system hypothesis* of Newell and Simon (1976) has been stated as follows:

> A physical symbol system has the necessary and sufficient means for general intelligent action.

Regardless of whether or not this conjecture ultimately turns out to be true, symbolic computation has become a reality, and its power and utility as a programming paradigm is impossible to deny.

The next few sections look at its implemenation and use in artificial intelligence.

7.3 Implementing symbol structures in LISP

Given that we want to be able to arrange physical symbols into structures, and perform operations on those structures, the question immediately arises as to what kind of structure we should use. The symbols of logic and mathematics are normally aggregated into *sets* and *sequences*. Each of these formal structures is well understood, but neither of these abstract entities is entirely suitable as a basis for a physical symbol structure.

Sets are unordered collections of elements, whereas physical symbols are forced to have location in a structure. (This location can be hidden from the programmer, to give the impression of a set, but it is none the less a reality of the implementation.) Sequences give terms a location, but an abstract sequence can be infinite.

A good candidate for a symbol structure is a *list*: it imparts a position to its members, but it is normally a finite physical entity. We can use a list to represent a set, of course; just as we can use various tricks to represent a sequence by extending a list indefinitely. However, the basic data structure remains ordered and finite.

7.3.1 LISP data structures

One of the first LISt Processing languages was LISP (McCarthy, 1960). This language has undergone a good deal of development over the last three decades, but the basic design has remained more or less the same. As McCarthy *et al.* (1965) point out, LISP differs from most programming languages in three important respects:

- Its main data structure is the list.
- Its programs are also represented by list structures.
- Its primitive operations are operations on lists.

The basic building block of LISP data structures is the symbolic expression, or *S-expression*, for short. Simple S-expressions are just atomic symbols, or *atoms*: strings of (not more than some implementation-dependent number of) alphanumeric characters beginning with a letter, for example PETER. An atom is represented internally as a cell in reclaimable memory. T is also a special atom that stands for 'true', while another special atom, NIL, stands for 'false'. NIL also serves as the *empty list*.

Complex expressions are implemented as memory cells combined to form arbitrary finite tree structures. There is a straightforward correspondence between finite trees and S-expressions. Thus, given an operator for combining cells into tree structures, the definition of an S-expression can be derived as follows:

Any atom is an S-expression.

If A_1 and A_2 are S-expressions, then $(A_1 . A_2)$ is an S-expression.

If $S = (A_1 . (A_2 . (\ldots . (A_{n-1} . A_n) \ldots)))$ is an S-expression for some $n > 0$, then S is a list if and only if $A_n = $ NIL.

By convention, if $n = 0$, then S is the empty list, NIL. This definition allows for lists of lists, as well as lists of atoms. If $S_1, S_2, \ldots, S_n$ are S-expressions, then we shall represent the list

$$(S_1 . (S_2 . (\ldots . (S_n . NIL) \ldots)))$$

as simply

$$(S_1 \ S_2 \ \ldots \ S_n)$$

Thus $(A . (B . NIL))$ is a list; it represents the list $(A \ B)$, but $(A . (B . C))$ is not a list, because $C \neq$ NIL.

S-expressions that are neither atoms nor lists are called *dotted pairs*. If $(A . B)$ is a dotted pair, then A is its *head*, and B its *tail*. Dotted pairs can be arbitrarily complex. Thus $((A . B) . C)$ is a dotted pair, as is $((A . B) . (C . D))$. Thanks to the correspondence between dotted pairs and lists, the notions of head and tail are defined for them too. Given that the list $(A \ B)$ is just $(A . (B . NIL))$, it should be obvious that although A is the head of $(A \ B)$, its tail is (B), not B. Finally, the tail of (B) is NIL.

Lists are very flexible data structures, being untyped and of arbitrary length. Thus there is nothing wrong with the list

$$("A" \ (9) \ (B . C) \ T \ (? \ (AAAAARGH!)) \ NIL \ 0.9)$$

even though it contains elements of rather different types: strings, fixed and floating point numbers, atoms, booleans, dotted pairs and other lists. Nevertheless, it is useful if lists are given some form of internal organization; a convenient structure is a list of dotted pairs called an *association list*, or *a-list*. For example, I could represent information about the city of St. Louis in an a-list like:

```
((NAME . ST-LOUIS)
 (STATE . MISSOURI)
 (POPULATION . 500000)
```

However, there are some obvious disadvantages with lists which have led to other data structures being added to LISP. LISP's lists are really stacks in that they can be accessed only from the front. Thus, to extract the population of St. Louis from the a-list shown above, we must write a program that cruises down the list until it finds the head marked POPULATION. There is no notion of access by position, as in an array, or by a key, as in hash tables. So although lists are still useful as repositories for temporary data, large amounts of permanent data are better represented in other kinds of structure. Modern LISP provides various alternatives – including arrays, hash tables, and record-like structures – which are more efficient in terms of storage space and speed of access.

7.3.2 LISP **programs**

We can easily get used to the idea of lists as data structures. Less familiar is the idea that a list can be a *program*; for example, the list

```
(+ X Y)
```

as a mathematical expression of the form

```
(<Function> <1st argument> <2nd argument>)
```

How could this work without causing confusion? Well, at least the following machinery is required.

- We must be able to *evaluate* expressions such as (+ X Y). To do this, we need to be able to look up some kind of function definition for + that tells us what sequence of primitive operations to apply to the arguments to compute the value.
- We must be able to *define* functions in the first place, and apply their definitions to arguments (actual, not formal, parameters). The mechanisms of function definition and function application are based on a logistic system, called the *lambda calculus* (see Church, 1941). Unlike first-order predicate calculus, lambda calculus is functional rather than relational; the primitive notion is that of many-to-one relations, rather than many-to-many relations. Thus *father* is a functional relation, because for each person there is only

one father, whereas *brother* is a more general relation, because each person may have more than one brother. I shall touch on the relation between LISP and the lambda calculus later in this section.

- We must be able to *access* the current values of variables (or formal parameters) like X and Y. The evaluation of each S-expression is performed relative to an *environment* of variable bindings. We need to be able to save and restore these environments, as we compute the value of a complex S-expression by computing and combining the values of any subexpressions contained therein.

- In the evaluation of complex S-expressions, which may involve both the application of more than one function and the composition of functions, we need to be able to store the *current* S-expression; namely, the one we are evaluating at a given moment. We need to be able to *copy* S-expressions pending evaluation so that we can save them during subcomputations. We also need to store intermediate results.

- Finally, we must be able to inhibit the evaluation of lists that are not program statements but merely data structures. Thus, we don't want to try to evaluate the list

```
((NAME . ST-LOUIS)
 (STATE . MISSOURI)
 (POPULATION . 500000)
```

by looking to see if we have a definition for the non-existent function

```
(NAME . ST-LOUIS)
```

This is achieved by the special form QUOTE: for all X, (QUOTE X) returns X.

The standard way of implementing functional languages like LISP is to use a four-stack machine, called the *SECD machine*. These four stacks keep track of partial results, values for variables, the current expression, and copies of the current state of the computation for restoration after subcomputations. Without going into details, the evaluation of an S-expression performed by such a machine implements the basic operation of function application as defined by the lambda calculus (see Henderson, 1980; Glaser *et al.*, 1984).

7.3.3 Functional application and lambda conversion

In understanding the relationship between lambda calculus and LISP, it is useful to bear in mind Church's original distinction between a *denotation* and an *abstraction*. The expression (X * X) *denotes* a particular number; which number depends on the value of X. However, it can also be taken as a function square(X), in which X is *bound* rather than being *free*. This function is an abstraction, because it can apply to many different values of X. To distinguish between the denotation and the abstraction, the latter is represented by

  (λX)(X * X)

in the lambda calculus. The lambda operator, λ, is said to bind the variable X, rather as a quantifier binds an individual variable in the predicate calculus. Thus (λX)(X * X) can serve as a definition of the square function:

  square(X) = (λX)(X * X)

Now in applying the square function to a particular number, say 3, we have to substitute the 3 for the variable X somehow, so that 3 is the value of X and evaluating (X * X) returns 9. When we apply the function definition (λX)(X * X) to the argument 3, we use an inference rule called *lambda conversion*. Let (λX)M stand for any lambda abstract, and let S(a, X, M) stand for the result of uniformly substituting a for X in M.

> **Lambda conversion** Replace any part (λX)M of a formula by S(a, X, M), provided that the bound variables of M are distinct both from X and from the free variables of a.
>   If we let ((λX)M)(a) stand for the application of the function definition (λX)M to the argument a, then

  ((λX)(X * X))(3) = (3 * 3) = 9

What has this to do with LISP? Well, the LISP definition of the square function is something like

  (DEFINE SQUARE (LAMBDA (X) (* X X)))

The exact details depend on the dialect and implementation of the language, but the intent is clear. In fact, in COMMON LISP, one would simply use the shorthand

  (DEFUN SQUARE (X) (* X X))

Either way, the intent of the definition is to associate a function name, like SQUARE, with a lambda expression that constitutes its definition. (LAMBDA (X) (* X X)) is just a syntactic variant of (λX)(X * X). In fact

(SQUARE 3) = ((LAMBDA (X) (* X X)) 3) = ((λX)(X * X))(3) = 9

in any LISP at all, once SQUARE has been defined. Thus evaluating

((LAMBDA (X) (* X X)) 3)

binds X to 3 by lambda conversion, so that (* X X) now *denotes* the number 9, in Church's terminology. Remember that LAMBDA is *not* a function; it is a special operator in the lambda calculus.

The basic syntax of a LISP function call is just a list of the form

(<Function> <Argument> ... <Argument>)

This is not the most complicated syntax in the world, but together with QUOTE, LAMBDA, and the form of the conditional statement (see below), it is all you need to know. People who are irrationally attached to commas, full stops, colons, semicolons, palindromes (*if ... fi, case ... esac*) and the like may find this a bit hard to take, but having parentheses as the only delimiter has one amazing advantage. LISP programs are just LISP data structures. Thus LISP programs can read, write and manipulate other LISP programs as if they were data. No, not as if they were data; they *are* data.

The conditional in COMMON LISP has the form (IF X Y Z). If the S-expression X evaluates to anything other than NIL, then Y is evaluated, else Z is evaluated. Again, IF is not a function. Thus

```
(DEFUN ASSOCIATE (ATTR ALIST)
     (IF (= ALIST NIL) NIL
          (IF(= (FIRST (FIRST ALIST)) ATTR)
              (REST (FIRST ALIST))
              (ASSOCIATE ATTR (REST ALIST)))))
```

defines a recursive function for extracting the value of an attribute from an association list. FIRST is a function that returns the head of a list, while REST is a function that returns its tail. The function is recursive because it calls itself, but it always terminates because either the attribute is in the a-list, in which case we return its value, or we reach the end of the list, in which case we return NIL. As successive calls to ASSOCIATE are evaluated, with new values for the formal parameters ATTR and ALIST, the SECD machine stores away old variable bindings and keeps track of the computation.

This recursive style of programming is typical of functional programming languages, and there are various tricks in the writing and compilation of such functions that can render them relatively efficient to execute.

7.3.4 List processing

LISP is a formal language that can be given a very concise description. Most LISP programs can be specified in terms of only *five* primitive operations on S-expressions and one special form (a conditional expression). It is easy to overlook the beauty and elegance of pure LISP, because most implementations supply a host of additional operations. Modern LISP is also smothered in FORTRAN-like features, some of which are useful, and some of which are an abomination. (Needless to say, some are both.)

The five operations are the following; these are not the LISP names for them, however.

Let S be the set of S-expressions. We shall write, for example:

$$E(X, Y): S \times S \rightarrow \{T, NIL\}$$

to signify that E is a function from the product of S and S to the set of truth values. Thus E is a function of two arguments, both of which are S-expressions, and its value is either T or NIL.

(1) $E(X, Y): S \times S \rightarrow \{T, NIL\}$ tests if two atoms are equal.

(2) $A(X): S \rightarrow \{T, NIL\}$ tests if an S-expression is an atom.

(3) $H(X): S \rightarrow S$ takes the head of a non-atomic S-expression; if X is an atom, the result is undefined.

(4) $T(X): S \rightarrow S$ takes the tail of a non-atomic S-expression; if X is an atom, the result is undefined.

(5) $C(X, Y): S \times S \rightarrow S$ assembles S-expressions; thus, if A and B are S-expressions, we can form the S-expression (A . B).

Together with function composition and the conditional form, these operations are sufficient for computing all general recursive functions. (Function composition is the ability to make the value of one function the argument of another.) In fact, the system consisting of:

(1)   the single atom NIL;

(2)   an equality test of the form "*if* X = NIL *then* ... *else* ...";

(3)   the functions $H(X), T(X), C(X, Y)$.

together with function composition is sufficient to represent a Turing machine (see Minsky, 1972, Chapter 10).

7.4 Why LISP is almost wonderful

We have seen that LISP has a very compact core, even though modern LISP manuals are heavier than some computers. This underlying simplicity means that implementing or embedding a representation language *in* LISP is not as complicated as it might be in a more conventional language, where there is that much more syntactic baggage to start off with. Also, the correspondence between programs and data means that 'meta-programs' can write or transform other programs at run-time with an ease that most other programming languages cannot hope to emulate. These two features (simplicity and meta-programmability) make LISP almost infinitely extensible and customizable. Add to this the fact that LISP is first and foremost an interpreted language, and one has a language designed for exploratory programming.

So, you ask, why isn't LISP the answer to all our knowledge representation needs? After all, LISP is eminently capable of storing, manipulating and controlling the evaluation of symbol structures; doesn't this provide much of what we need to implement a physical symbol system for intelligent action? The answer, like the answer to all good questions, is 'yes and no'.

Certainly the *medium* of symbolic computation is well suited to the implementation of structures for representing knowledge, but the symbolic level of analysis does not tell you *what* those structures should be. This is rather like the problem we encountered with the predicate calculus. Logic lets you represent and reason about the world, but it does not tell you *how* to organize your representation or go about your reasoning – that's your problem.

LISP's attitude is rather similar: 'So you want to represent your knowledge of the world as a multiply-embedded list 1 000 000 elements long with a maximum depth of 1 000 sublists, with some atoms standing for this and some for that, and some heads of sublists being relations and others being functions and others being special symbols? Go ahead – make my day!'

This laid-back approach to knowledge representation gives us plenty of options, but it doesn't constrain the space of possible solutions very much.

In a perfect world, there would be a level of analysis above the symbol level which, properly understood, would constrain the set of possible representations for solving some problem. Newell (1982) calls this the *knowledge level*, and suggests that knowledge should be characterized *functionally*, in terms of what it does, rather than structurally. The author goes as far as to say that knowledge cannot be represented by structures alone at the symbol level; we require both symbol structures and symbol processes.

It seems to follow from Newell's analysis that we cannot represent knowledge adequately without knowing what it will be used for. Perhaps that is one of the things that serves to differentiate between *facts* and *knowledge*. The fact that the Normans invaded England in the year 1066 is just a fact; but my knowledge of it can be put to various uses, such as passing History examinations, or provoking fights between Englishmen and Frenchmen. If the former is my goal, my representation had better be linked to other facts about King Harold and King William. If the latter is my goal, my representation ought to be linked to other inflammatory material, such as British soccer violence or the Common Agricultural Policy of the European Community. Thus there is no 'correct' way to represent some fact, but there are more or less useful representations of knowledge of some fact.

Newell also has something to say about the role of logic in knowledge representation, which will enable me to close the file on both LISP and PROLOG before going on to special-purpose knowledge representation languages. Newell argues that logic is primarily a tool for *analysis* at the knowledge level. This issue is separable from the merits or demerits of logic programming languages as vehicles for expert systems implementation. I have argued elsewhere (Jackson, 1986, Chapter 12; 1987) that PROLOG is neither more nor less suited than LISP as such a vehicle, because, once one gets down to real programming in either language, the formal niceties of the underlying calculus do not get you very far.

It is perhaps not too surprising that neither lambda calculus nor predicate calculus is sufficient to unlock the mysteries of intelligent behaviour; they were not designed for that purpose.

Bibliographical notes

Winston and Horn (1984) is one of the better LISP textbooks. Charniak *et al.* (1980) is also worth consulting for advanced AI techniques. Bratko (1986) provides a good introduction to AI programming in PROLOG.

STUDY SUGGESTIONS

7.1   Let L be the list

       (a (b) c ((d) e (f)) g)

What is the value of the following function composition?

```
first(first(rest(rest(rest(L)))))
```

7.2   The function f is defined by

```
f(X Y) = (λX)(if Y = 0 then 1, else X * f(X, Y − 1))
```

What is the value of the function application f(2 3)?

7.3   It is interesting to contrast LISP's use of a-lists (see Section 7.3.1) with the facilities provided by PROLOG for storing and accessing information. Given a database such as

```
year-of-birth(peter, 1948).
place-of-birth(peter, barbados).
```

we can easily retrieve such information by a process of resolution with unification, as described in Chapter 5. Thus the goal

```
:− year-of-birth(peter, X).
```

would succeed with X bound to 1948, via a single step of resolution.

Design a query to extract the same information from the more complex formula:

```
birth-data(peter, year(1948), place(barbados)).
```

You can use '_' to signify parts of the pattern for which variable bindings are not required.

7.4   The PROLOG language also has list-processing facilities built into it. It is interesting to contrast the different ways that the two languages achieve this. Below is the PROLOG definition of the member function.

```
member(X, [X | _ ]).
member(X, [ _ | L ]) :− member(X, L).
```

Lists are data object delimited by square brackets in which elements of whatever kind are separated by commas. Thus the following are all PROLOG lists:

```
[a, b, c]
[a, X, c, Y]
[father(john), mother(mary), sister(mary, john), brother(paul, X)]
```

The notation [X | Y] represents a pattern which, when it unifies with a list, binds (unifies) X with the head of the list and Y with its tail. Thus the unification of

```
[a, b, c]
```

and

```
[X | L]
```

would bind X to a and L to [b, c]. So the goal

    :— member(b, [a, b, c])

would fail to unify with first clause

    member(X, [X | _])

but succeed with the head of the second clause

    member(X, [_ | L])

with substitution {X/a, L/[b,c]}. As noted in Exercise 7.3, the use of '_' in place of a variable name merely indicates that we do not care about the binding achieved. After all, we are just going to throw the head of the list away if it is not equal to whatever X gets bound to.

    Thus, the first clause states that X is a member of any list that starts with X. The second clause states that otherwise X is a member of the list if X is a member of the tail of that list. I think you will agree that the definition is rather elegant, once you master the notation.

(a) What subgoal is set up after

    member(b, [a, b, c])

unifies with

    member(X, [_ | L])?

(b) Define delete as a PROLOG procedure such that the goal

    :— delete(b, [a, b, c], Answer).

returns with Answer bound to [a, c]. Then repeat the process in LISP, defining a function DELETE such that

    (DELETE 'A '(A B C))

returns the value (A B).

(c) If you are a novice in both languages, compare these two experiences. What differences in thinking obtain between the relational and functional styles of programming?

⑧ Production Systems

Introduction

It is probably an axiom of artificial intelligence that intelligent behaviour is rule-governed. Even in the world at large, people have a tendency to associate intelligence with *regularities* in behaviour, and we often *explain* behaviour by appeal to such regularities. Take the example of speaking one's native language. We all behave as if we have complete knowledge of the rules of English, although we do not, of course. (Anyone who did could write it all down and enjoy a dazzling career in Linguistics.)

The point is that intelligent behaviour, such as using a language appropriately, appears to be executed in a way that is respectful of rule, even if intelligent agents do not know precisely what the rules are. In artificial intelligence, rules play a rather more direct role in the production of behaviour. We say that an agent behaves in the way that he does because he possesses a representation of rules relevant to the generation of the behaviour in question.

Production rules are a formalism which saw some use in automata theory, formal grammars and the design of programming languages, before being pressed into the service of psychological modelling (Newell and Simon, 1972) and expert systems (Buchanan and Feigenbaum, 1978).

In the expert systems literature, they are sometimes called *condition–action* rules or *situation–action* rules. This is because they are usually used to encode empirical associations between patterns of data presented to the system and actions that the system should perform as a consequence.

Thus production rules serve precisely the function that we discussed above; they are intended as generative rules of behaviour. Given some set of inputs, the rules (interpreted in a particular way) determine what the output should be. As such, productions define a programming paradigm, just as the functions of LISP or the relations of PROLOG do.

The difference is that the way production rules are typically employed in expert systems is much more imperative (or prescriptive) than the rather declarative (or descriptive) use of functions and relations that one finds in pure LISP and pure PROLOG. Rather than representing true statements about the world or computing the values of functions defined over data, such rules normally determine how the symbol structures that represent the current state of the problem should be manipulated to bring the representation closer to a solution. One can encode such behaviour in LISP or PROLOG, of course; the point is that production rule languages are specifically designed to do this, and as a result they do it rather well.

8.1 Canonical systems

Productions are really grammar rules for manipulating strings of symbols, sometimes called *rewrite rules*. Post (1943) studied the properties of rule systems based on productions, which he called *canonical systems*. A canonical system is a kind of formal system based on:

- an *alphabet A* for making strings;
- some strings that are taken as *axioms*; and
- a set of *productions* of the form:

$$\alpha_1 \$_1 \ldots \alpha_m \$_m \rightarrow \beta_1 \$'_1 \ldots \beta_n \$'_n$$

where

(a) each α_i and β_i is a fixed string,
(b) α_1 *and* α_m are often null,
(c) some or all of the α_i or β_i may be null,
(d) each $\$_i$ is a variable string which can be null,
(e) each $\$_i$ is replaced by a certain $\$'_i$.

$\alpha_1 \$_1 \ldots \alpha_m \$_m$ is often called the *antecedent* of the rule and $\beta_1 \$'_1 \ldots \beta_n \$'_n$ the *consequent*, by analogy with the material conditional of propositional logic. However, it is not a good idea to confuse → with ⊃, because of the imperative flavour of →.

The definition of a canonical system is best understood with the aid of an example. Let A be the alphabet $\{a, b, c\}$ and let the axioms be

a, b, c, aa, bb, cc

Then the following productions generate all and only the palindromes based on this alphabet, starting from the axioms:

(P1) $\$ \rightarrow a\$a$
(P2) $\$ \rightarrow b\$b$
(P3) $\$ \rightarrow c\$c$

Furthermore, in this case we can trace the rule applications that must have given rise to a particular palindrome. Thus *bacab* must have been generated by applying **P1** to the axiom c and then applying **P2** to the result. In other words, given c as an axiom, we can derive *aca* as a *theorem*, and so add this to the axioms. From *aca*, we can then derive the further theorem *bacab*. Note that this set of productions is not commutative; if we apply the same rules starting with a particular input but in a different order, we get a different result. Applying **P2** then **P1** to c would give us *abcba*.

Canonical systems may seem rather trivial at first sight; all they do is rewrite one string of symbols into another. But there is a sense in which all calculi of logic and mathematics are just sets of rules that tell you how to manipulate symbols. It is easy to forget this, because the symbols of logic and arithmetic often have some meaning for us, unlike strings such as *abcba*.

It turns out that any formal system can be realized as a canonical system (see Minsky, 1972, Chapter 12). (Actually, there is a trivial proviso that says that a system may need to help itself to the letters of an auxiliary alphabet to use as a kind of punctuation in complex proofs.) Thus the ability to scan a string of symbols, dissect and rearrange it (perhaps adding and deleting symbols) is all the machinery that is required to verify proofs in some formal system or to carry out *any* effective procedure.

8.2 Production systems for problem solving

Production rules in the service of expert systems differ from productions as rewrite rules in certain superficial respects, but the fundamental principles and formal properties remain the same. For example, we are not interested in the grammar of symbol structures *per se*, as we were in the palindrome example. Rather we are interested in taking a representation of some problem and transforming it until it satisfies some criterion that says: 'This is a solution to the problem'.

8.2.1 The syntax of rules

Nowadays, production rules are usually implemented as rules that manipulate symbol structures such as lists or vectors, rather than strings of symbols. This is largely due to the influence of languages such as LISP and the data structures that they provide. (Early implementations used the string-manipulation language SNOBOL for its pattern-matching capabilities.)

Thus the alphabet of canonical systems is replaced by a vocabulary of symbols or atoms, and a rather simple grammar for forming symbol structures. The vocabulary normally consists of three sets:

- a set N of names of objects in the domain;
- a set P of property names that impute attributes to objects;
- a set V of values that these attributes can take.

In practice, N and V may overlap.

The grammar typically used is that of *object–attribute–value* triples. If $v \in N$, $\pi \in P$ and $\omega \in V$, then (v, π, ω) is such a triple, for example, (Peter year-of-birth 1948). This is often generalized, so that instead of having a number of triples for some object v in order to represent the various attribute value pairs

$$(\pi_1, \omega_1), \ldots, (\pi_n, \omega_n)$$

associated with v, we combine them into a vector of the form

$$(v, \pi_1, \omega_1, \ldots, \pi_n, \omega_n)$$

In the most popular production rule language, OPS5, the fact that I was born in Barbados in 1948 would be represented by the vector

```
(Peter ^year-of-birth 1948 ^place-of-birth Barbados)
```

We shall use this syntax from now on, since we will be looking at OPS5 in more detail in Appendix B and Chapter 17.

Once we have a vocabulary of symbols and a grammar for generating symbol structures, we can encode the initial state of some problem we are interested in. This representation corresponds to the axioms of a canonical system; these are the symbol structures that we are going to progressively rewrite in a series of rule applications.

Finally, we come to the rules themselves. These are no longer string manipulation rules, as in the palindrome example, but rules whose antecedents match against symbol structures and whose consequents contain special operators which manipulate those symbol structures. The details will become clear in the next section, where we consider the computational mechanism for applying such rules.

A *production system* consists of a *rule set* (sometimes called *production memory*), a *rule interpreter*, which decides when to apply which rules, and a *working memory*, which holds the data, goal statements and intermediate results that make up the current state of the problem. The working memory is the central data structure which is examined and modified by productions. The rules are triggered by this data, and the rule interpreter controls the activation and selection of rules at each cycle.

Schematically, rules in a production system have the general form:

$$P_1, ..., P_m \rightarrow Q_1, ..., Q_n$$

with the reading

> if *premises* P_1 and ... and P_m are true
> then perform *actions* Q_1 and ... and Q_n

The premises are sometimes called 'conditions', and the actions 'conclusions', because one kind of action is to conclude, if certain conditions are met, that a particular proposition is true or probable, as we saw in Chapter 3. Another piece of terminology is that the premise is sometimes called the 'left-hand side' of the rule, while the action is called the 'right-hand side', for obvious reasons.

Premises are usually represented by object–attribute–value vectors like

```
(Person ^Name Peter ^Age 40 ^job none)
```

One can imagine a rule that includes this condition, for example

```
(p unemployed
    (Person ^Name Peter ^Age 40 ^Job none)
    →
    (MAKE Task ^Claim welfare ^For Peter))
```

This rule is in the particular syntax of the language OPS5, where rules have the form

```
(p <rule-name>
   <premise₁>
   ...
   <premiseₘ>
   →
   <action₁>
   ...
   <actionₙ>)
```

Premises are patterns that are meant to match vectors in working memory. Actions, like (MAKE ...) in the above example, modify working memory, for example:

```
(MAKE Task ^Claim welfare ^For Peter)
```

adds the new vector

```
(Task ^Claim welfare ^For Peter)
```

to working memory.

Thus our unemployed rule signifies that, if Peter is 40 years old and unemployed, he ought to claim welfare. This is not a very general rule, as it applies only to Peter at a certain age. Suppose we want to make the statement that *anyone* who is unemployed should claim welfare in 1988. (Politicians are always generous in an election year.) This requires that we introduce variables which do not denote particular objects or values, but can be seen as 'place holders' that will match against suitable values and become bound to them. In the following expression, variables are those symbols surrounded by angle brackets:

```
(p bonanza
   (Person ^Name <N> ^Job none)
   (Place ^Country America)
   (Date ^Year 1988)
   →
   (MAKE Task ^Claim welfare ^For <N>))
```

As one might expect, all occurrences of a variable in the premises must be instantiated to the same value when the rule is interpreted. The pattern matching performed by OPS5 is 'one way'; data do not contain variables. Thus the algorithm is somewhat simpler than that for the full unification required by resolution theorem proving.

8.2.2 The working memory

The basic function of the working memory (WM) is to hold data in the form of object–attribute–value vectors. These data are used by the interpreter to activate the rules, in the sense that the presence or absence of data elements in the working memory will 'trigger' some rules by satisfying the patterns in their premises. An example will make this clear.

If working memory contains the following vectors:

```
(Person ^Name Peter ^Age 40 ^Job none)
(Place ^Town St-Louis ^State Missouri ^Country America)
(Date ^Month 12 ^Day 29 ^Year 1988)
```

then at the next cycle the interpreter will look to see which rules in production memory have conditions capable of being satisfied. If a condition contains no variables, it is satisfied just in case an identical expression is present in working memory. If a condition contains one or more variables (if it is a pattern), then it is satisfied just in case there exists an expression in working memory with an attribute–value pair that matches it in a way that is consistent with the way in which other conditions in the same rule have already been matched. In the simplest case, a match is just an assignment of constants to variables which, if applied as a substitution, would make the pattern identical to that part of the expression that it matched against.

Thus, (Person ^Name Peter ^Age 40 ^Job none) satisfies the premise (Person ^Name <N> ^Job none) with substitution {<N>/Peter}. Note that we can disregard attribute–value pairs, like ^Age 40, which are not mentioned in the premise. The other premises are satisfied by other vectors without the aid of pattern matching, so

```
(Task ^Claim welfare ^For Peter)
```

is added to working memory.

8.3 Controlling the behaviour of the interpreter

The interpreter for a set of production rules can be described in terms of the *recognize–act cycle*, which consists of the following sequence of steps:

(1) *Match* the premise patterns of rules against elements in working memory.

(2) If there is more than one rule that could fire, *choose* one to apply; this step is called *conflict resolution*.

(3)   *Apply* the rule, perhaps adding a new item to working memory or deleting an old one, and then go to step 1.

Usually, a 'start-up' element is inserted into the working memory at the beginning of the computation to get the cycle going. The computation halts if there is a cycle in which no rules become active, or if the action of a fired rule contains an explicit command to halt.

In step 2, the system has a set of pairs consisting of rules and the variable bindings derived from pattern matching; these pairs are called *instantiations*. Conflict resolution corresponds to the system 'making up its mind' which rule to fire. Of course, it is possible to design a rule set such that, for all configurations of data, only one rule is ever eligible to fire. Such rule sets are called *deterministic*; you can always determine the 'right' rule to fire at any point in the computation. Most of the rule sets in which we are interested from an expert systems point of view will be non-deterministic; there may often be more than one piece of knowledge that might apply at any given time.

Controlling the behaviour of rule-based systems can pose non-trivial problems. There are two general approaches to this: *global control* and *local control*. Global control regimes tend to be domain-independent, in that the strategy employed does not use domain knowledge to any significant extent. All of the conflict resolution strategies listed in the next section are examples of global control, because they apply across the board in all applications. Such strategies are usually 'hard-coded' into the interpreter, and they are therefore difficult for programmers to change. Local control regimes tend to be domain-dependent, in that special rules are required which use domain knowledge to reason about control. Such rules are sometimes called *meta-rules*, because they reason about which (object-level) rule to fire, rather than reasoning about objects or relationships in the domain. Local techniques are usually 'soft-coded' in the sense that the programmer can write explicit rules to create particular effects.

8.3.1   Conflict resolution

The conflict resolution strategy has a marked effect on the behaviour of a production system, so it should be chosen with care. Good performance from an expert systems point of view depends on both *sensitivity* and *stability*. Sensitivity means responding quickly to changes in the environment reflected in working memory, while stability means showing some kind of continuity in the line of reasoning (McDermott and Forgy, 1978; Brownston *et al.*, 1985, Chapter 7). Conflict resolution mechanisms vary from system to system, but three are very popular, and are often used in combination to form a global control regime.

- *Refractoriness*. A rule should not be allowed to fire more than once on the same data. The obvious way of implementing this is to discard from the conflict set instantiations which have been executed before. A weaker version deletes only the instantiation that fired during the last cycle. The latter is used specifically to prevent loops. If a loop is what you want, there is sometimes a 'refresh' function that will allow you to explicitly override refractoriness whenever you wish.

- *Recency*. Working memory elements are time-tagged in OPS5, so that you can tell at which cycle an item of data was added to working memory. The recency strategy ranks instantiations in terms of the recency of the elements that took part in the pattern matching. Thus rules that use more recent data are preferred to rules that match against data which has been loitering in working memory for some time. The idea is to follow the 'leading edge' of the computation, if possible, rather than doubling back to take another look at old data. Such doubling back may, of course, occur if the current line of reasoning fails.

- *Specificity*. Instantiations derived from more specific rules, such as rules that have a greater number of conditions and are therefore more difficult to satisfy, are preferred to more general rules with fewer conditions. The idea is that more specific rules are 'better' because they take more of the data into account. This strategy can be used to deal with exceptions to general rules. For example, the following rule might be used to eradicate postgraduate unemployment in Election Year; it would always fire in preference to the rule bonanza.

```
(p not-you-doc
    (Person ^Name <N> ^Job none ^Degree PhD)
    (Place ^Country America)
    (Date ^Year 1988)
    →
    (MAKE Task ^Arrange execution ^For <N>))
```

OPS5 uses all three strategies to good effect. Without such aids, a production system would have no simple methods for dealing with non-determinism, handling exceptions or focusing attention on a particular line of reasoning. In other words, the representation would lack *heuristic power*, in that the behaviour of such a program could be very hard to control, even if the knowledge it represented were essentially correct.

8.3.2 Forward and backward chaining

At the global level of control, production rules can be driven forward or backward. We can chain forward from conditions that we know to be true towards problem states which those conditions allow us to establish, or we can chain backward from a goal state towards the conditions necessary for its establishment. This is rather like the difference between forward and backward strategies in resolution theorem proving that we met in Chapter 5.

OPS5 is essentially a forward-chaining system, while we saw in Chapter 3 that the production rules of MYCIN were mostly backward chaining. In OPS5, we always match the left-hand sides of rules against working memory, and then perform the manipulation described by the right-hand side of the instantiation that emerges victorious from conflict resolution. In MYCIN, it is the right-hand side of a rule that drives the reasoning; thus if we wish to establish the identity of an organism, we find all the rules that draw conclusions about organisms in their right-hand sides, and then see which, if any, of them have conditions that can be satisfied by data.

Perhaps the easiest way to think of this forward and backward distinction is in terms of grammar rules, like those given in Section 8.1. As we saw earlier, we can use rules like

> **(P1)** $\$ \rightarrow a\$a$
> **(P2)** $\$ \rightarrow b\$b$
> **(P3)** $\$ \rightarrow c\$c$

in two distinct ways.

Firstly, we can use them to generate palindromes. Given any start symbol from the alphabet, any sequence of rule applications will result in a palindrome; thus the sequence of rule applications **P1**, **P1**, **P3**, **P2**, **P3** to the start symbol c generates, in order, the strings

> *aca*   *aacaa*   *caacaac*   *bcaacaacb*   *cbcaacaacbc*

This is an example of forward chaining, because we match c, and each successive string generated, against the left-hand side of a rule, and detach the instantiated right-hand side.

Secondly, we can use the rules to recognize palindromes. We saw earlier that, given a string like *bacab*, we can trace the sequence of rule applications that led to its construction. *bacab* matches against the right-hand side **P2**; we sometimes say that the right-hand side of **P2** 'accepts' *bacab*. The instantiated left-hand side of **P2** is *aca*, which matches the right-hand side of **P1**. The instantiated left-hand side of **P1** is just the axiom c, and therefore our recognition procedure terminates with success. Thus we have verified that *bacab* is indeed a palindrome. This is an example of backward chaining, since we match each substring of *bacab*, including *bacab* itself, against the right-hand side of a rule, and detach the instantiated left-hand side. Given a string like *acbcb*, there is no rule whose right-hand side accepts *acbcb*, and so it cannot be a palindrome.

In the theorem-proving literature, forward chaining is typically associated with 'bottom-up' reasoning (that is, reasoning from facts to goals) while backward chaining is associated with 'top-down' reasoning from goals to facts. However, these terms are not, strictly speaking, synonymous where production systems are concerned. For example, it is possible for a forward-chaining production system to perform top-down reasoning, if it is informed by a local control regimen, such as an explicit ordering on goals.

As an example, consider the rule set fragment in Figure 8.1, for choosing an electric guitar and amplifier based on the kind of music you want to play. Given the following working memory elements:

```
((start) (Music ^type Blues ^period 1960s))
```

the program will proceed to solve the problem in a top-down fashion, first choosing the guitar and then choosing the amplifier. However, this will be accomplished entirely by forward chaining. The start-up rule will make choosing the guitar the first task: its insertion of the task token (Task ^choose guitar) will effectively prevent any amplifier rules from firing until the change-task rule is satisfied that we have a guitar hypothesis at an adequate level of certainty (>0.75). Having made this selection final, by setting its CF equal to 1, the program then proceeds to set up the task of choosing an amplifier.

This whole process of problem reduction could be made more elaborate, for example by breaking the task of choosing an amplifier down into further choices, such as preamp, speakers and effects. The point is that the strategy is top-down, even though the rules are forward chaining on data, and hence operating bottom-up. Thus it is sometimes necessary to draw a distinction between the directionality of the *chaining* and the directionality of the actual *reasoning*. These two activities are really on different levels of analysis. Obviously, the chaining implements the reasoning and not vice versa, but the reasoning strategy *controls* the chaining, in this case by manipulating task tokens.

This kind of distinction highlights a common problem in talking about the way in which AI programs work. Most complex systems, whether they are pieces of software, physical devices, or some combination of the two, can be understood at various levels of description, as Newell (1982) noted. To adopt Newell's terminology, chaining is a phenomenon of the symbol level, where we are only interested in 'left-hand sides' and 'right-hand sides' of rules, whereas reasoning is something that occurs at the knowledge level, where we can distinguish between facts and tasks.

It was stated earlier that most production rule sets of interest in artificial intelligence applications are non-deterministic. In forward chaining, there may be more than one rule whose conditions are satisfied

```
(p start-up
   (start)
   →
   (MAKE Task ^choose guitar))

(p choose-guitar
   (Task ^choose guitar)
   (Music ^type Blues ^period 1960s)
   →
   (MAKE guitar ^make Fender ^model Stratocaster ^CF 0.80))

(p choose-guitar
   (Task ^choose guitar)
   (Music ^type Blues ^period 1970s)
   →
   (MAKE guitar ^make Gibson ^model Les-Paul ^CF 0.80))

(p change-task
   (Task ^choose guitar)
   (guitar ^make <X> ^model <Y> ^CF > 0.75)
   →
   (REMOVE 1)
   (REMOVE 2)
   (MAKE guitar ^make <X> ^model <Y> ^CF 1.00)
   (MAKE Task ^choose amp))

(p choose-vox-amp
   (Task ^choose amp)
   (Music ^type Blues ^period 1960s)
   (guitar ^model Fender ^CF 1.0)
   →
   (MAKE amp ^make Vox ^model AC30 ^CF 0.70))

(p choose-marshall-amp
   (Task ^choose amp)
   (Music ^type Blues ^period 1970s)
   (guitar ^model Gibson ^CF 1.00)
   →
   (MAKE amp ^make Marshall ^model JTM-45 ^CF 0.85))
```

Figure 8.1 A rock 'n' roll rule set.

by data, while in backward chaining there may be more than one rule that can help establish a goal. Thus control issues are crucial, regardless of the direction in which the rules chain, and a production system that is ill-controlled may produce spurious conclusions, or no conclusions at all (because of looping or premature termination).

We saw in Chapter 3 that an *AND/OR tree* is a useful device for representing the search space associated with a set of production rules. Nodes in the tree correspond to states of working memory, while branches correspond to possible rule applications. The tree diagram is typically laid out in a backward-chaining style, with the main goal at the top, the subgoals in the middle, and the data at the terminal nodes.

Thus the *root node* of the tree is the start state of the problem, while the *leaf nodes* contain candidate solutions. Non-terminal nodes, on the other hand, will be of two kinds: AND nodes and OR nodes. AND nodes correspond to rule applications which rewrite a goal as a conjunction of subgoals, while OR nodes correspond to alternative rule applications. Thus, in the terminology introduced in Chapter 2, the possible rule applications generate a *search space* and determine its underlying structure.

Rule-based programming does not abolish combinatorial explosion, since the AND/OR tree for any problem may branch exponentially. But, in practical applications, it is hoped that the conflict resolution strategy employed by the interpreter will tend to choose a rule that leads to a reasonable solution. The next section reviews a more strong-arm approach to the control of search.

8.3.3   Rules and meta-rules

The code for each production rule is meant to be self-contained, so that one rule never directly calls another, and all necessary context for rule activation is provided by the premises. Rule R_1 at cycle C_1 may facilitate the subsequent firing of rule R_2 at cycle C_2, but this is only via the changes that it makes to the contents of working memory. However, some production system interpreters allow the programmer to write *meta-rules*, which reason about which rules should be considered for firing.

Meta-rules are distinguished from ordinary rules in that their role is to *direct* the reasoning required to solve the problem, rather than to actually *perform* that reasoning. This distinction between different levels of reasoning is often referred to as the distinction between *meta-level* and *object-level*. Thus, one might have meta-rules which reason about which (problem solving) rule to apply next, thereby performing conflict resolution, or enhancing an existing conflict resolution strategy.

For example, MYCIN's production rules are indexed by the clinical parameters appearing in their action parts. Thus it is easy to retrieve for consideration all of the rules that might apply in determining the value of a given parameter. This information is used by meta-rules which, instead of applying to subgoals, apply to the rules that apply to subgoals. Given that we wish to achieve subgoal G, say finding the identity of an organism, there may be as many as 30 rules that could apply. Meta-rules are used to prune and order the list of rules applicable at any one point.

Here is a sample pruning rule for MYCIN, taken from Buchanan and Shortliffe (1984, Chapter 28):

> METARULE001
> IF: (1) the culture was not obtained from a sterile source, and
>   (2) there are rules which mention in their premise a previous organism, which may be the same as the current organism
> THEN: it is definite (1.0) that each of them is not going to be useful

It states that, when trying to identify organisms from a non-sterile site, rules that base their identification on other organisms found at that site are not going to be very useful. Other meta-rules are there to re-order relevant domain rules, and they encode strategic knowledge of the kind 'try this before trying that', for example:

> METARULE002
> IF: (1) the infection is a pelvic-abscess, and
>   (2) there are rules which mention in their premise Enterobacteriaceae, and
>   (3) there are rules which mention in their premise Gram positive rods,
> THEN: there is suggestive evidence (0.4) that the former should be done before the latter

Note that meta-rules also admit of uncertainty, since their conclusions may be qualified by a certainty factor that is less than 1. Thus our basic pattern of reasoning at the meta-level is that same as at the object-level. It is simply that meta-rules reason about the object-level rules, while the object-level rules reason about the domain itself.

Finally, here is an example of a very general meta-rule, since it refers to general problem-solving strategy, rather than specific medical knowledge.

> METARULE003
> IF: (1) there are rules which do not mention the current goal in their premise, and
>   (2) there are rules which mention the current goal in their premise

THEN: it is definite (1.0) that the former should be done before
the latter

Meta-rules can either be relatively domain-specific or domain-free,
although the former is more usual. A domain-specific meta-rule is one
that encodes a particular piece of strategic knowledge about the domain;
for example, in medical diagnosis, one might wish to encode the fact that
special groups of patients, such as alcoholics or people suffering from
burns, are especially prone to particular kinds of infection, and write
meta-rules that point the program in the direction of the rules that seem
most applicable to such cases. A relatively domain-free meta-rule might
be one that advises the program to consider rules that generate small
search spaces before rules that generate larger ones.

However, it is important not to be misled by this distinction, as a
lot depends on the level of abstraction at which the knowledge is expressed. For example, a meta-rule such as

if x is an alcoholic, then consider rules for determining this disease
before rules for determining that disease

could be abstracted along the lines of

if x is some reason for believing that y is of category z, and there
are special rules associated with category z, then apply those rules
before trying other applicable rules

The latter is less domain-dependent, insofar as it could be applied to
a greater variety of problems. A particular domain-specific application
of this principle, such as the example concerning alcoholics, could be
regarded as an instantiation of a more general meta-rule. At present,
there is considerable interest in the possibility of identifying abstract
problem-solving principles capable of being applied in different domains
(see Clancey, 1983, and Chapters 14, 15, 17 and 18).

We shall return to the topic of meta-level reasoning in Chapter 11.
For now, observe that it is a powerful idea, but one that should be
applied selectively. If a program spends too much time thinking about
how it should proceed, it will not achieve its goals in a timely fashion.

Bibliographical notes

An excellent introduction to rule-based approaches to AI problems can
be found in Nilsson (1980). Davis and King (1977) do a good job of
summarizing the strengths and weaknesses of production systems as a
programming paradigm.

Appendix B is provided for readers who are interested in trying their hands at programming with production systems. It contains an introduction to the rule-based language OPS5, which has been widely used in expert systems applications. The intention is to illustrate some of the concepts introduced in the text, rather than to impart an encyclopaedic knowledge of the language. For more details, the interested reader is referred to Brownston *et al.* (1985). Nevertheless, the appendix contains enough information for readers to create non-trivial programs.

STUDY SUGGESTIONS

8.1 Encode the following medical rules of thumb as OPS5 production rules. Think carefully about the design of working memory vectors (and hence rule conditions and actions).

> recurrent pain in upper abdomen & poor appetite & weight loss
> →
> stomach tumour
>
> recurrent pain in lower abdomen & recurrent diarrhoea & nausea & no fever
> →
> inflammation of large intestine
>
> recurrent pain in lower abdomen & recurrent diarrhoea & fever
> →
> inflammation of large intestine
>
> recurrent pain in upper right abdomen & no fever
> →
> gallstones
>
> recurrent pain in upper right abdomen & vomiting & fever
> →
> gallbladder inflammation
>
> abdominal pain & vomiting & diarrhoea & ate at university canteen
> →
> food poisoning
>
> abdominal swelling & swollen ankles & breathing difficulty
> →
> congestive heart condition

abdominal swelling & yellow skin & yellow eyes

$\rightarrow$

liver cirrhosis

abdominal swelling & weight gain

$\rightarrow$

obesity

abdominal swelling & morning nausea

$\rightarrow$

pregnancy

8.2 Given a conflict resolution strategy that involves specificity, which rule from the rule set in Exercise 8.1 will fire if the working memory is given as follows?

WM = (pain in abdomen & diarrhoea & no fever)

8.3 Implement the rule set in Study suggestion 8.1 as an OPS5 program and run it on test cases, such as

pain in abdomen & diarrhoea & no fever

Refer to Appendix B for details of how to build and run simple OPS5 programs.

8.4 Embellish the program in Study suggestion 8.3 by adding certainty factors in the MYCIN style. I leave the assignment of weights to you, but avoid floating point numbers by using certainties in the range $[-10, 10]$. Another piece of advice is the following:

Assign tallies to rules so that if the conditions of rule r1 subsume those of rule r2, then the tally of r1 should be less than or equal to the tally of r2

The set of conditions C1 subsumes the set of conditions C2 if all data satisfying C2 will satisfy C1 too. Thus the set of OPS conditions containing just

```
(abdomen ^symptom pain ^location upper ^CF <X> <= 5)
(fever ^CF - 10)
```

is subsumed by the set containing only

```
(abdomen ^symptom pain ^CF <X> <= 3)
```

but not conversely. (The expression <X> $\Leftarrow$ 5 in the value slot of the ^CF attribute denotes a restriction to the effect that the variable <X> must be bound to a value less than or equal to 5 for any match to succeed.)

The rationale behind this assignment strategy is that more specific rules should not generate weaker hypotheses than more general rules.

Rerun the program with data such as

pain in abdomen (9) & diarrhoea (7) & fever (-10)

where the numbers after symptoms indicate weights.

9 Associative Nets and Frame Systems

Introduction

I shall follow Nilsson (1980) in using the generic term *structured object* to refer to any representational scheme whose fundamental building blocks are analogical to the nodes and arcs of graph theory or the slots and fillers of record structures. I shall systematically contrast this kind of representation with schemes which have been derived either from the rewrite rules of formal grammars or the well-formed formulas of various logics. Structured object representations are essentially ways of grouping information in a more or less natural way, and providing equally natural access paths.

We saw in the last chapter that production rules are a good representation for linking conditions with actions. However, sometimes 'what to do when' is not the main focus of interest; sometimes it is the properties and interrelationships of complex objects in the domain that determine the solution to a problem. It is not very convenient to represent knowledge about objects, events and arbitrary relationships between them (including type–subtype, part–whole, before–after and so on) in the rather limited format of rewrite rules and working memory elements. Nor are predicate–argument expressions of the kind encoun-

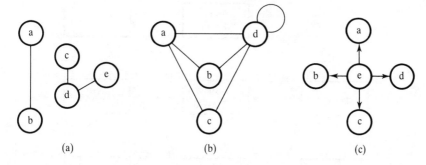

Figure 9.1 Some graph structures: (a) a simple graph; (b) a connected graph with a self-loop; and (c) a simple digraph that is also a tree.

tered in Chapters 4 and 5 a very effective mechanism for storing this kind of information. In addition, neither of these formalisms is very efficient for such purposes, either in terms of how knowledge is stored or how it is accessed.

The next two chapters explore more suitable representations for structural knowledge, paying attention to some of the difficulties that researchers and practitioners have encountered.

9.1 Graphs, trees and networks

The terminology of graph theory has been imported into artificial intelligence and computer science to describe certain kinds of abstract data structure. The following definitions are phrased in such a way as to reflect their current usage in describing structured objects, rather than their original definitions in their home discipline.

All the definitions assume that there exist two kinds of primitive entity, *nodes* and *links*. The nodes are the sources and destinations of links, and they usually have labels to distinguish them. The links may or may not have labels, depending on whether or not there is more than one kind of link. Nodes are sometimes called 'vertices', and links are sometimes called 'edges', which is the standard graph-theoretic terminology.

> **Definition**   If N is a set of nodes, a *general graph*, G, is any subset of $N \times N$. If the order of the pairs in $N \times N$ is material, G is also a *digraph*, or directed graph.

Note from Figure 9.1 that a graph need not be connected. If we outlaw self-loops in a graph, by adding the restriction that the pairs must

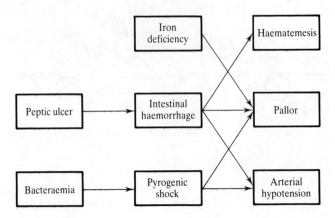

Figure 9.2 Portion of a causal network, adapted from Pople (1982).

contain distinct nodes, the result is a *simple graph* (or simple digraph). If we outlaw circuits as well (paths through the graph which begin and end with the same node), then *G* is a *forest*.

> **Definition**   If *G* is a simple graph on *n* nodes with *n* − 1 links and no circuits, then *G* is also a *tree*.

In other words, a tree is a connected forest. It is usual to designate one of the nodes as the 'root' of the tree, such as node *e* in the digraph of Figure 9.1 (c). The rest of the nodes form a loop-free, branching structure consisting of successors of the root. Nodes with no successors are called *terminals*, or 'leaves', of the tree, while the others are *non-terminals*.

In graph theory, a *network* is simply a weighted digraph – a directed graph with numerical labels associated with links. These labels normally indicate the cost of traversing the link, or the distance between links, as in a road map. In AI, the labels on links can stand for anything at all; they signify arbitrary relations between nodes.

The following definition of a network is probably closer to current AI practice than the original graph-theoretic one.

> **Definition**   If *L* is a set of labelled links and *N* is a set of nodes as before, then a *network* is any subset of *N* × *L* × *N*, where the order of the triples is material.

Links in networks are almost always directed, because the relations that labelled links stand for need not be symmetric.

Simple graphs are useful for analogical representations of spatial

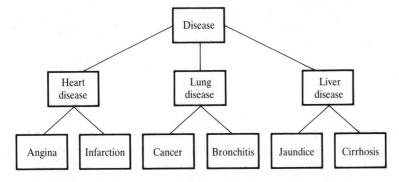

Figure 9.3 Simplified tree classifying diseases by organ location.

and temporal relationships. They are also used to represent more abstract relationships, like causal connections between medical disorders (see Figure 9.2). Accessing such information involves graph search, for which various algorithms are already available (see Pearl, 1984).

Trees, on the other hand, are useful for representing classification hierarchies and discrimination nets. For example, one might wish to classify different kinds of disease according to organ location (see Figure 9.3). The resulting tree would have the set of all diseases as its root node, and the successors of this node would be nodes standing for such categories as heart disease, liver disease, kidney disease, and so on. Each of these nodes could have successors which specialize their ancestor node in different ways, and so on. Terminal nodes might stand for actual diseases that one can diagnose and treat, such as a liver disease like cirrhosis.

Semantic nets (somewhat misleadingly named) are a kind of network commonly used to structure more general kinds of information. These are constellations of nodes and links in which the nodes stand for concepts and the links stand for relationships between them. They are so named because they were originally employed to represent the meaning of natural language expressions.

Figure 9.4 shows fragments of a semantic net. The first fragment represents the verb *give*, showing that it has three associated roles: a donor, a recipient, and an object that is given. The node labels at the end of these links state what kind of entity is allowed to fill the role in question. Thus the donor and the recipient are typically persons, while that which is given is normally a thing.

The second fragment shows an instance of giving, which we shall call *give-256*, in which John gives Mary a copy of the book *War and Peace*. This can be seen to be a valid instance of *give*, as the fillers for the roles obey the restrictions on the appropriate nodes. We assume that

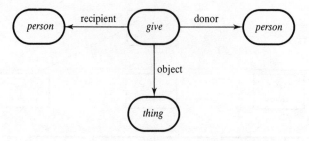

(a) A network representing the verb 'to give'

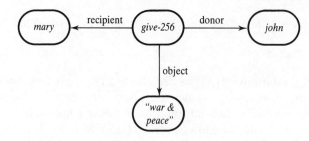

(b) A network representing an instance of giving

Figure 9.4   Fragments of a semantic network.

mary and *john* are both instances of *person*, and that *"war & peace"* is an instance of a class such as *book*, which is a kind of *thing*.

Similarly, *give-256* would normally be connected to *give* by a link which signifies that this particular act of giving is an instance of the general concept of giving. This special link is often called the ISA link. It is used to attach specific instances, which normally represent data, to the concepts in the network.

The term *associative nets* is better for our purposes, being more neutral with regard to what the network is used for. The use of some form of network for the modelling of domain-specific objects and relationships is becoming more and more widespread in expert systems, so it is worth looking at their underlying assumptions in more detail.

9.2   The rise of associative networks

The systematic use of networks for knowledge representation begins with Quillian's (1968) work on language understanding. Quillian questioned the notion that our ability to understand language can be characterized, even in principle, by a set of basic rules. He suggested that text understanding involved 'the creation of some mental symbolic representation', which led to a concern with how the meanings of words might be stored so that a computer could make human-like use of them. Quillian was not the first to stress the importance of general knowledge in language understanding; this had already been discovered by the machine translation community. However, he was among the first to suggest that human memory could be modelled by a network of nodes representing concepts and relations, and propose a processing model for memory retrieval.

The practical problem for expert systems is to determine how much semantic information the system needs to represent. In Appendix B, we note that our simple OPS5 program for arranging bricks held very little knowledge concerning the different kinds of objects that it reasoned about. Thus it was not represented anywhere that the hand it controlled could only hold one brick; it just so happened that the conflict resolution strategy ensured that the program always behaved as if this were the case. One difficulty with such an impoverished representation is that the program cannot avoid anomalous states in unusual circumstances. In the OPS5 example, if conflict resolution had not done the right thing, the program would have gone on trying to pick up bricks with a full hand before getting rid of the brick in its hand.

If we want more robust programs, and ones that remain reliable in the face of modifications, a program should be able to make reasonable assumptions where knowledge is missing and monitor the integrity of its own knowledge. This in turn places a constraint on the representation of knowledge employed; the knowledge should be organized in a way that facilitates integrity checking. The kinds of knowledge structure explored in this chapter (and the next) are relevant to these goals.

9.2.1 The type–token distinction and cognitive economy

There are two aspects of Quillian's memory model that are particularly relevant to subsequent semantic net systems, and so I shall emphasize these at the expense of other features.

Firstly, there is a *type–token* distinction made between concept nodes. The type node for a concept is connected to a configuration of tokens of other concept nodes which constitute its definition. This is rather like a dictionary, in which each entry is defined in terms of other entries, which are defined elsewhere in a similar fashion. Thus the meaning of token nodes is derived with reference to the corresponding type node, just as, in order to understand a word used in a dictionary definition, you may need to refer to the entry for that word. Localization of this kind aids the construction and maintenance of representations of knowledge.

For example, one might choose to define the meaning of 'machine' as an assembly of connected components which transmit force to perform work. This would require connecting the type node for 'machine' to tokens representing 'assembly', 'components' and so on. However, in addition to links within this definitional plane, there will be paths to other tokens, such as those standing for 'typewriter' and 'office', which represent knowledge to the effect that typewriters are a kind of machine for office use.

Another interesting feature of the memory model is usually referred to as *cognitive economy*. Thus, if we know that a machine is an assembly of interconnected parts, and we know that a typewriter is a machine, then we can deduce that a typewriter is an assembly. It doesn't make sense to store this information explicitly by attaching it to the type node for 'typewriter'. If we allow 'typewriter' to have the property of being an assembly by virtue of its standing in a certain relation to 'machine', we can save some storage space and still get the information that we need, so long as we can draw the right inference.

This convention, known today as the *inheritance of properties*, is extremely widespread in knowledge representation schemes which employ any kind of structured object. As we shall see later in this chapter, a number of extra features have been added to this facility in later years, but the basic idea remains the same. Inheritance of properties is a particularly clear example of the storage space *versus* processing speed trade-off that the designers of knowledge representation schemes need to consider. However, we shall see that it poses a number of non-trivial problems, particularly if we allow exceptions, for example, token nodes that do not inherit all the properties of their type. Furthermore, although meaning is still localized within the network, for a given node, bits and pieces of its definition may be distributed here and there among its type nodes. In our example, only part of the meaning of 'typewriter' is now stored at the type node for typewriter; the rest of it is with the 'machine' node.

Thus, in addition to the space/speed trade-off, there is also a trade-off between the space saved by modularizing definitions and the intelligibility of those definitions from the user's point of view. However, if this idea is correctly implemented, a program will always know how to retrieve and assemble the definition of a given concept. The main advantage is that we can store an arbitrary amount of semantic information at a node, for example, ranges for the values of properties that tokens of a type must possess. This is simply not practical in a formalism like production systems, where exhaustive checking of the consistency of working memory would have to be performed either by special rules representing integrity constraints or by the problem-solving rules themselves. Either way, this activity would consume computational resources needed for problem solving, and it would be hampered by the unstructured nature of the working memory.

9.2.2 Assessing the adequacy of associative nets

The basic information retrieval operation in the processing model that goes with Quillian's memory model can be described as an *intersection search*. The idea is that, if you want to know whether or not a typewriter is a machine, 'activation' of some kind will spread out in all directions from both the 'machine' type node and the 'typewriter' type node. At some point, this spreading activation will intersect, establishing that there is indeed a relationship between these two concepts, because there is a path from each to the other.

It is interesting to note that Quillian's ideas enjoyed only a limited success as a psychological model of human memory organization and functioning. Collins and Quillian (1969) tested the model by measuring the time that human subjects took to answer questions about category membership and properties of concepts, and found that response time did increase with the number of assumed nodes involved in the intersection search. However, this result held only for positive responses. There were indications in the data that negative responses would cause trouble for the theory, and subsequent experiments by other researchers showed that this was indeed the case.

These results do not detract from Quillian's contribution to research in knowledge representation, however. His work anticipated a decade of research into network-based formalisms for conceptual encoding. Although modern associative nets differ substantially from the original conception in their overall structure, and are often employed to ends other than natural language understanding, many of the basic principles derive from the ideas described above.

Nevertheless, a number of problems have dogged network representations. During the 1970s, various critiques of net-based formalisms were published, of which the most influential was probably that of Woods (1975). Using nodes and links to represent concepts and relations may sound straightforward, but experience has shown that it is strewn with pitfalls for the unwary:

- Network architects were not always scrupulous in the way in which they assigned meanings to nodes. Thus, faced with a type node labelled 'typewriter', it was often unclear whether it stood for the concept of a typewriter, or the class of all typewriters, or a typical typewriter. Similarly, token nodes were open to many interpretations, such as a particular typewriter, an indefinite singular typewriter, an arbitrary typewriter, and so on. Different interpretations support rather different sets of inferences, and so these are not idle distinctions.

- Reducing inference to intersection search does not abolish the problems associated with the combinatorial explosion noted in

Chapter 2. Hence it was felt that a memory organization in terms of constellations of nodes, with spreading activation as the main retrieval process, resulted in a system whose behaviour was insufficiently constrained. For example, negative responses to queries seemed to involve extravagant amounts of search, because it is only after the activation has spread as far as it will go that you can be sure that two concepts do not in fact stand in the hypothesized relation.

Thus it was realized that early associative network formalisms were lacking in two respects: logical and heuristic adequacy.

- Nets were logically inadequate because they could not make many of the distinctions that logic can make, for example, between a particular typewriter, at least one unspecified typewriter, all typewriters, no typewriters, and so on. The meaning of nodes and links was often inextricably bound up with the retrieval and inference capabilities of the system. This confounding of semantics with details of implementation resulted from the fact that nets were meant to represent, retrieve and draw inferences about knowledge using a uniform set of associative mechanisms; understandably, the distinctions between these three functions sometimes got blurred.

- Nets were heuristically inadequate because searches for information were not themselves knowledge-based. In other words, there was no knowledge in such systems which told you how to search for the knowledge that you wanted to find. These two shortcomings interacted in unpleasant ways; for example, if you were unable to represent negation or exclusive alternation (logical inadequacy), this led to gaps in your knowledge as to when you could safely terminate a failed search (heuristic inadequacy).

Various formalisms and mechanisms were proposed to deal with these problems, but few of them were widely adopted. For example, many network systems were enriched so that they were closer to various logics in their expressive power, thus making it possible to represent some of the distinctions described earlier (Schubert, 1976). Others were given enhanced heuristic power by attaching procedures to nodes which could be executed whenever the nodes became active (Levesque and Mylopolous, 1979). Nevertheless, the basic organization of the memory in terms of nodes and links remained the same, even in cases where extra structures, such as 'supernodes' standing for partitions of nodes, were added (Hendrix, 1979). The resulting systems were often unwieldy and the original simplicity was sometimes lost, with not much gain in capability.

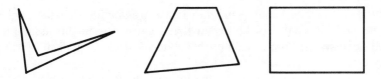

Figure 9.5 Typicality among quadrilaterals.

9.3 Representing typical objects and situations

This section reviews a mechanism, called a *frame system*, for representing real-world knowledge in a way that attempts to integrate declarative notions about objects and events with procedural notions about how to retrieve information or achieve goals, thereby overcoming some of the problems associated with semantic networks.

9.3.1 Introduction to frame concepts

One of the intuitions behind frame system theory was that conceptual encoding in the human brain is not much concerned with strictly defining the properties that entities must possess to be considered exemplars of some category. As we saw in Chapter 6, many of the categories that we use are not sharply defined, being based on rather vague concepts. Humans seem to be more concerned with the salient properties associated with just those objects which are somehow typical of their class.

Such objects have been called 'prototypical objects' or *prototypes*. Thus a prototypical bird, like a sparrow, can fly, and so we tend to think of this as being a property of birds, even though there are birds, like the emu, which cannot fly. There is a sense in which a sparrow is a better exemplar of the bird category than an emu, because it is more typical of the class. Nevertheless, the existence of exceptional birds, such as the emu, forces us to qualify generalizations such as 'birds fly'.

Even with mathematical objects, such as polygons, one suspects that we have well developed notions of typicality. Given the three quadrilaterals in Figure 9.5, there can be little doubt that typicality increases as we proceed from left to right. Quadrilaterals with obtuse inner angles are somehow less typical than convex quadrilaterals, possibly because we are used to correlating area with perimeter, and this correlation makes more sense where angles are more or less equal.

Frame systems attempt to reason about classes of objects by using prototypical representations of knowledge which hold good for the majority of cases, but which may need to be deformed in some way to capture the complexities of the real world. Thus if I know nothing about the area of a more or less rectangular plot of land, but I know the length of the sides, then I may estimate the area, assuming that the angles are more or less equal. To the extent that I am wrong in this assumption, I will overestimate the area, but this state of affairs is typical of heuristic devices.

In practical problem solving, exceptions to rules abound and there are often rather fuzzy boundaries between classes. Frame systems are useful because they provide a way of structuring the heuristic knowledge associated with the application of rules and the classification of objects. Instead of being peppered here and there in the code of an applications program, or gathered together into a pool of meta-rules, heuristics are distributed among the kinds of object that they apply to, and exist at levels of control in a hierarchy of such objects.

9.3.2 Complex nodes in a network

Minsky (1975) described frames as 'data structures for representing stereotyped situations' to which are attached various kinds of information, including what kinds of object or event to expect in that situation, and how to use the information in the frame. The idea is to use a single data structure as a focus for all the knowledge that might be useful about a given class of objects or events, rather than distributing that knowledge among smaller structures, like logical formulas or production rules. Such knowledge will either be contained in the data structure itself, or will be accessible from the structure (if it is stored in some other, related structure, for example).

Thus a frame is essentially a way of bundling both declarative and procedural knowledge about some entity into a record structure, consisting *slots* and *fillers*. The slots are like fields in a record, and the fillers are like values stored in those fields. However, frames differ from familiar structures, like Pascal records, in a number of significant respects, as we shall see.

A frame has a special slot filled by the name of the entity that it stands for, and the other slots are filled with the values of various common attributes associated with the object. Attached to such slots, there may also be procedures, which are called whenever a slot is accessed or updated. The idea is that problem-solving computations occur largely as a side-effect of the flow of data in and out of a frame.

A frame can be thought of as a complex node in a special kind of associative network. Frames are typically arranged in a loose hierarchy (or heterarchy) in which frames 'lower down' the network can inherit values for slots from frames 'higher up'. (A heterarchy is a 'tangled hierarchy'; that is, an acyclic graph in which nodes can have more than one predecessor.)

The fundamental idea is that properties and procedures associated with frames in the properties of nodes high up in the frame system are more or less fixed, insofar as they represent things which are typically true about the entity of interest, whereas frames in the lower levels have slots that must be filled with more contingent information. If such information is absent, owing to incomplete knowledge of the prevailing state of affairs, slot values for lower frames can be inherited from global values in frames higher up the hierarchy. Otherwise, local values supplied lower down are allowed to overwrite the heuristic information held higher up.

The main link types in a frame system are between instances and classes and between classes and superclasses. Thus the `Computer` node would stand in a class–superclass relationship to the node `Machine`, while the node `Edai`, representing a particular computer (Edinburgh University AI Department's long-suffering VAX 750), would stand in an instance–class relationship to the `Computer` node. Properties and relationships that would normally be encoded by labelled links between nodes in a typical semantic network are now encoded using the slot-filler representation. In addition, slots can have all sorts of extra information attached to them, such as procedures for computing a value for the slot in the absence of one, procedures for updating the value of one slot when another slot is updated, and restrictions on the values that a slot can take.

9.3.3 Defaults and demons

Let us imagine that we are real estate agents, and our job is to estimate the price of plots of land as they come on the market, even if we do not have all the information that we need to set an exact price. We are so eager to make money and get deals rolling that we are prepared to make assumptions about plots we haven't even seen on the basis of incomplete descriptions. Most plots are convex quadrilaterals, so our price estimates are based on this assumption, unless we have information to the contrary.

Suppose that Figure 9.6 encodes knowledge about planar geometry for reasoning about such plots. Each node in the hierarchy consists of a record structure with the following format

```
NAME:
Number of Sides:
Length of Sides:
Size of Angles:
Area:
Price:
```

We could leave the slots of the `Polygon` record blank, because there is nothing we can say about the sides and angles of a typical polygon.

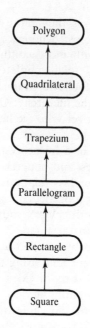

Figure 9.6   A hierarchical representation for geometric figures.

However, we might hazard a default value of 4 for the slot Number of sides, since plots of land are typically four-sided. The force of this assignment would mean that all plots of land not known to have a number of sides other than 4 would be treated as if they has four sides, for the sake of argument.

We cannot fill the Area slot, but we know how to compute the area of a polygon given other information, since any *n*-sided polygon can be divided into *n* − 2 triangles whose areas can be summed. We can encode this as a procedure which, given the requisite information, computes the value and places it in the slot. We attach this procedure to the slot itself. Procedures which are attached to data structures and are triggered by queries or updates are sometimes called *demons*. Those which compute values on demand are called *IF-NEEDED* demons.

It would also be useful to have a demon which computed the price of a plot once the area was known. This can be implemented as an *IF-ADDED* demon attached to the Area slot, so that if the value of this slot is added (or updated), the price is automatically (re)computed and placed in the Price slot. We may want to recompute the price if extra information becomes available that allows us to make a better estimate of the area.

Looking further down the hierarchy, we can obviously fill in the Number of Sides slot of Quadrilateral; the value of this slot really is 4. This value will be inherited by each successor frame in the hierarchy. We can compute the area and price of a four-sided plot in the same manner as any other polygon, so we allow Quadrilateral to inherit these procedures from Polygon.

Nothing else is known about quadrilaterals in the general case, but we might like to be able to estimate the area of a four-sided plot of land if we know the length of its sides, even if we don't know the angles. A reasonable heuristic would be to multiply the average of one pair of opposing sides with the average of the other pair. If the plot is not convex, we may overcharge the client, but that has never broken an estate agent's heart, as far as I know.

This heuristic could be encoded in an IF-NEEDED procedure attached to the area slot of Quadrilateral which does one of three things:

- It calls the corresponding IF-NEEDED demon associated with Polygon if there is side and angle information available to enable the exact computation of the area.

- It uses the heuristic approach if only side information is available.

- If no information is available, it does nothing, but 'watches' for incoming information.

Each of Trapezium, Parallelogram, Rectangle and Square inherit the value of Quadrilateral's Number of Sides slot. However, in each case, we can do a rather better job on the area calculation; for example, the area of a trapezium is the height multiplied by the average of the parallel sides. Rectangle and Square can both inherit Parallelogram's procedure, which multiplies the base by the height.

The point of this simple example is that the use of defaults and demons renders frame systems more useful than ordinary record structures. Of course, we could have a ordinary Pascal-type record structure and then write Pascal procedures that answer queries based on the records and similar heuristics, but the frame system is in many ways a neater solution. Data, definitions and procedures are packaged up together in modules which can share data and procedures by inheritance mechanisms.

9.3.4 Multiple inheritance and ambiguity

Frame systems extend and regularize the notion of inheritance found in Quillian's work in a couple of respects. It is often convenient to allow a frame to inherit information from more than one ancestor in the frame system. Thus the organization of frames becomes more like a lattice than a tree, because a node can have more than one predecessor, although a single root node is typically retained.

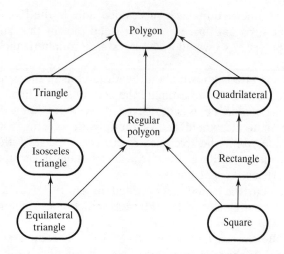

Figure 9.7 A heterarchical representation for geometric figures.

Such an arrangement is shown in Figure 9.7. The new frame `Regular Polygon` cuts across the initial classification of polygons in terms of the number of sides to introduce another attribute, regularity. It is useful to allow `Equilateral Triangle` and `Square` to inherit certain information directly from this node, instead of having to encode it more than once elsewhere. For example, we know that the inner angles of regular polygons are equal, and `Regular Polygon` is the best place to store this information, in accordance with the criterion of cognitive economy.

This arrangement causes no problems as long as the information contained in alternative inheritance paths is not in conflict. But consider the example shown in Figure 9.8. (This is a great favourite in the literature; it is often called the 'Nixon diamond' for reasons that will become apparent.)

Suppose that we assume by default that Quakers are Pacifists (so the `quaker` frame has `true` in its `pacifism` slot) and that Republicans are not (so the `republican` frame has `false` in its `pacifism` slot). Remember that this does not rule out pistol-packing Quakers or Republicans who are Doves. It simply means that, in the absence of further information about an individual Quaker or Republican, we make the corresponding assumption.

But what can we say about a Republican Quaker, such as former US President Richard Nixon? (In the absence of any further information, that is.) Is he a pacifist or not? In other words, where should `republican quaker` inherit the value of its `pacifism` slot from, assuming that the value is not defined locally?

In the above example, the defaults are in conflict, and so we cannot

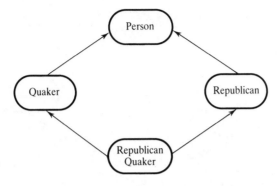

Figure 9.8 A recipe for conflicting defaults among frames.

decide about Nixon's pacifism using just information in the heterarchy. Some inheritance systems would draw no conclusion here, because the evidence is in conflict; such reasoners are called *skeptical* (see Horty *et al.*, 1987). Other systems recognize the ambiguity and allow multiple alternative conclusions to be drawn; such reasoners are called *credulous* (see Touretzky, 1986).

Whatever theoretical position we adopt, we have to be careful to allow for this kind of eventuality when implementing a frame system. For example, we might argue that a peaceful Republican is less exceptional than a Quaker who supports military action, and either order the search of the ancestors accordingly or simply set the pacifism slot of republican quaker to true. Alternatively, we might attach an IF-NEEDED demon to the Pacifism slot of Republican Quaker which uses special knowledge to resolve the ambiguity. Thus Republican Quakers might be deemed non-pacifist by default in election year in accordance with party guidelines; otherwise they revert to their natural inclinations and are pacifist by default.

It should be pointed out that inheritance networks are simpler than frame systems, because nodes in the network need not contain the paraphenalia of slots or attached procedures. All that is required to generate ambiguities of the kind noted above is a set of nodes {*A*, *B*, *C*, ...} structured into an acyclic graph by two kinds of link: positive links which denote that *A is a B*, and negative links which denote that *A is not a B*. Thus we could have represented the Nixon problem of Figure 9.8 as the network of Figure 9.9, where pacifist is a node in its own right, and the negative link between republican and pacifist is shown by a crossed through arrow.

A related aspect of multiple inheritance networks is that we can look at nodes from different perspectives. It is often useful to distinguish between the properties that a node inherits from different inheritance

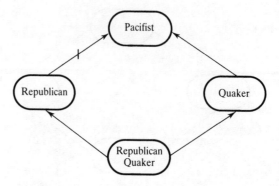

Figure 9.9 The Nixon problem as an inheritance network.

paths. Thus, the human brain can be considered having certain properties, such as localization of function, by virtue of the fact that it is a complicated piece of electrical circuitry. Yet it has other properties, for example global states such as sleep, by virtue of the fact that brain circuitry is suspended in an electrochemical soup. Looking at complex objects in different ways is often helpful to understanding.

It is clear that, in a heterarchical system, the potential for rich interconnections is that much greater than in a strict hierarchy. Higher level nodes may share lower level successors, indicating an indirect (and often analogical) relationship between them; for example, the relationship that holds between an equilateral triangle and a square. However, in frame systems the values of slots in a frame can also be pointers to other frames (see the CENTAUR system in Chapter 16), thereby yielding yet other dimensions along which frames can be structured.

9.3.5 Comparing nets and frames

In summary, the majority of associative networks failed to provide a satisfactory answer to the following questions:

- What do nodes and links really stand for?
- How can we process the stored information efficiently?

Frames are typical of more recent approaches to structured object representations, which attempt to provide answers to both of these questions. They attempt to clarify the semantics of nodes and links by sharpening the type–token distinction and using only a small number of links. They attempt to solve the problem of efficient processing by attaching procedures to nodes which know how to compute values of variables in response to queries and how to update values of variables in response to assertions.

The use of frames as data structures for storing expectations about typical objects and events has become quite widespread in artificial intelligence applications (see Chapter 19); most software tools for building expert systems provide such facilities in one form or another (see Chapter 20). In many cases, we wish to score frames representing hypotheses according to how well they account for data, such as a collection of symptoms or other observations. A match between data and the slot values of a frame provides evidence for the hypothesis represented by the frame, as well as generating expectations concerning what other data to look for; for example, additional symptoms whose presence or absence would confirm or disconfirm the hypothesis in question (see Chapter 16).

Of course, some form of external program or interface is required to get the frame system to do useful work. Although individual frames may contain procedures attached to their slots, this local code is insufficient to organize a whole computation. Some form of interpreter is needed which handles information requests and decides at what point the goal of the query has been achieved. For this reason, frames are mostly used in conjunction with other representations, such as production rules. In the next chapter, we review a style of programming which to some extent liberates structured objects from the need for external control, by allowing objects to pass messages to each other, thereby initiating more complex computations.

Bibliographical notes

Both Bobrow and Collins (1975) and Findler (1979) contain papers that are representative of the heyday of associative networks. Minsky's paper in Winston (1975) is essential for a proper understanding of the origin of various frame concepts, such as typicality and default values. The related notions of *script theory* are also worth pursuing in Schank and Abelson (1977).

Touretzky (1986) discusses some of the theoretical issues involved in inheritance networks, and provides a sound procedure for reasoning about exceptions. Later papers worth chasing up include Touretzky *et al.* (1987), Horty *et al.* (1987) and Selman and Levesque (1989). The latter paper shows that Touretzky's procedure is NP-hard; that is, it is computationally intractable for large, richly connected networks.

STUDY SUGGESTIONS

9.1 Read the paper by Hayes in Brachman and Levesque (1985). Are frames no more than an implementation device for a subset of predicate logic, or do they capture genuinely extralogical aspects of human reasoning?

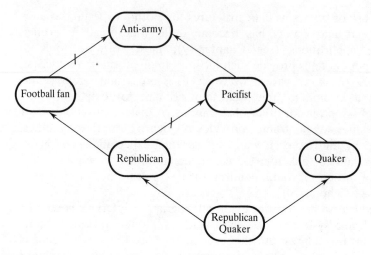

Figure 9.10 An inheritance network with cascaded ambiguity.

9.2 Ambiguities such as those found in the Nixon problem can be cascaded to produce even more puzzling examples. The one in Figure 9.10 is taken from Touretzky *et al.* (1987).

(a) What would a credulous reasoner conclude about a Republican Quaker's attitude towards the army?
(b) What would a skeptical reasoner conclude?

9.3 The inheritance example in Figures 9.11 and 9.12 are also taken from Touretzky *et al.* (1987). They show two topologically identical inheritance networks, which differ only in the labels assigned to nodes. The first shows that royal elephants are exceptional, because they are elephants that are not grey, while the second shows that chaplains are exceptional, because they are men who do not drink beer.

(a) Touretzky's reasoner would conclude in both cases that multiple interpretations are possible. Do you agree or disagree, and what are your reasons?
(b) Sandewall (1986) argues that the correct interpretation for Figure 9.11 is to allow the direct path from royal elephant to grey thing to dominate the indirect path via elephant. What are your intuitions here?
(c) For Touretzky, the example of Figure 9.12 shows that changing the node labels can change one's intuitions about how inheritance should proceed. He argues that concluding that a marine chaplain is not a beer drinker (as Sandwall's approach would advocate) is less appealing than the elephant example. The reasons that Touretzky advances for his judgement are:

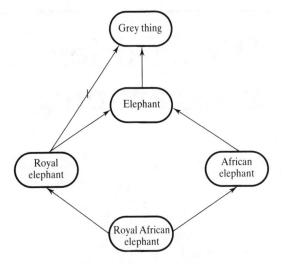

Figure 9.11 The royal elephant problem.

- that neither chaplains nor marines are typical men, and are very different from each other, so it is hard to decide what a marine chaplain would be like; and
- that although we know that chaplains abstain, we know nothing about the rate of beer drinking among marines, which might be high and include marine chaplains.

Whom do you agree with, or are there arguments for both sides?

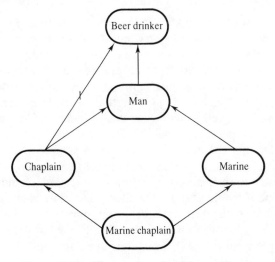

Figure 9.12 The marine chaplain problem.

10 Object-oriented Programming

10.1 Prototypes, perspectives and procedural attachment

10.2 FLAVORS and LOOPS

10.3 COMMON LISP Object System (CLOS)

Bibliographical notes

Study suggestions

Introduction

Many experimental knowledge representation languages have been produced in the last 10 years, and most of them are *object oriented*. As with frames, the fundamental organizing principle in such schemes is the packaging of both data and procedures into structures related by some form of inheritance mechanism. They differ from the formalisms described in the last chapter in that procedures can be inherited (and combined) as well as data, and such objects can communicate with each other via a special message-passing protocol.

In this chapter, we first look at a precursor of some of today's software tools, a system called KRL (standing for a Knowledge Representation Language), with a view to understanding why these tools developed as they did. Then we see how some of the difficulties associated with this style of programming are handled in the later systems, FLAVORS and LOOPS. Finally, we review the COMMON LISP Object System (CLOS), which has been adopted as part of the COMMON LISP standardization process.

10.1 Prototypes, perspectives and procedural attachment

KRL (Bobrow and Winograd, 1977) was a self-conscious attempt to integrate much of what had been learned from earlier work on structured objects into a single system that was both theoretically defensible and of practical utility. The building blocks of the representation were called 'conceptual objects' and were similar to Minsky's frames in that they stood for prototypes and their associated properties. Their basic idea is well described by the following quotation from their 1977 paper (p. 5):

> .. to explore the consequences of an object-centred factorization of knowledge, rather than the more common factorization in which knowledge is structured as a set of facts, each referring to one or more objects.

This orientation led to a declarative, description-based language, in which conceptual objects are viewed, not in isolation, but from the perspective of other prototypical objects. The fundamental intuition is that the properties of an object that appear relevant, interesting and so on are a function of how you perceive the object and for what purpose. Thus, if you are to play a piano at a concert, you are interested in the quality of the sound and whether or not it is in tune, whereas if you are to carry a piano upstairs, you are interested only in its size and weight, and you couldn't care less about its musical properties!

Seen in this light, description can be viewed as a process of comparison, in which one specifies a new entity by saying in what way it is similar to, but different from, existing objects. Thus a van is very like a car except that it has no seats or windows in the rear. This is a holistic view of representation, rather than a reductionist one. In other words, a complete constellation of concepts can be defined in terms of each other, rather than in terms of some smaller set of primitive ideas. The trouble with the use of primitives in semantic representations is that no-one can ever agree on which are the primitive concepts, or how they should be combined to form more complex ideas (but see Schank, 1975 and Schank and Abelson, 1977 for attempts in this direction).

The procedural aspect of KRL also constituted a departure from more conventional programming methods. It is customary to associate procedures with particular operations that need to be performed. Such procedures are often strongly typed, in that the formal parameters will only accept actual parameters of a particular data type. Less often, these procedures will be *polymorphic*, in the sense that they can be given different classes of data that have to be manipulated differently, but they can still be relied on to do the right thing. An example would be procedures that 'know' how to deal with both fixed and floating point numbers.

In KRL, general procedures (as opposed to demons hovering over slots) are attached to classes of data object. Bobrow and Winograd integrated this kind of procedural attachment with the underlying frame structure, and made it possible for subclasses to inherit procedures as well as data from their associated superclasses. This turned out to be a liberating idea.

The intuition behind the inheritance of procedures is that it is useful to be able to program in terms of *generic operations* whose implementation details can be defined differently for different classes of objects. Just as abstract data types allow the programmer to forget about the details of how data are actually stored in the machine, generic operations allow one to forget about how operations on such data objects are actually implemented. An example will help to make this clear.

Suppose you are Commander-in-Chief of a combined forces operation. You have at your disposal tanks, ships and aircraft, awaiting your order to attack. When you ask different units to attack, they will respond in totally different ways – aircraft may drop bombs, ships may fire missiles, and so on. However, underlying this variety of attacking behaviour, implemented in terms of various lethal devices being unleashed, is a very general concept, namely that of offensive action. As Commander-in-Chief, you are interested only in a particular level of description; you want implementation decisions about which buttons to press, and so forth, to be made locally in the units themselves, while you settle back and enjoy your cigar.

The notion of attack is even more general than this, of course. If we read that one politician has attacked another, we assume a verbal attack, rather than a punch on the nose, and we are right (most of the time). Our interpretation of the use of generic concepts, such as attack, is extremely *context dependent*.

To return to KRL, the idea behind an object-centred organization of procedures was to try to learn from studies of human information processing how more naturalistic styles of reasoning might be programmed. In particular, it was assumed that the control of inference would be done locally, in contrast with the more global regimes associated with both production systems and automatic theorem proving. In other words, as well as knowing how to implement generic operations, classes of objects would also know *when to invoke* the various procedures to which they had access.

KRL had other features of interest, such as scheduling agendas and process frameworks, which are less central to the present discussion, although they were equally influential. Lehnert and Wilks' (1979) critique of KRL is also worth a look, as is Bobrow and Winograd's (1979) reply. KRL was really a vehicle for research into the theoretical foundations of knowledge representation; next we look at two systems with a more practical orientation.

10.2 FLAVORS and LOOPS

FLAVORS is a representation language embedded in LISP which incorporates many of the features of object-centred programming described above and extends the basic paradigm to handle multiple inheritance gracefully. As outlined in Section 9.3.4, multiple inheritance is where we arrange frame-like entities into a lattice, allowing a frame to have more than one parent node. Some mechanism is then required to implement inheritance along more than one pathway, resolving conflicts as and when they arise.

The object-oriented style of programming is particularly suited to problems that require detailed representations of real-world objects and dynamic relationships between them. The classic application is simulation, achieved by mapping the components of a complex system onto data structures armed with procedures which govern their behaviour. The first language recognizably in this tradition was probably Smalltalk-80 (Goldberg and Robson, 1983), which saw application in office systems that support the 'desk-top metaphor', where icons on the screen represent familiar pieces of office equipment.

The central notion is that the whole program is built around a set of objects, each of which has a set of operations defined over it. Instead of representing such objects in terms of passive data structures, object-oriented systems permit representational units a more active role, in which they are capable of interacting with other units by *passing messages*. The resultant emphasis is therefore less on the design of a global control structure that will invoke procedures in the ordinary way (as in Pascal, say) than on the specification of the objects themselves, the roles that they perform, and the communication protocol between them.

10.2.1 Method combination in FLAVORS

Objects have their own internal representations of data, like the slots of a frame, and their own mechanisms for updating and using the information so encoded. They are armed with private procedures, which are usually local implementations of generic operations. In addition to data passed as arguments, these procedures can reference local variables whose values are the fillers of the structure's slots.

The following example, taken from the LISP Machine Manual (Moon *et al.*, 1983), illustrates this quite well. Here is one way of representing the class of ships as a conceptual object; I have simplified the actual FLAVORS code.

```
(defflavor (ship)
    x-position
    y-position
```

```
            x-velocity
            y-velocity
            mass)
```

defflavor is a LISP function whose invocation will create a LISP object to
stand for 'ship' and associate with it the properties x-position, y-position,
x-velocity, y-velocity and mass.

We can now create an instance of ship, called 'Titanic', by
executing the LISP expression

```
(setq titanic
    (make-instance ship
        x-velocity 3
        y-velocity 4))
```

which simply assigns the LISP object returned by the call to make-instance
to the LISP variable titanic, at the same time instantiating the x-velocity
and y-velocity slots of the new instance with initial values.

Something like the following procedure could then be defined to
calculate the speed of a ship.

```
(defmethod (ship speed)
    (sqrt (+ (^ x-velocity 2)
             (^ y-velocity 2))))
```

defflavor is a LISP function rather like defun (see Chapter 7 or
Appendix A). This definition states that the speed of a ship can be
calculated by taking the square root of the sum of the squares of its
velocities with respect to the x- and y-coordinates. Such a procedure
belongs to the abstract data type representing ships, and is therefore a
method of the class ship.

The idea is that as well as encoding declarative knowledge about
ships (attributes commonly associated with the prototypical ships), we are
also able to encode procedural knowledge (methods for using declarative
knowledge to solve problems). To invoke this procedure to calculate the
speed of a particular ship, such as the Titanic, we send a message to the
object titanic which causes an appropriate implementation of the speed
operation to be executed in the context of the data values associated with
this object, and returns the answer 5. titanic is an instance of the class
ship, and so it inherits the speed procedure from ship.

This seems very straightforward, but as a way of life it only works
if certain conventions are observed.

Firstly, programs designed in this way must institute and observe a
protocol or 'contract' between objects, such that each object communic-
ates with others only in a well understood way. In other words, the

interface between such units must be properly designed and then strictly adhered to. The best way to see this is by example.

To find out the *x*-position of the Titanic, the program must send a well-formed request to the object titanic, saying 'tell me your *x*-position'. How the *x*-position is actually stored and retrieved is that object's business and nobody else's. Neither objects in other classes, nor any non-object-oriented parts of the overall applications program need to know this. Indeed, the actual access mechanism should be hidden from them, in case they use these mechanisms directly instead of going through the object itself.

Secondly, it is clearly redundant to define separate methods for calculating the speeds of different classes of object moving in the same coordinate system. The method defined above for ships will do just as well for any object travelling in a similar coordinate system, since calculating the speed of such objects constitutes a generic operation. Therefore it makes sense to associate this method with a superordinate class, like mode of transport or weapon platform, and have instances of subclasses like ship and tank inherit this method from higher up the class structure.

This is little more than cognitive economy, or inheritance of properties, extended to the procedural side of things. Performing a generic operation is thus assimilated into the message-passing paradigm, with both the name of the operation and the arguments to the operation being transmitted according to the protocols defined. Sending a message is not the same thing as procedure invocation, because it gets things done without the caller having to know which method will be employed, or where it will be inherited from. All the caller knows is the name of the generic operation and the arguments to that operation. The data object that is the recipient of the message determines which function is actually used.

Finally, the novelty of the FLAVORS system lay in the ability to 'mix' flavors; that is, to support multiple inheritance and combined methods (Cannon, 1982). This extension allows objects to have more than one parent, and therefore to inherit data and procedures from more than one place. Thus the organizing principle is not a hierarchy of objects, but a heterarchy of the kind seen in the last chapter, and is therefore represented by a lattice rather than a tree. Why would you want to do this? Consider the following example (taken from Cannon's paper).

The window-oriented display of AI workstations is often implemented in the object-centred style. That is to say, windows on the screen are represented internally as LISP objects, which record both properties of windows, such as length, breadth and position, and procedures for opening, closing and drawing windows. These windows come in a variety of designs – with and without borders, with and without labels, and so on.

Thus the class window with border is a subclass of the class window,

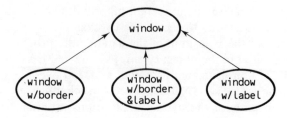

Figure 10.1   A hierarchical solution to the window problem.

and so is window with label. In a hierarchical system, these would each be disjoint subclasses of the same superordinate class. They would inherit certain methods, such as refresh from the window class, and have more specialized methods of their own, for drawing borders or labels, as appropriate.

What happens if you want a bordered window with a label? This new class, representing window with border and label, could be treated as a subclass of window in a hierarchical system, disjoint from either the window with border or window with label subclasses, which would be its siblings in the tree structure (see Figure 10.1). However, this would be wasteful, as well as counter-intuitive. What we really want is to mix two existing 'flavors' of window to get a new flavor. We would like this new kind of window to inherit from both its parents, window with label and window with border, and combine the properties and methods so derived in the right way (see Figure 10.2).

The question is: how do you achieve this so that the mix does what you want? The problem is in two parts:

- Find suitable methods higher up the lattice.
- Combine them to achieve the desired effect.

One mechanism that works well is to have *before* and *after* code that is executed on either side of the main method. Thus, in the example of the windows given above, you could compose a method for drawing a window with border and label by having instances of the mixed class inherit the refresh method from window itself, via either parent, and then inherit more specialized after methods from each of its parents. The combined method would then consist of executing the more general method from window first, and then executing both the 'border' and 'label' specializations afterwards (in that order) to produce a labelled, bordered window.

All this requires some extra machinery, of course, which makes the basic inheritance mechanism for methods more complicated than the original conception, just as allowing default values to overwrite inherited

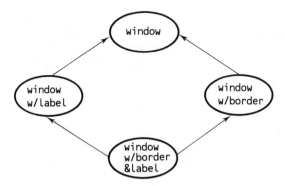

Figure 10.2 A heterarchical representation of the window problem.

data complicated the simple model of cognitive economy. It calls for careful organization of the system architecture, with clear conventions for the programmer to observe in designing the behaviour of the object-oriented system. The next section looks at method combination in another object-oriented system, LOOPS, with a view to seeing how such things are typically done.

10.2.2 Method combination in LOOPS

As Cannon noted, it is relatively easy to combine behaviours if they do not interact. The whole idea of hierarchical inheritance systems was that, in creating new classes and instances, you only ever *added* LISP code. Either old values and procedures would automatically be inherited by new objects, or they would completely overwrite them. Therefore the process of expanding a knowledge-based system was one of incremental programming. You simply told the system about more objects and, as long as you placed these new objects at the right point in the hierarchy, inheritance would always do the right thing.

However, it is often the case that behaviours do interact. Thus, when redrawing a labelled bordered window, the basic window needs to be drawn first, then the border, then the label. Get the order wrong, and the display is spoiled.

Thus if W is a window, of whatever kind, we would like to be able to send W the refresh message

(← W refresh)

and let w work out what to do, depending on what kind of window it is.

Often it is only necessary to augment an inherited method. This is the case when you only want a window with a border, or a window with a label. LOOPS provides a special method invocation mechanism ←Super (pronounced 'send super') for doing this (Bobrow and Stefik, 1983, Chapter 6). This message-passing function will invoke the next more general method of the name supplied, so that the more specialized method can combine it with local code, along the lines of

```
(BorderedWindow.Refresh
  [LAMBDA (self)
    (←Super self Refresh)
    (← (@ :border) Display)
    self])
```

This is a method which invokes the more general method returned by ←Super from window (see Figure 10.2) before executing local code to draw the border, and then returning its own name, the binding of self, as the value of the function. The expression

```
(← (@ :border) Display)
```

sends the display message to the border, which is an object in its own right, stored in the border slot of the window; the subexpression (@ :border) accesses this slot.

LOOPS had a bewildering array of special forms of this kind, so if you find them confusing you are probably in good company. The details of the syntax are less important than the principle of getting a more general method from elsewhere and executing it, before doing something more specialized, defined locally.

Inheriting one method, the 'nearest' one up the hierarchy, may not be enough however. Given a class like window with border and label, you may want to inherit methods from each super class. The function ←SuperFringe is like ←Super, except that it invokes the next more general method of the same name for each of the superclasses of the current class. These superclasses are kept in a list associated with the current class, and inheritance proceeds depth-first and left-to-right. Special code must now be written to make sure that the methods returned by ←SuperFringe are executed in the right order, and that nothing goes amiss (for example, that the window is not refreshed twice, once by each method).

LOOPS also provides a more general method invocation function, called DoMethod. This is even more powerful than the functions described above: one can use it to invoke a method from anywhere in the lattice and execute it in the context of the current object. Thus

```
(DoMethod W refresh window)
```

will execute the refresh method associated with the class window in the context of W, regardless of whether or not W would ordinarily inherit its refresh function from window. This facility is potentially dangerous, of course, because it does not conform to the conventions outlined in Section 10.1. It should only be used as a last resort – when only an axe will do.

The point of these examples is not to impart a detailed knowledge of the syntax and behaviour of LOOPS programs, but to show that simple ideas quickly become complicated when you attempt to apply them to even the most straightforward problems in the real world, like managing the window display of a workstation. Object-oriented programming buys you a great deal in terms of program organization for problems that involve complex interactions between data objects and procedures, but it still requires you to make a number of important low-level decisions; for example, about how the lattice above a class should be searched. Method combination also adds an extra dimension to the problem of debugging; it is not always easy to see where the code that has been executed has been misinherited from, and to work out why this has happened!

10.2.3 Meta-classes in LOOPS

LOOPS differed from FLAVORS in that it provided *meta-classes* – classes that have other classes as members. Meta-classes originally surfaced in the Smalltalk system, early implementations of which had the single meta-class Class, whose members were all the classes in the system (including itself). In later implementations of Smalltalk, a meta-class is created automatically every time a new class is created, and the class automatically becomes an instance of that meta-class. Meta-classes in Smalltalk-80 are not themselves instances of meta-classes, but belong to the single meta-class, Metaclass. I shall sometimes refer to classes that are not meta-classes as 'object classes'.

The purpose of meta-classes is to support the creation and initialization of instances. Usually, we send messages to instances, not classes, and instances inherit their behaviours from their (object) classes. Occasionally, we want to send messages directly to classes; for example, the message that says 'make an instance of yourself with these properties'. Classes inherit their behaviours from their meta-classes, giving a pleasing uniformity to the system as a whole. (Ordinarily, we do not send messages to meta-classes but, if we did, they would inherit their behaviours from the meta-class Metaclass, to which they all belong, including Metaclass itself.)

LOOPS did not create a meta-class for every class, but had a simpler class structure of the kind shown in Figure 10.3. Ellipsoidal nodes stand for object and meta-classes, while rectangular nodes stand for instances of object classes. The thinner arrows denote the relation '*A* is a subclass of

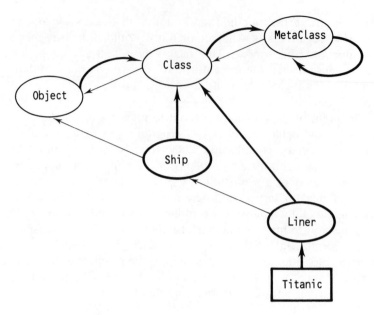

Figure 10.3 The class structure of LOOPS.

B', and the thicker arrows denote the relation 'A is an instance of B'.

LOOPS provided three standard meta-classes: Object, Class and MetaClass. The thinner arrows of Figure 10.3 show that Object is a superclass of Class, and that Class is a superclass of MetaClass. In other words, some objects are classes and some classes are meta-classes. In addition, Object is a member of Class, Class is a member of MetaClass, and MetaClass is a member of itself. Thus Object is the root of the class hierarchy (having no superclasses), and MetaClass is the root of the instance hierarchy (having no class other than itself).

Nodes with thicker outlines, such as ship and liner, are meant to be typical user-defined classes. Note that all such classes are members of Class, and from which they inherit their behaviour. Thus, to create the instance Titanic, we send a new message to liner, which inherits its new behaviour from Class. Titanic inherits its behaviour via liner, of course.

Making some objects metaclasses has the advantage that certain kinds of structure and behaviour can be programmed into an object-oriented system as defaults at the highest level. Thus, instances of object classes such as liner will normally be created in a standard way but, if we wish to override this behaviour, we have only to interpose a user-defined metaclass (say metaliner) between liner and class that introduces the required modification (as in Figure 10.4). Thus the LOOPS class structure combines power and flexibility in a principled way.

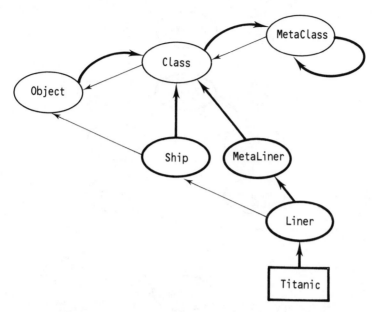

Figure 10.4 Inserting a user-defined meta-class.

10.3 COMMON LISP Object System (CLOS)

The future of LISP appears to lie with COMMON LISP: an attempt to standardize the LISP language and prevent both the proliferation of new dialects and the divergence of existing dialects, such as INTERLISP, ZETALISP and Franz LISP. Similarly, the future of object-oriented programming in LISP seems to lie with the COMMON LISP Object System (CLOS), which has been adopted as part of the standardization process. This section attempts to do no more than show how CLOS combines and extends ideas found in FLAVORS and LOOPS; for a programmer's guide to the language, the reader is referred to Keene (1989).

10.3.1 Multiple inheritance in CLOS

Multiple inheritance is handled more or less as it was in LOOPS. The order in which the direct superclasses of a class are listed in the definition of that class determine the order in which those superclasses will be consulted in the search for data or procedures. This convention, together with the rule that a class always takes precedence over any of its superclasses, ensures that it is always possible to compile an unambiguous *class precedence list* for a given class.

    Thus, given the class hierarchy of Figure 10.5, and a CLOS definition of student which lists the superclasses as

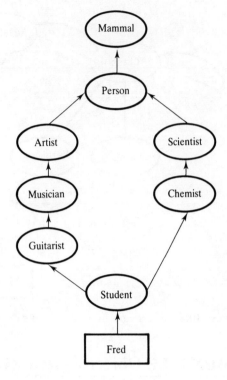

Figure 10.5 A hypothetical class hierarchy.

(chemist guitarist)

we can expect the class precedence list of student to be

(chemist scientist guitarist musician artist person mammal)

Thus, if the typical artist and scientist conflict on some property (degree of political awareness, perhaps), any instance of student, such as Fred, will inherit from scientist and not from artist.

Note that all subclasses of person must be consulted before person itself is consulted and we are allowed to go on to mammal. This convention is sometimes called the 'up-to-the-joins' convention, for obvious reasons.

10.3.2   Method combination in CLOS

FLAVORS and LOOPS adopted rather different solutions to the problem of how to combine behaviours. In FLAVORS, the basic mechanism was to use before and after methods, while in LOOPS super-sending was the main trick that got things done. (FLAVORS had a variety of additional mechanisms which are to some extent regularized in CLOS, as we shall see.)

CLOS supports both before and after methods and a form of super-sending. As usual, there is a primary method which does most of the work of a generic function, such as refresh in the window example. As in FLAVORS, 'before' methods can be used to set up the computation performed by the primary method, while 'after' methods can be used to clean up, or add finishing touches.

In addition, CLOS supplies a kind of method called an *around method*, which provides a way of wrapping a layer of code around the core framework of before, primary and after methods. This is for situations where the core framework does not do the right thing; for example, when you want the before method to set a local variable to be used in the computation performed by the primary method, or when you want to wrap the primary method up in a special control structure. In the core framework, before and after methods are executed for their side-effects; the value of a method invocation is the value returned by the primary method, unconstrained by any external control structures.

The most specific around method associated with a message is called before calling the appropriate before, primary or after methods. The core framework is invoked by evaluating the system function call-next-method in the body of the around method. This is rather like super-sending in LOOPS; FLAVORS used special (not to say weird) methods called *wrappers* and *whoppers* to similar effect.

Standard method combination is summarized in Figure 10.6 (after Keene, 1989).

CLOS supplies a variety of additional method combination types, as well as the ability for users to create their own types. For example, *or combination* returns the value of the first method component to return non-nil. Users can create their own combining functions using logical, arithmetical and list operators.

It should be pointed out that standard method combination is probably adequate for 90% of a programmer's needs. Neverthless, it is nice to have strong-arm techniques available for tricky computations. It seems that CLOS has struck a good balance between the unbridled power of the original FLAVORS and the rather limited facilities provided by LOOPS.

Finally, it is worth mentioning that method definition in CLOS is in some ways more powerful than FLAVORS or LOOPS. As before, methods are effectively generic functions, whose applicability depends on a specialized parameter which states the class of the first message argument. They are called just like LISP functions (there is no 'sending' function, as in LOOPS), with the recipient of the message as the first argument, and the rest of the arguments as normal parameters to the function.

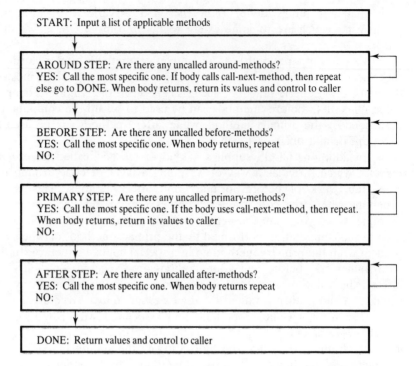

Figure 10.6 Standard method combination in CLOS.

However, there are also *multi-methods*, which allow the behaviour to depend on the class of more than one argument. For example, people from different cultures not only eat different foods but eat them in different ways. Thus Japanese eat more fish than Americans, but they also eat more raw fish. Thus the prepare-meal method should be sensitive to both the nationality of the message recipient and the type of dish proposed. For example, in

```
(prepare-meal X Y)
```

the implementation of prepare-meal might depend on both the class of X (the cook) and the class of Y (the dish).

10.3.3 Meta-classes in CLOS

In CLOS, classes and metaclasses are better integrated with the LISP environment than was the case in LOOPS. In fact, every LISP object is an instance of a class. For example, there is a class array corresponding to the COMMON LISP data type array.

CLOS provides three basic metaclasses:

- standard-class. This is the default class of any class object defined by the user using the primitive function defclass. Thus

```
(defclass father (man parent)
    (:name)
    (:occupation)
    (:documentation "The class of male parents"))
```

defines the ordinary class father, with superclasses man and parent, slot specifiers for the name and occupation of instances of the class, and a little documentation. Most user-defined classes will be of this kind.

- built-in-class. This is the class of class objects that are implemented in some special way; for example, some of the classes might correspond to COMMON LISP data types. Many system-defined classes are of this kind.

- structure-class. This is the class of class objects defined using defstruct rather than defclass. defstruct is a COMMON LISP function which creates frame-like objects consisting of slots and fillers with automatically defined access functions, but it does not support multiple inheritance. Occasionally, LISP programmers with existing LISP programs may wish to use defstruct to implement extant data objects.

There are also classes that contain objects representing methods, but we shall not delve any deeper into the details of this side of CLOS. The functionality associated with basic metaclasses like standard-class is meant to be adequate for most applications. However, as in LOOPS, one has the option of specializing standard-class to obtain more exotic behaviours.

In summary, the philosophy and techniques of object-oriented programming appear to have a great deal to offer the designers of expert systems:

- The philosophy of representing our knowledge of the world in terms of interacting objects and agents provides an appropriate framework for many classes of problem, particularly those (like planning and scheduling) which have a strong simulation component.

- The techniques of procedure and data abstraction encourage AI programmers to think about the kinds of object and behaviour that are relevant to the problem, instead of becoming engrossed in the implementation of functions and data objects at too early a stage in the design.

This is not to say that object-oriented programming solves all our problems. As we shall see in Chapters 20 and 21, it leaves the expert system designer with plenty of difficult decisions to make. However, the object-oriented paradigm makes it easier to think about certain kinds of design decision, and facilitates implementation once those decisions have been made. This seems to be all that one can legitimately ask of current software technology.

Bibliographical notes

For a general review of object-oriented computing, covering both concepts and implementations, the papers in Peterson (1987) are recommended. A more specialized review of object-oriented systems in artificial intelligence can be found in Stefik and Bobrow (1986). Keene (1989) provides a very clear account of CLOS.

STUDY SUGGESTIONS

10.1 Consult the class lattice in Figure 10.7. Suppose that the superclass lists associated with various classes are as follows.

```
Lecturer: (Physicist Singer)
Physicist: (Experimentalist Theoretician)
Singer: (Performer Musician)
```

(a) What is the class precedence list of Lecturer?
(b) On the sobriety attribute, if Scientist is teetotal by default and Musician is alcoholic by default, what value will Freda inherit?

10.2 Consult the class lattice in Figure 10.8. Suppose that the superclass lists of classes with multiple superclasses are as follows:

```
wkg-man: (man worker)
father: (parent man)
wkg-woman: (worker woman)
mother: (parent woman)
wkg-father: (wkg-man father)
wkg-mother: (mother wkg-woman)
```

Suppose further that man, parent, worker and woman have the following methods for making breakfast:

```
man: bacon and eggs
parent: muesli and fruit
worker: coffee and doughnut
woman: lemon tea and croissant
```

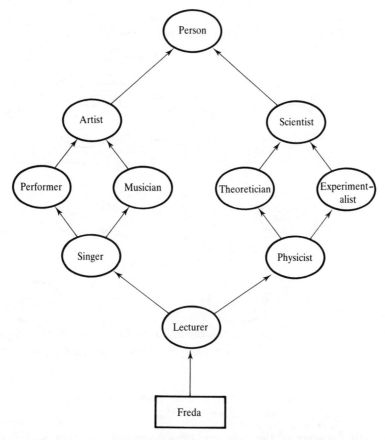

Figure 10.7   The class lattice for Study suggestion 10.1.

To determine what the subclasses of these classes will do about breakfast, here are some LOOPS-style method specifications in pseudo-code:

```
(wkg-man.breakfast
   [LAMBDA (self)
      if hangover then coffee
      else (←Super self breakfast)])

(mother.breakfast
   [LAMBDA (self)
      if weekend then (DoMethod self man breakfast)
      else (←Super self breakfast)])

(wkg-mother.breakfast
   [LAMBDA (self)
```

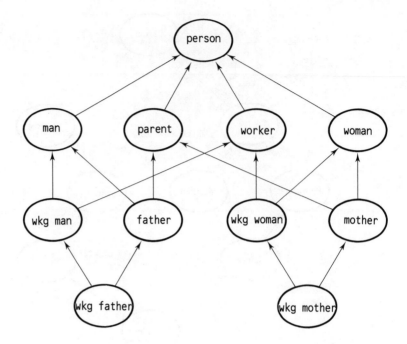

Figure 10.8 The class lattice for Exercise 10.2.

```
if late then (DoMethod self woman breakfast)
else (←Super self breakfast)])
```

How will instances of the following classes respond to the message breakfast?

(a) father
(b) mother
(c) wkg-man
(d) wkg-woman
(e) wkg-father
(f) wkg-mother

11 Procedural Deduction

Introduction

In Chapter 5, we looked at the theoretical foundations of automated reasoning systems, and the way in which they are usually implemented as resolution theorem provers. We noted that such systems typically suffer from major problems of control, as well as a number of organizational problems.

In this chapter, we look at the evolution of *procedural deduction systems*: reasoning systems which use procedures to:

- add extra control features to guide proof search; and
- represent knowledge that does not lend itself to a purely declarative characterization.

These developments are instructive, because they demonstrate the departures from standard logic and additional machinery that are normally required to get a theorem prover to do useful work from an AI point of view.

11.1   Procedural deduction in PLANNER

PLANNER (Hewitt, 1972) was one of the first designs for an AI programming language based on the idea of an extended theorem prover. The full conception was never realized, but a significant subset of the language, called MICRO-PLANNER, was implemented (Baumgart, 1972) and saw application in planning and question answering applications (notably Winograd, 1972). Here the discussion will be confined to those aspects of PLANNER which impinge on knowledge representation issues (rather than, say, issues of programming language design).

PLANNER modelled the state of some universe of discourse in terms of an associative database containing both *assertions* and *theorems* which functioned as procedures. Assertions were predicate–argument lists, such as

```
(BLOCK B1)
(ON B1 TABLE)
```

and 'theorems' were really patterns which enabled inferences to be drawn. Thus a theorem along the lines of

```
(ANTE (BLOCK X) (ASSERT (ON X TABLE)))
```

is really a procedure which says 'if X is asserted to be a block, then also assert that X is on the table'. So, if (BLOCK B1) is asserted, (ON B1 TABLE) will be asserted too. The function ASSERT adds its instantiated argument to the database.

This is an example of an *antecedent theorem*, so called because we are only interested in reasoning from the antecedent to the consequent (by analogy with *modus ponens*) and not from the negation of the consequent to the negation of the antecedent (by analogy with *modus tollens*). We say that such a theorem is really a procedure because it contains control information; indeed, it functions rather like a demon in a frame system (as described in Chapter 9).

PLANNER also provided a second kind of procedure, called a *consequent theorem*, such as

```
(CONSE (MORTAL X) (GOAL (MAN X)))
```

This procedure effectively says 'to show that X is mortal, show that X is a man'. Thus, if (MORTAL SOCRATES) is a goal to be proved, (MAN SOCRATES) will be set up as a subgoal. The function GOAL initiates a search of the database for its instantiated argument. However, one cannot use this theorem to go from the assertion of (MAN SOCRATES) to the assertion of (MORTAL SOCRATES).

Consequent theorems can also manipulate the database. For example, to put block B1 (whose surface is clear) on another block B2 (whose surface is clear), we need to find the surface that B1 is already on, delete the old assertion to this effect, and then make the new assertion that B1 is on B2.

```
(CONSE (ON X Y)
      (GOAL (CLEAR X)) (GOAL (CLEAR Y))
      (ERASE (ON X Z)) (ASSERT (ON X Y)))
```

Given the goal (ON B1 B2), so long as B1 and B2 are clear, PLANNER will perform the desired manipulations of the database. Consequent theorems therefore provide a mechanism for implementing STRIPS-like operators for planning applications (see Chapter 4).

The reader can see from this sketch that, in PLANNER, control information was represented explicitly in the database of procedures, rather than being concealed in the strategic component of the theorem prover, as in resolution refutation systems. The power of this approach is that we can decide when certain classes of inferences are to be drawn. We can also model changes of state in a reasonably efficient way.

One problem with procedural deduction relates to the concept of completeness. The reader will recall from Chapter 5 that a proof system is *complete* if all tautologies can be derived as theorems. This is clearly not the case for PLANNER; we noticed that we could not generate (MORTAL SOCRATES) from a database containing

```
(MAN SOCRATES)
```

```
(CONSE (MORTAL X) (GOAL (MAN X)))
```

Arguably this is the kind of price you pay if you want to mix control information with propositional representations. Unfortunately, PLANNER was not *that* much more efficient than a resolution theorem prover. This was because its control information is rather short-sighted. There is no overall strategy for satisfying a goal, just a collection of theorems whose local decisions may or may not add up to the desired effect. Also, there was no facility in PLANNER for reasoning about control; for example, using meta-rules of the kind described in Chapter 8. We shall see that later systems attempted to address this problem of how to perform *meta-level inference* in a principled way.

11.2   PROLOG and MBASE

We saw in Chapter 5 that we can render a proposition such as

> 'If a philosopher beats someone in a race, then that person will admire him'

in first-order predicate calculus, e.g.

$$(\forall X)(\forall Y)(PHILOSOPHER(X) \wedge BEATS(X, Y)$$
$$\supset (ADMIRE(Y, X))$$

and that such a formula could be rendered in conjunctive normal form as follows:

$$\{ADMIRE(Y, X), \neg BEATS(X, Y), \neg PHILOSOPHER(X)\}$$

We also saw that if we write this as

```
admire(Y, X) :- philosopher(X), beats(X, Y).
```

with the single positive literal on the left side of the :− operator and the negative literals on the right side, we have a Horn clause statement in the syntax of the logic programming language PROLOG. The following sections explore the problem of how to control the application of such rules.

11.2.1   Backtracking in PROLOG

A statement such as

```
admire(Y, X) :- philosopher(X), beats(X, Y).
```

is rather like a consequent theorem in PLANNER. Given the goal 'someone admires someone', which can be represented by the clause

```
:- admire(V, W).
```

the statement says that 'to show that Y admires X, show that X is a philosopher, and then show that X beats Y'. Thus, a goal that unifies with admire(Y, X) can be construed as a *procedure invocation*, and the unifier can be considered as a mechanism for passing actual parameters to the other literals, which constitute the body of the procedure. The subgoals in the body are implicitly ordered; this is called PROLOG's *left–right search rule*.

As with PLANNER, and earlier resolution-based systems, the goal is easily attained if the database contains just the assertions

    philosopher(zeno).

    beats(zeno, achilles).

and we get the answer

    admire(achilles, zeno).

If the database contains other relevant information, the program may have to *backtrack* before achieving its goal. Backtracking is where the variable bindings achieved by a subgoal are undone because those bindings have caused a later subgoal to fail, and new bindings are sought. If the database contained just the additional clause philosopher(socrates) then, if we find this formula before we find philosopher(zeno), the next subgoal beats(socrates, W) will fail, and we will have to look for another philosopher. As we pointed out in Chapter 5, the amount of work that the theorem prover typically has to do to achieve a goal like admire(V, W) depends on what else the database contains.

Suppose the database knows of 249 philosophers apart from Zeno, that is, it contains another 249 statements of the form philosopher(x) for some x other than zeno. It is an unfortunate fact of life that in the worst case the program will backtrack 249 times between the two subgoals before it demonstrates the goal. If the order of the subgoals were exchanged, the program would succeed without backtracking with this database, but would perform less well in the context of a database where we have only one philosopher but a lot of races going on.

Alternatively, the database may contain other rules which interact with our statement about admiration. For example, 'x beats y' might be deemed a transitive relation, in which case we might have the rule

    beats(X, Y) :- beats(X, Z), beats(Z, Y).

or we might define a philosopher as someone who loses at least one footrace to a tortoise:

    philosopher(X) :- beats(Y, X), tortoise(Y).

The presence of such rules will greatly complicate the search space and multiply opportunities for backtracking. The next section describes an extension to PROLOG, called MBASE, which was used to implement a knowledge-based system called MECHO for solving high-school problems in Newtonian mechanics. What follows is a somewhat simplified account of the extra-logical devices used by MBASE to control proof search.

11.2.2 Controlling proof search in MBASE

One obvious way of controlling search when trying to prove a goal is to order the clauses carefully in the database. PROLOG searches the database from top to bottom when looking for facts or rules to unify with the goal; this is called the *top-down computation rule*. We can sometimes take advantage of this convention to keep proofs short:

- *Particular facts* (ground atoms) should appear before rules that have the corresponding predicate as a goal, to minimize the cost of rule invocation. For example,

    ```
    beats(achilles, zeno).
    ```

    should appear before

    ```
    beats(X, Y) :- beats(X, Z), beats(Z, Y).
    ```

- *Exceptions* to general rules should also appear earlier in the database than the rules to which they constitute exceptions. Thus,

    ```
    flies(X) :- penguin(X), !, fail.
    ```

    should appear before

    ```
    flies(X) :- bird(X).
    ```

    The `fail` literal is a way of expressing negation in PROLOG: it is a subgoal that always fails. The ! literal, called 'cut', is PROLOG's way of saying 'if you fail back to this point, then fail back to the last procedure call'. This *cut and fail* combination is a very common means of controlling backtracking. It prevents the interpreter from pursuing a depth-first search for all possible solutions. Unfortunately, this convention can also make the flow of control hard to understand (see Study suggestion 11.1). Note also that the database is now inconsistent from a purely logical point of view.

- *Default assumptions* can be implemented by asserting non-ground clauses at the bottom of the knowledge base. For example, a clause of the form

    ```
    pacifist(X) :- quaker(X).
    ```

    should appear after all clauses of the form

    ```
    pacifist(nixon) :- !, fail.
            . . .
    ```

    if we want Quakers to be pacifists by default; that is, unless we have information to the contrary.

In summary, clauses in the knowledge base are typically ordered so that special cases occur first; particular facts and exceptions come first, then general cases, in the form of inference rules, and finally defaults, which can be assumed if they cannot be proved one way or the other.

MBASE used all these devices, but in addition it provided facilities for controlling depth of search; one could call a literal to three different depths:

- A *database call* (DBC) involves restricting the search to ground literals in the database and thereby avoiding rule applications. This facility was achieved by the simple expedient of wrapping ground literals in the predicate DBC, thus the fact that b1 was a block would be represented by the clause

    ```
    DBC(block(b1)).
    ```

    Subgoals of the form DBC(x) for some clause x were then effectively database only calls. This is for cases where PROLOG would try too hard.

    The cut and fail combination described above can also be used in conjunction with DBC as a trap to stop silly searches for goals that cannot be satisfied, such as trying to prove that a block is in two places at once, for example:

    ```
    at(Block, Place1) :-
        DBC(at(Block, Place2)),
        different(Place1, Place2), !, fail.
    ```

    Note that, without the use of the DBC predicate in the procedure body, the program would quickly go into a loop.

- An *inference call* (DBINF) applies rules in the usual way, using PROLOG's top-down and left–right search conventions.

- A *creative call* (CC) generates place-holders for intermediate unknowns and pursues the computation where an inference call would fail and give up. This is useful for mathematical computations in which we do not have values for all the variables in an equation, but we keep the variables around because we may be able to eliminate some of them later on. So, in some applications, we actually want to try harder than PROLOG.

    The use of cut and fail to encode negation, exhibited above in the 'penguin' example, is usually regularized by defining not as a proper procedure, along the lines of

    ```
    not(P) :- call(P), !, fail.
    ```

    ```
    not(P).
    ```

call is a special PROLOG system predicate which evaluates a goal passed in as a parameter. The idea is that, if the call succeeds, the not goal fails, and the cut disables backtracking. Otherwise, we fall through to the second clause, and the not goal succeeds straightforwardly.

Some of the problems of completeness associated with PLANNER can also be present in PROLOG. Thus the use of cut and fail to encode negation, as shown above, can sacrifice completeness and consistency. There are various different ways in which negation can be incorporated into Horn clause logic, but the conditions under which they have desirable properties are rather restricted (see Shepherdson, 1984, 1985).

However, it was found that the global control mechanisms described so far were still insufficient to guide computations to a successful conclusion. The problem was that they were only based on knowledge local to the current state of the computation. MBASE addressed the problem of how to supplement local control by two further mechanisms – schemata and meta-predicates – to which we now turn.

11.2.3 MECHO's use of schemata and meta-predicates

The associative mechanisms employed by MECHO are called 'schemata', and they are mainly used to encode general knowledge about such things as pulley systems, for example:

```
sysinfo(pullsys,
    [Pull, Str, P1, P2],
    [pulley, string, solid, solid]
    [ supports(Pull, Str),
      attached(Str, P1),
      attached(Str, P2) ]).
```

sysinfo is a predicate which takes four arguments, each of which is like the slot of a *frame* (see Chapter 9):

- The first argument, pullsys, says that this schema is meant to represent a typical pulley system, so this is the name slot.
- The second argument, [Pull, Str, P1, P2], is simply a list of the parts of a pulley system: a pulley, a string and two particles.
- The third argument, [pulley, string, solid, solid], contains type information about these components.
- The fourth argument contains a list of relationships that hold between these components.

Note that there is nothing very propositional about such representations (for example the way in which type information is represented by an implicit mapping between two lists). Neither is obtaining such information deduction, in any interesting sense, even though it involves resolution theorem proving. It is far more like accessing information in a frame (except that it is unlikely to be as efficient).

The cueing of schemata is only one of the ways in which MECHO attempts to package the background information that the program needs to solve such problems. Various additional kinds of structure are also needed which say which formulas to use to solve for which quantities. Thus

```
kind(a1, accel, relaccel(. . .)).
```

states that a1 is a quantity of type accel, which is defined in the relaccel assertion, that is, in the context of relative acceleration, while

```
relates(accel, [resolve, constaccel, relaccel]).
```

states that the formulas called resolve, constaccel and relaccel contain variables of type accel, and can therefore be used to solve for acceleration. This is the kind of extra indexing that the type–token distinction of an associative network would supply. Here it has to be represented in logic, using structures that are not typically found in the first-order predicate calculus.

Finally, there are *meta-predicates*, whose role is to select the inference method most suited to the solution of a particular goal. Consider the following example:

```
solve(U, Expr1, Ans) :-
    occur(U, Expr1, 2),
    collect(U, Expr1, Expr2),
    isolate(U, Expr2, Ans).
```

This procedure states that Ans is an equation that solves for unknown U in the expression Expr1 if

- Expr1 contains two occurrences of U;
- Expr2 is Expr1 with these two collected together;
- Ans is Expr2 with U isolated on the left-hand side.

Meta-predicates like solve are really plans that serve to structure a computation, in this case putting an equation into a form such that it can be used to solve for an unknown. Like meta-rules in production systems, they can be used to reason about how reasoning should be performed. Together with facilities for packaging information and extra indexing, such extensions to PROLOG made it possible to harness a theorem prover for the purposes of complex problem solving. Without such devices, it is doubtful whether much useful work could have been done.

11.3 Meta-level inference in MRS

MRS (Genesereth, 1983) stands for Meta-level Representation System. Superficially this programming language resembles PLANNER, in that computations arise as a result of asserting or querying propositions. However, like MBASE, MRS has taken seriously the problem of providing extra control facilities, although it has gone about this in a slightly different way.

11.3.1 Control options in MRS

MRS provides the equivalent of meta-predicates at the system level, that is, at a level which is quite independent of the domain of application. One example is the predicate PREFERRED, which is used to order subgoals. Thus given the rule

```
(IF (AND (beats &X &Y) (philosopher &X))
    (admires &Y &X))
```

the meta-level statement

```
(IF (= today Saturday)
    (PREFERRED (philosopher &Z) (beats &X &Y)))
```

would be a way of saying that we should search for instances of philosopher before searching for instances of beating on Saturdays (perhaps because there are more races on Saturdays, and so the philosopher search space is easier to traverse).

This is a rather low level of control, of course, but at a higher level MRS allows a user to schedule tasks by placing them on an agenda and then executing them in a preferred order. The basic idea is that, at each task step, MRS enters a deliberation–action loop, where the task at the meta-level is to compute the next object-level action. This action, for example to assert or query a proposition, is then executed before control returns to the meta-level.

The basic operation of the scheduler is to find executable tasks and carry them out. In MRS, a task is essentially a function application, where the function involved is either a LISP function, a control primitive such as a do statement, or an MRS operation. MRS operations can be defined by the user by means of the DEF statement; thus

```
(DEF (philosopher &X)
     (beats &Y &X)
     (tortoise &Y))
```

defines the discovery of a philosopher as a task whose subgoals consist of finding someone who beats the candidate philosopher in a footrace and then showing that that someone is a tortoise.

Needless to say, tasks such as the above bear a more than passing resemblance to PROLOG procedures such as

```
philosopher(X) :- beats(Y, X), tortoise(Y).
```

The primary difference is that such tasks can be held on an agenda and their execution can be reasoned about, where in basic PROLOG one is stuck with the depth-first search strategy. Of course, one could implement a scheduler in PROLOG (or in BASIC, for that matter), but MRS gives you these options for free, plus a lot of meta-predicates for reasoning about control.

In addition to PREFERRED and EXECUTABLE, the most important are:

- (APPLICABLE *x*), which states that task *x* is executable unless disqualified (see below);
- (DISQUALIFIED *x*), which states that task *x* is disqualified.

A task is executable if it is applicable and not disqualified. Obviously, it is up to the user to put the meta-predicates to work. For example, one might deem a task to be applicable if certain conditions are satisified, but one might disqualify it if there is a preferred task.

A full description of the control facilities of MRS is beyond the scope of this book; we have concentrated on the most novel aspects here. MRS also provides the means to:

- attach procedures to predicates;
- control the direction of chaining;
- distinguish between inference and look up.

The power of the language derives not so much from any individual feature, but from the way in which these features can be combined. The reader is referred to the manual (Russell, 1985) for further technical details.

11.3.2   Organization options in MRS

We noted earlier that knowledge representation implies organization. Simply translating verbal reports of human knowledge into first-order predicate calculus is to do only half the job. Thus it is also to MRS's credit that the user is supplied with a number of options concerning the way in which knowledge is to be stored.

In MRS, it is possible to set up more than one database; these are called *theories*. Every proposition has a theory property; the default value for this property is global, the main database. There are many reasons why one might want to partition knowledge in this way.

- If there is a natural decomposition of the domain knowledge into, for example, knowledge about electrical properties of a device and knowledge about its mechanical properties, then it might pay to partition along this dimension. Different modes of inference may be appropriate for different knowledge partitions. For example, in one partition we may be able to assume complete knowledge, while in another partition we may not.

- We might wish to use different theories to represent the beliefs of different agents involved in an application. For example, in a war game, one would want to keep the beliefs of the opposing commanders distinct; otherwise there could be no element of surprise. One could do this in a single database, by some special indexing mechanism, but it is perhaps more natural to keep the theories in separate databases.

- It is useful to be able to reason about alternative states of the world. For example, in reasoning about some device, one might want to consider what the world would be like if things were more or less as they are, except that such and such a component failed (see Chapter 24).

- In planning and scheduling applications, it is often useful to consider different states of the world that could be brought about by performing different actions or allocating resources in different ways.

MRS allows the user to set up such theories and then manipulate them as if they were objects. For instance, theories can be arranged hierarchically by means of the includes predicate. If we want our theory about tortoises to be available whenever we reason in our theory about athletes, we simply declare that the latter includes the former.

Another important feature of MRS is that the user is given options concerning:

- the syntactic form in which propositions are stored; and

- the way in which propositional representations are actually implemented in the machine.

The default is that a proposition is given a unique identifier, such as P666, and then the corresponding list structure is stored under a LISP property of the identifier. Predicates and arguments occurring in the list structure are then indexed on. Only items implemented in this way are accessible to all the various commands for manipulating theories.

However, there are a number of other useful options:

- conjunctive normal form – as a conjunction of disjunctions (see Chapter 5);
- disjunctive normal form – as a disjunction of conjunctions;
- plus various tabular representations which are good for storing the values of properties, functions and binary relations.

MRS goes some way towards answering the criticisms levelled at logic-based systems concerning lack of control and cost of access. However, meta-level inference costs something. It is up to the programmer to make sure that this cost buys a genuine saving at the object-level, otherwise programs will run even more slowly! In other words, there has to be enough meta-knowledge to guide the object-level computation. The amount of indexing done by MRS must cost something too; on small machines, space costs speed. Needless to say, there is no such thing as a free lunch; if you want the additional power of meta-level inference, you have to pay the price (and you had better know how to use it).

Bibliographical notes

Weyhrauch (1980) is an early theoretical paper on the subject of meta-level inference in formal systems. Genesereth and Nilsson's (1987) textbook covers a lot of interesting ground relevant to this topic, especially their Chapter 10. Van Harmelen (1989) provides a useful review of the main approaches to meta-level reasoning.

STUDY SUGGESTIONS

11.1   Suppose that our goal is :—bachelor(fred).

   (a) What would the following PROLOG program conclude about Fred's marital status?

```
man(fred).
man(george).
```

```
wife(george, georgina).
bachelor(X) :— man(X), not(wife(X, Y)).
not(P) :— call(P), !, fail.
not(P).
```

(b) What would the following program conclude?

```
man(fred).
man(george).
wife(george, georgina).
bachelor(X) :— man(X), not(wife(X, Y)).
wife(X, Y) :— !, fail.
wife(fred, freda).
not(P) :— callP),!,fail.
not(P).
```

11.2 Suppose that our goal is :— enemy(fred).

(a) What would the following MBASE program conclude about Fred?

```
DBC(friend(george)).
republican(fred).
enemy(X) :— not(DBC(friend(X))).
friend(X) :— republican(X).
not(P) :— call(P), !, fail.
not(P).
```

(b) What would the following program conclude?

```
DBC(friend(george)).
enemy(X) :— not(DBC(friend(X))).
friend(X) :— not(communist(X)).
not(P) :— call(P), !, fail.
not(P).
```

11.3 Suppose that the goal of an MRS program is to show that Fred is sober, that is, to prove (sober fred).

(a) What would the following MRS program conclude about Fred?

```
(DEF (sober &X)
  (OR (walking-normally &X)
      (AND (NOT (singing &X &Y))
           (OR (nautical-song &Y) (evangelical-hymn &Y)))))

(DEF (evangelical-hymn &X)
     (OR (in &X songs-of-praise) (in &X redemption-hymnal)))
```

```
(IF (wearing &X new-shoes)
    (PREFERRED (singing &X) (walking-normally &X)))

(IF (= today Sunday)
    (PREFERRED (hymn &X) (nautical-song &X)))

(= today Sunday)

(IF (wearing &X new-shoes)
    (OR (good-fit new-shoes &X) (NOT (walking-normally &X))))

(wearing fred new-shoes)

(NOT (good-fit new-shoes fred))

(singing fred hearts-of-oak)

(nautical-song hearts-of-oak).
```

(b) In what order would the search space be traversed, that is, in what order will goals and subgoals be expanded?

12 Comparison of Representations

Introduction

The formalisms outlined in Part III do not constitute mutually exclusive choices with regard to the organization and implementation of expert systems. For example, a number of systems combine production rules with semantic nets or frames, as we shall see in Parts IV and V. Also, relationships exist between the syntax and semantics of the formalisms, and exemplars are sufficiently diverse to resist easy generalizations.

Nevertheless, we have covered quite a lot of ground in Part III, and it is worth attempting some general remarks which compare and contrast alternative representations.

12.1 The pros and cons of production rules

Davis and King (1977) give an excellent summary of production systems, in terms of their basic characteristics and their strengths and weaknesses. It is worth recapitulating some of their analysis here. However, the authors do not compare production rules with other formalisms, such as object-oriented languages, since these were not in routine use at the time of writing.

12.1.1 Rules as primitive actions

One way of looking at production systems is to view production rules as procedures whose internal form is more constrained than usual, and whose communication with other similar procedures is also highly constrained. On the one hand, the form of a production rule limits the body of the procedure to a simple conditional statement. On the other hand, rules are not allowed to call other rules directly, as procedures are, neither can they pass values around. As far as a typical (non-meta) rule is concerned, there may be *no other rules* in the rule base. All a rule can do is side-effect the working memory, and let some other rule pick up the computation from there.

This is obviously a very different arrangement from an object-oriented system. In such systems, objects must know of each other's existence if they are to send messages directly to one another. Also, the format of methods is almost completely unconstrained; they can contain arbitrary LISP code. However, there is a production rule language called OPS83, in which the action part of rules is really just a procedure body, and can contain all the usual programming constructs. Indeed, the action part of therapy rules in MYCIN was just a procedure invocation, so you can see how difficult it is to make generalizations about these programs.

The constrained format of both production rules and their communication channel (working memory) clearly enhances the modularity of rule-based programs. Modularity is something of a virtue, because it makes programs easier to understand and modify. However, one often wonders if modifying the behaviour production systems is really all that easy. Adding and deleting rules often has unexpected effects, as does modifying the conditions of a rule. Local changes to the rule set can cause global changes in behaviour, just as in any program.

12.1.2 The ordering of rule concepts

Clancey (1983) presents a critique of the use of unstructured sets of production rules in expert systems, based largely on his experience in attempting to adapt MYCIN for teaching purposes in the GUIDON project (Clancey, 1987a). His main argument is that the uniform '*if . . . then*' syntax of production rules hides the fact that such rules often perform very different functions and are correspondingly constructed in different ways. Certain structural and strategic decisions about the representation of domain knowledge are therefore implicit in the rules, and not explicitly represented anywhere.

We have already seen that production rules of the general form

IF: (1) The infection is meningitis,
(2) Only circumstantial evidence is available,
(3) The type of infection is bacterial,
(4) The patient is receiving corticosteroids,
THEN: There is evidence that the organisms involved are
E.coli (0.4)
Klebsiella pneumoniae (0.2) or
Pseudomonas aeruginosa (0.1).

Figure 12.1 A simplified version of MYCIN rule no. 543.

$$P_1, \ldots, P_m \to Q_1, \ldots, Q_n$$

have an informal reading along the lines of

if *premises* P_1 and ... and P_m are true,
then perform *actions* Q_1 and ... and Q_n

Now the order of the P_i is immaterial with respect to this declarative reading, since P_1 & P_2 is entirely equivalent to P_2 & P_1 in any standard logic. However, the order of the P_i *is* material to the procedural interpretation of such rules, just as it is material in procedural deduction (see Chapter 11). Different orderings of conjuncts will produce quite different search spaces, which will be traversed in different ways, as we saw in the last chapter. Similarly, the order in which rules for a goal are tried will affect the order in which subgoals are generated. Making sure that conflict resolution tries the most 'likely' rules first can save search effort in the majority of cases.

The problem is that the criteria for rule and clause ordering are only *implicit* in the rule set. Knowledge about which rules to try first and the best order for considering conjuncts is really meta-knowledge – knowledge about how to apply knowledge. There is little doubt that such knowledge is a crucial aspect of expertise that is difficult to capture and codify.

Clancey argues that rule-based systems require an epistemological framework which somehow makes sense of the domain-specific know-ledge one is seeking to represent. In other words, inference rules relevant to some problem domain are often implicitly embedded in knowledge of a more abstract kind. The best way to explain this is to use Clancey's own example; look at the rule in Figure 12.1.

The ordering of the conjuncts in this rule is extremely significant. Obviously one needs to establish a hypothesis concerning the nature of the infection (1) before one can decide whether or not the evidence for it is circumstantial (2). Bacterial meningitis is a subclass distinct from viral meningitis, and so condition 3 can be seen as a refinement of condition 1. Finally, the decision to delay the test at 4 is probably a strategic one. Making this the first clause would alter the shape of the search space, perhaps causing subsequent tests to be pruned if this one failed.

Knowledge representation means making knowledge explicit, but production systems leave a number of general principles for controlling search implicit. This is probably why adding and deleting rules or conditions often has unexpected effects. A purely declarative reading of the rules leads us to expect one outcome, but their procedural interpretation determines another outcome.

Clancey offers an attractive analysis of the different kinds of knowledge that make up the epistemological framework of a rule-based system. The main components are described as structural knowledge, strategic knowledge and support knowledge. It is worth considering each of these in turn.

Structural knowledge consists of the different levels of abstraction through which one can view the knowledge domain. Taxonomy is perhaps the most obvious example of a source of knowledge which is not normally represented explicitly in production rules. The knowledge that meningitis is an infection which can be either acute or chronic, bacterial or viral, etc., is implicit in many of the premises.

Strategic knowledge is knowledge about how to approach a problem by choosing an ordering on methods and subgoals which minimizes effort in the search for a solution. For example, the rule of thumb that compromised hosts (for example, alcoholics) are likely to have an unusual aetiology can lead the expert to focus on less common causes of infection first. Such knowledge typically interacts with structural knowledge, for example, such a heuristic might be linked to bacterial meningitis, rather than viral.

Support knowledge is typically knowledge involving a causal model of the domain of discourse which explains why certain contingencies typically hold. Thus, the MYCIN rule which links steroid use with Gram-negative rod organisms causing bacterial meningitis has as its rationale the fact that steroids impair the immunological system. Again, such knowledge makes contact with structural knowledge concerning the classification of diseases and the classification of organisms.

It should be clear that much of this background knowledge does not lend itself to being explicitly represented by production rules. Structural knowledge is best represented by complex data objects, such as frames, while some kinds of control information may be inherently procedural. Support knowledge may be relegated to the documentation of the program, but it must be accessible to the explanation program.

12.1.3 Flexibility and efficiency of production systems

Production systems typically do forward chaining, matching data in working memory against the left-hand sides of rules and then executing the right-hand sides. (MYCIN is a notable exception to this general rule, of course. MYCIN does exhaustive backward chaining to gather evidence for and against hypotheses.) However, a more goal-driven effect can be achieved in a forward-chaining system by having task statements in working memory and making the first condition of each rule a test for the current task (see Chapters 8 and 17). This layers the rule set according to the particular task in hand, so that when one task is done the right-hand side of the rule that concludes the task will usually set up the next task, and so on.

It is worth remembering that most production rule interpreters do not support backtracking. Modifications to data structure are destructive, which makes it very difficult to return to an earlier state of the computation. This is very efficient, of course; it obviously saves space to alter the representation of working memory surgically at the end of each recognize–act cycle instead of stacking old states.

12.2 The pros and cons of structured objects

One can see that structured object representations were first developed in accordance with a very simple intuition, namely that one could devise ways of representing the world that were much more analogical than either production rules or predicate logic. As is so often the case, some of the attractive simplicity of these ideas was lost in early implementations, as researchers attempted to use the formalisms to solve complex problems. However, the standardization effort that produced CLOS shows that some of this simplicity can be regained.

12.2.1 Using frame and object representations

The main advantages of frame and object representations appears to be that they are relatively easy to use. Unlike production systems and logic programming, they extend conventional procedural programming practice in comprehensible ways. The greatest barrier to understanding program behaviour is, not surprisingly, method combination. Like conflict resolution in production systems (and computation and search rules in logic programming languages), method combination is something of a black box. When modifications to a method cause unexpected behaviour, it is usually necessary to rethink the way in which method roles have been combined.

12.2.2   Theoretical problems with structured objects

In an early critique, Hayes (1978) suggested that the frame idea added very little to our understanding of knowledge representation; rather its significance was at the level of implementation, i.e. how to package information into useful bundles. Hayes suggested that frames were just 'bundles of properties', and that anything that could be represented by a frame could be represented in logic. While there is some truth in this assertion, there is also a great deal of difference between the role of a formula in a set of such formulas and the role of a frame in a frame system.

In standard logic, the meaning or truth value of a formula is in no way affected by the presence or absence of other formulas in the set. The same is clearly not true of frames in a frame system: the presence or absence of other frames can affect slot values in a frame. Perhaps the simplest way to say this is that frames derive some positional value from being in a certain place in the hierarchy, whereas formulas in a set derive no such value: a formula is either in or out.

Hayes also suggested that default reasoning 'can be easily and naturally expressed in logic' if we distinguish between different knowledge states. Thus default assumptions hold until we obtain new information that changes our knowledge state. With the benefit of hindsight, one can say that Hayes' treatment was too simplistic; it turns out that the representation of patterns of default reasoning in logic is by no means straightforward (see Reiter, 1980).

Nevertheless, Hayes had a point when he characterized frame theory as 'a loose collection of related ideas'. The question that arises is whether it is possible or profitable to pin the theory down any further, or whether the pragmatic solutions offered by implementors are not sufficient for most purposes. The experience in applications of logic programming is that one has to unpin the theory to get much useful work done, so one wonders what pinning frame theory down is likely to achieve, at least in practical terms.

In a later critique, Brachman (1985) pointed out that, if you allow unrestrained overwriting of inherited properties, it becomes impossible to represent either definitional conditions (such as 'all squares are right-angled quadrilaterals with equal sides') or contingent universal statements (such as 'all the flowers in my garden are roses'). Many frame systems did not incorporate any distinction between 'essential' properties (those that an individual must possess to be considered an instance of a concept) and 'accidental' properties (those that all the instances of a concept just happen to possess). Instead, instances usually inherited 'typical' properties, which are susceptible to cancellation or alteration anywhere in the hierarchy. This makes it impossible to express universal truths, or even to construct composite concepts out of simpler conceptual units in a reliable way.

Some programming tools, like LOOPS, do tend to make a distinction between 'class variables', which contain information about the class as a whole, and 'instance variables', which contain information specific to an instance. In CLOS, there is a similar distinction between 'shared slots' and 'local slots'. This would appear to take some of the force out of Brachman's argument.

12.2.3 Flexibility and efficiency of structured objects

Frames are a good implementation device for exploiting inherent structure in rules and data. They also lend themselves to model-fitting approaches, such as looking for a best match between data and some hypothesis. Context-dependent interpretation and local flow of control can be very useful for certain applications; for example, where data is noisy or of uncertain import, or where data changes fast and where data dependencies demand that updates be propagated through a set of objects.

Like production systems, frame systems do not usually support backtracking, and for the same reason (destructive modification of data structure). However, the whole idea of most of these systems is that the records contain enough information for the interpreter to be able to make sensible decisions about what to do next that will not normally need to be revoked. Some systems do allow for a kind of iterative refinement – alternative hypotheses are processed in successive stages using different strategies until one of them wins (see Chapter 16).

Objects offer mechanisms for dealing with things like exceptions and defaults, which are not easy or efficient to handle in standard logic. However, the freedom that object-oriented programming gives should be used wisely. One should resist the temptation to create a new slot every time one comes up against a new problem, and then fill it with some special flag or piece of code that solves the problem in a less than principled way. Networks of communicating objects must be carefully designed, and their communication protocols strictly adhered to, if their behaviour is to be coherent.

12.3   The pros and cons of procedural deduction

In the past, applications of logic to AI have been hampered by problems of control. Thus Green's (1969) question-answering system QA4 could handle relatively simple queries, but failed to cope with more difficult ones, thanks to the combinatorial explosion inherent in resolution theorem proving. Systems that replaced resolution theorem proving with more procedural methods of inference, such as PLANNER, attempted to give the programmer more control over the way in which inferences were drawn. However, procedural deduction languages of this kind are typically quite limited in expressive power, as Moore (1975) has pointed out. Even today, the trade-off between logical and heuristic adequacy, mentioned in Chapters 2 and 4, is not well understood.

12.3.1 Logic programs as specifications

It is difficult to disagree with Newell (1982) when he suggests that logic is the primary tool for the analysis of human knowledge. Thus one can make a case for the adoption of logic as a specification language, even if one prefers not to implement expert systems using a logic-based representation language. Kowalski's (1982) suggestions concerning the creation of 'runnable specifications' using logic programming techniques are interesting, although rather short on detail. The following questions immediately arise:

- How should the specification be derived during the design process?
- How can one integrate the syntax and semantics of extended logics for dealing with such things as time and uncertainty?
- How does one get from a runnable specification to a performance system?

Thus the process of deriving a specification ought to depend on some classification of expert systems tasks, and some criteria for mapping such tasks onto problem solving methods, representation schemes and control regimes (see Reichgelt and van Harmelen, 1985; Chandrasekaran and Mittal, 1984; Clancey, 1985; McDermott, 1988). We shall pursue this topic in Part IV. However, the logic programming community has contributed surprisingly little to this debate. The problem of compiling runnable specifications of expert systems architectures into high-performance systems is one that has to be solved by any proponent of the logic-based approach. The reader is invited to consult van Harmelen (1989) for a review of the issues and a number of proposals.

12.3.2 Some problems with procedural deduction

Successful applications of logic programming, such as the MECHO program (described in Chapter 11), usually exhibit a number of explicit departures from the syntax of the first-order predicate calculus and its procedural interpretation in standard PROLOG. As in PLANNER, the architects' avowed intention was to work towards a computational logic for natural reasoning which contained control primitives. Of particular importance were the meta-predicates, which manipulated formulas as if they were objects and affected the way in which they are employed to compute unknowns. Also, the cueing of schemata played a crucial role in dynamically generating contextual information and assumptions necessary to the computation. One can see how this mechanism is analogous to the use of frames and scripts in introducing ideas about typical objects and events.

Some of the syntactic and semantic limitations found in MECHO are still common in today's logic-based systems, for example:

(1)   Functions and equality are often deliberately avoided. Intermediate unknowns are represented by specially generated constant symbols, rather than functions. The equality axioms are combinatorially explosive and computationally intractable, and therefore cannot be used directly.

(2)   Objects are usually assumed to have unique names. Along with the banishment of function symbols, this helps to side-step the whole problem of deciding whether or not two entities described by different terms are distinct. For example, a route planner could waste time and effort deciding that the west end of one road was the east end of another.

(3)   The program is assumed to have complete information about the domain. Thus all the relevant objects are deemed to be known to the system, as are all the relationships between them. If some proposition cannot be proved, it is assumed to be false.

Both Bundy (1978) and Bundy *et al.* (1979) contain interesting self-criticisms by the authors of the MECHO system regarding the way in which the meta-level is implemented. Because PROLOG has only one level of syntactic structure, PROLOG variables are used to range over both individuals at the object level of the domain (for example, strings, pulleys and particles) and units of knowledge at the meta-level (for example, facts and formulas). The mixture of object- and meta-level assertions in MECHO's code is conceptually confusing, and could well make the system hard to adapt or extend.

MRS offers a number of advantages over strict logic programming, in that one has access to a genuinely procedural language (LISP) in attaching procedures to predicates. But the main difference between MRS and MBASE (the PROLOG extension in which MECHO was implemented) lie in the fact that MRS has taken more of a programming language approach, supplying the user with primitives that can be used to build complex control structures. In the hands of a skilled programmer, the possibilities are very great indeed; most of the limitations listed above can be fixed in MRS. MBASE supplied the user with a much smaller number of primitives, and therefore demanded even more ingenuity in the encoding of meta-knowledge. Also, the organizational options of

MBASE were much more limited than those of MRS. In summary, the difference between the two is that between a research tool and a more practical programming language.

12.3.3   Flexibility and efficiency of procedural deduction

It is quite easy to emulate a backward-chaining production system in PROLOG; it is also possible to write a simple interpreter for forward-chaining without very much effort. Either way, the ground literals function as the working memory, while the non-ground clauses function as rules. Modification of working memory is achieved by `assert` and `retract` operations which add or remove formulas from the database. It is less easy to mimic the local flow of control associated with frame systems, although we saw some examples of how this effect can be achieved in Chapter 11, by packaging procedures and data together. We also saw ways of handling defaults and exceptions, although these take you outside of standard logic, and seem to be no more principled than other (less formal) solutions.

Logic programming languages give the knowledge engineer facilities for quantification and pattern matching which are generally more powerful than those afforded by production rule interpreters and semantic nets. Although there certainly exist rule and net systems which offer the power of first-order logic, such capabilities are usually purchased at the price of greatly complicating the original formalism. However, the power of logic-based systems is not purchased without price: theorem proving with full unification is computationally expensive in terms of both memory and CPU. For this reason, it has often been argued that resolution refutation is infeasible as a computational device for reasoning about problems of realistic complexity.

Today, improvements in both the theory and practice of logic programming and procedural deduction generally hold out more hope for expert systems applications. Nevertheless, as Russell (1985) notes, 'Logic does not rhyme with magic'. In other words, logic does not solve all the computational problems associated with knowledge representation and reasoning, and it is asking rather a lot to suppose that it should!

In conclusion, the reader should be aware that some of the material in this chapter is fairly controversial. There is as much argument as agreement in the literature as to the strengths and weaknesses of the various formalisms. Neither is there absolute accord on the question of which formalisms are best for which kinds of problem.

We shall return to knowledge representation formalisms in Part V, where we discuss some important expert system tools and architectures in depth. These programs typically combine and instantiate techniques and structures described in Part III. Because of their complexity, their discussion will be deferred until we have looked at a number of expert system applications in Part IV, and attempted a classification of the problem-solving paradigms that they employ.

Bibliographical notes

Readers who wish to pursue the general topic of knowledge representation in more detail are recommended to consult Reichgelt (1990), Brachman and Levesque (1985), and Bobrow and Collins (1975) for additional background.

STUDY SUGGESTIONS

12.1 Read Brachman's (1985) critique of frame systems with inheritance.

(a) Should expert systems architects worry about these issues or not?
(b) Should the designers of frame systems build integrity constraints into such systems, or provide tools for users to enforce their own constraints?

12.2 (a) Implement the missionaries and cannibals puzzle described at the end of Chapter 2 in the object-oriented style. Represent the boat as an object, with slots that indicate what bank it is on and what passengers it is carrying. Give the boat class various methods, such as embark, cross and disembark, which serve to take on passengers, transport them across the river, and deposit them on the other side.

(b) Compare the object-oriented program with the search programs that you wrote earlier.

(c) Solve the same problem using a production system, and compare this experience with building the object-oriented program. Which was easier to design, or to debug?

12.3 (a) Recode the medical knowledge base given in the exercises to Chapter 8 in predicate logic, and reimplement the OPS5 program as a backward-reasoning program in PROLOG, paying particular attention to the question of control.

(b) Compare and contrast the two programs and the experience of building them. Does the logic programming approach convey any advantages?

12.4 If you had to combine a production system and a frame system in a single programming paradigm, how would go about it? Here are some questions to think about.

(a) Do you need a working memory as well as frames for storing data?
(b) Do you still need procedures in the slots of frames if you have production rules to side-effect data structures?
(c) Would you have a single rule set, or one that was partitioned or structured in some way?

Part IV

Practical Problem Solving

13 Knowledge Elicitation

Introduction

Chapter 1 cited Buchanan's definition of *knowledge acquisition* as

> the transfer and transformation of potential problem-solving expertise from some knowledge source to a program.

Knowledge acquisition is a generic term, as it is neutral with respect to how the transfer of knowledge is achieved. For example, it could be achieved by a computer program that learns to associate symptom sets with diagnostic categories by processing a large body of case data. The term *knowledge elicitation*, on the other hand, often implies that the transfer is accomplished by a series of interviews between a domain expert and a knowledge engineer who then writes a computer program representing the knowledge (or gets someone else to write it).

However, the term could also be applied to the interaction between an expert and a program whose purpose is:

- to elicit knowledge from experts in some systematic way – for example, by presenting them with sample problems and eliciting solutions;

- to store the knowledge so obtained in some intermediate representation; and

- to compile the knowledge from the intermediate representation into a runnable form, such as production rules.

The use of such programs is advantageous because it is less labour intensive, and because it accomplishes the transfer of knowledge from the expert to a prototype in a single step.

In this chapter, we shall examine the knowledge elicitation problem in more detail, looking at both theoretical analyses and practical approaches. Section 13.1 suggests ways in which knowledge acquisition can be broken down into different stages of activity or levels of analysis. Section 13.2 reviews some early work on automated knowledge elicitation, which focused on the syntax of rules, and Section 13.3 compares this with more recent developments, which focus more on the semantics of the domain.

13.1 Theoretical analyses of knowledge acquisition

Chapter 1 mentioned that knowledge elicitation interviews generates between two and five 'production rule equivalents' per day. The reasons why productivity is so poor include the following:

- The technical nature of specialist fields requires the non-specialist knowledge engineer to learn something about the domain before communication can be productive.

- Experts tend to think less in terms of general principles and more in terms of typical objects and commonly occurring events.

- The search for a good notation for expressing domain knowledge, and good framework for fitting it all together, is itself a hard problem, even before one gets down to the business of representing the knowledge in a computer.

As with any difficult task, it is beneficial to try to break the process of knowledge acquisition down into subtasks that are easier to understand and simpler to carry out.

13.1.1 Stages of knowledge acquisition

Buchanan *et al.* (1983) offer an analysis of knowledge acquisition in terms of a process model of how to construct an expert system (see Figure 13.1); it is worth summarizing these stages here.

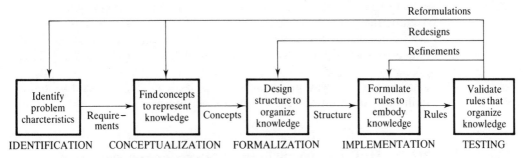

Figure 13.1 Stages of knowledge acquisition.

(1) *Identification*. Identify the class of problems that the system will be expected to solve, including the data that the system will work with, and the criteria that solutions must meet. Identify the resources available for the project, in terms of expertise, man-power, time constraints, computing facilities and money.

(2) *Conceptualization*. Uncover the key concepts and the relationships between them. This should include a characterization of the different kinds of data, the flow of information and the underlying structure of the domain, in terms of causal, spatiotemporal, or part–whole relationships, and so on.

(3) *Formalization*. Try to understand the nature of the underlying search space, and the character of the search that will have to be conducted. Important issues include the certainty and completeness of the information, and other constraints on the logical interpreta-tion of the data, such as time dependency, and the reliability and consistency of different data sources.

(4) *Implementation*. In turning a formalization of knowledge into a runnable program, one is primarily concerned with the specifica-tion of control and the details of information flow. Rules will have to be expressed in some executable form under a chosen control regime, while decisions must be made about data structures and the degree of independence between different modules of the program.

(5) *Testing*. The evaluation of expert systems is far from being an exact science, but it is clear that the task can be made easier if one is able to run the program on a large and representative sample of test cases. Common sources of error are rules which are either missing, incomplete or wholly incorrect, while competition between related rules can cause unexpected bugs.

As Figure 13.1 suggests, the primary consideration in designing an expert system is the class of problems that you want the system to solve. It is a mistake to begin either with a particular conceptual analysis of the domain or with a particular organization of knowledge in mind. This is because one suspects that the way in which we represent concepts to ourselves and the way in which we organize our ideas depend to some significant extent on our current needs and purposes.

13.1.2 Different levels in the analysis of knowledge

The distinction drawn between identification, conceptualization and formalization can also be found in the work of Wielinga and Breuker (1984) who distinguish between five different levels of analysis: knowledge identification, knowledge conceptualization, epistemological analysis, logical analysis and implementational analysis.

- *Knowledge identification* simply refers to the recording of what one or more experts report on their knowledge. This is the stage of the in-depth interview, in which a knowledge engineer encourages experts to talk about how they do what they do. The results will normally be recorded in a natural language, although it may also use some special notations of mathematics or physical science.

- *Knowledge conceptualization* aims at the formal description of knowledge in terms of primitive concepts and conceptual relations. At this level, one is probing rather deeper into the content of the interview protocols. The aim is to eliminate the inevitable redundancy and ambiguity of the natural language description.

- *Epistemological analysis* is concerned to uncover the structural properties of the conceptual knowledge, such as taxonomic relations. These properties and relations will tell us something about the way in which the knowledge might be organized in a representation. This analysis should also tell us something about the relationship between the specialized knowledge of the domain and commonsense or everyday knowledge that everyone possesses.

- *Logical analysis* is concerned with knowledge about how to perform reasoning tasks in the domain. Thus some tasks may require nothing more than deduction, such as reasoning from known causes to their effects, while others may require something resembling *abductive* inference, such as reasoning from observed effects to possible causes. In some applications, special inference rules may be appropriate, for example, for temporal or spatial reasoning.

- *Implementational analysis* deals with the mechanisms on which other levels of analysis are based: pattern matching, slot filling, and so on. This is the appropriate level for experiments and other forms of empiricial analysis, such as user surveys or assessment by experts. For Wielinga and Breuker, testing is part of this level, which is consistent with Buchanan's diagram in which testing feeds back into implementation.

Another knowledge-level analysis for expert problem solving is called *ontological analysis* (Alexander *et al.*, 1986). This approach describes systems in terms of entities, relations between them, and transformations between entities that occur during the performance of some task. The authors use three main categories for structuring domain knowledge:

- *static ontology*, which consists of domain entities, together with their properties and relations;
- *dynamic ontology*, which defines the states that occur in problem solving, and the manner in which one state may be tranformed into another;
- *epistemic ontology*, which describes the knowledge that guides and constrains state tranformations.

There is some obvious overlap here with the *knowledge conceptualization* and *epistemological analysis* levels of Weilinga and Breuker's framework. However, there is less of a correspondence with lower levels, such as the *logical* and *implementational* analyses. Ontological analysis assumes that the problem under study can be reduced to a search problem, but does not focus on the method of search.

These analyses may seem rather abstract, but they are valuable because they help to structure an ill-structured task. Anyone who has attempted to elicit knowledge from an expert knows how hard it is to find a suitable framework around which the knowledge can be organized. Too often, people say 'let's use frames!' or 'let's use rules!' as if that takes care of the whole issue, when they should be deferring the choice of implementation vehicle until they have understood both the nature of the knowledge and the key inferences that will have to be drawn to solve problems.

13.2 Expert system shells

Early expert systems were built 'from scratch', in the sense that the architects either used the primitive data and control structures of an existing programming language to represent knowledge and control its application, or implemented a special-purpose rule or frame language in an existing programming language, as a prelude to representing knowledge in that special-purpose language.

The special-purpose languages typically had two different kinds of facility:

- *modules*, such as rules or frames, for representing knowledge; and
- an *interpreter*, which controlled when such modules became active.

The modules, taken together, constituted the knowledge base of the expert system, while the interpreter constituted the inference engine. In some cases, it was clear that these components were reusable, in the sense that they would serve as a basis for other applications of expert system technology. Because such programs were often abstractions of existing expert systems, they became known as expert system *shells*.

13.2.1 EMYCIN as architecture and abstraction

For example, EMYCIN (van Melle *et al.*, 1980) was a domain-independent framework for constructing and running consultation programs. Its name stands for 'Empty' MYCIN (or 'Essential' MYCIN), because it can be thought of as the MYCIN system minus its domain-specific medical knowledge. However, it was more than just an abstraction of MYCIN, as it offered a number of software tools to help expert system architects build and debug performance programs.

EMYCIN provided a number of features which have since become widespread in expert system shells:

- An abbreviated rule language, which is neither LISP nor the subset of English used by MYCIN, but an ALGOL-like notation, as in Figure 13.2, which is easier to read than LISP and more concise than the English subset used by MYCIN.
- An indexing scheme for rules, which also organizes them into groups, based on the parameters that they reference. Thus MYCIN had CULRULES that applied to cultures, ORGRULES that applied to organisms, and so on.
- A backward-chaining control structure like MYCIN's, which unfolds an AND/OR tree, the leaves of which are data that can be looked up in tables or requested of the user.
- An interface between the final consultation program and the end-user, which handled all communications between the program and the user (for example, the program's requests for data and provision of solutions; the user's provision of data and requests for explanations).

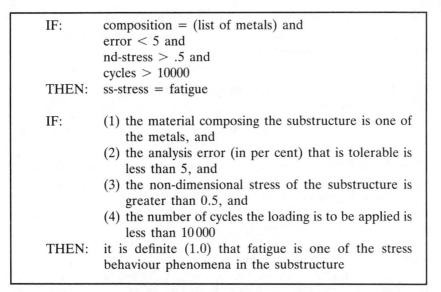

IF: composition = (list of metals) and
           error < 5 and
           nd-stress > .5 and
           cycles > 10000
THEN: ss-stress = fatigue

IF: (1) the material composing the substructure is one of
                the metals, and
           (2) the analysis error (in per cent) that is tolerable is
                less than 5, and
           (3) the non-dimensional stress of the substructure is
                greater than 0.5, and
           (4) the number of cycles the loading is to be applied is
                less than 10 000
THEN: it is definite (1.0) that fatigue is one of the stress
           behaviour phenomena in the substructure

Figure 13.2   An EMYCIN rule in the Abbreviated Rule Language from the SACON system, together with its English translation.

- An interface between the system designer and the evolving consultation program, providing tools for displaying, editing and partitioning rules, editing knowledge held in tables, and running rule sets on sets of problems.

As part of its interface with the system designer, EMYCIN included a program called TEIRESIAS (Davis, 1980b). As we shall see in the next subsection, this was a 'knowledge editor' devised to help with the development and maintenance of large knowledge bases. TEIRESIAS concentrated on the syntax of the production rules in an evolving expert system, making sure that new rules referenced medical parameters referenced in similar, extant rules. However, TEIRESIAS had no knowledge of either the domain of application or the problem-solving strategy to be employed by the system under construction.

This turns out to be both a strength and a weakness. The strength of the method lies in its generality; such a syntactic analysis can be applied to rules in almost any domain. The weakness lies in the fact that it places a considerable burden on both the expert and the knowledge engineer; they are the sole repositories of all the background knowledge about the domain on which the decision rules are based. In other words, they alone are responsible for ensuring that the rules make sense at any level deeper than that of syntactic conformity. Nevertheless, TEIRESIAS contained many innovations which are worth looking at in more detail. Knowledge elicitation programs that delve deeper into the semantics of the domain are discussed in Section 13.3.

13.2.2 Maintaining and debugging knowledge bases in TEIRESIAS

Experts know more about their field than they realize, or can put into words spontaneously. It is not very helpful to ask them general, open-ended questions like

What do you know about blood infections?

in an attempt to uncover this knowledge. A better approach, adopted by TEIRESIAS, is to let them bring their expertise to bear on some sample problem that will elicit the required knowledge.

Given an initial rule set, representing a prototype expert system, TEIRESIAS runs the rules on stored problems and invites the expert to criticize the result. New rules, or rule modifications, proposed by the expert are monitored for consistency and coherence using *rule models*. These are essentially generalizations about the kinds of rules that are found in the performance program.

For example, MYCIN's rules for attempting to establish the identity of an organism almost invariably have conditions in their premises which mention the parameters for culture site and infection type. So, if the expert wishes to add a new rule of this kind, it seems reasonable for the system to expect this rule to reference these parameters. If they are not referenced, it can at least point this out to users, and give them the option of doing something about it.

Another rule model might note that the rules referencing culture site and infection type in their premises also mention the portal of entry of the organism as another of their conditions. Again, the system can prompt the user for this information if it is not provided by the new rule. Furthermore, it can probably deduce which portal of entry is usually associated with the other clinical parameters found in the rule, and fix the bug itself.

Rule models are really a kind of *meta-rule* (see Chapter 8), in that they make general statements about rules, instead of statements about objects in the domain of application. In particular, TEIRESIAS has meta-rules which refer to the attributes of object-level rules, instead of referring to other rules direct. Such rules might suggest that, in some circumstances, it is better to investigate certain parameters before trying to trace others when fixing a bug in the rule set.

Facilities also exist for helping an expert add a new instance of a data type. Errors that commonly occur with this task are giving the new instance the wrong structure, and not integrating the new instance properly into the system. For example, if one wishes to introduce a new clinical parameter to MYCIN, that parameter should inherit the structure of attributes associated with other parameters of that context type, and values for those attributes should fall within the allowed ranges.

A data abstraction used to guide the creation of instances is called a *schema*. Schemas (or schemata) are descriptions of data types, just as data types are generalizations about data. As such, they can be organized into a hierarchy, where each schema inherits the attributes associated with its superordinate, and has additional attributes of its own.

Creating a new instance then involves tracing a path from the root of the schema hierarchy to the schema representing the appropriate data type. At each level, there will be attributes which need to be instantiated, until the instance is completely described. Relations between schemas will indicate updating tasks that the system might need to perform.

TEIRESIAS therefore distinguishes between three levels of generality:

- *domain-specific* knowledge about data objects;
- *representation-specific* knowledge about data types;
- *representation-independent* knowledge about declarations.

In summary, an expert can use TEIRESIAS to communicate with an expert system like MYCIN to find out what the performance program is doing and why. Given that the program is incomplete, and prone to error, one can then ask the question 'What do you know that the program doesn't know?' Faced with a specific problem to solve, experts can focus their attention on assigning credit or blame to individual rules, debugging old rules and adding new ones.

TEIRESIAS used a number of facilities for monitoring the behaviour of a rule set, provided by the shell EMYCIN:

- EXPLAIN. After each consultation, a terse explanation is provided which tells the user how the conclusion was reached. Each rule that was activated is printed along with the cumulative certainty factor of its conclusion.
- TEST. In this mode, the expert can compare the results of the current run of the program with stored correct results and explore the discrepancies. EMYCIN has a question–answer facility that can be used to ask why new values were concluded, and why correct ones were not concluded.
- REVIEW. The expert can review system conclusions about a

stored library of cases. This helps to monitor the effects of alterations in the rule set – the debugging effort may well introduce new bugs. Batch runs between debugging sessions can be used to see if alterations to improve performance on some cases degrade performance on others.

It should be stressed that there is no well-understood or widely accepted methodology for incrementally extending knowledge bases in the manner of REVIEW. However, some work has been done on evaluating individual rules (Langlotz *et al.*, 1986) and optimizing rule sets (Wilkins and Buchanan, 1986). This work is reviewed in Chapter 26.

13.3 Automating knowledge elicitation in OPAL

The program described in this section, OPAL (Musen *et al.*, 1987), attempts to provide acquisition strategies which are guided by knowledge of the domain. We saw that TEIRESIAS concentrated on identifying errors in an existing rule set, drawing the knowledge engineer's attention to faulty or missing rules, and allowing him or her to test the performance of the modified set. TEIRESIAS did not use any knowledge of the domain of application as a basis for constructing the initial rule set, or monitoring changes to the rule set as it evolved. By contrast, OPAL attempts to conceal from the user much of the detail of how knowledge is represented and deployed, and sets out to elicit knowledge from an expert directly by an 'interview' session conducted at the terminal. OPAL is not a general-purpose program, however; it uses knowledge about a particular domain of application (cancer therapy) to elicit treatment plans from which decision rules can be generated.

13.3.1 A graphical interface to a domain model

OPAL expedites knowledge elicitation for the expert system ONCOCIN (Shortliffe *et al.*, 1981), which constructs treatment plans for cancer patients. Its interest lies in its use of a *domain model* to acquire knowledge directly from an expert via a graphical interface. It also uses domain knowledge to translate the information acquired at the terminal into executable code, such as production rules and finite state tables.

To understand how OPAL works, it is necessary to understand a little bit about the domain. Cancer treatments are called *protocols*, and these specify combinations of drugs given over a period of time, together with laboratory tests and (sometimes) radiation therapy. ONCOCIN derives therapy recommendations from a knowledge base of cancer protocols, stored as skeletal plans. The program works by first *selecting* a suitable protocol, and then instantiating it by filling in details of drugs, routes of administration, and so on. This problem solving method is sometimes called *plan refinement*.

ONCOCIN employs three different representations of knowledge:

- a *hierarchy of objects*, representing protocols and their components, such as drugs;
- *production rules*, which are linked to frames and which conclude the values of medical parameters during plan refinement;
- *finite state tables* (explained below) which represent sequences of therapies to be administered over time.

Entering a new protocol into ONCOCIN therefore involves creating a hierarchy which represents its components, linking suitable production rules to the new objects, and filling in a finite state table that specifies the order in which component treatments should be administered. OPAL achieves the entry of a new protocol by eliciting knowledge via a graphical interface, encoding the knowledge in an intermediate representation, and finally translating this representation into the format used by ONCOCIN, generating the appropriate production rules. The intermediate encoding and the ultimate steps of translation and generation are facilitated by OPAL's model of the cancer therapy domain, to which we now turn.

OPAL's domain model has four main aspects, and it was derived using ontological analysis, as outlined in Section 13.1.2:

- *Entities and relationships*. Entities are therapeutic elements, such as drugs, which form part of the static ontology of the domain. Much of the domain knowledge is structured around the attributes of various alternative drugs, such as dosages and routes of administration. The relationships between therapeutic elements are compositional, in the sense that they hold between levels of specificity in treatment plans. Thus a drug may be part of a chemotherapy, and a chemotherapy may be part of a protocol.

- *Domain actions*. Given the compositional relationships, refining a plan to administer can proceed by invoking plans to administer the component drugs. In other words, the process of plan refinement is implicit in the hierarchical organization of domain entities. Thus the domain model in OPAL is able to concentrate on the task, rather than the search method employed. However, component plans may need to be modified to suit individual patients, for example by altering dosage, or subsituting one drug for another. Concepts such as altered dosage and drug substitution form part of the dynamic ontology of the domain.

- *Domain predicates*. These concern conditions under which plan modification is considered, and include such things as the results of laboratory tests and symptoms exhibited by the patient (such as drug toxicity). This knowledge forms part of the epistemic ontology of the domain; it is the knowledge which guides and constrains domain actions. At the implementation level, rules that modify treatments are predicated on such conditions; these predicates appear in the 'left-hand sides' of ONCOCIN production rules. Such a rule is attached to an object in the planning hierarchy so that it applies only in the context of a particular drug in a particular chemotherapy in a particular protocol.

- *Procedural knowledge*. Because treatment plans are administered over time, knowledge about the way in which protocols can be carried out forms an essential part of the domain model. This knowledge enables OPAL to elicit the information that will eventually reside in the finite state tables that describe possible sequences of therapies, and it forms another part of the epistemic ontology. At the implementation level, OPAL uses a special programming language to describe such procedures, enabling an expert to create complex algorithms by manipulating icons.

OPAL uses this domain model to elicit and display knowledge about treatment plans via a variety of visual representations, such as icons that stand for elements of plans, graphical forms to be filled with information about drugs, and a visual language for representing the procedural aspects of treatment.

Entities and relationships are entered via graphical forms in which the user normally selects items to be entered into the blanks from a menu of alternatives. These forms are then turned into frames, where the blanks are slots and the items of information elicited are slot values (or fillers). This new object is then automatically linked to other objects in the hierarchy; for example, drugs are linked to the chemotherapies of which they are components.

Domain actions are also entered by form-filling. Here the forms stand for skeletal plans, such as administering combinations of drugs, and available actions (such as *attentuate dose* or *delay dose*) can be selected from menus. This approach is feasible because the list of possible actions is fairly small. Unlike TEIRESIAS, OPAL does not require users to concern themselves with details of implementation, such as which medical parameters are referenced by such actions in the internal workings of ONCOCIN. All relevant information concerning medical parameters, such as platelet counts and white blood cell counts, is attached to the forms. Like the domain actions, the domain predicates are limited in number, so OPAL can display predefined lists containing laboratory tests known to the system when eliciting information about how a protocol should be modified in the light of different test results. The translation into expressions that evaluate ONCOCIN parameters is concealed from the user.

The acquisition of procedural knowledge is facilitated by a *visual programming* language. The graphical interface allows the user to create icons standing for plan elements, and arrange them into a graph structure. By positioning these elements and drawing connections between them, the user can create charts which mimic the control flow of conventional programming languages.

These programs are ultimately converted into *finite state tables* (which should be familiar to computer scientists). In general, such tables say, for any given state of some process or machine and any new input, what new state the process should go into, and what outputs should be generated as a function of the transition. In the present context, the states are treatment plans, and inputs and outputs are medical data.

13.3.2   Efficacy of OPAL and related efforts

Musen *et al.* (1987) note that knowledge acquisition posed considerable problems in developing the original prototype of ONCOCIN. It took 2 years and about 800 hours of an expert's time to encode the protocols for lymph node cancer, and adding additional protocols took months at a time. The rationale for developing OPAL was to speed up the acquisition process by reducing dependence on the knowledge engineer as the transcriber and translator of expertise.

Using OPAL, specifications of new protocols can be entered in a matter of days, with about three dozen new protocols being entered during the first year. Clearly it is the incorporation of domain assumptions into OPAL which makes the form-filling approach effective. Needless to say, outlining these assumptions itself involves a knowledge engineering effort. Yet, once that investment has been made, subsequent knowledge elicitation is greatly facilitated. The success of OPAL illustrates the benefit of viewing domain knowledge at different levels of abstraction instead of focusing solely on implementation details.

The technique of eliciting domain knowledge from an expert by an interview conducted at the terminal is a feature of many new acquisition systems, such as ETS (Boose, 1986) and Student (Gale, 1986) which use something analogous to form-filling to read information into structured objects like frames. However, not all such systems have the graphical sophistication of OPAL, and not all compile such knowledge directly into decision rules. On the other hand, knowledge elicitation in OPAL is made easier by the highly structured and stylized nature of cancer therapy plans, as the authors themselves acknowledge.

What seems to be clear is that *knowledge acquisition is greatly facilitated by being itself knowledge based*. In other words, a knowledge-elicitation program needs some knowledge in order to acquire new knowledge effectively, just as knowledge engineers need to have some knowledge of a domain before they can communicate effectively with an expert. Perhaps this result is not surprising, given the lessons of knowledge-based approaches to problem solving. Knowledge elicitation is a substantial problem in itself, and there is no reason to suppose that there is a single general method that will be effective in all domains, any more than there is reason to suppose that there are general problem-solving methods that will always be effective. The knowledge that one needs in order to acquire more knowledge can be viewed as a form of meta-knowledge. It is mostly knowledge about *structure* and *strategy*, involving information about ways of classifying phenomena (such as diseases) and ways of deciding between alternative courses of action (such as therapies). Not surprisingly, this is also the kind of knowledge needed to explain solutions (as shown in Chapters 12 and 19).

Knowledge elicitation by interview based a domain model is not the last word in automated approaches to acquisition. Later chapters will consider two further approaches: acquisition strategies organized around a particular problem solving method, and machine learning from examples. We shall deal with acquisition strategies based on problem solving methods as we deal with the methods themselves throughout the rest of Part IV. We defer a discussion of machine learning until Part VI, as it is something of an advanced topic for an introductory text. Nevertheless, the reader should be aware that each of these alternatives appears to be increasingly viable as a practical solution to the knowledge acquisition bottleneck.

Bibliographical notes

Van Melle (1981) gives a detailed account of the systems-development aids in the EMYCIN framework. Boose and Gaines (1988) contains a representative sample of research papers on knowledge acquisition, including a paper on OPAL. Also included in the collection is Boose and Bradshaw's account of ETS and AQUINAS. These knowledge elicitation programs contain many different techniques and tools for expediting the construction of prototype expert systems. For a panoramic view of knowledge acquisition strategies in the 1980s, plus an extensive bibliography, see Neale (1988).

STUDY SUGGESTIONS

13.1 Why is knowledge acquisition such a bottleneck in expert systems development?

13.2 Find a problem that you are interested in, and specify it thoroughly. For example, you might want to buy a new car, but this is not a well-defined problem unless you also specify how much money you want to spend, the primary purpose of the vehicle, makes and models you are definitely not interested in, and so on. Most major purchases, from houses to hi-fis, are good for this kind of exercise.

13.3 (a) List the key concepts and relationships involved in the problem you chose for Study suggestion 13.2. In the car example, these would obviously include such things as makes and models of cars, their various properties, such as engine size and fuel consumption, and their relationship to key factors in your lifestyle, such as amount of driving you do, whether or not you have a horse or a dog or a boat, and so on.

(b) Find some way of formally representing these concepts and relationships. For example, makes and models of cars could be collected under various classes, such as sedan, sports, station wagon. However, there may be more than one dimension along which concepts can be grouped and differentiated, in which case you will be forced to cope with aspects of multiple inheritance. Priorities among properties may also be important, as well as some means of resolving conflicts. If you want a powerful car, but at the same time low fuel consumption, how will you effect a compromise?

13.4 Implement a simple advice-giving program that helps a user step through the important stages of decision making in the problem you chose for Study suggestion 13.2. This means deciding how the representation of concepts and relationships derived in Exercise 13.3 will be realised in data structures. You will also have to design a control regime that respects both the structure of the search space (such as the way that cars are classified) and any mechanisms for prioritizing properties or resolving conflicts (such as deciding what to do when faced with incompatible demands).

14 Heuristic Classification (I)

Introduction

In Chapter 13, we saw that the inference engine and knowledge representation of a successful expert systems application could often form the basis of another application. Thus the EMYCIN architecture, derived from MYCIN, was used as a vehicle for a number of other systems. However, the designers and implementors of EMYCIN never claimed that it would be suitable for arbitrary applications.

This chapter asks a number of rather difficult questions about the various problem-solving methods that are available to expert systems practitioners, and the kinds of application that they are most suitable for. In particular:

- Can we attempt a *classification of expert systems applications* on the basis of easily identifiable features of the task or the domain?

- Can we identify a well-differentiated *set of problem-solving methods* which are relevant to classes of expert system applications?

- Can we specify what *styles of representation and inference* are most suitable for a given problem-solving method?

The answers are based on the best of current thinking on these topics, but they are hardly definitive or complete. Needless to say, these topics are of great theoretical and practical interest. If expert systems technology is to have a firm basis in theory, we must understand why the technology works (and sometimes does not work) better than we do now. On the practical side, helping expert system builders to make the right design decisions with respect to the methods and representations most suitable for their application will do much to prevent the frustration and disillusion that often accompany bad decisions.

The plan of this chapter is as follows. First, it takes a critical look at classifications of expert system tasks that have been suggested in the literature. We shall see that few of these classification schemes take us very far. Then we examine Clancey's (1985) analysis of a problem-solving method known as *heuristic classification*, which appears to characterize the behaviour of a large number of expert systems which perform tasks such as diagnosis and data interpretation. Finally, heuristic classification will be contrasted with other problem-solving methods, which appear to succeed on tasks where heuristic classification is unsuitable.

14.1   Classifications of expert system tasks

Hayes-Roth *et al.* (1983) offer a classification of expert systems which reflects the different kinds of task that can be addressed by expert systems technology. Their classification scheme has received some criticism over the years, largely because it appears to mix up different dimensions, and because the categories employed are not mutually exclusive. Nevertheless, the categories are described briefly here to provide a starting point for our discussion, since their scheme has not been substantially improved on by anyone else. They are as follows:

- *Interpretation systems* infer situation descriptions from observations or sensor data. Typical tasks include signal understanding and chemical structure elucidation.

- *Prediction systems* infer likely consequences from situations or events. Typical tasks include weather forecasting and financial forecasting.

- *Diagnosis systems* infer system faults from symptom data. This category includes a broad spectrum of tasks in medical, mechanical and electronic domains.

- *Design systems* develop configurations of objects that satisfy certain constraints. Typical tasks include circuit design and producing optimal arrangements of machinery in a confined space.

- *Planning systems* generate sequences of actions that achieve stated goals. Most typical tasks are planning robot motions and route planning.

- *Monitoring systems* study observations of system behaviour over time to guard against deviations that threaten stated goals. Typical applications involve air traffic control and monitoring of power stations.

- *Debugging systems* generate remedies for system faults. Typical applications involve computer-aided instruction and aids to computer programmers.

- *Repair systems* generate and administer remedies for system faults. Typical applications involve avionics systems and computer networks.

- *Instruction systems* diagnose and treat students' misconceptions concerning some domain.

- *Control systems* govern the behaviour of a system by anticipating problems, planning solutions and monitoring the necessary actions. Typical tasks involve battle management and mission control.

This classification has a number of shortcomings. Reichgelt and van Harmelen (1986) argue that some of the categories seem to overlap with or include others; for example, *planning* can be seen as a special case of *design*, namely the design of actions (as Hayes-Roth *et al.* (1983) point out). Similarly, Clancey (1985) asks 'Is automatic programming a *planning* problem or a *design* problem?' There are also obvious overlaps among debugging, repair, monitoring and instruction systems.

Clancey proposes an alternative analysis in terms of *generic operations* on a system. Instead of attempting to categorize problem-solving programs directly in terms of the kind of problem that they set out to solve, one can ask what kinds of operation such a program can perform with respect to a real-world (mechanical, electrical or biological) system. Such systems might include manufacturing machinery, VLSI chips or the organs of human respiration.

(There is a possible source of confusion here, because we also use the term 'system' to denote suites of programs. The kind of system that Clancey is talking about here is obviously distinct from the expert system itself. By the general term 'system' we usually intend some complex arrangement of interacting objects, existing in some environment and engaged in some process, involving the exchange of energy and information with that environment.)

Clancey distinguishes between *synthetic* operations that *construct* a system and *analytic* operations that *interpret* a system. These very general concepts can be specialized, resulting in a heirarchical analysis of the kinds of operation that a program can be called on to perform. The

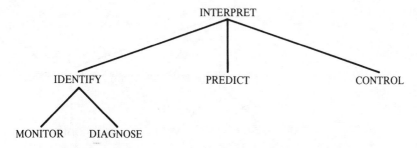

Figure 14.1 Generic operations for analysing a system.

hierarchies for interpretation and construction are shown in Figures 14.1 and 14.2 respectively (adapted from Clancey, 1985).

Looking at Figure 14.1, we can see how the different kinds of INTERPRET operation relate to the notion of a system. Given input–output pairs, the IDENTIFY operation tells us what kind of system we are dealing with. Given a known system, PREDICT tells us what outputs to expect for a class of given inputs. CONTROL, on the other hand, takes a known system and determines inputs which achieve a desired output. Thus the three specializations of INTERPRET cover all the possibilities in which one member of the set {*input, output, system*} is an unknown quantity. IDENTIFY can be further specialized for faulty systems. The MONITOR operation detects discrepant behaviour, and DIAGNOSE explains it.

Looking at Figure 14.2, the CONSTRUCT operation can be specialized in three ways. SPECIFY states the constraints that any system design must satisfy, DESIGN generates an arrangement of parts which satisfies those constraints, and ASSEMBLE realizes the design by putting the parts together. The DESIGN process can itself be specialized in two ways. CONFIGURE concentrates on the actual structure of the system, and PLAN concentrates on how that structure will be assembled.

It is worth looking back at the categories proposed by Hayes-Roth *et al.* (1983) to see how they fit in with Clancey's analysis:

- *Interpretation* is now a generic category that covers any task which involves describing a working system. *Prediction* and *control* are now varieties of interpretation task.

- *Monitoring* and *diagnosis* are now varieties of identification task, which is itself a kind of interpretation task. *Debugging* is assimilated into *diagnosis*, although it also includes a modification task (to put things right).

- *Design* remains a basic category, but *instruction* is assimilated into a modify operation, as is *repair*. *Planning* is now a specialization of *design*.

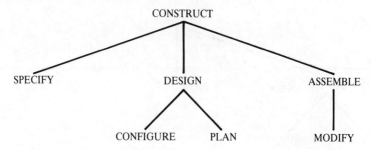

Figure 14.2   Generic operations for synthesizing a system.

As we observed earlier, our interest in classifying expert system tasks is not purely theoretical. Ideally, we would like to map problem-solving methods onto tasks, in such a way that we can say, for any given task, which methods are most appropriate. Clancey's contribution to this topic was the identification of a particular problem-solving method, heuristic classification, and it is to this method that we now turn.

14.2   Classification problem solving

Classification is a problem common to many domains. For example, in botany and zoology, experts are interested in placing new species in a taxonomy of existing plant or animal types. The classes involved usually have a hierarchical organization, in which subclasses possess the discriminating features of their superclasses, and classes which are 'siblings' in the hierarchy are mutually exclusive with respect to the presence or absence of some set of features.

4.2.1   Heuristic matching

Clancey argues that the essential characteristic of classification is that the expert *selects* a category from a set of possible solutions which has already been enumerated. In simple problems, the salient features of an object are sufficient for its classification, so the match between data and category is immediate. For more complex problems, the salient features may be insufficient to identify the correct branch and level in the hierarchy. In this case, we may resort to what Clancey calls *heuristic classification*: a *non-hierarchical* association between data and category requiring inter-mediate inferences, possibly involving concepts in *another* taxonomy. This is best understood schematically, as in Figure 14.3 (after Clancey,

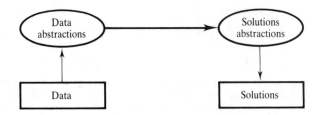

Figure 14.3 Inference structure of heuristic classification.

1985), which shows the three basic steps in heuristic classification: data abstraction, matching data abstractions to solution abstractions (the heavy arrow), and solution refinement.

- *Data abstraction*. It is often useful to abstract from the data of a particular case. Thus, when diagnosing illness, the important fact may not be so much that the patient has a body temperature of 105.6°, but that the patient's temperature is above normal. Usually we want to reason in terms of temperature ranges, not continuous values.

- *Heuristic match*. Although the match between the raw data of a particular case and the final diagnoses is hard to perform, it is often easier to perform a match between data abstractions and broad classes of illness. Thus high body temperature indicates fever, suggesting infection. Data 'trigger' hypotheses, but only at a relatively high level of abstraction. This matching process is heuristic because the map from data to hypotheses may not be one to one at any level, and there may well be exceptions to general rules. Observing data that fit the data abstraction merely makes solutions that fit the solution abstraction more likely.

- *Solution refinement*. Having identified a solution abstraction which narrows the solution space, we still need to identify and rank candidate solutions in that space. This may require further reasoning about the actual data values (for example), or it may require the gathering of further data. Either way, the goal is to rule out some of the competing hypotheses in the solution space and rate those that remain.

Clancey differentiates between three varieties of data abstraction:

- *Definitional*. This involves essential features of a class of objects, and therefore resembles the taxonomic approach of botany and zoology.

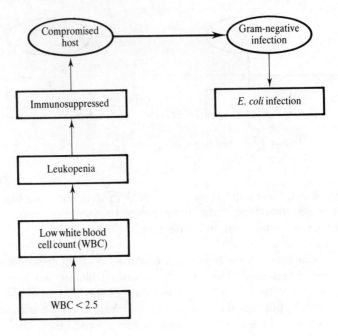

Figure 14.4 Inference structure of MYCIN.

- *Qualitative.* This involves abstracting over quantitative measures, as in the example of body temperature, given above.
- *Generalization.* This involves abstraction in a hierarchy; for example, immunosuppressed patients are compromised hosts.

Figure 14.4 (adapted from Clancey), illustrates heuristic classification in the context of the MYCIN program discussed in Chapter 3.

Thus the original datum concerning the patient white blood cell count can be qualitatively abstracted as a low count which defines the condition of leukopenia (lack of leukocytes). Leukopenia is a kind of immunosuppression (an impairment of the body's ability to defend itself against infection), while an immunosuppressed patient is a kind of 'compromised host' (someone more liable to infection than normal). The generic category compromised host suggests a Gram-negative infection (infection involving a particular class of bacteria), while the details of the case suggest the organism *E. coli*.

In MYCIN's case, the match between data and solution abstractions performed by production rules, and the heuristic nature of this match, is represented by the certainty factor. This can be thought of as a measure of how strong the correspondence encoded by the rule is deemed to be. Other rules will refine the match, thereby adjusting the certainty factor.

14.2.2   The generality of heuristic classification

The interesting thing about Clancey's analysis is that it identifies a wide range of expert systems in different domains which appear to function in more or less the same way. His paper applies this analysis to a number of systems other than MYCIN, including the following.

The SACON program (Bennett *et al.*, 1978) advises engineers concerning the use of a software package (MARC), which uses finite-element analysis to simulate the mechanical behaviour of objects; for example, metal fatigue in bridges. MARC is a powerful and complex program that offers users a lot of options; SACON's role is to help MARC users set up the kind of simulation that they want. The output of SACON is an *analysis strategy*, which is inferred from load and substructure descriptions supplied by the user.

SACON has knowledge of over 30 classes of analysis. In identifying the type most suitable for a user's problem, it employs two steps of heuristic matching similar to those described by Clancey. The first step involves choosing a mathematical model for estimating stress and deflection under various conditions, based on the input data about loadings and structure geometries. The second step involves choosing an analysis strategy based on the worst-case stress and deflection behaviours derived from the chosen model.

Both steps involve selection from a set of alternatives and heuristic match between abstractions. There is no solution refinement step, however, because the second step identifies only useful classes of the MARC program, although the analysis strategy does come with recommendations about specific features provided by MARC. Unlike MYCIN, there is no qualification of the match by certainty factors; SACON's conservative use of worst-case behaviours allows for categorical recommendations, even though the match is inexact.

As Clancey points out, many expert systems perform more than one of the generic operations outlined in Figures 14.1 and 14.2. Thus MYCIN's therapy recommendations involve *monitoring* the patient's state, *diagnosing* the disease category, *identifying* the bacteria and *modifying* the state of the patient (or the state of the organism). SACON, on the other hand, *identifies* types of structure, *predicts* how such structures will behave in terms of a mathematical model and then *identifies* appropriate analyses.

Another program that Clancey analyses is SOPHIE (Brown *et al.*, 1982), which troubleshoots electronic circuits. The main purpose of this program was as a research vehicle for ideas about computer-assisted learning, but its problem-solving modules were capable of classifying an electronic circuit in terms of the component that caused the faulty behaviour. Thus its pre-enumerated solution space contains descriptions of valid and faulty input–output pairs.

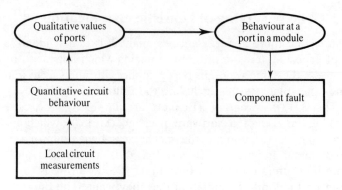

Figure 14.5 The inference structure of SOPHIE.

Figure 14.5 (after Clancey, 1985) shows how we can see SOPHIE's inference structure as an instance of heuristic classification. Measurements taken at various points in an electronic circuit allow SOPHIE to make quantitative statements about circuit behaviour, such as the voltage across two points. The program can then turn these into qualitative statements about behaviour, such as 'high voltage', which can be heuristically mapped to faults at the level of the module. Solution refinement then consists in deciding which components of the module are faulty. Thus, in terms of the task analysis of Figure 14.1, SOPHIE can be seen to MONITOR the state of a circuit and DIAGNOSE faulty modules and components.

Clancey's analysis is worthwhile because it addresses some of the questions we posed at the beginning of this chapter. In particular it identifies a generic problem-solving method which seems to be applicable across a number of different domains. The next section attempts to sharpen the distinction between heuristic classification and other methods by identifying a class of problems for which heuristic classification is not well suited.

14.3   Classification versus construction

The distinguishing feature of heuristic classification is that the solution set can be enumerated in advance. Thus, in the diagnostic phase of MYCIN, the program selects from a fixed set of offending organisms. However, in many tasks, solutions are *constructed* rather than selected. For example, MYCIN's therapy program recommends some combination of antibiotics at various dosages. In theory, one could compile an enormous table of drug–dosage combinations, but such an approach does not make much sense. Similarly, DENDRAL's structural hypotheses are generated at run-time by a graph-enumeration algorithm, rather than being prestored in a vast library of chemical structures.

Constructing a solution to a problem normally involves having some model of the structure and behaviour of the complex object one is trying to build. This model must contain knowledge concerning constraints that the finished product must satisfy. These will include:

(1)   constraints on the *configuration* of solution components;
(2)   constraints on the *inputs and outputs* of any processes; and
(3)   constraints on any *interactions* between 1 and 2.

For example, in generating a plan for a robot to attain some goal, there will be constraints that rule out certain actions, or sequences of actions. There will be *physical constraints* that state how objects can be handled or placed, in terms of the inputs and outputs of handling and placing actions. (In Chapter 4, these were called pre- and post-conditions.) These constraints will partially determine *temporal constraints* on how handling and placing actions can be strung together, that is, they determine the configuration of solution components. We also need to pay attention to constraints on interactions between such components. Thus, if our goal is to decorate a house in a single day, we should probably paint the upstairs rooms first.

Typically, such problems do not lend themselves to a solution in terms of heuristic classification. The space of possible sequences of actions for open-ended planning tasks is essentially infinite, so there is no way that all such sequences could be prestored for selection. The order in which things are done is also important in other constructive tasks, such as assembly and configuration. Unlike classification, construction problems involve permutations of possible solution elements, as well as the possibilities themselves. This usually militates against merely selecting and refining a solution by heuristic matching.

Nevertheless, it is important to maintain Clancey's distinction between the *task* and the problem-solving *method* used to perform it. All diagnostic tasks are not classification problems, because we may need to create new classes of faults or modify existing ones, as we gain experience with a new device. Similarly, it may be possible for a domain-specific planner to select from a library of plans or plan skeletons, as we saw in our discussion of ONCOCIN in Chapter 13. It all depends on how constrained the problem-solving situation is. Even an obvious construction task, like building a new house, can be approached in more than one way. At one extreme, one could employ an architect to design the house from scratch (construction method); at the other extreme, one could merely select a design from a catalogue (classification method).

Clancey claimed that his work had the following implications for expert systems research:

- It provides a framework for decomposing problems into operations in such a way that they can be more easily classified.

- Understanding a method like heuristic classification can be seen as a prelude to specifying a special knowledge engineering tool for that purpose.

- It provides a basis for choosing applications. If a problem appears to be amenable to heuristic classification, there is good reason to believe that it can be solved by expert systems technology.

In the next chapter, we shall see how tasks, methods and tools can be related using high-level concepts such as construction and heuristic classification. In particular, we shall be interested to see the implications of such analyses for automated knowledge elicitation. It turns out that knowledge-based knowledge acquisition gains in power if programs for interviewing an expert know something about the problem-solving method to be employed, as well as knowing something about the domain.

Bibliographical notes

In addition to references cited in the text, there is an early taxonomy of problem solving types due to Chandrasekaran (1983a). Chandrasekaran (1986) and Chandrasekaran and Mittal (1984) also attempted to build a theoretical framework for looking at knowledge-based problem solving in terms of 'generic tasks'; this work was linked to a project known as MDX (Chandrasekaran, 1983b), which investigates diagnostic problem solving in the domain of liver disease. For a recent exposition of the generic task approach, with commentators and discussion, see Chandrasekaran (1988).

Clancey's work on heuristic classification grew out of an interest in intelligent tutoring systems, which (unlike early 'teaching machines') use a representation of expert knowledge for the purposes of automated instruction. A full account of this work can be found in Clancey (1987a), while a shorter tutorial on the main theoretical issues can be found in Clancey (1987b). A prototype shell designed specifically for heuristic classification problems, called HERACLES, is described in Clancey (1987c).

STUDY SUGGESTIONS

14.1 Study Hayes-Roth's classification of expert system tasks.

(a) Are there any additional kinds of task that you can think of which are not well covered by this scheme?

(b) Where would an expert system that gave legal advice (a system which advised clients concerning their rights under the law, and advised various courses of action, such as litigation) fit into this scheme?

14.2 Study Clancey's task analysis (given in Figures 14.1 and 14.2).

(a) Where would a computer dating system fit into this analysis?

(b) Can you think of ways of extending or embellishing this analysis? For example, are there different kinds of CONTROL task?

14.3 Are the following tasks primarily classification tasks, construction tasks, or a mixture of the two?

(a) Deciding what courses to take at college.

(b) Deciding on and organizing a vacation.

(c) Changing one's vacation plans because of unforeseen circumstances.

(d) Preparing your tax return.

14.4 What follows is an outline of a Wine Advisor in OPS5 (after a Teknowledge OPS5 tutorial by Rand Waltzman). This program takes as input the kind of meal that one is having, and returns suggestions as to which wines might be suitable. It works by heuristic classification, since it assumes a rough mapping between gross features of the meal (meat or fish, kind of sauce, and so on) and broad classes of wine (such as colour, body and sweetness).

(a) Your task is to flesh out the rule base and make certain design decisions about how to organize the knowledge about food and wine, how to handle uncertainty, how to move between various stages of the reasoning. The program contains comments to help you understand what is going on and to suggest ways in which you might extend the program. Consult Appendix B for guidance (and go easy on the knowledge acquisition).

```
; DECLARATIONS

; First select the conflict resolution strategy...

(strategy mea)

; then declare any external LISP functions...

(external minimum)
(external maximum)
```

```
; and declare the attributes of working memory elements.

(literalize task name)
(literalize wine property is cert)
(literalize meal property is)
(literalize decision re is)

; Production rules of the form

; (p <rulename> <RHS> → <LHS>).

;; RULES THAT FIND OUT ABOUT THE DISH.

; This corresponds to the data abstraction stage.

; dish-type is the rule invoked first because its calling
; pattern is put into WM by the initialization procedure,
; init (see end of program).

    (p dish-type
       (task ^name dish)
       (meal ^property dish-type ^is unknown)
       →
       (write
         (crlf)
         Is the main dish of the meal "MEAT," FISH or POULTRY?
         (crlf))
       (modify 2 ^is (accept)))

; meat finds out more about the dish, if it is meat.

    (p meat
       (task ^name dish)
       (meal ^property dish-type ^is meat)
       →
       (write
         (crlf)
         What kind of meat? " e.g. STEAK, VEAL, LAMB"
         (crlf))
       (make meal ^property meat-type ^is (accept)))

; You can write a similar rule for fish distinguishing, for example,
; wet fish from shell fish; also a rule for poultry.

;; RULES THAT SUGGEST WINE PROPERTIES
```

```
; This is the heuristic matching stage.

; steak is an example of a meat rule which suggests wine properties.

   (p steak
      (task ^name dish)
      (meal ^property meat-type ^is steak)
      →
      (make wine ^property colour ^is red ^cert 1.0)
      (make wine ^property body ^is full ^cert 1.0)
      (make wine ^property flavour ^is dry ^cert 0.7)
      (make wine ^property flavour ^is sweet ^cert 0.2)
      (make task ^name attributes)
      (remove 1))

; You can write similar rules for lamb, veal, and so on.
; We remove the dish task once we know what the dish is.
; Then we set up the task of deciding upon wine attributes.

; You should have default rules for meat, fish and poultry, which
; catch any cases, such as alligator, that you have not anticipated.

;; RULES THAT HANDLE CERTAINTIES

; If there are two structures in WM with the same value for
; the same attribute but with different certainties
; then attribute-update creates a third structure with a new value
; and deletes the other two.

; The formula for computing the new CF is
;      cf = cf1 + cf2(1 − cf1)

   (p attribute-update
      (task ^name attributes)
      (wine ^property <attribute> ^is <value> ^cert <cert1>)
      (wine ^property <attribute>
            ^is <value>
            ^cert {<cert2> <> <cert1>})
      →
      (bind <newcert>
         (compute <cert1> + (<cert2> * (1 − <cert1>))))
      (make wine ^property <attribute> ^is <value> ^cert <newcert>)
      (remove 2)
      (remove 3))
```

```
; Write a rule called preference, which is only invoked if there is
; more than one possible value for an attribute in working memory.
; The rule should ask the user's preference and change the certainty
; of the relevant attribute-value combination to unity, deleting the
; other values from working memory.

; Write a rule called choose-value which fires if there are two
; structures in working memory which carry different values
; under the same attribute. The rule should choose the structure
; with the greater CF and delete the other.

; Write a rule called unique, which fires if there is only one
; candidate value for an attribute, and declares the attribute done.

; Write a rule called unity, which fires if a particular value is
; definite (has CF = 1) and declares the attribute done.

; if all the attributes of the wine are done then report them

    (p all-attributes-done
        (task ^name attributes)
        (colour done)
        (body done)
        (flavour done)
        (wine ^property colour ^is <colour>)
        (wine ^property body ^is <body>)
        (wine ^property flavour ^is <flavour>)
        →
        (write
          (crlf)
          I recommend a <flavour> <colour> wine with a <body> body
          (crlf))
        (remove 1)
        (remove 2)
        (remove 3)
        (remove 4)
        (make task ^name brand))

; RULES FOR THE WINE

; Select a wine, given an attribute-value description.
; This corresponds to the solution refinement stage.
; Generate all the candidates before you offer selections to the
; user.
```

```
; Write a rule called go-choose which selects the highest scoring
; wine when no other rules will fire to propose any more wines.

; soave is a sample wine rule. Write as many as you like.

   (p soave
      (task ^name brand)
      (wine ^property colour ^is white)
      (wine ^property flavour ^is dry ^cert <cf1>)
      (wine ^property body ^is fine ^cert <cf2>)
      →
      (make wine ^property brand
                 ^is soave
                 ^cert (minimum <cf1> <cf2>)))

; I define minimum as an external LISP function (see end of program).

; RULES FOR PRESENTING SELECTIONS

; The user responds to these by typing 'yes' or 'no'.

; Write a rule called selection which finds the highest scoring wine
; and offers it to the user.

; Write a rule called rejection which deals with a negative response
; to the current suggestion.

; acceptance ends the session on the correct obsequious note.

   (p acceptance
      (task ^name choice)
      (decision ^re <candidate> ^is yes)
      →
      (write (crlf) Sir/Madam has impeccable taste (crlf))
      (halt))

; LISP functions

; init clears working memory, indicates that the dish is unknown and
; puts the first task token in working memory

   (defun init nil
      (remove *)
      (make meal ^property dish-type ^is unknown)
      (make task ^name dish)
      t)
```

```
; The following incantation is necessary to define a LISP function in
; the version of OPS that I'm using if I want to invoke it in a rule.

(defun minimum fexpr (liz)
    ($value (apply 'min (mapcar '$varbind liz))))
```

(b) How easy would it be to change the search strategy, for example to generate candidate wines in rough order of 'goodness' and offer them to the user as they appear, rather than generating all possible candidates first?

15 Heuristic Classification (II)

15.1 Mapping tools to tasks
15.2 Heuristic classification in MUD and MORE

15.3 Evaluating MORE
Bibliographical notes
Study suggestions

Introduction

This chapter continues to develop the distinction between classification and construction tasks outlined in Chapter 14. The emphasis will be on problem-solving methods, including different kinds of knowledge representation and inference engine.

In particular, we shall:

- look more closely at the kinds of software tool that are most suitable for constructing systems that use methods of heuristic classification;

- examine a more up-to-date example of heuristic classification than MYCIN and its EMYCIN derivatives; and

- see how an automated knowledge-elicitation system for this example can benefit from the possession of knowledge concerning the problem-solving method to be employed.

15.1 Mapping tools to tasks

Clancey (1985) notes that, although rule-based languages such as EMYCIN omit many of the refinements of his model of heuristic classification, they have provided a good programming tool for classification tasks, such as diagnosis. Thus neither MYCIN nor EMYCIN-based systems contained a specific taxonomy of symptoms or disorders, as Clancey recommends, but the fact that solutions are enumerated in advance means that backward chaining can be employed to reason from solution abstractions to relevant data via data abstractions which are implicit in the rules. The fact that productions in the rule set are indexed in terms of the medical parameters that they cite renders this goal-directed strategy easy to implement.

Other features of the rule-based paradigm that we have already observed in MYCIN are:

- the rejection of backtracking in favour of destructive modification of working memory; and
- the exhaustive nature of the basic search strategy (apart from various heuristic devices, such as pruning branches of the tree when certainty falls below a certain level).

These two features are closely related. We never need to backtrack because we pursue multiple lines of evidence independently and rank hypotheses at the end. If the search were not more or less exhaustive, some form of backtracking would be required in the course of best-first search, as we saw in Chapter 2.

In constructive problem solving, such a simple control regime is seldom appropriate. Design and configuration problems typically present a problem solver with many alternative ways to proceed, not all of which turn out well. In many cases, there are no good evaluation functions that one can employ to guide a search, because the suitability of a solution is not dependent on isolated features of a design, but rather more global properties that are only discernible in the finished product. For example, when arranging furniture in a room, there are certain *constraints* that one might wish to satisfy – desk by the window, bookcase by the desk, sofa opposite the television, and so on. However, a proposed solution can satisfy such constraints while failing to satisfy other more global properties, such as allowing a clear path across the room, or having the furniture evenly distributed.

We shall see in Chapter 18 how additional methods for controlling search are typically required by constructive tasks. These include *least commitment* (deferring decisions that constrain future choices for as long as possible), *propose and revise* (attempting to fix constraint violations as you go along), and various forms of *backtracking*. Mapping such methods to types of task is still a research issue.

Nevertheless, Clancey's identification of a level of task analysis that is grounded in problem-solving methods, such as heuristic classification, is essential to the task of identifying and choosing software tools to do the job. This level appears to be situated between the 'higher' conceptual and epistemological levels that we met in Chapter 13, and the 'lower' logical or implementational levels. Without it, we appear to lack useful generalizations that link task types to inference structures and representation languages.

15.2   Heuristic classification in MUD and MORE

In this section, we examine some of the consequences of Clancey's analysis for knowledge acquisition. First we review an expert system for drilling problems (MUD) that uses the method of heuristic classification to good effect. Then we describe a knowledge-elicitation prototype (called MORE) for this system, which links acquisition strategies to the problem-solving method employed.

As in MYCIN, MUD's knowledge-acquisition process is mostly concerned with the mapping between solutions and data. However, other kinds of knowledge, such as hierarchical relationships between data and solution abstractions, heuristics for unfolding the search space, and so forth, tended to be only implicitly represented in MYCIN's rules (as we saw in Chapter 12). The 'MUD and MORE' approach makes this knowledge more explicit since, like OPAL (see Chapter 13), it uses an intermediate representation that serves as a model of the domain.

15.2.1   A model of the drilling fluid domain

The MUD system (Kahn and McDermott, 1984) assists an engineer in maintaining drilling fluid at installations such as oil rigs. It does this by diagnosing problems with the fluid, based on a description of its properties, and suggesting various causes and remedies. Changes in the fluid, such as sudden increase in viscosity during drilling, can be caused by a variety of factors, such as high temperature or pressure, or a wrong mix of chemical additives.

MUD is implemented in OPS5, and its rules map changes in fluid properties (data abstractions) to possible causes of these changes (solution abstractions). The following rule, given in an English translation, is typical:

```
IF:    (1) there is a decrease in density of the fluid, and
       (2) there is an increase in viscosity (of the fluid),
THEN: moderately (7) suspect that there has been an influx
       of water.
```

The numbers in parentheses are certainty factors; these are combined in the manner of MYCIN (see Chapter 3). Thus, to determine the likelihood of an influx of water, each rule that could contribute evidence for or against this hypothesis is considered. Measures of belief and disbelief are derived as described in Chapter 6, and the certainty in the hypothesis is the difference between these two measures.

Kahn's experience was that experts often found it difficult to provide the necessary rules for the heuristic classification approach. The rule format did not always correspond to the way in which they thought about their knowledge or communicated it among themselves. Experts sometimes have problems assigning certainty factors to new rules, and typically like to review rules they have already written, for the purposes of comparison. Often experts use the certainty factors to produce a partial ordering with respect to a particular conclusion. Buchanan and Shortliffe (1984, Chapter 7) also found that experts sometimes need to know details of the control regime and the propagation of certainty factors in order to write effective rules.

In building heuristic classification programs like MUD and MYCIN, rule writing and refinement is essentially a six-step process:

(1)   The expert tells the knowledge engineer what rules to add or modify.

(2)   The knowledge engineer makes changes to the knowledge base.

(3)   The knowledge engineer runs one or more old cases for consistency checking.

(4)   If any problems arise with old cases, the knowledge engineer discusses them with the expert, and then goes to step 1.

(5)   The expert runs the modified system on new cases.

(6)   If no problems are discovered, then the process halts, else we return to step 1.

As we saw in Chapter 13, the architects of MYCIN kept this basic framework, but attempted to improve the efficiency of some of the steps with various tools, such as the abbreviated rule language and explanation facility of EMYCIN, and a library of test cases for running in batch mode.

Kahn and his coworkers (Kahn *et al.*, 1985; Kahn, 1988) took a different route in the construction of the MORE system: a knowledge-elicitation program which uses both knowledge of the domain and knowledge of the problem-solving strategy to flesh out the MUD knowledge base. Like OPAL, MORE has a domain model incorporating important relationships between domain concepts. It uses this knowledge to guide the interview with the expert, recognize errors in the assignment of confidence factors, and generate rules that perform heuristic classification.

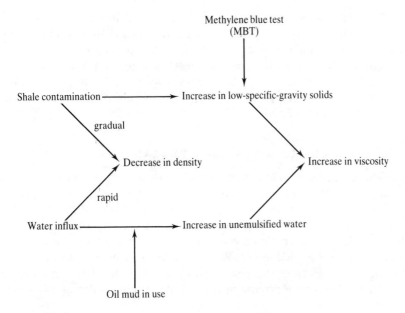

Figure 15.1   A fragment of a MORE model of the MUD domain.

A domain model for MORE has the following ingredients:

- *symptoms* that we may observe during diagnosis and seek to explain;
- *attributes* that serve to further discriminate symptoms, such as rapid increase or decrease in some property;
- events that are possible causes of symptoms and therefore serve as *hypotheses*;
- *background conditions* which make symptoms more or less likely given the occurrence of a hypothetical cause, and conditions which make hypotheses more or less likely;
- *tests* that can be used to determine the presence or absence of any such background conditions;
- *test conditions* that have a bearing on the accuracy of the tests.

This knowledge is organized into a network that makes explicit the connection between causes and symptoms, as well as the connection between conditions and the states or events that they facilitate or inhibit. Figure 15.1 shows a network fragment from the MUD domain, adapted from Kahn (1988).

Shale contamination and *water influx* are hypotheses which between them cause the four symptoms *decrease in density*, *increase in low-specific-*

gravity solids, *increase in unemulsified water* and *increase in viscosity*, which are all properties of the drilling fluid caused by contamination. Note that causal links can be qualified by the degree of onset of the symptom. *MBT* (the methylene blue test) is a test for the increase of solids in the fluid, while *oil mud in use* is a background condition that has a bearing on the causal connection between the influx of water and the increase in unemulsified water.

15.2.2 Knowledge acquisition strategies

Kahn and his colleagues attacked the knowledge-elicitation problem from two directions. On the one hand, they noted the interview techniques used by knowledge engineers in the construction of the MUD system. On the other hand, they analysed these techniques in terms of the problem-solving method of heuristic classification used by MUD. As a result, they identified eight knowledge-acquisition strategies, which are worth summarizing below. Each of these strategies is used by the MORE program to elicit knowledge for confirming or ruling out hypotheses during diagnosis.

- *Differentiation*. Seek symptoms that distingush between hypotheses; for example, symptoms that have only one cause. Such one-to-one mappings between symptom and disorder are called *pathognomic* associations in the medical literature.

- *Frequency conditionalization*. Determine any background conditions that make a particular hypothesis more or less likely. In decision-theoretic approaches to diagnosis, the degree of evidential support lent by a symptom to a disorder should depend on the prior probability of the disorder.

- *Symptom distinction*. Identify special properties of symptoms that indicate the underlying cause. Thus, in Figure 15.1, we see that a rapid decrease in the density of the drilling fluid suggests an influx of water, rather than shale contamination.

- *Symptom conditionalization*. Find out the conditions under which different symptoms might be expected to manifest themselves, given a particular disorder. Such conditions set up expectations which may serve to rule out hypotheses if they are not confirmed.

- *Path division*. Attempt to uncover intermediate events between a hypothesized disorder and an expected symptom, which have a higher conditional probability of occurrence than the symptom itself. Failing to observe such intermediate events constitutes stronger evidence against a hypothesis than failing to observe the symptom.

- *Path differentiation*. As in path division, elaborate causal pathways between disorder and symptom. Here the motivation is to discover intermediate events that will allow us to differentiate between disorders that have similar symptoms.

- *Test differentiation*. Determining the degree of confidence to be placed in test results. Evidence is normally the result of tests which have varying degrees of reliability.
- *Test conditionalization*. Determine the background conditions that affect the reliability of tests. Such information has a bearing on the significance of observations in particular cases.

MORE begins by eliciting from an expert some basic information concerning diagnosable disorders and observable symptoms. Then it evokes knowledge-acquisition strategies selectively, based on its current state of knowledge. It is worth looking at MORE's knowledge representation in more detail, to understand the conditions under which the different strategies are deployed.

The MORE domain requires three kinds of production rule:

- *Diagnostic rules*. These perform the heuristic mapping between symptoms and hypotheses typically found in systems like MYCIN, ONCOCIN and MUD.
- *Symptom confidence rules*. These qualify the data abstraction implicit in the symptom space with estimates of test reliability under different background conditions.
- *Hypothesis expectancy rules*. These qualify the solution abstraction implicit in the hypothesis space with estimates of the prior probability of hypotheses under different background conditions.

MUD's diagnostic rules differ from MYCIN's in that they have two confidence factors associated with them: a positive and a negative one. The positive factor represents the degree of support for the conclusion when the rule's conditions are satisfied, while the negative factor represents the amount of disbelief in the conclusion when the rule's condition is not satisfied. Symptom confidence and hypothesis expectancy rules use only one confidence factor. For symptom confidence rules, the value represents the degree of change in the system's confidence in an observation. For hypothesis expectancy rules, the value represents degree of change in the expected likelihood of a hypothesis, given the rule's conditions.

MORE maintains both an *event model* and a *rule model*. The event model consists of symptoms, hypotheses and conditions, connected together by links, as in Figure 15.1. This representation is used to generate the required production rules, rather as OPAL generates rules from its domain model.

More precisely, MORE generates whole *families* of diagnostic rules, one for each diagnostic hypothesis. For example, MORE might generate the following diagnostic rule directly from the MUD event model:

```
If there is an increase in chlorides            [rule 1]
Then there is salt contamination.
```

However, this rule is too general. It needs qualifying, for example by the strategy of symptom distinction, which identifies the effect of background conditions upon the significance of a symptom. The following rule might therefore be added to the *salt contamination* rule family:

```
If there is an increase in chlorides            [rule 2]
and the drilling fluid is undersaturated
Then there is salt contamination.
```

MORE manages its rule families in the following way. When it learns of a new condition relevant to a hypothesis, it creates a new, single-condition rule and adds it to the rule family for that hypothesis. If this condition is relevant to other rules already in the rule family, then this condition will be added to those rules. (If the new condition does not manifest itself with other conditions in a rule, then that rule is not modified.) Rules to which a new condition has been added are called *constituent rules*; these are discussed further in the following section on confidence factors.

Symptom distinction is an example of a strategy which serves to refine existing diagnostic rule families. It is called into play when a family contains no rules with extreme positive confidence factors. The initial rule given above is too general to be given a high confidence factor and, since it is the only rule in the rule family, symptom distinction is called on to refine the rule. Eventually, rules like rule 1, whose conditions are subsumed by those of other rules, are eliminated from the family. This can be seen as enforcing (in advance) the preference for more specific rules found in most conflict-resolution strategies.

Symptom conditionalization, on the other hand, is evoked when there are no rules in a family that have extreme *negative* confidence factors. In this case, MORE attempts to elicit background conditions that make a symptom more or less likely, given the hypothesis. Knowledge of conditions that increase the likelihood of a symptom allows the problem solver to rule out a hypothesis if a strongly suggested symptom does not occur.

Other strategies – such as differentiation, path differentiation and path division – serve to create *new* rule families. The differentiation strategy is pursued when MORE discovers a pair of hypotheses, H_1 and H_2, which have no *differentiating symptom* (that is, there is no symptom in the event model which is linked to H_1 but not to H_2) and are therefore, for all practical purposes, in the same family. MORE elicits such a symptom, and adds it to the event model with appropriate links. This more elaborate event model will then be used to generate a distinct rule family for each of H_1 and H_2.

The path differentiation strategy is selected when a symptom in the event model is linked to two different hypotheses. MORE elicits from the expert an intermediate event that causes the symptom, and is caused by one hypothesis but not the other. Observing such an event will help discriminate between the competing explanations of the symptom, and so a rule family is created for it.

The path division strategy is evoked when a rule family is found to lack a rule which associates a high negative confidence factor with failure to observe a symptom of that family's hypothesis. MORE then seeks an intermediate event which is caused by the hypothesis. Failure to observe such an event will constitute stronger evidence against the hypothesis than failure to observe the symptom, and so a rule family is created for it.

The remaining strategies – frequency conditionalization, test differentiation and test conditionalization – are pursued when a rule family lacks a rule with either a high or a low positive or negative confidence factor. In such a situation, the rules are not informative enough to solve the classification problem. Eliciting information about new tests and test conditions, and estimates concerning the prior probabilities of hypotheses under various background conditions, will tend to either increase or reduce the confidence factors of heuristic rules mapping symptoms to hypotheses. Information of the first kind is ultimately turned into symptom confidence rules, while information of the second kind is turned into hypothesis expectancy rules.

15.2.3 Confidence factors in MORE

It was mentioned earlier that experts often have problems assigning certainty factors to rules, and like to review rules that they have already written, for the purposes of comparison. They are obviously striving for some notion of consistency in both the degree of significance that they accord to different pieces of evidence and the strength of the association between evidence and hypotheses. The question then arises as to how experts can best be helped with this task.

MORE entertains expectations about the assignment of confidence factors to rules. If the values assigned to rules violate any of these expectations, MORE cautions the knowledge engineer, and explains the inconsistency. The user then has the option of modifying one of the conflicting confidence factors.

MORE's expectations concerning confidence factors are as follows.

- Suppose that a disorder D leads to a symptom, S_1, and S_1 leads to another symptom, S_2, then MORE expects that the negative

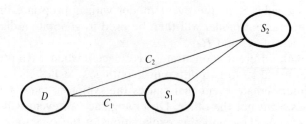

Figure 15.2 Negative confidence factors in causal chains.

confidence factor associated with the rule that maps S_1 to D will be greater than or equal to the negative confidence factor associated with the rule that maps S_2 to D. In Figure 15.2, we expect that $C_1 \geq C_2$, where C_1 weights the association between S_1 and D, and C_2 weights the association between S_2 and D. The intuitive idea behind this expectation is that failure to observe S_1 is stronger evidence against D that failure to observe S_2, all other things being equal. Referring back to Figure 15.1, the negative association between *water influx* and *increase in unemulsified water* should be greater than that between *water influx* and *increase in viscosity*.

- The diagnostic significance of a symptom is an inverse function of the number of hypotheses that could account for that symptom. In Figure 15.3, MORE expects that $C_1 > C_2$, because S_1 is only caused by D_1, whereas S_2 could be caused by other disorders.

- MORE has expectations regarding the relative values of confidence factors associated with rules in the same rule family. (Recall that rule families are formed by rules that draw conclusions about the same hypothesis.) For example, when we add to a rule family a symptom condition which increases the conditional likelihood of the symptom, this should result in rules which have greater negative confidence factors than their constituent rules. (Recall that constitutent rules are the extant rules to which the new condition was added.) The rationale behind this expectation is that the more we anticipate a particular symptom, given a particular hypothesis, the greater our shift towards disbelief in the hypothesis if that symptom is not observed.

Thus each of these expectations attempts to enforce certain qualitative notions of consistency on the assignment of confidence factors to rules within a family. The notion of a rule family is crucial here, as it was in the implementation of MYCIN, where rules were also grouped according to the parameters that they updated.

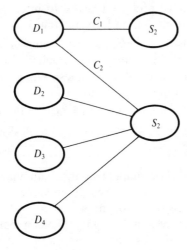

Figure 15.3   Positive confidence factors where there are many causes.

15.3   Evaluating MORE

In his thesis, Shortliffe (1976) acknowledged the need for a knowledge-elicitation mechanism to help the expert with problems such as consistency and independence in assigning weights to MYCIN production rules. Buchanan and Shortliffe (1984, Chapter 10, Section 5) reprint a number of memos which discuss some salient issues. These are also worth reading because they discuss the question of how easy it is to add rules to the rule set and modify existing rules.

MORE clearly goes some way towards helping to enforce notions of consistency which are both intuitively reasonable and easy to understand. However, MORE does not address the problem of independence that Shortliffe raised. We saw in Chapter 6 that the application of Bayes' theorem requires that evidences be independent if we are to combine weights of evidence using a simple multiplication scheme.

Shortliffe suggested that dependent pieces of evidence should be grouped into single rather than multiple rules, and treated as a 'super symptom' whose weight approximates that of the conjunction of individual symptoms. MORE does not appear to enforce this preference, although it has some of the necessary information in the event model, given that the latter encodes causal relationships. Such empirical studies as have been performed confirm that confidence factors diverge most widely from probabilities when independence assumptions are violated (Buchanan and Shortliffe, 1984, Chapter 11, Section 5).

Kahn acknowledges a number of other problems with the MORE prototype.

- Users would have preferred MORE to infer rule weights somehow from the event model, and ask far fewer questions in general.

- Concepts such as *hypothesis* and *symptom* were not familiar to domain experts in factory-floor applications, whose knowledge appeared to be encoded in troubleshooting procedures for dealing with different kinds of breakdown.

- A conventional alphanumeric interface to the system was judged to be 'completely inadequate' even for the purposes of experimenting with the prototype.

The last point shows how important the man–machine interface to an expert system is. Unless users can easily understand what they see on the screen, and search effectively for the information they need, they will not understand what the system is doing. Development and debugging is greatly enhanced by the use of mouse- and window-oriented graphic displays which enable a user to interleave the activities of browsing, editing and executing programs.

Another problem was that MORE was implemented in OPS5, and so the event model had to be coded in terms of complex vectors held in working memory. Such a representation is not well suited to the encoding of causal knowledge, and so the event model was hard to build, modify and maintain. With the benefit of hindsight, we can see that a structured object representation (see Chapter 9) should have been used.

Since MORE, a number of programs have been written which set out to elicit knowledge for expert systems that do heuristic classification, and we shall encounter one of these programs (TDE) in the next chapter.

Bibliographical notes

MOLE (Eshelman and McDermott, 1986; Eshelman *et al.*, 1987; Eshelman, 1988) is another interesting expert system shell for classification problem solving. It is rather more sophisticated, and perhaps harder to understand, than MORE. Briefly, it distinguishes between *covering knowledge* (knowledge that maps data to hypotheses) and *differentiating knowledge* (knowledge that allows one to choose between competing hypothesis), and uses this distinction to structure the processes of knowledge elicitation and knowledge base refinement.

STUDY SUGGESTIONS

15.1 Represent the following knowledge about automotive troubleshooting as a MORE-style domain model in the manner of Figure 15.1. (It is taken from the *Owners Workshop Manual* for the BMW 320.) Non-programmers can just draw the graph, but programmers may wish to use a rule-based language to encode the finished model.

Symptom	Causes
● Engine fails to turn...	
No current at starter motor	Flat battery Loose battery leads Defective starter solenoid Engine earth strap disconnected
Current at starter motor	Jammed starter motor drive pinion Defective starter motor
● Engine turns but will not start...	
No spark at spark plug	Ignition leads damp or wet Distributor cap damp or wet Dirty contact breaker points Incorrectly set contact breaker points Faulty condenser (early models) Defective ignition switch Faulty coil (early models)
No fuel at carburettor jets	No petrol in tank Vapour lock in fuel line (hot climate or high altitude) Blocked needle float chamber valve Blocked jets Faulty fuel pump
● Engine stalls and will not restart	
Carburettor flooding	Too much choke Float damaged Float lever incorrectly adjusted
No fuel at carburettor jets	No petrol in tank Petrol tank breather choked Obstruction in carburettor Water in fuel system

15.2 (a) Encode the knowledge in Figure 15.1 (or Study suggestion 15.1, if you prefer) using a structured object representation.

(b) Write a program that compiles this representation into a production rule format, for example in the OPS5 syntax.

16 Hierarchical Hypothesize and Test

Introduction

In this chapter, we consider three systems that employ a method that combines aspects of both heuristic classification and constructive problem solving, known as *hierarchical hypothesize-and-test*. As in heuristic classification, we are still interested in the mapping between data abstractions and solution abstractions, but there is the added complication that solution elements so derived may need to be combined into a *composite hypothesis* to explain all the data. A classic example is differential diagnosis, where a patient presents with a variety of signs and symptoms, and the clinician's job is to postulate the presence of one or more disease processes that account for them all.

Admitting composite hypotheses complicates matters considerably, and calls for a structuring of the search space to make it more manageable. Hierarchical hypothesize and test attacks the problem by reasoning with an explicit taxonomic representation of the space of hypotheses; this is usually a tree whose leaves are solution elements. Not surprisingly, the knowledge representation is normally based upon structured objects organized in a hierarchy, and the pattern of hypothesis activation is guided by this organization, as well as by some overall control regime.

The CENTAUR system (Aikins, 1983) is considered first, because it is well documented and easy to understand. Then we consider another system, called INTERNIST (Pople, 1977), which is large and complex enough to address many of the problems associated with this approach. Finally, we examine a more recent system, called TEST (Kahn *et al.*, 1987), which shows that the hierarchical strategy also has some implications for knowledge elicitation.

16.1 Motivation and overview

In a system like MYCIN, which deals with only a fraction of a small branch of medicine (the blood infections), exhaustive depth-first search with pruning may be an acceptable way for a machine to approach the problem of checking out alternatives.

But what if you were interested in the whole of internal medicine? The number of distinct diseases that a clinician is likely to encounter is not huge (estimates vary between 2000 and 10 000 diagnostic categories), yet it is not unknown for a patient to be suffering from ten or more concurrent diseases. As Pople pointed out, in the worst case, an exhaustive backward-chaining program would need to consider about 10^{40} diagnostic categories!

When the solution space is potentially very large, hierarchical hypothesize-and-test is extremely beneficial. The search space can then be thought of as a tree which represents a taxonomy of solution types, with nodes higher up standing for 'vaguer' solutions than nodes lower down, and with terminal nodes standing for actual solutions. The process of refining hypotheses is now very much easier, because the structure of the solution space can be used to derive focusing and scheduling heuristics, as we shall see.

Figure 16.1 shows a portion of the disease hierarchy used by the CENTAUR system. The root node is PULMONARY-DISEASE, and all other nodes represent kinds of pulmonary disease (lung disease). The immediate successors stand for subtypes of lung disease, such as an obstructive defect, while leaf nodes stand for kinds of obstructive defect which can be diagnosed and treated.

Of course, to represent the whole of internal medicine in this manner, the tree would be very large indeed. In INTERNIST, the tree is organized around the various organ systems – lungs, liver, heart, and so on. Although the hierarchical organization aids search, it does not abolish the problem of finding the best explanation of a set of case data, given that disease hypotheses may need to be combined to cover all the signs and symptoms.

This variation of hypothesize and test is particularly useful in cases where:

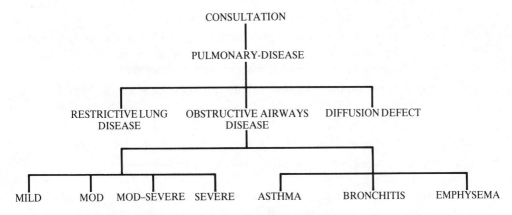

Figure 16.1 A hierarchical representation of lung diseases.

- the association between evidence and hypotheses which correspond to solutions is weak or noisy, but the association between initial data and 'non-terminal' hypotheses is reasonably good, and there exist methods for refining hypotheses and discriminating between them once they have been established;

- a fully expanded set of rules might be highly redundant, because of a large number of shared conditions associated with many of the conclusions, or else might obscure some important structural principles implicit in the domain;

- we are interested in explicitly representing and manipulating the space of hypotheses which are competing at any one time, rather than pursuing competing hypotheses independently;

- the conditions are not equally easy to establish, either computationally or according to other criteria such as cost or risk, and so the process of evidence gathering must itself be represented and reasoned about;

- multiple solutions and partial solutions may be possible or acceptable, for example, a patient may be suffering from more than one disease, or knowing the general class of disease or the principal alternative diseases may be sufficient for some form of treatment.

A simple algorithm for hierarchical hypothesize-and-test can be sketched as follows:

(1) Read in initial data.

(2) For each evoked hypothesis, give it a score which reflects what proportion of the data it accounts for.

(3)   Determine the best scoring node, n.

(4)   If n is a terminal node, then quit, else partition the whole hypothesis space into two sets, K and L, where K contains the successors of n, and L puts n's competitors on hold.

(5)   Gather more data that will discriminate between the hypotheses in K, and rate them.

(6)   Let k be the best scoring node in K and l be the best node in L.

(7)   If k scores better than l, then let n be k, else let n be l.

(8)   Go to 4.

The general approach used in CENTAUR involves seeing how well some (possibly idealized) representation of a hypothetical disease actually fits the facts. Nodes in CENTAUR's disease tree are activated by data, instantiated and scored on the basis of how much of the data they account for and how well they predict other data points. High scoring nodes are placed on an agenda, to be followed up. Roughly speaking, following up means seeing how well each of the node's successors explains the data. In this way, the program converges on a set of high-scoring terminal nodes which constitute good hypotheses.

16.2   Structured objects in CENTAUR

To explain how CENTAUR works, it will help if we first summarize the domain of application. CENTAUR reconstructs a medical expert system called PUFF (Kunz *et al.*, 1978; Aikins *et al.*, 1984), originally implemented in EMYCIN. PUFF's task is to interpret measurements gained from certain tests of pulmonary function (the working of the lungs). Typical measurements are the amount of gas in the lungs, and the rates of flow of gases into and out of the lungs. The purpose of the tests is to determine whether the patient shows signs of lung disease, and gauge the severity of his or her condition.

16.2.1   The structure of prototypes

The basic idea in CENTAUR is that frame-like structures provide an explicit representation of the context in which production rules do their reasoning. This allows one to separate strategic knowledge about how to control the reasoning from situational knowledge about what can be inferred from what set of facts. In theory, this allows inferential knowledge to be put to different uses in different contexts, with gains in both economy and coherence for the knowledge representation.

Thus production rules can be conceived of as simply one kind of value for a particular kind of slot in a frame. Associating rules with slots in frames provides one mechanism for organizing rules into what appear to be natural groupings. The other slots in a given frame provide the explicit context in which its rules are applied.

The frame-like structures used in CENTAUR are *prototypes*, *components* and *facts*. Of the 24 prototypes, 21 represent disease patterns in pulmonary function, one represents knowledge common to all such diseases, while the other two represent relatively domain-free knowledge about how to run a consultation and how to review the evidence. Thus knowledge is organized around the diagnostic categories themselves, rather than this organization being implicit in a set of unstructured rules.

Prototypes in CENTAUR contain both object-level and meta-level knowledge. They are arranged in a network. At the top of the hierarchy is the CONSULTATION prototype, which effectively controls the way in which the consultation develops through various stages, such as initial data entry and the triggering of hypotheses. Then there is a layer of prototypes which represent different pathological states, such as RESTRICTIVE LUNG DISEASE and OBSTRUCTIVE AIRWAYS DISEASE, which we have already seen in Figure 16.1. Finally, diseases are specialized according to their subtypes and degree of severity. Thus OBSTRUCTIVE AIRWAYS DISEASE can be categorized as MILD, MODERATE, MODERATELY SEVERE or SEVERE, while its subtypes are ASTHMA, BRONCHITIS and EMPHYSEMA.

Each prototype has slots for a number of components, which point to subframes of knowledge at the object level. Thus, associated with each pulmonary disease prototype, there are slots which represent lung tests, each of which is a frame-like structure in its own right, with its own internal structure. For example, the OAD (Obstructive Airways Disease) frame has 13 components, each with its associated name, range of plausible values, and importance measure. In addition, a component frame often contains a special slot, called 'inference rules', which holds a set of production rules for inferring a value for that component. If no such rule set is provided, or if the rule set fails to return a value, the system questions the user. This provision of a rule set is rather like procedural attachment: the main differences are the stylized syntax in which rules are written and the gain in modularity over the use of general procedures. Conventional procedural attachment can involve arbitrarily complex pieces of LISP code which are hard to understand and modify.

The facts that the program works with are frames with six slots, containing information about the name of the parameter, its value, the degree of certainty, its source, classification and justification.

As well as domain-specific knowledge, prototypes contain *control slots*, meta-level knowledge about how to reason with these knowledge structures. The slots hold LISP clauses for:

- instantiating a prototype, by specifying a set of components for which values should be determined;
- reacting to its confirmation or disconfirmation, by specifying the set of prototypes to be explored next;
- printing statements that summarize the final conclusion.

Each control slot can be considered as the consequent part of a rule whose condition is that the situation must match that described by the prototype.

16.2.2   Rules embedded in prototypes

The reader will remember that it is the prototype components which represent the majority of the domain-specific object-level knowledge, because it is these structures which contain information about the tests which can be used to diagnose a particular pulmonary disease. These components are the values of slots in the disease prototypes, but they have their own internal structure and are therefore prototypes in their own right. Thus, in addition to having production rules embedded in prototypes, it is true to say that there are also prototypes embedded in other prototypes. This introduces another dimension of organization in the arrangement of prototypes in addition to the hierarchical one explicitly represented in terms of types and subtypes of disease. Data structures which can be embedded in themselves in this way are often called 'recursive'.

There are five different kinds of rules used by CENTAUR:

- *Inference rules.* These are associated with components representing clinical parameters, and specify ways in which their values may be determined.
- *Triggering rules.* These are antecedent rules associated with clinical parameters which serve to advance prototypes as hypotheses with some degree of certainty.
- *Fact-residual rules.* After a conclusion has been reached, in the form of a set of confirmed prototypes, these rules attempt to account for any case data that has been left out.
- *Refinement rules.* These suggest further tests, and their execution returns a final set of prototypes with an indication of which ones account for which facts.
- *Summary rules.* These have actions which cause the information in prototypes to be translated into English and printed.

Other slots include those for general book-keeping, such as name of the author, source of the information, and those that record the circumstances under which the prototype was evoked for explanatory purposes.

CENTAUR's rules are therefore classified according to their function. In the EMYCIN implementation of PUFF, all rules are classified as inference rules, even though many of them do other things, such as summarizing evidence and setting default values. Also, because CENTAUR rules are the values of slots, their context of application is made explicit. For example, in the EMYCIN implementation of PUFF, rules for inferring the values of clinical parameters are indexed according to which parameter features in the conclusion, or action, side of the rules, as is the case in the original MYCIN program. In CENTAUR, rules for inferring a particular parameter are stored in a slot value in the prototype component representing that parameter, and only applied within in the context of that prototype, that is, when that prototype is active.

We shall see in Chapter 22 that this 'distributed' approach to the organization of production rules is taken even further in what are called *blackboard systems*. However, CENTAUR illustrates many of the benefits of associating rules with a context of application. As well as being good software engineering, this way of structuring heuristic knowledge also aids the construction of explanations (see Chapter 19).

16.3 Model-based reasoning in INTERNIST

INTERNIST is a program that sets out to model the actual steps of diagnostic reasoning performed by human clinicians. Typically, a pattern of symptoms will evoke one or more hypotheses about what could be wrong with the patient, and these in turn give rise to expectations concerning the presence or absence of other symptoms. Further observations may lead to some hypotheses being discarded or confirmed, or they may lead to new hypotheses being entertained. The initial setting up of hypotheses is *data driven*, in the sense that a particular manifestation will trigger a number of conjectures. The subsequent gathering of new data in an attempt to support or refute a hypothesis is *model driven*, in the sense that it is based on stereotypical or schematic ideas about the way in which different diseases manifest themselves.

In many reasoning tasks, including medical diagnosis, one cannot always reason directly towards one's goal (whether in a forward or a backward direction). This is because the clinician often begins with insufficient information even to formulate the problem properly. For example, there may not be enough information to delineate the space of possible diseases, or the signs and symptoms may point in more than one direction (after all, people are quite capable of suffering from more than one disease).

INTERNIST has to distinguish between a set of mutually exclusive disease hypotheses to arrive at a diagnosis. If a patient is suffering from more than one disease, the program must find a set of diseases that account for some or all of the symptoms. It does this by considering the most likely hypothesis first, noting the symptoms covered, and then proceeding to the next likely hypothesis and so on, until all the symptoms have been accounted for.

16.3.1 Representing knowledge in a disease tree

Pople describes diagnostic inference as a four-step judgemental process, along the following lines:

(1) Clinical observations must be able to suggest candidate diseases capable of causing them.

(2) These hypothesized candidates should then generate expectations with regard to what other findings might co-occur.

(3) There needs to be some method for choosing between hypotheses on the basis of available evidence.

(4) It must be possible to group hypotheses into mutually exclusive subsets, so that the acceptance of one subset means rejection of another, otherwise you would never be able to rule anything out.

The key lies in the bidirectional relationship between diseases and their associated signs and symptoms. INTERNIST considers this link as two separate relations, evocation and manifestation, as follows:

- The EVOKE relation accounts for the way in which a manifestation can suggest the presence of a disease.

- The MANIFEST relation describes the way in which a disease can manifest itself via signs and symptoms.

INTERNIST's medical knowledge is held in the *disease tree*: a hierarchical classification of disease types. The root node in this tree stands for all known diseases, non-terminals stand for *disease areas*, such as lung disease or liver disease, while terminals stand for *disease entities*, that is, actual diseases one can diagnose and treat. This is a static data structure, separate from the main body of the program, rather like MYCIN's knowledge tables. The difference is that the disease tree plays a far more active role in directing the reasoning of the program.

The INTERNIST knowledge base is constructed in the following way.

(1) The basic structure of the hierarchy is determined initially by dividing the 'root' of the disease tree into general areas of internal medicine, such as heart disease, liver disease and so on.

(2)   At the next level, subcategories are introduced which group together disease areas which are similar with respect to pattern of development (pathogenesis) and mode of clinical presentation (signs, symptoms and so on).

(3)   Further subdivision of these subcategories goes on until the level of 'disease entities' is reached, that is to say, individual diseases which can be diagnosed as such.

(4)   Then data are collected concerning the association between disease entities and their manifestations, including a list of all the manifestations associated with a particular disease, an estimate of the likelihood that the disease is the cause of the manifestation, and an estimate of the frequency with which patients suffering from the disease will exhibit each manifestation.

(5)   A list of associated manifestations $(M_1, \ldots, M_n)$ is attached to the representation of each disease entity, D, along with an evoking factor which estimates the likelihood $L(D, M_i)$ and a frequency factor which estimates $L(M_i, D)$, both factors being on a scale of 0–5.

(6)   As well as signs, symptoms and test results associated with some disease, D, there may be other diseases which are themselves manifestations of D, such as diseases caused by the original disease, D, and such causal links are also coded in the EVOKE and MANIFEST relationships.

(7)   Once all this information has been attached to the nodes representing the disease entities (which can be thought of as the 'leaves' or terminal nodes of the disease tree) there is a program which will turn the tree into a generalization hierarchy, that is to say, a tree structure in which non-terminal or 'branch' nodes share only those properties held in common by all of their successors.

(8)   Finally, data about individual manifestations are entered. The most important properties of manifestations are their TYPE (sign, symptom, laboratory finding) and IMPORT (an index on a 1–5 scale of how important a manifestation is).

Steps 1–3 create the 'superstructure' of the knowledge base, by determining its basic shape; for example, the range of categories and the levels of analysis within each category. Steps 4–6 correspond to the entry of basic medical knowledge into the database, represented in a manner that is convenient for the consultation program to use. The estimates of likelihood and frequency allow the consultation program to 'weigh the evidence' for and against a particular hypothesis.

At step 7, the program simply computes manifestations for non-terminal nodes representing disease areas by intersecting the manifestations of successor nodes. Consequently, all manifestations associated with a particular non-terminal node are also associated with every terminal or non-terminal node directly or indirectly below it in the hierarchy. For example, jaundice is a manifestation associated with particular kinds of liver disease, such as the various forms of hepatitis.

The reasoning behind this generalization procedure is as follows. It was pointed out earlier that the space of diagnostic categories for patients suffering from multiple diseases was extremely large. Because of this, conventional search methods such as depth-first search could not be expected to perform well on realistic cases. What is needed is some way of pruning this search space, or focusing the attention of the program on particular areas of the space, in such a way as to facilitate a speedy diagnosis.

The search problem would not be so acute, even in the case of multiple diseases, if there were more direct and reliable associations between diseases and their manifestations, such that the presence of a particular manifestation were sufficient to allow a clinician to conclude the presence of a particular disease. Such relations are termed 'pathognomonic', and they do actually occur. Unfortunately it is rare for a sign or symptom to be pathognomonic in this sense; it is a property more likely to be associated with findings that come from either expensive laboratory techniques or surgical procedures that one would not recommend as a matter of routine.

However, it is possible to establish quite robust associations between common manifestations and whole areas of disease at higher levels of a disease hierarchy. Thus jaundice suggests a liver problem, but bloody sputum suggests a lung problem. INTERNIST uses such associations to 'constrict' the search space, with the intention of homing in on the correct diagnostic category at a certain level of abstraction, before proceeding to the business of arriving at the right diagnosis at the level of disease entities.

The *constrictors* of a case, in Pople's terminology, are findings that cue the setting up of hypotheses within broad categories of the disease hierarchy. However, constriction is a heuristic device; it is not guaranteed to succeed. At higher levels of the hierarchy, while some manifestations are uniquely associated with disease areas, other are only predominant – they could be explained by other areas. This situation deteriorates as you go further down the hierarchy, of course.

Hence, step 7 is taken so that the consultation program can begin to make a differential diagnosis at a fairly high level in the hierarchy, using a generalization of the pathognomonic concept. This means that whole classes of diagnoses can be ruled out before going on to make an individual diagnosis. This is one of the mechanisms which make possible the use of the attention-focusing heuristics.

Step 8 elaborates on the properties of the manifestations themselves, as a further aid to the strategic level of diagnostic reasoning. For example, the TYPE property indicates how expensive it is to test for a manifestation, and how dangerous such a test might be for the patient, so that cheaper and safer manifestations can be followed up first. The IMPORT property indicates whether or not one can afford to ignore a particular manifestation in the context of a particular disease. Note that steps 5 and 8 represent a fairly informal method of handling uncertainty. Nevertheless, we shall see that the problems with INTERNIST were not caused by any imprecision or lack of rigour in this area; rather they derived from an imperfect formulation of the hypothesis space.

Finally, note how the hierarchical structure suggests strategies for eliciting knowledge from experts. Although this task was not automated in the building of INTERNIST, we shall see in Section 16.4 how a knowledge elicitation tool can be constructed which exploits such a representation.

16.3.2   Focusing attention in INTERNIST

An INTERNIST consultation proceeds in the following way. At the start of a session, the user enters a list of manifestations. Each of these evokes one or more nodes in the disease tree. The program creates a *disease model* for each such node, consisting of four lists:

(1)   observed manifestations not associated with the disease;

(2)   observed manifestations consistent with the disease;

(3)   manifestations not yet observed but which are always associated with the disease;

(4)   manifestations not yet observed but which are consistent with the disease.

Disease models receive positive scores for manifestations they explain and negative scores for ones they fail to explain. Both kinds of score are weighted by IMPORT, and a model receives a bonus if it is causally related to a disease that has already been confirmed. The disease models are then divided into two sets, depending on how they relate to the most highly rated model. One partition contains the top-ranked model and all those diseases which are mutually exclusive to it – its evoked 'sibling' nodes in the tree. The other contains all those diseases which are complementary to it, that is, evoked nodes in other disease areas.

Partitioning involves the concept of *dominance* in the following sense. Disease model D_1 dominates model D_2 if the observed manifestations not explained by D_1 (or any part diagnosis done so far) are a subset of those not explained by D_2. Given a top-ranked model, D_0, each member D_i of the evoked models list is compared with D_0. If D_0 either dominates it, or is dominated by it, then D_i is grouped with D_0 on the list of 'considered' hypotheses. Otherwise its consideration is deferred for the moment.

The rationale behind this kind of partitioning is that the set of models being considered at any one time can be treated as mutually exclusive alternatives. This is because, for any D_i and D_j in the set, the diagnosis consisting of D_i and D_j would add little or nothing to the explanatory power of either D_i or D_j on their own. Deferred models will be processed in similar fashion once the current problem of deciding between the models associated with D_0 has been resolved; partitioning will begin again with a new D_0, the model of best fit from among the deferred models.

After the initial input, some nodes will have been evoked and others not. The problem for the program is to transform the tree from this starting state to a solution state. A solution state consists of a tree with evoked terminal nodes which account for all of the symptoms.

Having partitioned the disease models, the program uses a number of alternative strategies, depending on how many hypotheses it is entertaining.

- If there are more than four hypotheses, it adopts a refutation strategy (RULEOUT mode), and tries to eliminate as many as possible, asking questions about symptoms that strongly indicate the presence of candidate diseases.

- If there are between two and four possibilities, it adopts a differentiation strategy (DISCRIMINATE mode), asking questions that will help decide between candidate diseases.

- If there is only one candidate, it adopts a verification strategy (PURSUING mode), asking questions that will confirm the presence of the disease.

This whole process is iterative. Responses to queries asked in any of these modes are processed in much the same way as the original input of manifestations by the user. Thus new nodes are evoked, old nodes are updated, models are ranked and partitioned, and a (possibly new) mode is selected resulting in further questions being asked.

16.3.3   Practical and theoretical problems with INTERNIST

In summary, the INTERNIST program worked like this. During the initial input phase, patient data could be entered in any order and any amount. Each positive finding evoked a differential diagnostic task that might involve both disease areas (non-terminal nodes standing for classes of disease) and disease entities (terminal nodes standing for actual diseases one can diagnose and treat). Hypotheses were given credit for explaining important manifestations observed so far; they were penalized when manifestations were expected but not found in the patient. Given a ranked list of hypotheses, two disease entities were considered to be in competition if their conjunction explained no more of the data than each would explain separately. Having determined a set of alternatives in this way, the program had formulated a differential diagnostic task. The set containing the highest scoring hypothesis and its competitors then became the current focus of the problem solver.

However, it should be stressed that INTERNIST did not actually employ a simple hierarchical hypothesize-and-test algorithm of the general form outlined in Section 16.1. This was because symptoms which evoked a particular non-terminal node might also be significant for other nodes in the disease tree. Thus the program could not assume that the disease that the patient was actually suffering from must therefore be found among the successors of the non-terminal node. So although cholestasis accounts for symptoms of jaundice, other diseases, quite unrelated to cholestasis in the disease tree, might also exhibit such symptoms, for example, alcoholic hepatitis. Thus, although the basic idea of the disease tree is that nodes which are close to each other in the hierarchy are those which have symptoms in common, the program must often gather hypotheses from further afield when postulating a differential diagnostic task.

This departure, although necessary, caused problems. Pople (1982) later expressed dissatisfaction with INTERNIST's performance on the grounds that sometimes important patient data were disregarded by the program's control heuristics, because of a preponderance of less important findings. Since the search for a solution did not converge in quite the same way as the algorithm outlined earlier, this tended to prolong interactive sessions on difficult cases, because the program would initially set up inappropriate diagnostic tasks. Thus clinical evidence from multiple organ systems might point in different directions when considered separately, misleading the program. An experienced physician would probably integrate the data at an earlier stage to converge on a key hypothesis. Thus the simple control scheme which made the program's behaviour so robust was really too simple as a model of how clinicians actually reason.

So, although hierarchical hypothesize-and-test worked well in the application of CENTAUR to PUFF, some problems arise in scaling up to a larger domain. The method did not fail, because the INTERNIST program was still able to solve difficult problems. However, users could see that it was sometimes taking a circuitous route to the solution.

Pople concluded that the basic strategy of hierarchical hypothesize-and-test needed to be augmented by new knowledge structures which represent what a clinician knows about well-structured sets of alternatives. It seemed that INTERNIST still did not contain enough different kinds of knowledge concerning which disease entities are in genuine competition with each other, what strategy to employ once the differential has been constructed, and what are useful criteria for ruling hypotheses in or out. In Clancey's terminology (see Chapter 12), there were structural and strategic aspects of medical problem solving which were not represented or rendered explicit in either the organization of the hypothesis space or the inference procedure which constructed and solved differential diagnostic tasks.

16.4 TDE as knowledge-engineering workbench

TDE (Kahn *et al.*, 1987) is a development environment for an expert system tool called TEST (Pepper and Kahn, 1987), which is primarily intended for solving classification problems, such as diagnosis. (TEST stands for Troubleshooting Expert System Tool, and TDE stands for TEST Development Environment.) However, these programs differ from both the MYCIN/EMYCIN approach (see Chapter 13) and that of MUD/MORE (see Chapter 15), in a number of important respects.

- The primary unit of representation is the structured object, rather than the production rule. (TDE is implemented in a frame-based language called Knowledge Craft, which is briefly described in Chapter 20.)

- Objects represent concepts that more closely resemble the way that troubleshooters think about equipment. Thus abstract notions such as *hypothesis* and *symptom* are replaced by more concrete notions, such as *failure mode* and *test procedure* (which are explained below).

- Users organize their knowledge by manipulating icons in a high-resolution, bit-mapped interface. (As we saw in Chapter 13, OPAL also uses graphical representations to good effect.)

- The representation of knowledge has a strong procedural aspect; for example, it associates test procedures with failure modes, in addition to computing degrees of belief in hypotheses as a function of the symptoms observed.

The failure mode is perhaps the most important concept in TEST and TDE: it denotes any deviation of the unit under test, whether a total breakdown or the malfunctioning of a small component. Thus, in the domain of car maintenance, 'failure to start' would be an obvious failure mode, but so would 'flat battery'. In a more traditional expert systems analysis, one would have to decide whether 'flat battery' was a hypothesis that accounted for data or a datum in itself. This distinction does not seem to be as central to TEST as it is to MUD and MYCIN. The other concepts around which knowledge is organized are:

- procedures for the test and repair of failures; and
- explicit causal relationships among failures.

Failure modes are organized into a tree, with the root node typically representing device breakdown and the leaf nodes representing the failure of individual components. Non-terminal nodes represent failures of function within the device, for example 'lights not working'. Many levels of such failures are possible between total breakdown and component failures.

As with CENTAUR and INTERNIST, this tree of disorders is the primary structure of a TEST knowledge base. A secondary level of structure is provided by procedures for performing tests and repairs, as well as various kinds of rule, which represent procedural knowledge associated with failure modes; for example, what measurements to make to confirm a failure, how to fix a failure, and how to search for component failures that account for a failure mode. Finally, there is a tertiary layer of declarative knowledge provided by various attributes associated with failure modes, which describe such things as important properties of components and relationships between them.

Although TEST's knowledge base is not structured around the traditional concepts of symptom and hypothesis, what TEST does is still recognizable as a form of heuristic classification. Failure modes higher up the tree represent data abstractions, while those lower down represent solution abstractions. The task that TEST performs is to construct a causal chain from high-level failure modes, such as 'failure to start', to lower level modes, such as 'battery flat'. The mapping between data and solution abstractions consists of *due-to* and *always-leads-to* relations between failure modes in the tree. The heuristic aspect is encoded by attaching rules to nodes in the tree, which guide the search for lower level modes.

TDE is a relatively new system, which makes a recognizable attempt to improve on aspects of MORE. It is not possible to attempt to evaluate the protoype at the time of writing, although certain trends in the design are obvious. For example, it is clear that the graphical interface gives users more freedom in how they go about building the knowledge base than MORE did. However, novices have the option of being led by interrogation techniques, which encourage them to elaborate the tripartite structure of the knowledge base in the order that the three layers are described above. It is possible to move between 'guided' and 'unguided' modes of interaction with the system.

Comparing TDE and MORE, once can see that there is more than one way to go about the business of designing tools for eliciting and structuring knowledge, even within a given problem-solving method, such as heuristic classification. There is a lot that we still do not know about how to compare and contrast such approaches for the purposes of evaluation. Nevertheless, prototypes such as MORE and TDE are essential data points in this empirical enterprise, because the problem of knowledge elicitation will not be solved by theorizing alone, however inspired.

Bibliographical notes

Pople (1982) gives a thorough account of INTERNIST and related research efforts. However, not all of the ideas expressed in this paper have been implemented or pursued. The CENTAUR architecture has been successfully applied to domains other than medicine; for example, the REX program, which advises a statistician on the analysis of regression problems (Gale, 1986). Gale (1987) describes a knowledge-elicitation program called Student, created for the REX domain, which has some similarities with the OPAL system outlined in Chapter 13, in that it is knowledge based, rather than being based on a particular problem-solving strategy.

STUDY SUGGESTIONS

16.1 This exercise requires a little background about pulmonary function test interpretation, but no previous medical knowledge is required to understand the simplified story I am going to give here. (Such that I know of this subject I owe to Drs Jeremy Wyatt and Patricia Tweedale. Any errors of fact or emphasis are obviously my fault, but they need not affect the validity of the exercise.)

Some important medical parameters in diagnosing respiratory defects are as follows:

- FEV1. Forced expiratory volume in 1 second, measured in litres. The associated test measures the amount of air you can expel from your lungs in a single second. It is an index of elasticity (and hence health) of lung tissue.
- IFEV1. This is the increment in FEV1 following the administration of a bronchodilator: a drug that helps your tubes relax.
- FVC. Forced vital capacity, that is, how much air your lungs can take in if you force them.
- IFVC signifies the increase in FVC after administration of a bronchodilator.
- TLC. Total lung capacity.
- RV. Residual volume, that is, the amount of air left in the lungs after expiration.

- RATIO1 = FEV1/FVC.
- RATIO2 = FEV1/FVC after administration of a bronchodilator.

In the specification I shall give below, the variable PRED will stand for the predicted value of any of the above parameters; context will make the parameter clear. (The predicted value of a medical parameter depends largely upon the gender of the patient.) Expressions such as

$$80\% < RATIO1 < 100\% \text{ (PRED-2SD)}$$

signify that RATIO1 is between 80 and 100% of the predicted value less two standard deviations from the mean value for the parameter in the relevant population.

RTB stands for Response To Bronchodilation

(a) Design frames for each of the following respiratory defects and their associated medical parameters, organizing them into a hierarchy along the lines of CENTAUR (see Figure 16.1), under the root note PULMONARY DISEASE.

> **AIRWAYS OBSTRUCTION**
> present if:
> > RATIO1 < PRED-2SD
> no RTB if:
> > RATIO2 < PRED-2SD
> good RTB if:
> > RATIO2 > PRED-2SD
>
> SLIGHT AIRWAYS OBSTRUCTION
> present if:
> > 80% < RATIO1 < 100% of (PRED-2SD)
> no RTB if:
> > IFEV1 < FEV1/10
> > IFVC < FVC/10
> good RTB if:
> > FEV1 > (PRED-2SD)/4
> > FEV1/3 < IFEV1
>
> MODERATE AIRWAYS OBSTRUCTION
> present if:
> > 55% < RATIO1 < 80% of (PRED-2SD)
>
> SEVERE AIRWAYS OBSTRUCTION
> present if:
> > RATIO ≤ 55% of PRED-2SD

RESTRICTIVE DEFECT
present if:
    RV < PRED+2SD
    TLC ≤ 80% of PRED-2SD
    RATIO1 > 80% of PRED-2SD

EARLY RESTRICTIVE DEFECT
present if:
    TLC < PRED-2SD
    RATIO1 > PRED-2SD

MILD RESTRICTIVE DEFECT
present if:
    RATIO1 > PRED-2SD
    80% < TLC < 100% of PRED-2SD

MODERATE RESTRICTIVE DEFECT
present if:
    RATIO1 > PRED-2SD
    60% < TLC < 80% of PRED-2SD

SEVERE RESTRICTIVE DEFECT
present if:
    RATIO1 > PRED-2SD
    TLC < 60% of PRED-2SD

You will need procedures to capture the diagnostic knowledge associated with them. Each frame needs to have slots which hold the predicted value of a parameter, together with the necessary standard deviation values. Thus the slot PRED-RATIO1 could hold the expected value for the parameter RATIO1, while the slot SD-RATIO could hold the standard deviation of this parameter. Clearly, for the purposes of this exercise, it does not matter what these values are. All your procedures need to do is reference the relevant slots.

For example, SEVERE-RESTRICTIVE-DEFECT could be a frame/object with a LISP procedure/method called PRESENT, defined along the lines of

```
SEVERE-RESTRICTIVE-DEFECT.PRESENT
    (and (> RATIO1 (- PRED-RATIO1 (* SD-RATIO1 2)))
         (< TLC (/ (* 6 (- PRED-TLC (* SD-TLC 2))) 10)))
```

which returns T if the relevant conditions are met.

(b) Encode the diagnostic knowledge associated with these frames in production rules instead of procedures. As with the procedures, assume that rules can reference slot values in a straightforward manner.

16.2 (a) Design and implement a simple knowledge-elicitation program that allows a user to declare a fault in some device and list possible causes of that fault. For example, in the automobile domain, the program should be able to elicit a TDE-style failure mode, such as 'engine does not turn', refine it with tests, such as 'is there current at the starter motor?' and associate possible causes with each refinement. Thus 'no current at starter motor' is explicable by causes such as 'defective battery'and 'defective starter solenoid'. Nodes such as 'defective battery' are amenable to further refinement, such as 'flat battery' or 'loose battery leads'. The program should store all this information in a tree structure, such as that described in Section 16.4.

(b) Test your program, either on someone other than yourself who is knowledgeable about the domain, or on yourself. If you are not yourself knowledgeable, and cannot find an expert, get the knowledge you need from some source. For example, troubleshooting knowledge about cars can be gleaned from workshop manuals, as in Study suggestion 15.1.

17 Constructive Problem Solving (I)

17.1 Motivation and overview
17.2 Case study: R1/XCON
17.3 Elicitation, evaluation and extensibility

Bibliographical notes
Study suggestions

Introduction

At the end of Chapter 14, we noted that the distinguishing feature of constructive problem solving was that solutions have to be built out of more primitive components. We contrasted this with classification problem solving, where solutions can be selected from some fixed set. The next two chapters describe artificial intelligence techniques that have been found useful for constructive problem solving, and illustrate these techniques with examples from the literature.

17.1 Motivation and overview

Typical tasks that require constructive problem solving are planning, design and certain kinds of diagnosis. In planning, the solution elements are actions, and solutions are sequences of actions that achieve goals. In design, the solution elements are components, and solutions are combinations of components which form a complex object that satisfies certain constraints. In the diagnosis of multiple disorders, the solution elements are disorders, and solutions are sets of disorders which account for the symptoms (as we saw in Chapter 16).

In each of these cases, it is infeasible to fix the solution set in advance. There are too many different ways in which actions can be ordered, components can be assembled, and faults can co-occur. Furthermore, actions can interfere with each other, components compete for space and connections, and disorders may interact in various ways, such as via causal relationships.

Relatively simple versions of each of these tasks can be solved by classification. For example, we saw in Chapter 13 that ONCOCIN planned cancer therapies by selecting from a library of skeletal plans which only needed to be instantiated appropriately before being proposed as solutions. Nevertheless, more complex problems require the ability to construct and revise plans more flexibly from primitive actions.

As we noted in Chapter 4, the naive approach to tasks such as planning runs into problems of computational complexity, because the size of the search space is an exponential function of the number of solution elements. This does not present too much difficulty if solutions are plentiful and we are not too fussy about the quality of the solution. Unguided search may find a satisfactory solution in a reasonable time. But, if we want a near optimal solution to a complex problem, unguided search is doomed to failure on even the most powerful computers. What is required is knowledge that can be used to constrict the solution space and focus the search on combinations of elements that make good solutions.

In the next section, we look at a system that uses a problem-solving method called *Match*. The Match method is useful when there is sufficient domain knowledge to recognize the right thing to do at any given point in the computation. It permits a 'propose and apply' approach to problem solving, in which the emphasis is on selecting the right operator to extend partial solutions. In Chapter 18, we shall see that this approach will not work for all constructive problems. However, when applicable, it is more flexible than consulting a library of partial solutions.

17.2   Case study: R1/XCON

R1 (McDermott, 1980, 1981, 1982a) is arguably one of the success stories of expert systems in the 1980s. It is a program that configures VAX computer systems by first checking that the order is complete and then determining the spatial arrangement of components. The commercial version of the system, developed by a collaboration between Carnegie-Mellon University and Digital Equipment Corporation, is called XCON; I shall sometimes distinguish the two when discussing the historical development of the program. R1/XCON is interesting because it shows what a relatively weak problem solving method can achieve if you have enough domain knowledge. Its story also illustrates the way in which a commercial system grows, and how that growth can best be managed.

R1's task is not trivial. Computer systems typically consist of 50–150 components, the main ones being the central processor, memory control units, unibus and massbus interfaces, all connected to a synchronous backplane. The buses can support a wide range of peripheral devices, such as tape drives, disk drives and printers, giving rise to a wide variety of different system configurations.

Given an order, R1 has to decide on both a combination of components that completes the specification and what their spatial arrangement should be. Deciding whether or not a configuration is complete is difficult, because it requires knowledge of individual components and their relationships. Deciding on a spatial arrangement is difficult, because there are many *constraints* that need to be taken into account. For example, assigning unibus modules to the backplanes involves taking into account features such as the amperage available on the backplane and the interrupt priority of the modules. This configuration task is therefore a classic construction problem that requires considerable expertise.

17.2.1 Components and constraints

Although both R1 and MYCIN are production rule programs, they differ substantially in a number of important respects. One difference is that MYCIN takes a *hypothesis-driven* approach to problem solving; it begins with some goal (producing a diagnosis) and then proceeds to generate subgoals, the conjoined solution of which solve the original goal (see Chapter 3). R1's approach is largely *data driven*; it begins with a set of components and tries to produce a configuration within the constraints imposed by the properties of these components and relationships between them. The program is implemented in OPS5 (see Chapter 5 and Appendix B).

R1 needs two kinds of knowledge:

- knowledge about *components* – voltage, amperage, pinning-type, number of ports and so on; plus
- knowledge about *constraints* – rules for forming partial configurations of equipment and then extending them successfully.

Component knowledge is stored in a database, which is separate from both the production memory of the production system and the working memory of transient data elements. The database is therefore a static data structure, while the working memory is dynamic. Unlike the production memory, the database does not consist of pattern-directed

modules, but of more conventional record structures which state, for each
component, its class and type plus a set of attribute–value pairs. Consider
the following example, which describes an RK611* disk controller.

RK611*
      CLASS: UNIBUS MODULE
      TYPE: DISK DRIVE
      SUPPORTED: YES
      PRIORITY LEVEL: BUFFERED NPR
      TRANSFER RATE: 212
      ...

Constraint knowledge is provided by each of the rules in R1's production
memory. The left-hand sides recognize situations in which partial configurations can be extended, while the right-hand sides perform those extensions.
The working memory starts off empty and ends containing the configuration. Components are represented in working memory by component
tokens implemented as the usual attribute–value vectors. R1 can perform
five actions in accessing the component database; it can generate a new
token, find a token, find a substitute for a specific token, retrieve the
attributes associated with an existing token, and retrieve a template for
filling out.

    As well as component tokens, the working memory contains
elements that represent partial configurations of equipment, the results of
various computations, and symbols which indicate what the current task
is.

    It is frequently the case that more than one R1 rule could fire at any
one cycle. The main conflict-resolution strategy used in R1 is called 'special
case' or *specificity* (see Chapter 8). If there are two rules in the conflict
set, Rule1 and Rule2, and Rule1's conditions are a subset of Rule2's,
then Rule2 will be preferred over Rule1. Another way of looking at this
is to regard Rule1 as more 'general' than Rule2; it acts as a default which
catches cases for which Rule2 is too specific. Rule2 might therefore deal
with an exception to Rule1, in which extra factors need to be taken into
account.

    Figure 17.1 shows an English translation of a sample R1 rule, taken
from Forgy (1982). The 'current active context' referred to in the first
condition of this rule will form the subject matter of the next section.

17.2.2   Using contexts to impose task structure

In addition to information about components and constraints, R1's
working memory contains symbol structures which specify the current
context of the computation. This helps to break the configuration task
down into subtasks. Moreover, these subtasks can be arranged into a

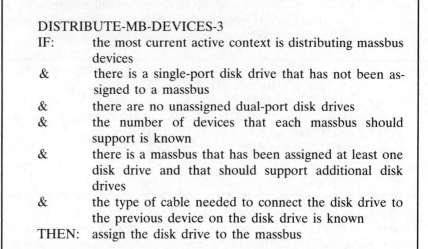

DISTRIBUTE-MB-DEVICES-3
IF: the most current active context is distributing massbus devices
 & there is a single-port disk drive that has not been assigned to a massbus
 & there are no unassigned dual-port disk drives
 & the number of devices that each massbus should support is known
 & there is a massbus that has been assigned at least one disk drive and that should support additional disk drives
 & the type of cable needed to connect the disk drive to the previous device on the disk drive is known
THEN: assign the disk drive to the massbus

Figure 17.1 An English translation of an R1 rule.

hierarchy with temporal relationships between them. In other words, the main task, say 'configure this order for a VAX-11/780' can be analysed into subtasks, like 'check that the order is correct' and 'arrange the components of the (possibly corrected) order'. Performing these two tasks constitutes performing the main task; however, they should obviously be performed in the order stated. It would make no sense to configure the components in the order, and then check that the order was correct afterwards.

Thus R1 analyses the configuration task into six immediate subtasks, each involving subtasks of their own:

(1) Check the order, inserting any omissions and correcting any mistakes.

(2) Configure the CPU, arranging components in the CPU and CPU expansion cabinets.

(3) Configure the unibus modules, putting boxes into the expansion cabinets and then putting the modules into the boxes.

(4) Configure the panelling, assigning panels to cabinets and associating panels with unibus modules and the devices they serve.

(5) Generate a floor plan, grouping components that must be closer together and then laying the devices out in the right order.

(6) Do the cabling, specifying what cables are to be used to connect devices and then determining the distances between pairs of components.

Such hierarchies can be thought of as being either *determinate* or *indeterminate* with respect to the ordering of subtasks. If there is a fixed order within the subtasks at every depth, we say that the task analysis is determinate, since the sequence of tasks is completely determined. If there is some latitude with respect to the ordering between some subtasks at some levels, the task analysis is indeterminate.

R1's task analysis is determinate, in that the tasks are always performed in the same order. This simplification is achieved as follows. Some of R1's rules serve mainly to manipulate context symbols: those working memory elements that tell the program where it has got to in the task hierarchy. Some rules recognize when a new subtask needs to be initiated; these add context symbols to working memory. Others recognize when a subtask has been completed; these remove context symbols from working memory. All other rules contain condition elements that are sensitive to context symbols, so that they only fire when their context is 'active', that is, when the requisite symbols are the 'recent' context symbols in working memory. To understand this, it is necessary to understand the conflict-resolution strategy employed by R1.

Each context symbol contains a context name, such as 'assign-power-supply', a symbol which states whether the context is active or not, and a time tag which indicates how recently the context was made active. The rules that recognize when a new subtask should be set up do this on the basis of the current state of the partial configuration. Rules which have the appropriate context symbol in their conditions will now receive preferential treatment during the recognize–act cycle. It is customary to put patterns that recognize context among the first conditions in the left-hand side of productions, so that the pattern matcher fails quickly on rules that lack the right context recognizers. Rules that deactivate contexts are simply rules whose left-hand side is composed solely of context symbols. Such a rule will fire only when all the other rules sensitive to that context have fired or failed. This is the 'special case' strategy referred to earlier, and the way it is used here ensures that R1 does all it can within a particular context before leaving it.

McDermott's justification for this use of contexts is not so much that it is somehow essential to the task of configuring a computer system. Rather, he argues that it reflects the way in which human experts actually approach the task. However, it is worth pointing out that R1 has no real knowledge of the properties of the contexts it deals with. Context names are just symbols, unlike components, say, which have all kinds of attributes and values associated with them. Consequently, R1 cannot reason about contexts in the same way that it can reason about components or constraints; it simply recognizes when a new context is needed and when it has done all it can in a particular context. This seems to be all the task requires.

17.2.3 Reasoning with constraints: the Match method

To illustrate the use of constraints by R1, let us consider subtask 3: the configuration of the unibus modules in their boxes and cabinets.

The main trouble with 'bin packing' problems of this kind is that there is usually no way of pruning the search space, because there is no suitable evaluation function for partial configurations. In other words, there is no formula that you can apply which will allow you to say that one partial configuration is better than some other partial solution. A system of functional and spatial relationships is a complex whole, and it succeeds or fails as such. It is not possible to tell in advance, by looking at some solution fragment, whether or not it will lead to a complete and acceptable solution, unless there are regularities in the system, such as various kinds of symmetry, which introduce redundancy.

In the context of subtask 3, there are certain constraints that can be used to inform the search for a solution:

- Each unibus module requires a backplane slot of the right pinning type.
- Each backplane in a box must be positioned so that its modules draw power from only one set of regulators.
- Regulators can supply only a certain amount of power, regardless of the number of slots available on the backplane.
- If a module needs panel space, the space must be in the cabinet that contains the module.
- Some modules may require supporting modules, either in the same backplane or in the same box.
- There is an optimal sequence for modules on the unibus, in terms of their interrupt priority and transfer rate, and so modules should be positioned as close to that sequence as possible.

Obviously there is a limited amount of box space. As a result, you cannot tell whether or not a module's configuration is acceptable until all the modules are on the unibuses. Sometimes R1 has to generate more than one candidate solution before an acceptable one is found.

Although R1 may have several attempts at a particular task, as in the above example, it never backtracks. In other words, it never makes a decision which it later has to go back and undo. At any point in the problem-solving process, it has enough knowledge to recognize what to do; this cuts down on trial-and-error search. Backtracking is computationally expensive, especially in terms of run-time storage, as well as making the behaviour of programs hard to understand.

The basic problem-solving method used by R1 is called, rather confusingly, 'Match'. All pattern-directed inference systems use matching to some extent, of course, but Match with a big M is more than this. A program using Match 'recognizes' what to do at any given point in its execution, rather than generating candidate solutions and then trying them out as in the generate-and-test paradigm used by expert systems like DENDRAL.

We do not usually think of matching as being search; pattern matching is normally a process whereby search is initiated, continued or terminated. For example, matching often determines whether or not an operator is applicable, or whether a solution has be found. However, Match can be considered as a search technique in which you look for an exemplar which instantiates some 'form', a form being a symbolic expression containing variables. An example of a form would be the left-hand side of a production rule: a symbol structure made up of one or more patterns which may share variables. The search space for Match is then 'the space of all instantiations of the variables in a form' (McDermott, 1982a, page 54), with each state in the space a partially instantiated form.

It is the form that embodies the domain-specific knowledge about constraint satisfaction, and it is the Match method which applies this knowledge to particular problems. However, McDermott lists two conditions which must be satisfied if this rather 'weaker' notion of search is to be successful in finding the solution to some problem:

- The *correspondence condition*. It must be possible to determine the value that a variable can take on 'locally', using only such information as is ready to hand at the point of correspondence when you compare the exemplar with the pattern. In the case of R1, 'ready to hand' information is that information which is available from the current context. Decisions must not depend on information that will only become available in 'daughter' and 'sister' contexts elsewhere in the hierarchy. This is not to say that contexts should be independent; merely that subsequent matches do not affect what has already been matched.

- The *propagation condition*. When an operator is applied, this should affect only aspects of the solution which have not yet been determined. In other words, there should be no 'retroactive' effects of decisions; decisions must be partially ordered. This condition is so called because the consequences of our decisions should propagate in one direction only: from a particular context to its daughter and (as yet unvisited) sister contexts, and not to its ancestors (or 'aunties').

McDermott divides R1's rules into three broad categories, depending on the role they play in the Match method:

(1) *Operator rules* create and extend partial configurations.

(2) *Sequencing rules* determine the order in which decisions are made, mostly by manipulating contexts.

(3) *Information-gathering rules* access the database of components or perform various computations for the benefit of the other rules.

It was noted earlier that the use of contexts in configuration had a certain psychological justification, in that human experts tended to approach the problem in this way, but no attempt was made to justify contexts by saying that they were somehow 'necessary' from a formal or computational point of view. With regard to Match, the situation is somewhat reversed. Humans frequently depart from the Match method, in that they tend to use a form of heuristic search that involves some backtracking. However, the computational advantages of Match are considerable, and there are practical reasons for supposing that heuristic search is not a good method for programming a solution to this problem, such as the inherent inefficiency of unnecessary backtracking.

17.3 Elicitation, evaluation and extensibility

In this section, we shall look at the problems of evaluation and extensibility, as well as knowledge elicitation. XCON's progress is rather better documented in this regard than most systems. Clearly, these three issues are linked, in that the quality of the knowledge determines performance, while the nature of the knowledge determines how difficult extensibility is. XCON's knowledge-elicitation problem is made harder by the sheer diversity of the knowledge required to perform the task. However, we shall see that a more penetrating analysis of the problem-solving method employed can facilitate knowledge elicitation, just as we saw in Chapters 14–16.

17.3.1 Knowledge elicitation in R1/XCON

McDermott (1982a) has a number of interesting observations to make about the initial phases of knowledge elicitation for R1.

- The experts had a reasonably clear idea of the regular decomposition of the main task into subtasks, and the temporal relationships *between* these subtasks.

- *Within* subtasks, however, their behaviour is more driven by exceptions than regularities, for example 'when performing subtask S, do X, unless Y'. Humans are not very good at recalling these exceptional circumstances on demand; they are driven by events.

This regularity of relations between tasks but irregularity within tasks is dealt with in the OPS5 implementation by the use of contexts and special cases. Refinement of rules and contexts provides a modular way of correcting erroneous behaviour during the initial stages of program development. However, McDermott (1988) points out that different kinds of knowledge were not always well differentiated within subtasks. In particular, two classes of knowledge tended to be confounded in the rules:

- knowledge about the different ways in which partial configurations could be extended; and
- knowledge about which competing extensions to select for actual execution.

Bachant (1988) joins Clancey (1983) and others in arguing for a more principled approach to this problem in which control is realized by explicit means. She notes that conflict resolution acts at too low a level to relate to the task itself, although it can obviously be used to effect decomposition into tasks, as we have seen. In a new methodology called RIME (which stands for 'R1's Implicit Made Explicit'), Bachant tries to strike a balance between over-controlling and under-controlling sequences of actions. Over-controlling involves over-specifying the order in which tasks are executed, and is typical of conventional sequential programming languages. Under-controlling is typical of the data-driven style of pattern-directed inference systems, where modules compete for the attention of the interpreter.

Bachant identifies the basic problem solving method of R1 as *propose-and-apply*, which can be analysed into the following steps:

(1) *Initialize-Goal*. This step creates a control element for the current task, removing any obsolete control elements for completed tasks.

(2) *Propose-Operator*. This step suggests plausible courses of action, rejecting those that are obviously inappropriate.

(3) *Prune-Operator*. This step eliminates operators according to global criteria, such as a predefined preference order.

(4) *Eliminate-Operator*. This step performs a pairwise comparison between any competing operators that remain and favours one over the other.

(5) *Select-One-Operator*. This step examines the results of steps 2–4 and chooses just one operator.

(6) *Apply-Operator*. This step applies an operator to the current problem state, extending a partial configuration.

(7) *Evaluate-Goal*. This step looks to see if the goal has been achieved

at the end of the cycle, terminating on success or failure, and iterating otherwise.

So what is the difference between Match and propose-and-apply? From Bachant's analysis, we can see that R1 used the weak problem solving method (Match) to implement a stronger, knowledge-based method (propose-and-apply). This is analogous to the use heuristic classification (strong method) makes of subgoaling (weak method) in MYCIN.

17.3.2 The evaluation and extension of R1/XCON

As mentioned in Chapter 3, evaluation is a difficult issue to address; it is even difficult to discuss. Expectations regarding expert system performance are often hazy. The program must run in a reasonable time and be able to deal with a collection of 'typical' cases, perhaps those cases used to elicit the knowledge from the domain expert. However, it is wishful thinking to suppose that one can devise some test or series of tests that will tell you when an expert system has reached some imaginary peak of performance.

In domains lacking the structure of formal systems like mathematics and logic, it is unlikely that you will ever be able to 'prove' that your expert system is indeed an expert in any rational sense. The evidence must be empirical, and yet the range of possible situations that your program might encounter will be vast in any non-trivial application. Even though XCON has to date processed tens of thousands of orders, it has only seen a small fraction of the space of possible orders it might receive.

McDermott reports that, in the early days of R1, it was predicted that the program would have to be 90% correct in its configurations before it began to be useful. R1 took 3 years to reach this goal, but experience showed that the prediction was in error. The program was able to assist with configuration before it reached this criterion, because it did no worse than its human predecessors. The configuration task is such that no single individual is entrusted to perform it alone; individuals typically lack both the knowledge and the time to take total responsibility for an order. So there was already sufficient redundancy in the system for R1 to usefully contribute its two cents' worth.

Is comparison with a human expert the criterion? This is a more difficult question than it sounds. In addition to the problem of finding a suitable set of test cases, there is the problem of making the right comparison. The configuration task is usually performed by technical editors; however, R1 does the job at a lower level of detail than this human expert, taking in aspects of the role of the technician who physically assembles the system. So should we compare R1 with the technical editor plus the technician? Well, it's not really that simple either: R1 doesn't really assemble the system, of course, so it's operating rather differently from the man who actually manipulates the components, and is therefore able to experiment with them directly. Surely this isn't comparing like with like?

In addition to adding new knowledge for the purpose of debugging old knowledge, there are three other reasons for extending a knowledge base:

(1)   You might want to add new knowledge about a wider class of data; for example, configuring new types of machine.

(2)   You might want to add new knowledge and introduce new subtasks which 'flesh out' the main task; for example, being more sophisticated about the placement of panels.

(3)   You might want to extend the definition of the main task; for example, asking R1 to configure multiple CPU orders.

When is the extensibility task complete? Judging from the experience with R1, the answer may be never. The domain of computer systems is constantly changing; this means there will be new components with new properties capable of entering into new relationships with each other, and so both the database and the production memory will be in a more or less constant state of flux. Furthermore, the system will always present the evaluation process with a moving target, making an already difficult task even more difficult. The experience with XCON is that incremental development leads naturally to redundancy and *ad hoc* solutions. In other words, unless vigorously opposed, the amount of disorder in the program will always increase. Rebuilding a system from scratch is expensive in terms of time, money and effort, but the investment can be worthwhile if it makes the program easier to extend.

XCON has recently (1988) been reimplemented in the RIME methodology. R1's top-down refinement of the computation into tasks (now called *problem spaces*) has been retained, but rules are now classified according to the steps they perform in the propose-and-apply method. Thus there are Propose-Operator rules, Prune-Operator rules, and so on, thereby regularizing R1's original representation of knowledge. However, the main utility of this framework is that it allows for a more systematic approach to knowledge elicitation. In particular, it helps with the problem of eliciting knowledge within subtasks noted by McDermott.

The next chapter looks at two systems which set out to solve constructive problems requiring a rather more complex control strategy. Problems arise because, in some applications, the correspondence condition discussed in Section 17.2.3 is not met. In other words, we cannot always determine locally what the next step should be, because the current state of the computation is underconstrained. In such situations, we can try to make decisions in such a way as to keep our options open, or we can be prepared to undo decisions if they later turn out to violate constraints. We shall see that such strategies can complicate the situation considerably, but that we can often use domain knowledge to manage that complexity.

Bibliographical notes

R1/XCON's progress has been well documented, although there is no single source that tells you all the details of its development. Bachant and McDermott (1984) is not a bad starting point, if what you want is an overview to supplement this chapter. Another interesting system to come from the collaboration between Carnegie-Mellon and Digital Equipment is XSEL: an OPS5 program which helps a salesperson select components for a VAX computer system and assists with floor layout (McDermott, 1982b, 1984).

STUDY SUGGESTIONS

17.1 Why are planning and design problems not always amenable to being solved by classification methods? Under what conditions *can* they be solved by classification?

17.2 What are the advantages in reimplementing XCON so that its propose-and-apply strategy is more explicit?

17.3 Describe in detail R1's use of contexts. Does R1 'understand' its problem-solving strategy of top-down refinement? That is, would the program be able to reason about its own strategy?

17.4 Consider automating the following configuration task, which is just complicated enough to be interesting, but not as complex as configuring a computer system.

Specification. The user is a budding electric guitarist who wants to replace his or her current gear with a stage set-up consisting of a new guitar, amplifier and effects pedals. The task of the expert system is to help the user choose a combination of makes and models of such equipment that will achieve the desired effect.

Data and knowledge. Data supplied to the system might include values for the following parameters:

- Kinds of music that the user intends to play (jazz, blues, rock).
- Style of playing (rhythm or lead, two-hand tapping, string bending, sliding).

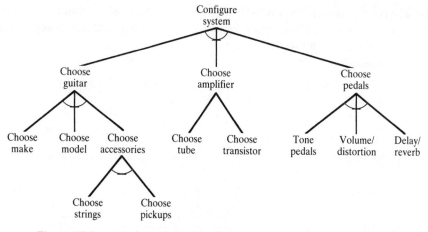

Figure 17.2   A task analysis tree for guitar-amp-effects configuration.

- Tonal preferences ('fat' sound versus a thinner sound, 'sweet' tone versus a more acerbic tone, degree of sustain).
- 'Guitar heroes' of the user (Clapton, Beck, Page, van Halen, Vai).
- Amount of money available for each major item.

Find your local guitar player (there is at least one in every class) and elicit this knowledge from him or her. It may also help to refer back to the example in Section 8.2.2. Look on this primarily as a design exercise, rather than an implementation exercise.

Task analysis. Use the same kind of task analysis that we observed in R1 – break tasks down into subtasks. The AND/OR tree of Figure 17.2 should serve as a reasonable starting point. Either try to develop your system to a uniform depth in this tree, or else specialize, for example, in guitars or in amps.

Traversal of the task tree by the program can be deterministic and proceed top-down and left-right. The most important single decision is the guitar, so complete that subtask before moving on to the amplifier, because it will have implications for other choices. Naturally, you have to determine the make and model before considering what strings to use and whether or not to bother with custom pickups.

Amplifiers fall into two main categories, depending on whether they use tubes (valves) or transistors. Each can be used with any kind of guitar, but certain kinds of music, coupled with certain choices of guitar and style of playing, indicate one kind of amp over another. Another dimension on which amplifiers differ is whether or not they offer built-in effects, such as reverb and chorus. This will have implications for the pedal requirements, because there is no point in duplicating the capabilities of the amplifier without special reason.

Pedal choices depend very much on the kind of music to be played. Some players use no pedals, others use them sparingly, while still others use many different combinations of sound effects. Options include distortion (the 'dirty' sound of heavy rock and metal), delay (pronounced echo effects), reverb (more subtle echo effects), and so on.

18 Constructive Problem Solving (II)

Introduction

In the last chapter, we examined a constructive problem solver that never needed to undo design decisions. However, not all construction problems can be tackled in this way, because it is not always the case that we have enough domain knowledge to make the right decision at each step. In this chapter, we explore both *least commitment* and *propose-and-revise* strategies, with the aid of examples, and review some more knowledge-acquisition tools for constructive problem solving.

18.1 Construction strategies

Imagine that you are arranging furniture in a room. The goal is to devise an arrangement that satisfies the physical constraints supplied by the dimensions of room (in terms of floorspace, width of alcoves, and so on) and the dimensions of the furniture, plus a set of preferences (desk by the window, sofa opposite the TV, and so on). Most likely, having taken some measurements and identified a number of possible locations for different items, you would 'anchor' one or two important pieces at suitable sites and then see if you could complete the arrangement in a satisfactory way.

If you are lucky, your first complete arrangement will work out, and you might well decide to keep things that way, rather than continue the search for an even better solution. But it is just as likely that some proposed extensions to the partial arrangement will violate physical constraints or preferences. However, when this happens, you will not necessarily backtrack all, or even some, of the way to square one. Rather, you will discover a fix, such as swapping the locations of two items, which does not violate the constraint. A good fix is one that un-does as little of your previous work as possible.

As mentioned earlier, construction problems are hard, because there is often no way of telling in advance whether a partial construct will work out. If one is arranging furniture, designing an electrical circuit, or planning a series of errands, then one had better be prepared to re-arrange, redesign or replan. The general, bottom-up strategy that we use for small problems appears to be something like the following.

(1) If possible, begin with a partial arrangement that satisfies the constraints. Otherwise begin at the very beginning.

(2) If the arrangement is complete, halt. Otherwise perform a 'promising' extension to the current arrangement.

(3) If the new arrangement violates a constraint, propose a fix that generates a new arrangement by undoing as little of the previous steps as possible.

(4) Go to step 2.

This strategy is impossibly general, of course, but it has a few interesting features, even at this level of vagueness. Firstly, whenever possible, start with something other than nothing. Thus, if you are planning some sequence of actions, start with a partial plan, extensions of which have worked in the past. It is not too fanciful to suggest that humans have a 'library' of skeletal plans for accomplishing common tasks. Secondly, promising extensions are often those which leave your options open. For example, when planning actions, a good heuristic is to select as your next action the one that least constrains the order and timing of the remaining actions. This is usually called a *least commitment* strategy. Thirdly, fixes do not necessarily involve chronological backtracking (undoing the last thing you did). Placing the desk may have obscured the TV, but maybe the TV is in the wrong place, in the sense that you will have to move it anyway if anything resembling the current plan is to work out.

For complex arrangements, it might seem that the search space is very large, and therefore that the problem is intractable. However, an arrangement task can often be simplified by considering it at different degrees of detail. For example, consider the problem of designing a house for a plot of land; in particular, consider the problem of room layout. As Rosenman *et al.* (1987) point out, configurations of rooms can be described at various levels of abstraction, for example:

- in terms of *adjacencies* (room A is next to room B);
- in terms of *orientations* (room A is north of room B); and
- in terms of *coordinates* which precisely determine the spatial relationship between rooms A and B.

At the highest level of abstraction, deciding that certain rooms need to be adjacent (kitchen and dining room, main bathroom and master bedroom) constrains the search space in a manner that produces exponential savings. At the next level down, deciding that the living room should face south for sunshine and that the kitchen should face north for coolness places constraints on the orientation of the dining room. Once adjacencies and orientations are established, we need heuristics for allocating space to rooms and resolving conflicts over space allocation, by committing space to the most important rooms first, and then splitting the remainder between less important rooms.

This hierarchical approach to problem solving is well known in the planning community, where the successors of the STRIPS program, such as NOAH (Sacerdoti, 1974) and NONLIN (Tate, 1977), sought to simplify the search space by:

- viewing actions at higher levels of abstraction that group whole sequences of actions into larger units;
- solving the planning problem in terms of a partial order of these units; and then
- filling in the details at successively lower levels of abstraction until the plan is fully specified.

This is a top-down approach to problem solving, and as such it resembles the task–subtask organization of the R1 program that we studied in the last chapter. However, it may sometimes be the case that (unlike R1) we need to remake decisions within a level of abstraction. This is the *revise* part of propose-and-revise. In really hard problems, we may even need to remake decisions at a higher level of abstraction, and then return to the current level. Clearly, we would like to avoid this if possible, hence the emphasis on generating good proposals while at the same time keeping one's options open.

In Section 18.2, we begin by looking at the MOLGEN system (Stefik,

1981a, 1981b) for planning experiments in molecular genetics; we shall de-emphasize the rather specialized domain here as much as possible. This system is a good example of the multi-layered approach to construction problems with a least commitment strategy, and it demonstrates the kind of organizational complexity that hard problems require. In Section 18.3, we look at a bottom-up problem solver called VT (Marcus *et al.*, 1988) for designing elevator systems using a propose-and-revise strategy, and then focus on an associated knowledge acquisition tool called SALT (Marcus, 1988), which helps elicit design knowledge.

18.2 An architecture for planning and meta-planning

MOLGEN is a multiple-layered system, in which each layer acts as a level of control for the layer beneath it. This kind of organization is obviously a generalization of the concept of *meta-level architecture* discussed in Chapter 11. The idea is that, in addition to the 'first-level' representation of the domain problem, there are higher levels which represent such things as possible actions on domain objects, and criteria for selecting and combining those actions.

In MOLGEN, the various layers of control are called *planning spaces*. The program uses three such spaces, each with its own objects and operators, which communicate with each via message-passing protocols (see Chapter 10). Their organization is shown schematically in Figure 18.1, with sample operators listed on the left-hand side of the box representing each space. The interpreter is MOLGEN's outermost control loop; it creates and executes strategies. As we shall see, these strategies implement a kind of meta-level reasoning, which controls the way in which the program addresses the basic design problem of planning experiments.

Beginning at the bottom, the *laboratory space* is the domain space that contains knowledge about the objects and operations of a laboratory. The objects are things that can be manipulated by operations that a laboratory technician can perform, such as sorting objects, merging two objects, and so on. We shall not say much about this layer of the program here; interested readers are referred to the original paper.

The *design space* contains knowledge about plans, in the form of classes of operators for:

- checking predictions and finding unusual features of objects (*comparison* operators);
- proposing goals and operations and predicting results (*temporal-extension* operators); and

● refining plan steps in accordance with constraints (*specialization* operators).

Thus *Propose-Goal* is a temporal extension operator which sets goals for laboratory steps to achieve. *Check-Prediction* is a comparison operator which compares the predicted results of performing a laboratory step with the current goal. *Refine-Operator* is a specialization operator which replaces abstract steps in a laboratory operation with more specific ones in a form of plan refinement.

Operators have priorities preassociated with them. In general, comparison operators tend to outrank temporal extension operators, which tend to outrank specialization operators. This ranking reflects the overall least commitment strategy, since it obviously takes less 'committing' to perform comparisons and make predictions than to refine plan steps. In MOLGEN's domain, the expertise being modelled by these operators is that of someone who designs experiments, but the general principles involved in their organization would apply to many other constructive domains.

The following three operations on constraints are important in MOLGEN, and relevant to most applications of constructive problem solving:

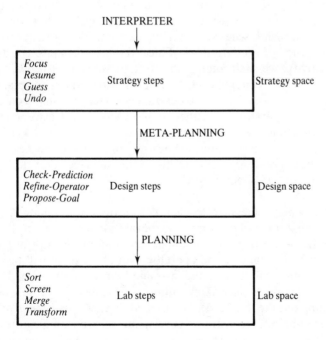

Figure 18.1   MOLGEN's planning spaces (after Stefik, 1981b).

- *Constraint formulation* creates constraints that limit the solution space. An example in the room layout domain would be deciding that the kitchen and dining-room must be adjacent.

- *Constraint propagation* passes information between subproblems which are almost, but not quite, independent of each other. Thus resolving the layout of the upstairs and downstairs of a house are nearly independent subproblems, but they interact along some dimensions, such as stairs and plumbing.

- *Constraint satisfaction* pools constraints from subproblems as the details of the design are worked out. Thus our house design might juggle the upstairs and downstairs arrangements to simplify the plumbing problem.

It is useful to characterize operations in terms of the constraints that currently act upon them. For example, if the problem is what to do on Saturday night, and the current operation is 'Go to the cinema', we say that the operation is underconstrained as long as there is more than one film showing in town. In general, an operation is *underconstrained* if there is not enough information available to realise it in terms of more detailed steps. On the other hand, the operation 'Go to a horror film' is overconstrained if there are no such films showing in town. In general, an operation is *overconstrained* if an attempt to execute it violates a constraint.

The *strategy space* reasons about the plan steps in the design space, using heuristics and a least commitment approach. Thus the design operators create and schedule domain steps, while strategy operators create and schedule design steps. Since the design steps constitute a planning activity, we shall refer to the strategy steps as *meta-planning*. In other words, at the strategy level, MOLGEN reasons about (or plans) how it is going to do its planning at the design level. Here we shall concentrate on the strategy operators, and their deployment in a least commitment cycle that sometimes resorts to heuristics.

MOLGEN's strategy space consists of the following strategy operators; these are described in terms of the messages that they pass to entities in the design space below.

- *Focus* sends a message to each design operator, telling it to 'find tasks' that it could perform to elaborate the current plan. Proposed operations are then put on an agenda in an order of priority determined by the rank of the operator. Not all of them will be executable; some will be underconstrained or overconstrained. *Focus* goes through its agenda executing such tasks as can be executed, sending out the 'find tasks' message after each successful execution, suspending underconstrained tasks, and relinquishing control to the *Undo* operator only when an overconstrained task is encountered.

- *Resume* is like *Focus*, except that it looks for suspended steps to restart, rather than creating new tasks.

- *Guess* is invoked when all the pending design steps are under-constrained. This represents a situation where there is no obvious best next step in the least commitment approach, and one can only use heuristics to guess what to do next. *Guess* sends each suspended step a message, asking it to estimate the utility of its various options, and then executes the one with the highest rating.

- *Undo* is invoked when the plan has become overconstrained. This represents a situation where the least commitment approach has failed and bad guesses have led the planner to a dead end, that is, to a state from which it cannot proceed, because the plan cannot be elaborated by a pending design step without violating a constraint. *Undo* as implemented in MOLGEN is fairly primitive; it looks for a 'guessed' step whose output is an input to the pending step and tells it to remove its effects from the plan.

This use of an agenda is more flexible than that described in the summary of INTERNIST and CENTAUR in Chapter 16. Although all three systems make the crucial separation between posting a task for execution and actually executing it, only MOLGEN's architecture allows for the case in which tasks may interact in non-trivial ways. As Stefik points out, if these interactions are not reasoned about explicitly at higher levels in a program, they tend to surface in confusing ways at lower levels. Of course, multi-layered architectures must ultimately simplify the problem, if we are to justify their employment. Thus, the kinds of task performed by higher levels must get simpler and simpler, until the top-level inter-preter is responsible for only trivial tasks, such as executing the task on the top of its agenda.

As noted earlier, a weakness of MOLGEN is that it is sometimes forced to guess when developing a plan, but has no very sophisticated method for backtracking. In other words, MOLGEN is better at proposing than revising, and does not always recover from bad guesses. The next section describes a system that solves problems in the propose and revise paradigm using a single architectural level but has a better revision process.

18.3 Eliciting, representing and applying design knowledge

VT (Marcus *et al.*, 1988) is an expert system for designing elevator systems that was generated using the knowledge acquisition system SALT (Marcus, 1988). The next section concentrates on the VT program itself, and its domain-dependent approach to guessing and revising, known as *knowledge-based backtracking*. The following section focuses on the elicitation and representation of design knowledge in SALT.

18.3.1 Knowledge-based backtracking in VT

The VT (Vertical Transportation) program is used by Westinghouse Elevator to custom-design elevator systems: a task that it performs unaided, although it can be run in interactive mode. The input to VT consists of a set of important parameters and their values, such as required speed, carrying capacity, and dimensions of existing shafts. Its output is a selection of appropriate equipment and a layout in the shaft that meets safety and performance requirements.

VT works by generating an approximate design and then refining it, dealing with constraint violations along the way. The first phase forward-chains rules which take as data either values of the initial parameter set or values of parameters computed by other procedures. A typical rule (confusingly called a PROCEDURE in VT) might be as shown in Figure 18.2.

This whole phase is data-driven: any design step can be taken as soon as it has enough information. However, unlike the rule shown in Figure 18.2, some of these initial steps will be underconstrained and, in the absence of fully constrained steps, they will be allowed to make guesses and propose extensions based on partial information. In other words, the correspondence condition we met in the last chapter will not always hold, but the problem solver proceeds anyway on the assumption that subsequent constraint violations can be fixed.

As the design is extended, VT keeps track of which values contributed to each derived value at each step by means of a *dependency network*. This kind of data structure is described in more detail in Chapter 22, but it is simply a directed acyclic graph. The nodes represent values computed for important parameters, such as CAR-JAMB-RETURN, and the links represent rule applications. Nodes and links are

---

> IF: values are available for the parameters
> DOOR-OPENING, PLATFORM-WIDTH and
> OPENING-WIDTH,
> and DOOR-OPENING = CENTER
> THEN: CAR-JAMB-RETURN
> = (PLATFORM-WIDTH − OPENING-WIDTH)/2.

Figure 18.2 A VT rule for a design extension, freely adapted from Marcus (1988b).

IF: there has been a violation of MAXIMUM-MACHINE-GROOVE-
          PRESSURE
THEN: try a downgrade for MACHINE-GROOVE-MODEL (1)
        try an increase of HOIST-CABLE-QUANTITY (4).

Figure 18.3   A rule that proposes two alternative fixes for a constraint violation, freely adapted
from Marcus *et al.* (1988).

created as rules are fired, so that the program can keep track of its
reasoning and subsequently identify decisions that contribute to constraint violations. Such decisions become potential backtrack points in the
revision process.

Constraint violations are detected by *demons* (see Chapter 9);
when enough is known to compute the effect on a value of the values that
constrain it, the comparison is made. Potential fixes have preference
ratings and are tried in order; an example of a fix is given in Figure 18.3.
The dependency network is then used to propagate the changes made by
the selected fix through the parameter values.

Figure 18.3 shows a rule that proposes two alternative fixes for
excessive pressure on the hoist cables: one that reduces the grip on the
cables and one that increases the number of cables. The former is
preferred, but if this fails to reduce the pressure enough, or interacts with
another fix, then the latter will be tried. The latter has a lower rating,
because changing the number of cables in the hoist has a knock-on effect
on other equipment sizes.

We say that two constraints are *antagonistic* if complying with one
constraint aggravates another. To return to our cinema example, if two
people want to go to the movies together, and one is bored by anything
but horror films but the other dislikes the sight of blood, then we have a
recipe for conflict. Gratifying either person will involve upsetting the
other.

Thus the problem of revision is complicated by the fact that fixes
can interact. As we saw above, changing the number of cables in the hoist
can affect constraints on other equipment; for example, there comes a
point where you have to upgrade the elevator model. VT's knowledge
base contains 37 chains of interacting fixes, and three of these contain
antagonistic constraints. For example, the constraint antagonistic to
MAXIMUM-MACHINE-GROOVE-PRESSURE   is   MAXIMUM-
TRACTION-RATIO. Reducing pressure on the hoist cables can result
in increased traction ratio, while reducing the traction ratio can increase
pressure on the cables.

If antagonistic constraints are violated simultaneously, one can conceive of a situation in which attempts to resolve one constraint aggravate the other constraint and vice versa, leading to an endless loop if the level of aggravation amounts to a violation. VT deals with this problem by treating the violation of antagonistic constraints as a special case. When a demon detects a violation in one of an antagonistic pair, it checks to see if the other has been violated. If it has, the demon resets each parameter value implicated in the violation to the last value that it had before the violation of *either* constraint, thereby undoing all fix attempts so far. Then it tries combinations of potential fixes in the following order:

(1) fixes that help both violation;
(2) fixes that help one but do not aggravate the other;
(3) fixes that help one but do aggravate the other.

In the third case, VT tries to fix the most important constraint first. Thus VT can be contrasted with MOLGEN in that it puts more effort into the revise part of the propose-and-revise strategy, whereas MOLGEN concentrates on managing its least commitment policy.

VT is implemented in OPS5 (see Appendix B) and its rule base consists of about 3000 rules. Published data are available on rule firings and CPU time per run; rule firings range between 2500 and 11 500, and CPU time on a VAX 11/780 with 20 Mb of memory ranges between 7 and 20 minutes. It is interesting to note that about 2000 of VT's rules are domain-specific ones generated by the SALT acquisition system (to which we now turn); the other 1000 handle input/output, explanation and control.

18.3.2 Acquiring propose and revise knowledge in SALT

The SALT system associated with VT assumes a *propose-and-revise* problem-solving strategy, and uses this assumption to impose structure on the process of knowledge acquisition. One method is to collect knowledge which fills particular roles within the problem-solving strategy. Identifying these roles, and understanding the relationships between them, turns out to be crucial to successful knowledge acquisition.

Domain knowledge is seen as performing one of three roles in any propose and revise system under construction; these are (with their SALT names in parentheses):

(1) knowledge that proposes an extension to the current design (PROPOSE-A-DESIGN-EXTENSION);

(2)   knowledge that identifies constraints on design extensions (IDENTIFY-A-CONSTRAINT); and

(3)   knowledge about how to repair constraint violations (PROPOSE-A-FIX).

SALT is an automatic system which acquires knowledge under each of these headings by interacting with an expert, and then compiles this knowledge into production rules to generate a domain-specific knowledge base. This knowledge base can then be coupled with an interpreter in a problem-solving *shell* (see Chapter 13) to create an expert system. SALT retains the original knowledge it acquired in a declarative form, which can be updated and recompiled as necessary.

The intermediate representation that SALT uses is a dependency network. Each node in the net is the name of a value, and can represent an input (such as TYPE-OF-LOADING), a design parameter (such as PLATFORM-WIDTH), or a constraint (such as MAXIMUM-MACHINE-GROOVE-PRESSURE). There are three kinds of directed links in the network:

- *contributes-to* links A to B if the value of A is used to compute the value of B;
- *constrains* links A to B if A is a constraint that restricts the value of a design parameter B;
- *suggests-revision-of* links A to B if A is a constraint, and a violation of A suggests a change to the current value of B.

The user of SALT can enter knowledge in any order, but each piece of knowledge must be either a PROCEDURE (for extending the design), a CONSTRAINT (for restricting the value of a design parameter) or a FIX (for repairing a constraint violation). There are schemas for each kind of knowledge, and the three kinds correspond to the three knowledge roles outlined above in an obvious way. Once a role has been chosen for elaboration, SALT will prompt the user for all the knowledge required by the role.

A PROCEDURE must be supplied for every design parameter that figures in a completed design, and should try to take into account all considerations relevant to that parameter's value. Where parameters are underconstrained, some preference between alternative values should be supplied. Thus the completed schema for computing the parameter CAR-JAMB-RETURN (as featured in Figure 18.2) might look as in Figure 18.4.

A CONSTRAINT is intended to capture interactions between parameter values which are not captured by the knowledge encoded in PROCEDUREs, but which need to be checked before a solution can be

1	Name:	CAR-JAMB-RETURN
2	Precondition:	DOOR-OPENING = CENTER
3	Procedure	CALCULATION
4	Formula	[PLATFORM-WIDTH − OPENING WIDTH] / 2
5	Justification	CENTER-OPENING DOORS LOOK BEST WHEN CENTERED ON THE PLATFORM

Figure 18.4   A filled-out PROCEDURE schema for CAR-JAMB-RETURN.

deemed complete. A FIX suggests revisions that can be tried in the light of a constraint violation, and involves changing one or more parameter values. Figure 18.5 shows a completed SALT schema for a fix to the violation of the constraint MAXIMUM-MACHINE-GROOVE-PRESSURE.

Given the stylized nature of the schemas, it is not hard to see how they could be automatically compiled into production rules. However, SALT does more than merely translate these schemata; it also analyses how the different pieces of knowledge fit together. To get the most of SALT's analytic abilities, the user should enter FIXes last, so that the implications of each fix can be analysed for the whole knowledge base.

SALT derives each link in the dependency network from a piece of knowledge supplied by the user. Thus it can work out that PLATFORM-WIDTH *contributes-to* CAR-JAMB-RETURN from the PROCEDURE that links these parameters. Similarly, the *constrains* and *suggests-revision-of* links can be derived from the declaration of CONSTRAINTS and FIXes respectively.

The task of the generated expert system is to find a path through the network and assign values at each node, in such a way that all constraints have been checked and satisfied, so that the network can settle into a stable state. It is the job of the compiler to proceduralize these paths, but also to determine compilability by confirming that there is indeed a unique and complete path for a set of inputs. Much of this work involves checking that the preconditions associated with PROCEDURES do not interact in detrimental ways. For example, if preconditions overlap for a set of inputs, this may affect path uniqueness, whereas, if there are gaps in the preconditions, some inputs may not result in the generation of a complete path. SALT also detects loops among PROCEDURES, which would prevent the system from converging on a solution.

Constraint Name:	MAXIMUM-MACHINE-GROOVE-PRESSURE
Value to Change:	HOIST-CABLE-QUANTITY
Change Type:	INCREASE
Step Type:	BY-STEP
Step Size:	1
Preference Rating:	4
Preference Reason:	CHANGES MINOR EQUIPMENT SIZING

Figure 18.5 A FIX for MAXIMUM-MACHINE-GROOVE-PRESSURE violation.

18.4 Summary of constructive problem solving

We have seen that some construction problems can be sufficiently constrained by domain knowledge to all but eliminate trial and error. Thus, in configuring a computer system, R1 never had to guess at the best next step in elaborating the current state of the problem, or go back and undo an extension to a previous partial solution. In this situation, an overall strategy of top-down refinement may be all that is required to control the bottom-up search for an acceptable arrangement of solution elements. Since you never need to look back, there is no need to keep a history of previous decisions. Neither is there any need to keep track of dependencies between decisions.

Yet many construction problems will remain insufficiently constrained by domain knowledge, because either

- the available knowledge is incomplete, or
- many near-optimal solutions are possible.

Incompleteness indicates that the problem solver should follow a least commitment strategy and be prepared to make a guess at the best extension to the current partial solution. Since guesses may turn out wrong, the program must be able to detect conflicts among constraints and either backtrack and try again or propose a fix for the conflict. However conflicts are resolved, some mechanisms for recording previous decisions and dependencies between them is essential; we shall return to this topic in Chapter 23. If there are many near-optimal solutions, the program may wish simply to adopt the first solution that it finds which meets some minimum set of requirements. Pursuing the search for an optimal or best-scoring solution will normally incur prohibitive computational cost.

Bibliographical notes

It is hard to find a good reference book on constructive problem solving, or even the subfield of planning. The last two chapters are an attempt to fill this gap in the context of expert systems research. However, many standard texts contain good chapters on planning – see, for example, Nilsson (1980), Genesereth and Nilsson (1987), and Charniak and McDermott (1985). See Sacerdoti (1974) for an early work on least commitment planning. See also Brown and Chandrasekaran (1989) and Coyne (1988) for descriptions of recent research into design problem solving.

STUDY SUGGESTIONS

18.1 Explain least commitment strategy, and contrast it with propose-and-revise.

18.2 Try to list as many tasks as you can think of which

(a) are amenable to solution by least commitment alone, and
(b) are not amenable to solution by least commitment alone.

Think of everyday tasks, such as planning a shopping expedition.

18.3 Consider the following arrangement problem. You have a room, as shown in

Table 18.1 Items of furniture to be arranged in Exercise 18.3.

Item	Size
2 bookcases	1 each
TV and hifi	3 altogether
2 couches	2 each
Coffee table	1
Desk	2
Music stand and guitar stand	2 altogether
2 chairs	1 each
Plant	1

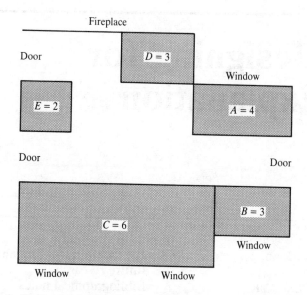

Figure 18.6 Room for furniture arrangement problem in Exercise 18.3.

Figure 18.6. The shaded areas are places in the room where furniture can be put without obscuring doors, fireplaces, or paths through the room. Each area is identified by a letter, and its rough size is given in some unit of space. Thus $A = 4$ denotes that A has four units of disposable space.

The task is to arrange the following items of furniture, given with their sizes in Table 18.1, subject to the following constraints:

- At least one couch must face the TV.
- The desk should face a window, with a chair.
- The coffee table should be next to at least one of the couches.
- The guitar stand and music stand must be together, with a chair.

19 Designing for Explanation

Introduction

There are two compelling reasons for the requirement that expert systems should be 'transparent', that is, able to explain their reasoning and justify their conclusions in a manner that is intelligible to users.

- The *clients* of automatic advice need to be convinced that the reasoning behind a conclusion is substantially correct, and that the solution proposed is appropriate to their particular case.

- The *engineers* of an expert system need to be able to satisfy themselves that the mechanisms employed in the derivation of a conclusion are functioning according to specification.

This chapter begins with a short survey of early work on explanations. It then discusses in detail how better explanations for clients were generated in the CENTAUR system, which we met in Chapter 16. Finally, it discusses a particular line of research, the Explainable Expert Systems project, which has concentrated on transparency from a knowledge engineer's point of view, and linked it to methods of knowledge elicitation.

19.1   Survey of early work on explanation

Such progress as has been made in the generation of explanations can be summed up briefly in the following way. The pioneering efforts of Stanford researchers in the 1960s and 1970s provided little more than high-level trace facilities in the first instance, although these were subsequently augmented by a range of debugging tools (see Chapter 13). This level of software engineering was satisfactory for a research vehicle, such as MYCIN, but left a lot to be desired for commercial systems. More recent efforts have concentrated on making more explicit certain issues to do with the control of inference and the underlying architecture. It has also been recognized that automatic explanation require access to a domain model, just as automatic knowledge elicitation does.

19.1.1   MYCIN's explanation system

The explanation module of the MYCIN system (see Chapter 3) was automatically invoked at the end of every consultation. To explain how the value of a particular medical parameter was established, the module retrieved the list of rules that were successfully applied and printed them, along with the conclusions drawn. It also allowed the user to interrogate the system about the consultation, and ask more general questions.

Thus all question-answering facilities were based on the system's ability to:

- display the rule invoked at any point in the consultation;
- record rule invocations and associate them with specific events, such as questions asked and conclusions drawn;
- use the rule indexing to retrieve particular rules in answer to queries.

As mentioned in Chapter 3, a consultation with a backward-chaining expert system involves a search through a tree of goals. Consequently, inquiries during a consultation fall into two types:

- those that ask WHY a particular question was put;
- those that ask HOW a particular conclusion was reached.

To answer a WHY question, one must look up the tree to see what higher goals the system is trying to achieve. To answer a HOW question, one must look down the tree to see what subgoals were satisfied to achieve the goal. Thus the explanation process can be considered as a kind of tree traversal, and is thereby reduced to a search problem.

The fact that MYCIN keeps track of the goal–subgoal structure of the computation enables it to answer questions such as

Why do you ask if the stain of the organism is Gram-negative?

It can simply cite the production rule which states that Gram-negative staining, in conjunction with various other conditions, would suggest that the class of the organism was Enterobacteriaceae, and that the current goal was to identify the organism. MYCIN also maintains a record of the decisions it makes, and uses this record to explain and justify its decisions in response to HOW questions like

What made you think that Organism 1 might be a proteus?

In reply, MYCIN cites the rules that it applied, its degree of certainty in that decision, and the last question asked. General questions can also be asked; these reference the rules without considering the state of the dynamic database with respect to a particular patient. An example might be

What do you prescribe for *Pseudomonas* infections?

The reply could simply cite the therapy rules that mention the organism *Pseudomonas*.

However, the user cannot access the static knowledge contained in simple lists and knowledge tables, because these other sources of knowledge lack the uniform format of the production rules. Also, the mechanisms for creating the therapy lists and choosing the preferred drug are complex LISP functions which users cannot inspect, and probably would not understand if they could. Finally, the order in which rules are considered for application, and the order in which the conditions of premises are considered, are not aspects of the system that users are able to question.

Thus, although WHY and HOW questions appear to provide a neat and intuitively satisfying basis for finding out what a backward-chaining rule-based consultation program is doing, one must bear in mind that this approach does not cover every aspect of system function, and that a trace of rule applications will not be easy to follow if the chains of reasoning are at all long. (It just so happens that MYCIN's chains are typically not long, because the search space is relatively shallow.) Arguably, such traces tell clients more than they want to know, although their level of detail may be useful for the knowledge engineer.

With respect to *forward*-chaining systems, a mere trace of the rules applied so far is even less meaningful, because we are not in a position to know, at any given point of the computation, where the system's line of reasoning is headed, although the application of structuring techniques, such as R1's use of means–ends analysis (see Chapter 17), helps to provide the missing goal structure.

19.1.2 Explanation in MYCIN derivatives

It is well known that the problems associated with understanding, monitoring and correcting the behaviour of an expert system multiply as the knowledge base increases in size (Davis, 1980b). For example, it becomes more difficult to ensure that 'new' rules are consistent with 'old' ones, and to understand the flow of control in situations where large numbers of applicable rules may be in competition for the attention of the interpreter. Not much work has been done on how to monitor rule bases as they are extended in order to detect conflict or redundancy, but see Suwa *et al.* (1982) for one approach to this problem.

EMYCIN (van Melle, 1981) developed and elaborated MYCIN's facilities to some extent. Thus EXPLAIN, TEST and REVIEW commands were provided as debugging aids for the knowledge engineer (see Chapter 13). As in MYCIN, EXPLAIN worked by printing each rule that contributed to the conclusion, together with:

(1)   the certainty factor that resulted from the successful application of the rule;

(2)   the 'tally' value associated with the evaluation of the premises of the rule; and

(3)   the last question asked by the system before the conclusion was drawn.

The use of meta-rules in MYCIN and EMYCIN, which was intended to make some of the control choices explicit, opened the door to reasoning about problem-solving strategy, in addition to reasoning at the object level of the domain. It then became feasible to think about meta-level reasoning in the context of explanations, such that explanations of what had been inferred could be augmented by an account of why certain inferences had been drawn in preference to others.

Two rational reconstructions of the early Stanford work were begun at the end of the 1970s. One was the NEOMYCIN system (Clancey and Letsinger, 1984; Clancey, 1987c), which represented an attempt to take a more abstract approach to MYCIN-style medical problem solving, based on epistemological and psychological considerations. The focus of attention was on what kinds of knowledge clinicians actually used in routine diagnosis, and what their reasoning processes were like. Thus NEOMYCIN was much more concerned with the simulation of human problem solving (or *cognitive modelling*) than MYCIN had been. No-one had ever claimed that clinicians actually reasoned in the way that MYCIN did – all that mattered were the results.

This novel approach had implications for the explanation facilities. In NEOMYCIN, there was an emphasis on *strategic explanation*, in which one tried to make clear the overall plans and methods used in attaining a goal, instead of merely citing the rules employed (Hasling *et al.*, 1984). In other words, the program was expected to have some explicit representation of the problem-solving process, as well as domain knowledge. Rather as in INTERNIST, the collection and interpretation of data was focused by the current set of hypotheses (the *differential*: a term derived from the basic task of differential diagnosis). To understand the behaviour of the program, in terms of the questions it asks and the flow of control, the user has some access to the diagnostic strategies that the program is using.

NEOMYCIN had the following basic organization:

- Strategic knowledge was separated out from the medical knowledge and encoded in meta-rules.
- Diseases were organized taxonomically, as in INTERNIST, so that there was some explicit representation of the hypothesis space.
- Both of the above kinds of knowledge were kept separate from the rules that encode various kinds of association between data and hypotheses.

Thus the basic approach is still based on heuristic classification (see Chapter 14), but the mixed representation scheme structures and controls the use of domain rules, simplifying them in the process. In addition, the domain rules are themselves differentiated into four classes:

- *Causal rules* connect symptoms and diseases via a network of symptom and disease categories.
- *Trigger rules* associate data with hypotheses, enabling a kind of forward reasoning. When such a rule fires, the relevant hypothesis is placed in the differential.
- *Data/hypothesis rules* also associate data with hypotheses, but they work only on hypotheses already in the differential.
- *Screening rules* encode such things as restrictions on data, for example 'if the patient is male, then discount the possibility of pregnancy'.

The meta-rule shown in Figure 19.1 encodes a general strategy of looking for data that differentiates between two current hypotheses, such as data that are predicted by one hypothesis but not the other.

Thus, in NEOMYCIN, the execution of meta-rules replaces the MYCIN-style global control regime of backward chaining. The flow of control depends entirely on which meta-rules are executed. This is a rather more radical use of meta-rules than was found in MYCIN, where meta-rules merely served occasionally to order or prune domain rules that were being considered for application.

METARULE397

IF: There are two items on the differential that differ in
             some disease process feature

THEN: Ask a question that differentiates between these two
             kinds of processes

Figure 19.1   A NEOMYCIN meta-rule.

The other attempt at a reconstruction of MYCIN begun at the end of
the 70s was the CENTAUR system (Aikins, 1983). This program (described
in Chapter 16) experimented with a mixed representation of knowledge
in the reimplementation of the PUFF expert system for pulmonary
function test interpretation. Its architecture combined frames (or
prototypes) and production rules in an interesting way that made
explanation easier.

In CENTAUR, there was a particular emphasis on the *context* in
which reasoning was done, and the *stage-dependent* nature of expert-level
problem solving. To understand why a particular question was asked, one
needed to understand not merely the rule that fired but also the active
hypothesis that was being considered. Thus Aikins shares some of
Clancey's concerns, although her approach is a little less ambitious, as it
stops short of an attempt at cognitive modelling.

19.2   Explanations in CENTAUR

The original implementation of PUFF in EMYCIN (see Aikins *et al.*, 1984)
performed satisfactorily, in terms of solving the problems posed to it, but
the knowledge representation was found to be deficient in a number of
other respects.

- It was difficult to represent typical patterns of data or typical
  classes of patient.
- Adding or modifying rules to encode additional knowledge or
  refine existing knowledge frequently had unexpected effects.
- Changing the order in which information was requested from the
  user proved to be difficult, because the requests were automatically
  generated as the interpreter fired the rules.
- Generating clear explanations presented problems, because little
  more than a trace of rule activations was available.

Aikins argued, as Clancey had done, that the very modularity and uniformity of production rules, which had been cited positive features, had their negative aspect. Most rule sets contain implicit groupings, either using various kinds of indexing concealed in the interpreter (for example, the ORGRULES and PATRULES of MYCIN, which related to organisms and patients respectively), or having conditions and actions that manipulate goal tokens in working memory. This organization is often hierarchical, because of the taxonomic organization of hypotheses (in classification tasks), or the decomposition of goals into subgoals (in constructive tasks). Many of the problems cited above can be traced to the failure to differentiate between different kinds of knowledge, which may need to be represented and applied in different ways. As we saw in Chapter 16, CENTAUR attempted to combine the strengths of rule- and frame-based programming in a way that compensated for some of the weaknesses of the individual paradigms.

A run of the CENTAUR consultation program consists of an interpreter executing an agenda of tasks, rather than a chaining together of rules. A primary use for the agenda is to provide an explanation of why the system behaved as it did in the course of the consultation. Consequently, each task entry contains information about both the source of the task and the reason why the task was scheduled.

The source of the task will be a prototype (one that is a good match for the case data) or another task. Tasks are added to the agenda either by prototype control slots or in the course of executing tasks already on the agenda. The reasons are generated from the name of the prototype and the name of the control slot responsible for setting up the task.

During program execution, a prototype is always in one of three states:

- *inactive* – not being considered as a hypothesis;
- *potentially relevant* – suggested by data values;
- *active* – selected from the above and placed on the hypothesis list.

Disease prototypes represent hypotheses. The hypothesis list is simply a list of prototypes paired with their certainty factors, ordered in decreasing order of certainty. Two other lists keep track of confirmed and disconfirmed prototypes.

The key events in a CENTAUR consultation are:

- entering the initial data;
- triggering the prototypes using antecedent rules;
- scoring the prototypes and selecting one to be 'current';

- using known facts to fill in the current prototype;
- testing the match between the facts and the expected values;
- accounting for data left over by the initial diagnosis;
- refining the diagnosis accordingly;
- summarizing and printing the results.

Thus the consultation proceeds in *stages*, rather as a normal consultation might. As a session begins, the CONSULTATION prototype is selected as the current prototype, and the empty agenda is given two tasks: to FILL-IN and then CONFIRM the current prototype, courtesy of the TO-FILL-IN and IF-CONFIRMED control slots in the CONSULTATION prototype. The TO-FILL-IN slot of the prototype actually contains three tasks, each of which sets a variable for the consultation: the TRACING-LEVEL governs the amount of detail in the trace, AGENDA-PRINTING determines whether or not tasks are printed as they are added to the agenda or executed, and STRATEGY can take on the values CONFIRMATION (select the best match and attempt to confirm it), ELIMINATION (select the worst match and attempt to eliminate it), or FIXED-ORDER (use a predetermined order for evaluating hypotheses).

The first three tasks in the IF-CONFIRMED slot set other variables which control the consultation, such as setting the percentage of a prototype's slots that have to be filled in before that prototype can be considered confirmed. This allows the knowledge engineer to experiment with variations on the basic control regime, and possibly tune the system for different domains. The rest of the IF-CONFIRMED tasks control the stages of the consultation, as can be seen from the listing of the CONSULTATION prototype reproduced in Figure 19.2.

Once the domain of the consultation has been determined (in the present context this is pulmonary function), PULMONARY-DISEASE becomes the next current prototype, and it elicits the initial data from the user by asking a series of questions, as shown in Figure 19.3. In each exchange, the numbered line is a prompt printed by the program; acronyms on this line stand for laboratory data. The line prefixed by ** is the user's data entry response. Any comment that follows in square brackets is a message from the system, alerting the user to the fact that a prototype has been matched. Acronyms on this line stand for disease prototypes.

It can be seen from this transcript that data values trigger prototypes even as they are being entered. For example, the lines

6) FEV1/FVC ratio:
** 40
[Trigger for OAD and CM900]

CONSULTATION

TO-FILL-IN:
Ask for the TRACING-LEVEL for the CONSULTATION
Ask for the AGENDA-PRINTING for the CONSULTATION
Ask for the STRATEGY for the CONSULTATION

IF-CONFIRMED:
Set the confirmation threshold to 0
Set the percentage of filled-in slots necessary to confirm the
    prototype to 0.75
Set the default procedure for filling in slots to fill in slots in
    decreasing order of their importance measures
Determine the domain of the consultation
Select the current best prototype
Fill in the prototype
Apply tasks in the if-confirmed slot
Mark facts that are accounted for by the prototype
Apply the refinement rules associated with the confirmed
    prototypes
Apply the summary rules associated with the confirmed
    prototypes
Execute actions associated with the confirmed prototypes

Figure 19.2 Unfolding of tasks in CENTAUR.

indicate that the FEV1/FVC ratio of 40 activates the OAD (obstructive airways disease) prototype with a certainty measure of 900. (FEV1 stands for the forced expiratory volume in one second – the volume of air expelled in one second during a forced breathing out, starting with the lungs full of air; FVC stands for forced vital capacity – the volume of air expired during a rapid forced breathing out, starting with the lungs full of air and ending with whatever residual volume of air is left in the lungs after full expiration.)

Certainty measures range from −1000 to 1000 for computational convenience, and they indicate how sure the system is that the prototype cited matches the data for a particular case. They are therefore a measure of how well the actual values provided by the user fit into the prototypical or expected values stored in the slots of a prototype, and it is used to select the current best hypothesis. These measures are similar to the

--------PATIENT-7--------

1) Patient's identifying number:
** 7446
2) referral diagnosis:
** ASTHMA
[Trigger for ASTHMA and CM900]
3) RV/RV-predicted:
** 261
4) TLC (body box) observed/predicted:
** 139
5) FVC/FVC-predicted:
** 81
[Trigger for NORMAL and CM500]
6) FEV1/FVC ratio:
** 40
[Trigger for OAD and CM900]
7) the DLCO/DLCO-predicted:
** 117
[Trigger for NORMAL and CM700]
8) Change in FEV1 (after dilation)
** 31
9) MMF/MMF-predicted:
** 12
[Trigger for OAD and CM900]
10) The slope F5025:
** 9
[Trigger for OAD and CM900]

Figure 19.3 Questions and triggers in CENTAUR.

certainty factors found in MYCIN and EMYCIN, and the algorithm for combining more than one measure is the same. (Note that these values are not explained. Thus the algorithm for combining certainties is a 'black box' as far as the user is concerned.)

Figure 19.3 illustrates that the user can see immediately what is the impact of the input data on the disease prototypes. In a system that is wholly rule based, it is usually the case that data which activate the rule that 'wins' in the conflict resolution are the only data that appear in the trace. Thus one is left wondering what effect, if any, the other data might have had.

Hypothesis: ASTHMA, CM: 900, Reason: RDX was ASTHMA
Hypothesis: NORMAL, CM: 500, Reason: FVC was 81
Hypothesis: OAD, CM: 900, Reason: FEV1/FVC was 40
Hypothesis: NORMAL, CM: 700, Reason: DLCO was 117
Hypothesis: OAD, CM: 900, Reason: MMF was 12
Hypothesis: OAD, CM: 900, Reason: F5025 was 9

More specific hypotheses chosen: NORMAL, OAD
[New prototypes being filled in... NORMAL, OAD]

Figure 19.4 Summary of triggered prototypes.

After the initial data have been elicited, a summary of the triggered prototypes is printed out for inspection, as shown in Figure 19.4. NORMAL and OAD will be considered next, as these are immediate successors of the PULMONARY-DISEASE prototype. Consideration of the ASTHMA hypothesis will be deferred, because ASTHMA is a subtype of OAD, and is therefore considered after OAD in the overall strategy of top-down refinement. The hierarchical structure of the hypothesis space makes this overall strategy extremely clear and comprehensible to the user. In a system that is wholly rule based, the user might need to understand the conflict-resolution strategy (specificity) before understanding why some hypotheses are evaluated before others.

Note that not all of the data values entered were responsible for triggering a prototype, and also that more than one prototype has been triggered. In other words, some data values did not suggest any initial hypotheses, while some values suggested OAD, and others suggested normality. As the new prototypes for NORMAL and OAD are filled in, data values such as TLC (total lung capacity), which did not activate any prototypes, will be considered in the context of active hypotheses, and may cause their certainty measures to be altered. Thus, the TLC value of 139 casts doubt on the hypothesis of normality, as shown in Figure 19.5. Data values that fall outside the range of expected values stored in the slots of a prototype will tend to lower the certainty measure associated with that prototype.

Figure 19.5 shows that, although NORMAL was suggested as a hypothesis by two of the original test results, five other test results militate against this hypothesis being correct, and its certainty measure is reduced accordingly. All this can be gleaned from the trace. The hypothesis list is then constructed and ordered, with OAD as the current best prototype:

```
!Surprise value! 261 for RV in NORMAL, CM: 700
!Surprise value! 139 for TLC in NORMAL, CM: 400
!Surprise value! 40 for FEV1/FVC in NORMAL, CM: −176
!Surprise value! 12 for MMF in NORMAL, CM: −499
!Surprise value! 9 for F5025 in NORMAL, CM: −699
```

Figure 19.5 CENTAUR reporting unexpected data values.

Hypothesis List: (OAD 999) (NORMAL −699)
I am testing the hypothesis that there is Obstructive Airways
   Disease.

Eventually, the system will confirm the hypothesis that the patient is
indeed suffering from OAD, that the degree of OAD is severe, and that
the subtype of OAD is asthma. The consultation now moves into the
refinement stage, which causes further questions to be asked, such as the
degree of dyspnoea (shortness of breath). This stage is instigated by the
application of refinement rules, which are stored with the relevant
prototypes (see Figure 19.6).
      Now summary rules associated with the confirmed prototypes are
executed, as shown in Figure 19.7. These merely summarize the
information gained in the process of filling in the prototype, and require
no further interaction with the user. The printing out of findings is done
by the ACTIONS slot of the relevant prototype.
      The printing of the final conclusions is performed by the

```
[Refinement rules being applied...]
20) The number of pack-years of smoking:
** 17
21) The number of years ago that the patient stopped smoking:
** 0
22) The degree of dyspnoea:
** NONE
```

Figure 19.6 The application of refinement rules.

[Actions slot of OAD being executed...]
Conclusions: the findings about the diagnosis of obstructive airways disease are as follows:
Elevated lung volumes indicate overinflation.
The RV/TLC ratio is increased, suggesting a severe degree of air trapping. Forced Vital Capacity is normal but the FEV1/FVC ratio is reduced, suggesting airway obstruction of a severe degree.
Low mid-expiratory flow is consistent with severe airway obstruction. Obstruction is indicated by curvature of the flow-volume loop which is of a severe degree.
Following bronchodilation, expired flow shows excellent improvement as indicated by the change in the FEV1.
Following bronchodilation, expired flow shows excellent improvement as indicated by the change in the MMF.
Reversibility of airway obstruction is confirmed by improvement in airway resistance following bronchodilation.

Figure 19.7 Applying the summary rules.

ACTIONS slot of the PULMONARY-DISEASE prototype, as in Figure 19.8.

The stage-dependent behaviour of the program makes the program's output particularly easy to understand. At every stage of the process, it is clear what CENTAUR is trying to achieve, and which prototypes are active. This makes both debugging the program and understanding its conclusions easier than would be the case without the additional structure provided by the hierarchical frame system.

To summarize, Aikins argued that to understand a consultation, in terms of both the direction that it takes and the results that it returns, a user must be able to understand:

- the questions being asked;
- the reasons for asking them;
- the justification for intermediate conclusions.

Aikins argued that there were four principal shortcomings associated with the kinds of explanation generated by EMYCIN:

- The user needs to be able to follow the backward chaining of rules, and one suspects that this mode of reasoning is not typically employed by humans.

[Action slot of PULMONARY-DISEASE being executed...]
-----Prototype   Summary-----
-----Obstructive Airways Disease-----
Obstructive Airways Disease was suggested by the following findings
The fev1/fvc ratio of PATIENT-7: 40
The mmf/mmf-predicted ratio of PATIENT-7: 12
The f5025 of PATIENT-7: 9
In addition, Obstructive Airways Disease is consistent with
The tlc/tlc-predicted ratio of PATIENT-7: 139
The rv/rv-predicted ratio of PATIENT-7: 261
The f25 of PATIENT-7: 45
The severity of coughing of PATIENT-7: NONE
The degree of sputum production of PATIENT-7: NONE
The Obstructive Airways Disease accounts for the following findings:
The referral diagnosis of PATIENT-7
The fev1/fvc ratio of PATIENT-7
The f25 of PATIENT-7
The severity of coughing of PATIENT-7
The degree of sputum production of PATIENT-7

All facts have been accounted for by the confirmed prototypes.
Conclusions: Smoking probably exacerbates the severity of the patient's
airway obstruction. Discontinuation of smoking should help relieve the
symptoms. Good response to bronchodilators is consistent with an asthmatic
condition, and their continued use is indicated. The high diffusing capacity is
consistent with asthma. Pulmonary Function Diagnosis: Severe Obstructive
Airways Disease Asthmatic type. Consultation finished.

Figure 19.8   CENTAUR's final conclusions.

- The knowledge in the rules may not be complete, or may not be specified at a level of detail that makes rule applications easy to follow.

- Knowledge about context and control is not distinguished from knowledge about the content of the domain – there is no clear demarcation between meta-level and object level.

- Each rule application explains only the most recent question, with no broader context being supplied.

CENTAUR asks questions of the user if it fails to deduce some piece of
information it needs from its rules, or if it needs a value for a parameter

that is explicitly labelled 'ask-first'. Questions asked of the system by the user include the HOW and WHY of EMYCIN, but with a stage-dependent interpretation. Thus, a WHY question asked in the context of a particular prototype during the diagnostic stage will be interpreted as 'why are you considering this prototype?' In the review stage, however, such a question would be interpreted as 'why was this prototype confirmed?' CENTAUR always displays the current prototype, so that the context of the question and answer are clear.

CENTAUR's final interpretation consists of a list of confirmed prototypes, accompanied by a good deal of additional information, including:

- findings that suggest each prototype (the trigger values);
- findings consistent with each prototype (the plausible values);
- findings inconsistent with each prototype (error or surprise values);
- findings not accounted for by any prototype (residual facts).

Any test results not accounted for by any prototype on the confirmed list are listed, together with any other prototypes that might account for them. This helps to track down both possible errors in the tests and possible bugs in the knowledge base. Finally, a statement of conclusions and final diagnosis is presented along with a list of those prototypes which were disconfirmed during the consultation.

Like Clancey's work, this case study demonstrates that the task of explanation should not be relegated to some relatively independent module of an expert system. The issue of explanation has implications for many different aspects of representation and control which permeate the entire program. Thus the moral of the story is that explanation capabilities must be designed for in the system as a whole, if they are to be effective.

19.3 Explanations and automatic programming

Swartout (1983) agreed with Clancey and Aikins that traces of rule activations may describe program behaviour, but they cannot be said to justify it. This is because although the justification is part of the knowledge used to design and implement the program, this knowledge is nowhere represented explicitly in the code. In other words, the 'knowing how' of the system (the principles of reasoning in the domain) is typically confounded with the 'knowing that' (the model of the domain that the system reasons with).

19.3.1 Automatic programming in XPLAIN

The idea behind the XPLAIN system is a simple but powerful one which links the two processes of designing an expert system and obtaining coherent explanations from it. One way to design an expert consultation program is to specify the domain model and the domain principles, and then invoke an automatic programmer on this specification to generate the performance program. The process of integrating the prescriptive and descriptive aspects of the specification into the final system is recorded and used to produce explanations of the system's behaviour.

The domain model contains facts about the domain of application, such as causal paths and taxonomies. This concept corresponds quite closely to what Clancey would call 'structural knowledge' (see Chapter 12) – the kind of knowledge that underlies situation/action rules of the usual kind. The domain principles include methods and heuristics, which are usually either hard-coded into the interpreter or given to the interpreter as meta-rules. This corresponds quite closely to what Clancey would call 'strategic knowledge'. Swartout argues convincingly, as Clancey does, that separating out these different kinds of knowledge has positive effects on aspects of system performance other than the explanation facility, such as modifiability.

Swartout collected observational data on the kinds of questions that medical students and fellows asked when they ran the Digitalis Therapy Advisor. Three kinds of question were identified:

- questions about the methods employed by the program, such as how it calculates values for certain parameters;
- justifications of program behaviour, such as why are certain adjustments to therapy recommended;
- explanation of system questions, when there is some doubt about what kind of answer the system wants or expects.

The first type is the kind of question that most expert systems can answer without difficulty. All that is required is that the program be able to produce an English description of the code that is executed. The second type requires something more: the ability to represent and reference the medical knowledge underlying the code. The third type requires something more again: the ability to represent the user's understanding of the terminology in a question and resolve any conflicts between that understanding and the intended meaning. XPLAIN concentrates on the second type of question.

The automatic programming approach adopted in the XPLAIN system can be seen as a way of combining both the specification and implementation phases of constructing an expert system. The idea is that the specification of the domain model should be entirely declarative, because the program may want to use the same piece of knowledge in different ways. The domain principles are used to refine the goal structure associated with the task in a recursive manner until there are methods associated with each of the bottom-level steps that the program has to perform.

The kind of control exercised by domain principles is rather stronger than MYCIN's use of meta-rules, because domain principles do more than merely order or prune the application of domain-specific rules. The integration of the program fragments thus generated is a complex process that need not concern us here, as we are more interested in the principle of deriving explanations from declarative representations of domain knowledge. However, potential interactions between program actions have to be resolved, using knowledge that is also derived from the domain model and the domain principles.

19.3.2 The Explanable Expert Systems project

Swartout draws attention to the problem of 'computer artefacts' in previous explanation systems. These artefacts are aspects of the computation which derive not from the underlying domain model or the domain principles but from the simple fact that parts of the program are nothing more than low-level algorithms which are implemented so that the computer will run the consultation. Such computational artefacts are of no interest to physicians, and users are unlikely to understand either how they work or why they are necessary.

The ideas behind the XPLAIN system have since been generalized into an approach to expert systems design called the Explainable Expert Systems (EES) paradigm (Neches *et al.*, 1985). As we have seen, these ideas are compatible with the drive to differentiate and render explicit different kinds of domain knowledge, but they also include the crucial insight that many of the ultimate grounds for justification reside in the system development process. In the absence of formal machinery for recording and subsequently deploying these decisions, such information is typically lost in the implementation phase.

Figure 19.9 gives a global view of the EES framework. Note that the left-hand box containing the domain model and domain principles also contains other kinds of knowledge. For example, definitions of domain terminology are separated out from the domain model and principles; they had been a part of the principles in XPLAIN. Trade-offs are another kind of knowledge associated with domain principles, which indicate pros and cons of selecting a particular strategy to achieve a goal, while preferences are used to set priorities on goals based on their associated trade-offs. Integration knowledge is used to resolve conflicts between principles at the time that the automatic programmer is run, and optimization knowledge is concerned with the efficient execution of the

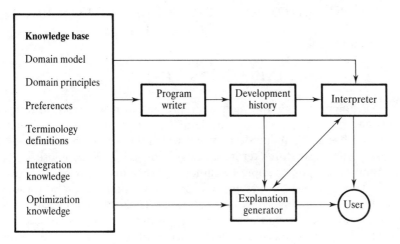

Figure 19.9 Global view of the EES framework, adapted from Neches *et al.* (1985).

expert system derived by the programmer. These ancillary sources of knowledge are a good illustration of kinds of meta-knowledge that go beyond the pruning and ordering of object-level rules at execution time that one associates with earlier expert system paradigms.

The specification of an EES system's knowledge base is represented in a semantic network formalism (see Chapter 9) called NIKL (Moser, 1983), which is a descendant of KL-ONE (Brachman and Schmolze, 1985). Like KL-ONE, NIKL builds constellations of concepts, which have an internal structure consisting of slots (or roles), and which are capable of entering into relations (or links) with other concepts. NIKL also contains a *classifier* which, given an existing network and a new concept with a particular structure, can place the concept at the correct location in a taxonomy. For example, given nodes representing ANIMAL, DOG and RABID-ANIMAL, the classifier will take the new concept RABID-DOG, create a new node for it, and correctly locate this node as a descendant of DOG and RABID-ANIMAL in the hierarchy. This facility is useful when a large domain model is being built incrementally.

Neches describes an application of the EES framework for building a Program Enhancement Advisor (PEA), which attempts to advise a programmer about ways of improving the readability of his code. The NIKL concepts in this domain are code transformations, such as changing a LISP COND (see Appendix A) into an IF-THEN-ELSE. The IF-THEN-ELSE concept is a kind of the KEYWORD CONSTRUCT concept which is, in turn, a kind of the concept EASY-TO-READ CONSTRUCT. Thus, the program might advise the user to replace

(COND ((ATOM X) X) (T (CAR X)))

by the more readable

(IF (ATOM X) THEN X ELSE (CAR X))

Problem-solving knowledge is represented in NIKL too, in terms of plans and goals organized into a hierarchy. Plans and goals are related; each plan has a 'capability description' which describes what the plan can achieve. NIKL also stores terminological knowledge which is used by the program writer, for example to gather together instances of concepts.

As in the XPLAIN system, the program writer works by top-down refinement, expanding goals into subgoals. Thus the main goal in PEA, *achieve enhanced program*, is refined into subgoals, such as achieve more readable program and achieve more efficient program. This is an example of what the authors call 'user-directed dynamic refinement', because the kind of enhancement performed is determined at run-time by user input. If achieve more readable program is chosen, then this goal will automatically be subject to goal/subgoal refinement, for example into scanning the program for transformation opportunities, confirming them with the user, and ultimately performing them. However, the EES program writer is also capable of reformulating goals that cannot be implemented directly. For example, a goal may need to be split into cases, instead of subgoals, as in perform action A on each instance of concept C, or a goal may involve a choice, as in perform action A on one instance of concept C.

The authors claim the following advantages for their approach:

- It is easy to express high-level strategies of the kind that are only implicit in the majority of expert systems, and show how they are refined into lower-level strategies.

- Separation of different kinds of knowledge makes a system more modular and easier to modify than first-generation expert systems.

- The automatic classification of new knowledge in a language like NIKL eases system development, because the knowledge engineeer need not worry about how new knowledge should be structured.

The EES approach has yet to address the problem of how to build expert systems with particular control structures, although it provides an interesting framework for thinking about the kinds of control issue we have considered. One way of looking at this problem is to concentrate on the interpreter that will execute the code output by the program writer. At present, the interpreter is kept very simple, and the control information is expressed in domain principles. Thus a MYCIN-like backward-chaining behaviour could be induced by a principle that said something like 'collect evidence for and against a hypothesis, so long as its certainty exceeds this threshold'. The domain model would contain the necessary information concerning what constituted evidence for and against which hypotheses, while evidence combination would be integration knowledge, in terms of the framework given in Figure 19.9.

19.4 Explanation facilities and future research

We saw in Chapter 16 how INTERNIST used hierarchical hypothesize-and-test as a technique for factoring a large solution space and building very large knowledge bases. However, a hierarchical approach to problem solving has other advantages, including transparency of program behaviour and flexibility of control. These properties were illustrated in this chapter by a case study of the CENTAUR system, which uses a frame hierarchy to supply the problem solving context in which production rules operate, and an agenda of tasks to control the order in which hypotheses are explored.

The EES research is a good example of a particular methodology for knowledge engineering (specification followed by compilation), which we have encountered in one form or another in most of the chapters in Part IV. The research is still in progress, and seems set to improve on various aspects of XPLAIN; for example, in the separation of terminological knowledge from domain principles. It is also envisaged that the refinement process will ultimately be an interactive one, which will admit of guidance from the user.

However, it is not altogether clear how this methodology allows one to mix different control strategies (as one can in CENTAUR, say); presumably the domain principles must be ordered or structured in some way. The main problem associated with such an approach is that it results in a large development history and requires a very powerful program writer, as Neches *et al.* point out in their discussion. The alternative strategy, making the interpreter more complex by giving it powerful control primitives, cuts the development history and simplifies the program writer but buries control decisions in the interpreter's code. Having the program writer produce both the interpreter and the code sounds interesting. This would effect an even greater separation between control knowledge and domain knowledge, but would presumably pose more integration problems.

As you can see, explanation is a complex topic, and the treatment given above is not meant to be exhaustive. However, it is intended to cover the main concerns and activities of researchers who are interested in both developing a methodology for building expert systems and improving the quality of explanations they produce. The critical issues appear to be:

(1) the differentiation of different kinds of knowledge;

(2) the explicit rendition of strategic and structural knowledge that tends to be hidden in program code;

(3) the modelling of individual users' knowledge or levels of skill.

We have concentrated upon issues 1 and 2 here, and neglected 3, which is still very much a research topic. A typical approach involves classifying users along some dimension of expertise, and then attaching various interaction modes to these classes. For example, users lacking in domain knowledge might need to have key concepts explained to them and be kept away from 'powerful' system commands, while users who are domain experts but who have never used the system before might be more interested in learning such commands and not need the explanation of concepts. User modelling is a difficult research area; there are few simple solutions to the problem of how best to maintain a representation of some user's understanding of a domain or a system.

Bibliographical notes

Self (1974) is still worth reading as an early review of 'student models' in computer aided instruction; many of his comments also apply to explaining expert systems. The interested reader is referred to Sleeman and Brown (1982) for early papers which address the topic of user modelling, and Polson and Richardson (1988) for more recent papers. Jackson and Lefrere (1984) provides a review of knowledge-based approaches to man–machine interaction that also touches on some issues relevant to explanation facilities.

STUDY SUGGESTIONS

19.1 What is wrong with simply providing the user with a trace of which rules have fired as an explanation of a program's reasoning?

19.2 Why is explanation often easier in a rule-based system if we distinguish between different kinds of rules?

19.3 Take any program that you have written for a previous exercise – such as the 'wine advisor' of Study suggestion 14.4 – and attempt to provide it with a satisfactory explanation facility. Try to differentiate between representations that perform rather different kinds of task, and use this classification to structure your explanations.

Part V

Software Tools and Architectures

20 Tools for Building Expert Systems

Introduction

This chapter is not meant to be a comprehensive, up-to-the-minute consumer guide to commercially available knowledge engineering environments. The intention is rather to outline the functionality of typical software tools which are now being used to construct expert systems, and capture the flavour of the current debate concerning what the tools of the future ought to be like. Although we have already met some of the toolkits to be discussed in this chapter, and considered a number of knowledge representation schemes from a theoretical point of view, this chapter makes a systematic attempt to categorize such tools according to the ways in which they are typically used and to assess their practical utility.

20.1 Overview of expert system tools

The majority of software tools for building expert systems seem to fall into five broad categories:

(1) *Expert system shells*, which are essentially abstractions over one or more applications programs. As we saw in Chapter 14, among the first of these was EMYCIN, which provided the production rule interpreter of MYCIN, together with all the ancillary data structures, such as knowledge tables, and their associated indexing mechanisms. A nicer rule language was provided to improve readability, and there was also software for maintaining a library of cases and monitoring the system's conclusions with respect to them. A more recent descendant of EMYCIN is S.1 (Teknowledge, 1985), a fairly sophisticated shell which combines the basic backward-chaining mechanism of EMYCIN with frame-like data structures and extra control facilities (see also Chapter 21).

(2) *High-level programming languages*, which to some extent conceal their implementation details, thereby freeing the programmer from low-level considerations of efficiency in the storage, access and manipulation of data. OPS5 (Forgy, 1982; see also Chapter 8 and Appendix B) is a good example of such a language; it is easy to learn and yet less constraining than a typical shell. Such languages have not usually been well packaged in the past, because most were research tools (and therefore available at low cost) rather than becoming commercial products, although this is now changing.

(3) *Multiple-paradigm programming environments*, sometimes called *hybrid systems*, which provide a set of software modules that allow the user to mix a number of different styles of artificial intelligence programming. Among the first to become available was a research tool called LOOPS (Bobrow and Stefik, 1983; see also Chapter 10), which combined object- and rule-based representations. A number of commercial products of this ilk are now available (at a price), and these provide the skilled user with a range of options that is potentially very large indeed.

(4) *Skeletal systems*, which provide the knowledge engineer with a basic problem-solving program to be instantiated. The most ambitious ventures in this direction to date are probably BB* (Hayes-Roth *et al.*, 1987) and the ABE project (Erman *et al.*, 1986). BB* is a 'blackboard architecture': a particular kind of problem-solving architecture which is described in detail in Chapter 22. ABE is a design for a software tool which facilitates programming with large communicating modules of code embedded in an operating

system. Such programs are meant to provide the user with an environment in which it is relatively easy to select, elaborate and combine skeletal systems.

(5) *Additional modules* for performing specific tasks within a problem-solving architecture. A good example of this kind of module is the dependency network used by VT (see Chapter 18) to keep track of which values of design variables depend on values determined by earlier decisions. These networks can also be used to propagate updates brought about by changing data or assumptions, in which case they are called *Truth Maintenance Systems* (TMSs).

It is worth saying a little more about each of these in turn, and trying to decide what their strengths and weaknesses are.

20.2 Expert system shells

Shells are intended to allow non-programmers to take advantage of the efforts of programmers who have solved a problem similar to their own. Thus the EMYCIN tool (van Melle, 1981) allowed the MYCIN architecture to be applied to another medical domain, for example pulmonary function test interpretation in PUFF, as well as a number of non-medical applications, such as the structural analysis program SACON. However, as was pointed out in Chapter 14, we need to consider more deeply the question of when this kind of technology transfer is appropriate.

20.2.1 Matching shells to tasks

It is clear that all shells are not suited to all tasks. Van Melle was among the first to point out that EMYCIN was *not* a general-purpose problem-solving architecture. Rather, he suggested that EMYCIN was suitable for deductive approaches to diagnostic problems, where large amounts of data are available and it is possible to enumerate the solution space of diagnostic categories in advance. Clancey has since dubbed these 'heuristic classification' problems (see Chapters 14 and 15). The approach appeared to be less well suited to what Van Melle called 'formation problems', which involve the piecing together of a complex whole that must satisfy some set of constraints. We have called these 'construction problems' (see Chapters 17 and 18).

Unfortunately, it is difficult to be rigorous in one's recommendations concerning what shell should be used for what problem. This is because we do not have very clear ideas concerning how the broad range of expert system tasks should be classified (but see Hayes-Roth *et al.*, 1983, Chapter 1; Chandrasekaran and Mittel, 1984; Reichgelt and van

Harmelen, 1986, for attempts in this direction). One feels that distinctions such as that between diagnostic and formation problems, though intuitively appealing, are not quite right. Many problems can be solved in different ways; for example, INTERNIST's approach to diagnosis shares many features of constructive problem solving (see Chapter 16), and really hard problems often require a mixed approach for their solution.

A great deal more will be said about the general problem of selecting an expert system tool in the next chapter (see Section 21.2). With respect to shells, the majority of commercial products provide the user with facilities that are adequate only for small search spaces, for example exhaustive backward chaining with limited control facilities. They are usually more suitable for classification than for construction problems, although the purveyors of these programs do not always point this out.

20.2.2 Shells and inflexibility

The advantageous simplicity of the knowledge representation language associated with most shells also has a number of disadvantages, as noted by Aikins (1983) in her critique of the EMYCIN implementation of PUFF.

- The production rule formalism employed by EMYCIN made it difficult to distinguish different kinds of knowledge – heuristic knowledge, control knowledge, knowledge about expected values for parameters. We saw in Chapter 19 that the ability to differentiate knowledge types has been advocated by other authors for reasons of understandability.

- The relatively unstructured rule set employed by EMYCIN made the acquisition of new knowledge difficult, since adding a rule to the set involved making changes elsewhere in the system, for example to knowledge tables containing information about medical parameters. This was, of course, one of the problems that the TEIRESIAS system (see Chapter 13) set out to solve.

- The exhaustive backward chaining employed by EMYCIN as its major mode of inference, involving both meta-level and object-level rules, made the generation of comprehensible explanations quite difficult. As Clancey (1983) pointed out, programming decisions about the order and number of clauses in a rule could have profound effects on the way the search space unfolds (see Chapter 12).

Other criticisms voiced by Aikins concerned not only the particular implementation of PUFF in EMYCIN, but the functionality of rule-based systems generally, and hence other shells which use production rules as the main representation language. A good deal of expertise consists of knowledge about typical patterns of data; typical in the sense of being either frequently occurring or idealized in some way. Experts can recognize familiar patterns of data with ease, and are capable of classifying possibly noisy and incomplete patterns in terms of a set of prototypical ideals. They also have valuable intuitions about what constitutes a relevant, interesting or surprising data value, and such clues contribute to decisions about what to do next when trying to solve some problem. None of this is very easy to represent using condition–action rules alone, unless one allows the formalism to become arbitrarily complex, which vitiates one of the advantages of using production rules in the first place.

Alvey (1983) also experienced problems with EMYCIN's explanation system in the creation of a 200-rule prototype system for helping with the management of terminally ill cancer patients. Like Aikins, he complained that although the system was capable of providing a trace of rule activations, the trace was often quite verbose. In general, there appeared to be an adverse trade-off between:

(1)   writing 'powerful' rules with many clauses which execute in an efficient and well-controlled manner, and

(2)   writing a greater quantity of smaller 'weaker' rules with fewer clauses which are probably less efficient, but which generate more comprehensible explanations.

Further criticisms of EMYCIN by Myers *et al.* (1983) are also instructive and grouped under two headings:

- The *run-time* interface. Consultations are always system-initiated, and the question–answer dialogue is rather rigid, permitting no intervention on the part of the user. The explanation system describes rather than justifies patterns of reasoning, as Clancey pointed out in the course of his work on NEOMYCIN (see Chapter 19).

- The *build-time* interface. Access to the knowledge base is limited. The knowledge engineer can access only a single rule or a single parameter at a time using the edit facilities provided, but there are obviously intimate connections between medical parameters and the rules that reference them.

They also found that the sharp division between 'running' and 'building' modes was quite inconvenient in practice. Ideally, one would like to be able to run the inference engine while building, or access the knowledge base at run-time, for the purposes of experiment and debugging. These criticisms may seem a little harsh, since EMYCIN was the first of its kind. However, we shall see in Chapter 21 that many of these problems remain in later tools, such as S.1.

A final criticism of shells concerns the handling of uncertainty. A shell like EMYCIN comes complete with a particular formalism such as certainty factors for performing inexact reasoning. However, most if not all of the formalisms employed by these shells are either inconsistent with probability theory or have properties that are simply hard to analyse. Although a pragmatic justification can often be given for a particular treatment of uncertainty in the context of a particular application (for example, Shortliffe's rationale for using certainty factors in MYCIN), it is a much more dangerous enterprise to adopt such a treatment simply because it comes with the shell one is using.

In fairness, shells have the advantage of being widely available for smaller machines, such the IBM PC and the Apple Macintosh. They are often implemented in 'non-AI' languages such as Pascal and FORTRAN, which can aid portability and interfacing to other software. Shells are also inexpensive compared with some of the other options. A shell might cost a few hundred dollars, but this compares favourably with the tens of thousands of dollars it might cost to purchase a multiple paradigm programming environment, not to mention the difference in hardware requirements. A company could afford to purchase more than one shell that runs on existing hardware, experiment with and evaluate each one, and then select the tool most suitable for a given application.

20.3   High-level programming languages

High-level languages give programmers a fast prototyping tool, so that more flexible designs can be explored and evaluated at relatively low cost in terms of time and effort. Typically, the run-time and build-time interfaces are closer together, so that code can be run and tested incrementally, as it is written. The user interface will typically not be as 'friendly' as that provided by a shell, but a fluent programmer will nevertheless be able to make rapid progress.

Production rule languages, object-oriented programming languages, and procedural deduction systems usually provide the expert system builder with a few more degrees of freedom than a shell with regard to the details of such things as the specification of control and the handling of uncertainty. As noted above, shells normally come with a particular control regime, such as backward chaining, and a particular approach to inexact reasoning, such as certainty factors, hard-wired into the program. This added flexibility is particularly important in the development of experimental system designs, where one is not exactly sure in advance what mechanisms will be required to solve the domain problem.

20.3.1 Constraints of production rule languages

In fairness, high-level languages typically impose their own constraints. Thus the dynamic memory of OPS5 programs is limited to vectors in working memory; this rules out recursive data structures, such as graphs or trees. The architects of the MORE system (see Chapter 15) found this a serious limitation (Kahn, 1988). Certain kinds of control flow, such as recursion and iteration, are also hard to engineer. Arguably, this is the price you pay for the comparative simplicity of OPS5 code, and the efficiency with which it can be executed.

Early production systems spent over 90% of their time doing pattern matching. However, Forgy (1982) noticed that there were several possible sources of inefficiency in naive approaches to this process. The *Rete match algorithm*, designed by Forgy and used by the OPS family of production rule languages, is based on two fundamental insights:

- The left-hand sides of productions in working memory often share conditions, and naive approaches will tend to match these conditions against working memory N times for N occurrences. This is an example of *within-cycle iteration*.

- Working memory is only modified a little each time, yet naive approaches tend to match all the patterns against all the working memory elements for each cycle. This is an example of *between-cycle iteration*.

The algorithm reduces the overhead of within-cycle iteration on productions by using a tree-structured sorting network. The patterns in the left-hand sides of the productions are compiled into this network, and the match algorithm computes the conflict set for a given cycle by processing this network. The between-cycle iteration on working memory is eliminated by processing a set of tokens that indicate which patterns match which working memory elements, and then simply updating this set when working memory changes. The absence of any control process other than the reflect–act cycle (see Chapter 8) makes the resultant conflict set easy to process. Conflict resolution simply applies an algorithm to the set, without regard for any other aspect of the current computational context.

Clearly, any attempt to introduce recursive data structures would greatly complicate the matching process. Similarly, any attempt to complicate the control regime would mean that conflict resolution would have to take extra information into account. The point is that such languages always face a trade-off between expressive power and efficiency of execution, and it is arguable that OPS5 has this trade-off just about right.

The solution to the shortcomings of rule-based programming is not to complicate such languages (thereby diluting their strengths), but rather to combine them with other programming paradigms which allow recursion in data and control. Thus, combining rules and frames, and allowing the conditions of a rule to match against the slots of frames, provides a pleasing solution to the data problem (see Section 19.4). Similarly, embedding rule sets in a larger computational framework, involving agendas and multiple knowledge sources, provides a basis for solving the control problem (see Section 20.5 and Chapter 22).

20.3.2 Evaluating object-oriented approaches

As we noted in Chapter 12, the rule-based format is well suited to the expression of knowledge of the form

under conditions $C_1, ..., C_n$, perform action A

but is less well suited to describing complex objects and the relationships between them. Object-oriented programming languages provide programmers with an alternative framework for organizing knowledge in terms of declarative representations of domain objects. The procedural side of the problem solver is factored with respect to these objects, which are armed with their own procedures and which communicate with each other via message-passing protocols.

Another pleasing aspect of object-oriented programming is that it is a rather more analogical style of knowledge representation than that found in systems based on predicate calculus or production rules. Instead of knowledge about a domain object being scattered among the many rules or axioms that reference it, the knowledge is collected in one place, which is a representation of the object itself. This chunking is virtual, in the sense that not all of the information about an object will necessarily be stored in the corresponding computational object, but it remains true that, to issue a command or request to an object, one deals directly with that representation by sending a message to it.

There are many real systems in the world where the exchange of energy and information between components can be represented by message-passing among computational objects, and this link with simulation technology is one that has benefits for artificial intelligence generally and expert systems in particular (see McArthur *et al.*, 1986). It is arguable that simulation is a powerful tool for model-based problem solving, and that, in the context of complex systems, such patterns of reasoning are sometimes easier to understand than those associated with a more conventional rule-based approach to inference. Object-oriented programming is also a useful way of integrating symbolic computation with computing environments based around graphical objects such as menus and icons. Although the provision of such devices does not solve the problem of transparency in expert systems, it does provide the programmer with tools for constructing better displays (see Richer and Clancey, 1985).

However, this does not mean that it is always easy to decide what the computational objects in the object-oriented program should represent. In the early object-oriented languages, where the principal application was the writing of software to perform simulations, this was less of a problem. Computational objects stood for classes or instances of the real objects in whose behaviour one was interested. Thus, simulating the behaviour of a production line would involve creating computational objects that represented the configuration of machines, while messages represented the exchange of information, energy and partly assembled products. The programmer's task is made relatively easy, because there is a comprehensible mapping from computational objects to objects in the world.

In many expert systems applications, one might need the computational objects to stand for far more abstract entities, if this style of programming is actually to be used to solve the problem. Hence objects might stand for facts and goals, sets of rules or individual hypotheses. It is then much less easy to decide what kinds of messages such entities should exchange, and what the meaning of those messages might be.

A lot depends on the level at which this kind of behaviour is going on. If objects are just the low-level implementation vehicle for getting a particular pattern of reasoning, then this need have no epistemological consequences at all. It is simply a feature of the host programming language for your expert system application, and the objects may well remain hidden from view. If, on the other hand, the objects are visible to both the expert during system development and the user during system performance, then the appropriateness of this mapping between abstract and computational objects needs to be established.

Even in genuine simulation applications, the object-oriented style of programming is not without its problems. Many important events occur as (possibly unintended) side-effects of other events which are hard to characterize in terms of message-passing. Klahr et al. (1982) cite an example from air battle simulation. Suppose an unauthorized aircraft penetrates airspace monitored by a radar installation. In a simulation program, the easiest way to 'wake up' the computational object representing the radar is to get the intruder to send the radar a message, saying 'I am here!' However, such behaviour clearly does not correspond to anything that is happening in the real world. Furthermore, even if the intruder was foolish enough to deliberately broadcast his position, such behaviour would require him to know the position of all the in-range radar stations: a piece of knowledge that he would not normally possess. In other words, although the unnatural solution is computationally tractable, it attributes knowledge to computational objects that their real counterparts do not have.

20.3.3 Logic programming for expert systems

In their criticisms of early expert systems tools, such as EMYCIN, a number of researchers and practitioners suggested that logic programming might provide an alternative approach to the construction of knowledge-based systems (Kowalski, 1984). Thus Clarke and McCabe (1982) suggest that a production system such as MYCIN could easily be reconstructed in PROLOG. Rules would be represented by Horn clauses (see Chapter 5) in which the head (positive) literal would stand for the conclusion to be drawn and the other (negative) literals would stand for the conditions.

PROLOG's built-in control regime approximates the backward chaining of MYCIN-style systems. Knowledge tables and other data could be represented by assertions. Recursive data structures, such as graphs and trees, can be created by PROLOG using clauses that contain complex terms. Programmers could develop their own handling of uncertainty, perhaps using certainty factors.

On the practical side, PROLOG gives you several useful things for free:

- an *indexed database* containing clauses which can be used to represent rules, procedures or data;
- *pattern matching* in the form of most general unification which allows both the datum and the pattern to contain variables and returns a substitution which would render them identical;
- a *control strategy* (depth-first search) with a top-down search rule (clauses nearer the 'top' of the database are accessed first) and a left–right computation rule (subgoals are processed in the left-to-right order in which they are listed).

On the strength of these facilities, a number of researchers suggested that one could also implement frames, or even objects, in PROLOG in a relatively straightforward manner. Both particular facts and 'type' information could be coded as unit clauses, for example:

```
fact(eb-virus, sequence, [C, A, G, ..., T, A, T]).

isa(eb-virus, herpes-virus).
```

which state that it is a database fact that the nucleotide sequence of the
EB virus is

```
[C, A, G, ..., T, A, T]
```

and that EB virus is a kind of herpes virus. In addition, inheritance
mechanisms could be implemented by PROLOG procedures.

There are a number of problems with this view, none of them
fatal, but none of them trivial either. This is a large topic, and we can
only consider some of the aspects here. Let us restrict ourselves to
looking at a couple of immediate issues to do with representation and
control.

One of the things that many implementations of PROLOG do not
provide is conventional data structures such as arrays or records, or
pointers for creating arbitrarily complex networks. Although these things
can all be simulated using complex terms or embedded lists, the accessing
and updating of these structures using pattern matching is, for the most
part, very much less efficient than 'lower level' representations which give
you uniform access to indices and fields by name, instead of by position.
There are some smart programming tricks that you can use to ameliorate
the situation, but then you're into Real Programming, rather than the
more high-level stuff that the knowledge engineer is supposed to do.
Also, the database indexing as provided probably isn't clever enough to
support efficient access to a large collection of frame-like clauses; this is
something else that a Real Programmer must do.

The built-in control structure can be something of a liability in non-
trivial applications. One cannot imagine a large frame-based system like
INTERNIST functioning adequately (or even at all) under a depth-first
search regime. Again a Real Programmer will have to write an interpreter
in PROLOG which implements the control strategy you need; it is not a
trivial task to do this in an efficient manner.

None of the above remarks militate against the use of procedural
deduction systems, such as MRS (see Chapter 11), which provide the requisite facilities for creating customized data structures and control regimes.
If we wish to compare logic-based approaches with rule- or object-based
ones, then a high-level language such as MRS is probably the correct standard
of comparison, rather than PROLOG. However, I think it is fair to say that
MRS has been used more as a research vehicle than a tool for developing
expert systems.

The moral of this story is (the not very surprising one) that
PROLOG is a programming language, just as LISP is. It is not a knowledge
representation language, any more than LISP is, because it doesn't have
built-in facilities for the flexible access and application of knowledge,
although you can create such facilities, as you can in LISP. The idea that
PROLOG is somehow easy to program in is a little misleading, and based

on an impression of the ease with which database entries and database queries can be constructed; this is not to be confused with Real Programming.

20.4 Multiple-paradigm programming environments

Multiple-paradigm programming environments allow skilled programmers to experiment with novel problem-solving architectures by selecting and combining different software modules. In the absence of a single universal knowledge-representation language suitable for arbitrary expert systems applications, practitioners may wish to avail themselves of more than one representational scheme, particularly when prototyping. Although there is no well-articulated theory of hybrid reasoning systems, experience with different schemes of representation and inference has shown that all have their weaknesses; thus the strategy of mixing schemes attempts to play as far as possible to their strengths.

We have already suggested that production rules provide a readable representation language for encoding empirical associations between conditions and actions, or observations and hypotheses, but they are less well suited to the encoding of arbitrary relations between domain entities, including such important relations as set/element and set/subset. Structured objects, such as frames, provide a flexible format for storing and accessing descriptions of domain entities, but the application of such knowledge is typically performed by arbitrary LISP code which can be hard to analyse. The rationale behind early attempts to marry the rule-and frame-based styles was the replacement of the procedural obscurity of demonic attachments with the clarity of productions, while setting production rules in a context which provided for a richer representation of data than that afforded by working memory.

LOOPS (Bobrow and Stefik, 1983) was the first AI programming environment to mix four programming paradigms within a message-passing architecture:

(1) *Procedure-oriented programming.* The basic LISP paradigm in which procedures are (for the most part) active and data are (for the most part) passive, even though LISP procedures are themselves data objects (lists). Procedures are allowed to side-effect data objects, permanently changing their public value.

(2) *Rule-oriented programming.* Like the above, except that condition–action rules play the role of procedures. In LOOPS, sets of rules were themselves objects, capable of being nested recursively so

that the 'action' part of a rule could invoke a subordinate rule set. Rule sets had control annotations attached to them which performed a rather primitive form of conflict resolution.

(3) *Object-oriented programming.* Structured objects have the characteristics of both program and data, and side-effects are normally local to objects, and allowed only through the 'proper channels' of the right protocol. Messages result in data values being broadcast or reset, but all data manipulation is done locally by the callee. How values are stored, modified or computed is no business of the caller.

(4) *Data-oriented programming.* Data access and data update trigger procedures, so that things happen as a side-effect of patterns in the data and the actions of other procedures on data. Variables that hold data values and have procedures attached to them, such as the slots in a frame, are often called *active values*. This style of programming is particularly useful in certain domains, such as simulation, where changes in data values need to be propagated across data structures.

LOOPS grew out of experiments with a representation language called Lore, but it has an acknowledged debt to a large number of earlier systems, including FLAVORS on the LISP Machine, KRL (Bobrow and Winograd, 1977), and UNITS (Stefik, 1979). Although the interface between production rules and objects was not particularly well engineered, LOOPS pointed the way and other better-engineered systems followed. UNITS' initial attempts to provide a 'rules language' also left quite a lot to be desired, as Rawlings and Fox (1983) pointed out, because it gave little more than a conventional programming language with GOTOs, assignment, iteration, and so forth.

However, KEE (Intellicorp, 1984; Kunz *et al.*, 1984), which is essentially 'Son of UNITS', surmounts most of these problems. Multiple inheritance of properties is supported, message-passing replaces procedure writing, and the rules language more closely resembles the syntax and semantics of productions. The package is embedded in a congenial programming environment that uses high-resolution graphics to display object hierarchies and windows representing individual objects.

KEE, and other environments such as Knowledge Craft (Carnegie Group, 1985), have also added a query language in the PROLOG style to the paradigms listed above. Different modules supporting different programming styles attain varying degrees of integration within the central object-oriented paradigm of such systems. Normally, both the conditions in production rules and logic clauses can be made to trigger on the slot values of structured objects, while rule actions may modify slot values. KEE allows the behaviour of an object to be described in terms of a set of production rules, rather as Aikins did in CENTAUR (see Chapters 16 and 19). Knowledge Craft, which began life as the frame language SRL (Wright and Fox, 1983), allows procedures attached to objects to initiate, or return control to, both the production rule and the logic programming modules.

Knowledge-engineering environments like KEE and Knowledge Craft are mostly concerned with providing the programmer with greater flexibility in the representation of knowledge and its procedural application, rather than imposing an overall framework on the business of building an expert system. Although rules, frames and logic can each be considered as frameworks in their own right, there is no overall unifying architecture within which the knowledge engineer is working. Rather it is up to knowledge engineers to create their own architecture, using the building blocks provided and the interfaces between them. This is not a trivial task, and few current tools provide much in the way of on-line assistance.

On the other hand, it is true to say that many of these knowledge-engineering environments have good user interfaces that use interactive graphics and mouse-driven menus creatively to make life easier for the programmer. As with high-level programming languages, the 'run' and 'build' interfaces are very close together, and this facilitates incremental system development. In addition to running on LISP machines, products such as KEE and Knowledge Craft also have implementations for VAX systems.

20.5 Abstract architectures

A new generation of software tools is slowly emerging from the research laboratories which attempt to help in the process of expert system construction without cramping the knowledge engineer's style. The components of these toolkits are various architectural building blocks (such as control mechanisms for coordinating the activities of multiple rule sets), task-oriented representation languages (such as languages for talking about faults in devices or arrangements of objects), and some kind of systems philosophy that helps the user put it all together. It is also worth noting that such tools typically satisfy some of the desiderata that we have discussed in earlier chapters to do with distinguishing different kinds of knowledge.

- They *separate* domain knowledge from control knowledge. It is usually possible to vary the control knowledge while holding the task and domain knowledge constant. This is clearly much harder to do in shells and high-level programming languages, while few multiple paradigm environments encourage or support this kind of design.

- They *differentiate* different kinds of both domain knowledge and control knowledge. Domain knowledge is often factored in terms of knowledge about actions, events and states. Control knowledge is often factored into global strategies (such as least commitment), foci (objects or attributes weighted to attract the attention of the interpreter), and heuristics (for deciding between competing foci).

- Modules are *reusable*, in that system builders can select, elaborate and combine existing modules as a basis for constructing new systems. Such architectures can be seen as a logical step in the progression from shells towards computing environments which attempt to combine the generality of high-level programming languages with the heuristic power of specially crafted knowledge representation and inference systems.

For example, Hayes-Roth *et al.* (1987; see also Chapter 22) describe an environment for building expert systems, called BB*, which makes an important distinction between three different levels of analysis:

(1) that of the particular *application* that the knowledge engineer is building;

(2) that of the task *framework* within which the knowledge engineer is working; and

(3) that of the problem-solving *architecture* which organizes and applies domain-specific knowledge to solve the task.

Looking at more than one level in this way enables us to analyse systems more easily, as well to experiment with alternative implementations of different modules, without endangering the grand design. Modularity means more reusability of knowledge structures, especially those which encode more general knowledge about task-dependent and task-independent reasoning strategies. Also, lower level knowledge structures may be put to a variety of uses, for problem solving, for explaining problem solutions, or for learning new problem-solving methods.

An important constraint placed on modules within a given level is that they meet uniform standards of knowledge content and representation – that they represent the same kinds of knowledge and do it in the same way. This is necessary from the point of view of the vertical organization of the hierarchy, because modules at higher levels will expect to be able to perform certain operations on lower levels, such as retrieving instances of concepts and instantiating generic concepts, even if they do not know how such knowledge is actually stored. In fact, uniformity helps to keep the interface between levels clean. From a horizontal point of view, uniformity allows modules at the same level to be combined in various ways – for example, into a pipeline – or to cooperate more loosely – for example, by sharing results.

Architecture is also important if you have a large problem that requires communication between quite heterogeneous programs. Thus your application might require complex signal processing and image interpretation as well as a classification or construction task, such as medical diagnosis or plan generation. One approach to this problem is to embed these programs in an operating system which facilitates the development of such applications. An example of this approach is the ABE project (Erman *et al.*, 1986), which aims to provide a full range of skeletal systems and programming tools for integrating different AI packages with other software. Here the emphasis is not on developing new knowledge representation languages or expert system shells but rather on providing an environment in which existing packages can be made to cooperate.

20.6 Additional modules

Facilities coming under the heading of additional modules are useful software tools that run in conjunction with an applications program. Generally, they perform some specialized function in an 'off the shelf' fashion that does not require either real programming in the host language or significant customization of the module. One example is KEE's Simkit: a software package for integrating simulation techniques with expert systems.

Another such facility is KEE-Worlds, a module which provides a mechanism for maintaining many different *contexts* in KEE. Roughly speaking, contexts are generated by branches in the search space where more than one operator is applicable. Imagine the following scenario, where there are two rules, each of which has its conditions satisfied by data in the current context of the computation:

```
[Rule1]  IF: today is a week day &
             illness is not present
        THEN: attend Computer Science class

[Rule2]  IF: today is a week day &
             weather is fine
        THEN: go sailing.
```

In most production systems, the conflict-resolution strategy will pick one of these rules to fire. However, in some applications it might be advantageous to 'split' the current context into two separate contexts, one in which we apply Rule1 and one in which we apply Rule2 (see Figure 20.1). These two contexts will differ in that different conclusions

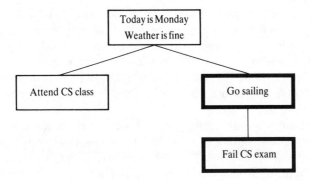

Figure 20.1 An example of multiple contexts.

will have been drawn; however, we may allow them to inherit information from their parent context. Thus, in each of the two contexts, today will still be Monday and the weather will still be fine.

We can now pursue the computation separately in each context, possibly branching again to generate new contexts. In this way, we may end by generating multiple solutions to the current problem, essentially by simulating different ways in which we might proceed, instead of making irrevocable control decisions.

However, there may come a point where a context can be deemed a failure, for example if it violates a constraint. Thus, in our example, the subsequent derivation of exam failure by an application of the rule

```
[Rule3]  IF: not attend Computer Science class
       THEN: fail Computer Science exam
```

might cause us to abandon the line of reasoning generated by Rule2. The context is then said to be *poisoned*. Typically, it is deleted, together with all ancestor contexts between itself and the choice point that gave rise to it, assuming that these are not also ancestors of other, extant contexts. Thus the contexts shown in dark outline in Figure 20.1 would disappear, leaving a single line of reasoning in which we attend our CS class.

Contexts therefore correspond to alternative decisions or assumptions made at different points in a computation. The problem of maintaining different assumption sets, and dependencies between them, is sufficiently difficult and sufficiently central to non-trivial applications to have developed its own literature, which goes under the headings of *truth maintenance*, or *reason maintenance*. This topic is discussed in detail in Chapter 23, where alternative computational mechanisms are explored.

The first expert systems tool to provide a context facility was ART, a derivative of the HEARSAY-III architecture described in Chapter 22. KEE and Knowledge Craft quickly followed. A procedural deduction system, called DUCK, provides a truth maintenance system defined over a facility managing multiple databases. Such facilities are generally expensive in terms of both memory and CPU time, but they can represent a natural solution to applications that may require multiple lines of reasoning. For example, in planning applications it is often beneficial to reason about alternative futures.

The trend towards 'add-on' modules is likely to continue as users demand additional facilities and the ability to interface to other kinds of software. In real applications, expert systems are rarely self-contained. They often require access to databases or robot arms, and receive data from signal processors or statistical packages.

This chapter has done no more than attempt a survey of the main types of expert system tool that are currently available, without going into detail about individual systems. In the next chapter, we concentrate upon the problems involved in selecting, learning to use, and actually deploying current tools. We shall see that many problems can arise in each of these phases, but that some of them are avoidable.

Bibliographical notes

Waterman (1986, Chapters 27–28) provides a catalog of expert systems tools, with a bibliography; unfortunately, such material quickly becomes out of date. Various magazines, such as *IEEE Expert*, do a reasonable job of reviewing new products as they become available. A critical comparison of some knowledge-engineeering environments, including KEE and Knowledge Craft, can be found in Laurent *et al.* (1986).

STUDY SUGGESTIONS

20.1 Compare and contrast the use of shells, high-level programming languages, and multiple paradigm programming environments for both classification and construction tasks.

20.2 Critique the expert systems tool with which you are most familiar. To be thorough, your evaluation ought to involve:

(a) detailing features of the tool that you like, and saying in what ways they make programming easier;

(b) detailing features that you dislike, and saying precisely how they conspire to make programming more difficult than it needs to be; and

(c) identifying additional features that you wish the tool supported

Under (c), try to distinguish between features that could easily be added to the tool and those that would incur substantial redesign or loss of efficiency.

21 Potential Implementation Problems

Introduction

Many difficulties arise in the implementation phase of building an expert system, although there has been very little systematic study of these problems. Such discussion as there is tends to be anecdotal, although we shall also examine some published reports of experiences and experiments. This chapter aims to give the reader some idea of: common pitfalls and how to avoid them; how to select a knowledge engineering tool; and how hard such tools are to learn and use.

21.1 Common pitfalls and how to avoid them

As an example of the anecdotal approach, Waterman (1986, Chapter 19) lists the following pitfalls, and suggests ways of avoiding them:

- The expert's domain knowledge becomes inextricably entwined with the rest of the program. In particular, it is impossible to separate it from general knowledge about search and problem solving. Waterman suggests that a rule-based organization can help achieve this, although we have seen from the comments of Clancey and Aikins that this is not always so.

- After extracting and representing hundreds of rules from an expert, the resultant knowledge base can still be radically incomplete and fail to solve simple problems, because fundamental concepts are missing or ill-represented. Waterman suggests that incremental development will help identify such problems early on. He advises testing at all phases of development, although we have seen that some knowledge-engineering tools make this easier than others.

- The development environment does not provide built-in explanation facilities, and adding such facilities to the completed system turns out to be non-trivial. Waterman suggests designing transparency in from the very beginning. This is good advice because, if there is no 'window' into what the program is doing, even the programmers will have a hard time understanding what is going on.

- The system contains a very large number of highly specific rules which slows execution and makes the system unwieldy. Waterman recommends collapsing the smaller rules into more general ones, where possible. Yet, as we saw in Section 20.2, there is generally an inverse trade-off between having rules that are powerful and rules whose justification and behaviour is easy to understand.

Here are some observations of my own, which I present without remedies, because it is not obvious what the remedies are.

- Incremental program development is all very well provided one is headed down (roughly) the right path. However, there appears to be no methodology for deciding when you have seen enough to decide that your approach is not working. Neither are there any guidelines for diagnosing what is wrong with your program, and deciding whether it can be repaired or whether it must be scrapped.

- There is very little evidence that knowledge-based programs are any easier to debug or modify than conventional programs; if anything they seem to be harder. Some 'high-level' languages are really not so high level after all, in that it can really help you to use them more effectively if you know something about how they are implemented. For example, the control regimes of languages such as OPS5 and PROLOG can be extremely puzzling to beginning programmers, even if they are experienced in other languages.

● In general, it is hard to know whether or not a particular programming tool or problem-solving method will 'scale up' from the kind of simple examples that one tends to use at the prototype stage to a full-blown application. In conventional programming, one can employ some kind of complexity analysis which tells you what the computational cost of your algorithm will be in the worst case, and then estimate how hard the typical case will be. In knowledge-based programming, the whole idea is that adding heuristic knowledge to your program should reduce complexity in the majority of cases. Consequently, it is often difficult to tell how significant worst-case results are. If you then encounter combinatorial problems, it can be difficult to tell whether you just need more knowledge or whether you need to rethink the whole design.

One could itemize other specific problems, but it is perhaps more fruitful to look at the general properties of tools for building expert systems (and the attitudes of programmers towards them) which are implicated in these and other difficulties. The following list is not intended to be exhaustive:

(1) Sometimes users (or their managers) select the wrong tool for the job, or use a tool just because they already have a software licence for it.

(2) Sometimes users underestimate the level of programming skill required by a tool.

(3) Sometimes users forget to practice the virtues of more conventional programming styles, such as thoughtful design and thorough documentation.

The next three sections seek to answer three important but difficult questions that arise from this list:

● How can one select the 'right' software tool?
● How easy to use are these tools *really*?
● What constitutes good programming style in such environments?

The answers are not easy to find, but everyone involved in expert system construction should care about these issues, and will be forced to think about them from time to time. My approach will be partly anecdotal, partly based on appeals to authority, and partly based on such relevant studies and surveys as have been performed. In the final section, I reproduce some useful maxims from the literature.

21.2 Selecting a software tool

Hayes-Roth *et al.* (1983, Chapter 1) propose some very general issues to consider when selecting an expert system building tool.

- *Generality*. Pick a tool with only the generality necessary to solve the problem. Thus, if you do not need complicated control facilities, there is no point in using them. Using features that you do not need is almost bound to cost you more in terms of money, personnel time and computational overhead.

- *Selection*. Let the problem characteristics determine the tool selected, rather than extraneous considerations, such as what software is ready to hand. Fortunately, the authors have something more to say on this topic in their Chapter 4, in terms of a classification of problem types, as we shall see below.

- *Speed*. When time is critical, choose a tool with built-in facilities for explanation and a good user interface. Building interfaces is time consuming, as well as being moderately tedious.

- *Testing*. Test the tool early on by building a small prototype. This is undoubtedly good advice, although the problem of determining the degree of scale-up one can expect remains unaddressed.

The critical question of problem characteristics is discussed in Stefik *et al.* (1983). They suggest a framework for analysing problems, mostly based on properties of the underlying search space. The main points are discussed below. My treatment is generalized to some extent, in that the authors distinguish eleven cases to my four. However, the basic principles remain the same.

(1) *Small solution space with reliable data and knowledge*. Suppose that there are not too many alternatives to consider when looking for a solution and you are certain that your data and rules are correct. Then it is possible to pursue a single line of reasoning exhaustively, backtracking where necessary, to find a solution. Thus there may well be an 'off the shelf' expert systems shell that will do what you want. One suspects that this approach works best if you want a *satisficing* solution, rather than an optimal one; that is, a solution that is 'good enough' rather than 'the best'. Bear in mind that anything that involves combining solution elements, in a consistent or optimal manner, may cause combinatorial explosion, even if the elements themselves are easy to find.

(2) *Unreliable data or knowledge*. If data or knowledge is unreliable, it will usually be necessary to combine information from diverse sources and employ some form of inexact reasoning. The authors

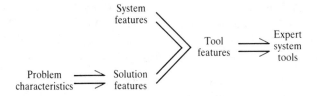

Figure 21.1 Basis for selection of an expert system tool.

wisely refrain from making specific recommendations, but the main candidates are certainty factors (see Chapters 3 and 6) and fuzzy logic (see Chapter 6). For a discussion of other alternatives, such as belief functions and Bayesian belief updating, see Chapter 25.

(3)   *Large but factorable solution space.* One finds two senses of the word 'factorable' in the literature, and they are not identical. A search space is said to be factorable if there exist 'pruning rules' that will reduce the size of the space early in the computation (Stefik *et al.*, 1983, page 99). However, a search space is also factorable if it can be decomposed into independent components which can then be processed separately (Nilsson, 1980, page 37), perhaps by different rule sets or different partitions of the same rule set. This is normally achieved by breaking the main problem down into non-interacting subproblems. The success of the main goal is then dependent on the success of a conjunction of more or less independent subgoals, and if any of these fails, then the whole computation fails without more ado. In either event, hierarchical generate-and-test is a reasonable method to employ, because you will be able to rule out large numbers of possibilities by pruning and/or decompose the solution space with respect to subproblems.

(4)   *Large, non-factorable solution space.* The solution space may not be factorable in either of the above senses. Many design problems are like this: partial solutions can only be evaluated in the global context of the whole design. One never knows whether one has succeeded or not until the last piece of the puzzle falls into place. A common method for dealing with large search spaces is to consider the space at various levels of abstraction, that is, descriptions of the space at different degrees of detail. Solving problems in this way corresponds to what is sometimes called 'top-down refinement' (see Chapter 17). One then achieves some high-level goal by achieving subgoals at lower (more detailed) levels of problem specification. The idea is to try to do away with expensive backtracking over levels, but this only works if there is no

significant interaction between subproblems. As we saw in Chapter 18, a least commitment strategy supplemented by guessing can be effective here, but it also helps to have domain-specific knowledge about how to resolve anticipated conflicts.

Hayes-Roth *et al.* represent the selection problem in terms of Figure 21.1. Problem characteristics suggest solution features, as in points 1–4 listed above. These are then combined with desired system features – such as production rules, forward reasoning, or explanation facilities – to suggest desirable tool features, which in turn suggest which tools might be appropriate. It has to be said that this is not as easy as it looks, but there is little doubt that this approach is more rational than most.

21.3　How easy is it to use these tools?

One of the 'selling points' of software tools for building expert systems, and the cause of much controversy, is the claim that many of them can be used by non-programmers, or at least by programmers with no previous grounding in artificial intelligence techniques. This section attempts a critical evaluation of such claims, citing studies and surveys as appropriate. The available evidence suggests that using a typical tool is not much easier than learning a new programming language, and that even experienced programmers make the kinds of mistake committed by beginning students of conventional programming.

Ward and Sleeman (1987) monitored experienced programmers learning to use the S.1 expert systems shell (Teknowledge, 1985), which is a modern derivative of EMYCIN. S.1 knowledge bases contain many different kinds of object: control statements, classes, class types, production rules, value hierarchies and functions. Thus, in extending EMYCIN with the addition of desirable features for representation and control, the architects of S.1 have also complicated the system to some considerable extent.

The S.1 shell has four modes of operation:

- knowledge base preparation (editing);
- knowledge base consultation (running the program);
- loading-break (a load or compile-time error);
- consultation break (a run-time error).

The programmers had difficulty navigating between these four modes, even though they were experienced in the usual process of creating a file, compiling it, running it, and recovering from errors. The error messages were no more helpful than those associated with conventional programming languages, in that they were unable to distinguish between the locus of error and the point in the execution of the code where the error manifested itself. Given the incremental nature of knowledge-base development, and exhortations by authorities which endorse such a strategy, the process of moving between these modes ought to be made as easy as possible, because the programmer is likely to have to perform the iteration even more times than in a more conventional programming task.

The study also found that if programmers stuck to the simplest possible model of computation – in which they input data, asked the system to determine the value of some parameter using a small knowledge base of rules and then display the result – there were few problems in deciding how to represent things and how to control search. As matters grew complicated – with the size of the knowledge base, the uncertain nature of the knowledge, or more complex control regimes – careful thought was needed on strategic matters. The following questions were among those that arose; they are all the more interesting because none of them are really specific to the S.1 tool.

- When should knowledge be represented by classes, and when should you use attributes? For example, if the class of aircraft in which you are interested can have one or more engines, should you simply let number-of-engines be a slot in the aircraft frame, or should you create new subclasses of the class aircraft, such as one-engined-aircraft, two-engined aircraft, and so on? The answer is not obvious without some thought; largely it depends on such pragmatic considerations as:

    do aircraft with different numbers of engines differ from each other on other attributes that are important to problem solving?

    If the answer is 'no', the attribute solution is probably best, all other things being equal. If the answer is 'yes', we need to consider if the information needed can be represented by creating a finite (preferably small) number of subclasses. If it can, the subclass solution is probably best; otherwise we must fall back on using attributes. Arguably, good programmers have more experience in making such design decisions (and getting them right) than non-programmers. This kind of problem is common to most representation schemes using structured objects, not just S.1.

- How should the premises and conclusions of a rule be organized, and how should different rules interrelate? Most rule-based systems allow us to gather evidence for and against hypotheses by using rules of variable grain size, depending on how many conditions we pile onto our rules. If premises P_1, ..., P_n all contribute to conclusion Q, we have the option of creating different rules that combine these premises in different ways, for example into n different rules:

> if P_1 then Q
> if P_n then Q

or into a single rule:

> if $P_1, ..., P_n$ then Q

or some combination of rules in between these two extremes. The point is that the 'n rules' situation will be more sensitive with respect to detecting evidence for Q than the single rule situation, where we demand that *all* the P_i be satisfied. Often this decision depends on how strong the mapping is between premises and conclusions: if the mapping is well understood, we can probably decide which premises should be grouped together and generate less than n rules. If, on the other hand, the association is more heuristic, we will get more robust behaviour if we do not make too many assumptions about which premises go together. Again, this kind of decision is non-trivial, and requires careful analysis of the nature of the link between evidence and hypotheses.

● What levels should be used for certainty factors in rules? It usually helps to have some idea of how long different chains of reasoning are likely to be before setting the 'tallies' on production rules. Otherwise, conclusions that are derived from long chains of reasoning may attain smaller certainty factors than conclusions derived from shorter ones. Sometimes this effect is desired; for example, if the length of the chain really reflects the tenuousness of the connection between evidence and hypothesis. But, in many instances, the length of the chain may reflect more or less arbitrary decisions about the grain sizes of rules.

Ward and Sleeman conclude that although learning to use S.1 seems to be no more difficult than learning a new programming language, such as Pascal, it is not any easier either. Their judgement is that claims made to the effect that personnel with no previous programming experience can easily learn to use such tools appear to be 'quite unjustified'. My own experience of supervising postgraduate students using a range of such tools (some simpler than S.1, and some more complex) is entirely in accord with their findings and conclusions: even good programmers have problems and do not always produce sensible code, as we shall see in the next section.

None of the above ought to be controversial. Programming is an intrinsically hard activity which is not for everybody. It is irresponsible to suggest that solutions to hard problems can be generated by non-programmers, given current tools and our current level of understanding as to how these tools should be used.

In fairness to S.1, it should be said that it is entirely adequate for certain kinds of task, and can be used to implement a range of problem-solving methods that are not restricted to heuristic classification (as its progenitor EMYCIN was). Thus Lan *et al.* (1987) used it to implement the solution to a construction problem: that of determining the location of printing plates on a newspaper printing press. They note that they had little serious difficulty, as long as they did not demand styles of inference from the system that it was not intended to support (such as hypothetical reasoning).

On a more general note, Robinson *et al.* (1987) point out, selecting an expert system tool is a hard problem, because:

- many of the more sophisticated tools are quite expensive, which prohibits speculative purchase;
- the time necessary to understand these systems by the average consumer prohibits a detailed evaluation of competing systems;
- manufacturers' terminology and notation is very diverse, even in the description of standard AI techniques, so it is hard to figure out just what is being offered.

There is a sense in which the last problem is just a special case of the general problem of software standardization. Programs of whatever kind are difficult to compare without extensive study. In the sector of AI tools, this problem has been compounded by the novelty of the technology.

21.4   What is good programming style?

In more conventional styles of programming, there exist notions of what constitutes good programming practice. Furthermore, whole books have been written which deal with aspects of program design, programming style and efficiency considerations. Even if some of these topics are controversial (what is good style?), such texts, together with word of mouth from more experienced programmers, help the novice learn the trade.

Such is less routinely the case in the context of AI programming in general, and knowledge engineering in particular. For many years, LISP primers contained horrendous programs that would make any 'structured programming' enthusiast shudder with horror. Sample programs were often peppered with non-standard flow of control, cavalier use of dynamic variable binding, and the careless manipulation of data structures such as property lists. This situation has improved dramatically in recent years –

compare Winston and Horn (1984) with Winston and Horn (1981), for example. Nevertheless, writing good LISP code is a skill that not many people acquire, and many famous AI programs contain the most appalling examples of bad programming practice.

The fact that it has taken 25 years for something resembling a good LISP programming style to become widespread does not augur well for the new languages, tools and environments that are currently emerging. It is pretty unclear to me what constitutes good KEE style, for example, and I have seen knowledge engineers who have years of experience in structured languages run amok when faced with a mix of procedural attachment, combined methods and active values! None of this is intended as a serious criticism of KEE (which I have unfairly singled out as the target of these comments), rather it is a sad fact of life that powerful tools require equally strong methodologies for their application if they are to serve our purposes. Perhaps we can take comfort from the example of OPS. It has taken only 5 years or so for a definitive text (Brownston *et al.*, 1985) to appear telling prospective knowledge programmers how to write effective OPS5 code.

Proponents of 'logic for expert systems' have contributed surprisingly little to the debate about programming style. Anyone who has ever marked a student exercise knows that it is as easy to commit gross errors of taste and substance in PROLOG as it is in LISP or FORTRAN-77, in terms of impenetrable flow of control and unprincipled side-effects. As Kluzniak and Szpakowicz (1984) point out, it is by no means self-evident that 'programming in logic' results in either better programs or less programming effort. Neither is it clear why a set of predicate calculus formulas should contain fewer bugs than a set of program statements, or be any easier to debug. Perhaps we need to make a clearer distinction between:

(1)   the use of logic-based knowledge representation for expert systems;

(2)   the use of deductive inference as a mode of problem solving;

(3)   the use of logic programming as an implementation strategy; and

(4)   the use of logic as a specification language for system prototypes.

In short, it seems that 'heuristic programming' is here for some time to come, in at least two senses:

- The programs will continue to be guided by the opportunistic application of imperfect knowledge.
- The programmers will continue to develop systems by rapid prototyping followed by incremental augmentation of the knowledge base and 'hand-tuning' on a largely experimental basis.

This is not altogether good news, but I suspect that it is the truth. The development of a more rigorous methodology is a desirable research goal, but a good deal more homework needs to be done before it can become a reality.

21.5   More maxims on expert system development

So as not to end this chapter on a depressing note, I include some selected maxims on how to build expert systems from Buchanan *et al.* (1983), plus a little commentary of my own. If expert system builders all followed Buchanan's advice, they could save themselves a good deal of unecessary grief.

- Select a task that is neither too difficult nor too hard for human experts.
- Define the task very clearly.
- Decide early how you will evaluate the system.

It is particularly important to draw a line around what the system will be expected to achieve; better still, state explicitly what the system will *not* be expected to do. It is better to have a reliable system that performs some fraction of a real task properly than an unreliable system that does most of the task correctly sometimes. Of course, reliability can only be ascertained if you have some criteria for judging the success of the system.

- Work intensively with a core set of representative problems, and keep a library of cases presented to the system.
- Separate domain-specific knowledge from general problem-solving knowledge, and aim for simplicity in the inference engine.

Make sure that your problems are representative, and either write or obtain some code that makes the running of examples easy. Software that logs a problem-solving session, including user inputs, is very useful if your system is highly interactive. We have already covered the issue of separating different kinds of knowledge in Chapters 12 and 19.

The authors also have good advice on rule writing:

- If a rule looks big, it is.
- If several rules are very similar, look for an underlying domain concept.

As in conventional programming, small is usually beautiful as far as chunks of code are concerned, and redundancy is usually a sign that a simplifying abstraction is possible.

The authors suggest building a Mark I system as soon as a typical example is well understood. However, the real nugget of pure gold is the following piece of advice: when building the Mark II system:

- Throw away the Mark I system!

In my opinion, many projects have foundered because programmers or system designers became irrationally attached to the first implementation of their ideas. This raises again the important question of when to stop elaborating and debugging Mark I: programmers often indulge in obsessional behaviour when building systems, 'perfecting' code that ought to be thrown away. Mark II should always build on the experience of Mark I, but only rarely on its actual code.

Finally:

- The process of building an expert system is inherently experimental.

Amen – this maxim is still true today. People who believe that expert systems can be built by unskilled personnel following some simple recipe are headed for a disappointment. One can always tell persons who have suffered from this experience, because they complain loud and long that AI has 'failed to deliver the goods'. Building a successful application requires the persistence and patience of a skilled programmer, as well as a genuine expert and a certain level of commitment from management.

Bibliographical notes

Papers in Hayes-Roth *et al.* (1983) provide some sensible advice about the practical business of building expert systems using special-purpose software. Much of this material has been referenced and discussed in the present chapter. It remains an open question as to how this technology can best be transferred from AI laboratories to industry at large. See Drummond *et al.* (1987) for some case histories and some useful discussion. Also, the paper by Robinson *et al.* (1987) referred to in Section 21.3, is worth reading in the original – it contains much good sense.

STUDY SUGGESTIONS

21.1 Devise some knowledge engineering maxims of your own, based on your experience so far (for example, with the Study suggestions from previous chapters). (Variations on Murphy's law don't count.)

21.2 Document your own progress in learning to use an expert systems tool. Try to classify any difficulties that you have. For example, you might begin by differentiating between the following kinds of problem:

- *Mode problems*. Finding your way around the user interface: editor, debugger, interpreter, and so on.
- *Syntactic problems*. Putting all the parentheses, semicolons, and so on in the right place.
- *Conceptual problems*. Difficulties in understanding procedural or declarative constructs of the tool, such as demons and contexts.

21.3 Get someone else to critique your code, and critique their code in return (but be nice to each other). It is better to use relatively small programs. You will find that just the prospect of someone else looking at your program will cause you to improve both the code and the documentation.

22 Blackboard Architectures

Introduction

Blackboard systems are a relatively recent phenomenon which provide the basis for an abstract architecture of great power and generality. They can emulate both forward- and backward-chaining reasoning systems, as well as being able to combine these forms of reasoning opportunistically. In addition, the blackboard model of problem solving encourages the hierarchical organization of both domain knowledge and the space of partial and complete solutions. It is therefore well suited to construction problems in which the problem space is large but factorable along some number of dimensions. Successful applications of the blackboard approach have included data interpretation (such as image understanding, speech recognition), analysis and synthesis of complex compounds (such as protein structures) and planning.

The basic organization of a blackboard system is as follows. Domain knowledge is partitioned into independent *knowledge sources* (KSs) which run under a *scheduler*, while solutions are built up on a global data structure, the *blackboard*. Thus instead of representing 'how-to' knowledge in a single rule set, such knowledge is encoded in a suite of programs. Each of these knowledge sources may be a rule set in its own right, or the suite may contain diverse programs that mix rules with procedures.

The blackboard now serves the function rather like that of a production system's working memory, except that its structure is much more complex. Typically, the blackboard is partitioned into different *levels* of description with respect to the solution space, each corresponding to a different amount of detail or analysis. Levels usually contain more complex data structures than working memory vectors, such as object hierarchies or recursive graphs. In modern systems, there may even be more than one blackboard.

Knowledge sources trigger on blackboard objects, but their instantiations may not be executed at once. Instead, *knowledge source activation records* (KSARs) are normally placed on an agenda pending selection by the scheduler. Knowledge sources communicate only via the blackboard, and thus cannot transmit data to each other or invoke each other directly. This is rather like the convention in production systems that forbids individual rules from calling each other directly; everything must be done through working memory.

This chapter reviews earlier work on blackboard systems and assesses recent attempts to use the blackboard model of problem solving as a basis for constructing general-purpose tools for building expert systems. The basic principles are illustrated with examples, but the emphasis is on architectural issues rather than the details of individual systems or applications. The final section briefly reviews recent attempts to deploy parallelism in the search for efficient implementations of blackboard systems.

22.1   The early years: HEARSAY, AGE and OPM

The blackboard architecture grew out of an attempt to build a speech-understanding system called HEARSAY (Erman *et al.*, 1980). Programming a computer to understand speech is an extremely hard problem, and one that requires:

(1)   complex signal processing,

(2)   some mapping from physical events in the speech waveform to symbolic units in a natural language, and

(3)   a search through a very large space of possible interpretations which combine these different units of analysis.

A dominant way of thinking about the speech problem is in terms of various levels of description, beginning from the physical domain of acoustic signals which are recorded and processed to yield outputs such as sound spectra, and progressing through increasingly rarified strata of linguistic abstraction, such as phonemes, syllables, morphemes, words, phrases and sentences.

22.1.1 Motivation for HEARSAY-II architecture

The intuition behind the genesis of blackboard systems was that there is a distinct body of knowledge associated with each of these levels of analysis: knowledge about signals, phonemics, lexical knowledge, knowledge of grammar, semantics and knowledge about the universe of discourse. No single body of knowledge is sufficient in isolation to solve the problem. Even if the signal processing preserves all the important features of the original waveform, and even if we can build a machine that perfectly decodes the output of signal processing into phonemes, we still will not be able to tell the difference between 'I scream' and 'ice cream' or 'please let us know', 'please lettuce no' and 'pleas letter snow' without additional information. Thus, although each body of knowledge is important, and can be considered and codified (more or less) without reference to the others, automatic (or human) speech understanding requires their co-operation.

The key problem that has to be addressed in speech understanding is the management of uncertainty. Firstly, the data is inherently noisy, incomplete and variable (both between and within speakers). Secondly, the mapping between levels is inherently ambiguous; for example, the mapping between phonemic and lexical levels in the 'I scream'/'ice cream' example. Thirdly, the role of both linguistic and extralinguistic context is crucial: the interpretation elements that surround a given segment of speech make alternative interpretations of that segment more or less likely. More traditional approaches to speech recognition use statistical models from communication theory to encode transition probabilities between segments, but a more knowledge-based approach requires a rethinking of uncertainty handling.

Erman *et al.* list the following requirements for a knowledge based approach to speech understanding to be effective:

(1) At least one possible sequence of operations (partial solutions) must lead to a correct interpretation. In other words, the 'bits' that form the correct interpretation must be in the hypothesis space somewhere.

(2) The procedure for scoring interpretations should rank the correct interpretation higher than all the competing complete interpretations. In other words, the correct interpretation of an utterance should outrank all other interpretations that span the utterance.

(3) The computational cost of finding the correct interpretation must satisfy some externally specified limit in terms of space and time

requirements. Thus a speech understander that takes several days to comprehend a single utterance, and requires many gigabytes of storage to do it, would not be deemed successful.

The central problem in speech understanding appears to be that requirements 1 and 3 are in serious conflict. To make sure that the right bits are somewhere in the space of partial interpretations, we usually have to be extremely generous at the hypothesis generation stage. This results in a combinatorial explosion of solution elements that render the search for the best spanning interpretation completely intractable for large vocabularies without extremely good heuristics for extending partial interpretations. Thus getting the scoring procedure of requirement 2 right is essential for success.

22.1.2 HEARSAY's use of knowledge sources

HEARSAY-II used diverse knowledge sources to generate, combine and extend possible interpretations of speech segments, and the blackboard was used to store these interpretations at different levels of abstraction.

Each KS can be thought of as a condition–action pair, even though it was not implemented as a production rule; conditions and actions were actually arbitrary procedures. The flow of control also differs from production systems in the following way. Instead of the interpreter checking to see if the conditions of knowledge sources are satisfied at each point in a recognize–act cycle, knowledge sources declare their activation conditions in advance, in terms of what kinds of data modification will trigger them. This results in an interrupt-driven polling action that is more efficient than the recognize–act of production systems: it more closely resembles the use of demons in frame systems, where control flow is governed by data update.

In general, knowledge sources are linked to levels on the blackboard in the following way. KS conditions will be satisfied by data modifications on a particular level, and KS actions will also write to a particular level (not necessarily the same as its data level). In HEARSAY-II, KSs were mostly organized so that they recognized data at a particular level of linguistic analysis and their actions operated on the next level up. Thus one knowledge source might be activated by data on the syllable level and post lexical hypotheses on the word level.

A schematic diagram of the HEARSAY-II architecture, simplified from Erman *et al.* (1980), shows the basic architecture of the system (see Figure 22.1). Arrows from blackboard levels to KSs denote the triggering of KS conditions, while arrows from KSs to levels denote the output of KS actions. Arrows that impinge upon the action arrows and connect them to the blackboard monitor record modifications to blackboard levels that act as triggers for other KSs and cause them to be scheduled.

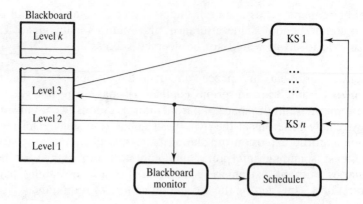

Figure 22.1 Simplified schematic of the HEARSAY-II architecture.

Further details of the HEARSAY program are not really relevant to our discussion. The most important thing to note about the architecture is that it does not dictate a particular control regime, such as top-down or bottom-up strategies. Thus, in the speech domain, one could proceed top-down, by hypothesizing a word and then gathering phonemic evidence for it, or else bottom-up, by assembling phoneme hypotheses into words. The monitor and the scheduler decide which KSs to activate, and this decision can be made as domain-free or domain-specific as you like. Ordinarily, KS activations are scored on the basis of how well their conditions fit the data, rather as the CENTAUR system scored tasks in Chapter 19.

22.1.3 HEARSAY-III: an abstract architecture

HEARSAY-III (Erman *et al.*, 1983) was an abstraction over the earlier HEARSAY systems, rather as EMYCIN was over MYCIN. In addition to the usual blackboard and knowledge source structures, HEARSAY-III had an underlying relational database for managing blackboard objects, and a scheduling blackboard which, together with scheduling knowledge sources, facilitated the selection of KSARs.

The database language was AP3 (Goldman, 1978), and it served a variety of functions in HEARSAY-III.

(1)   Blackboard units are typed AP3 objects. This helps to regularize the representation of both data and partial solutions.

(2)   Knowledge source triggers are implemented using AP3 pattern-directed demons. This regularizes the procedural side of things in the manner of frame systems.

(3)   Database contexts are supported by AP3, and the conditions for

poisoning contexts are expressed as AP3 constraints. Contexts can be used to support alternative ways of continuing a computation; for example, when a program is forced to guess (see Chapter 18), or to support hypothetical reasoning (see Chapter 23).

Knowledge sources consist of a *trigger*, some *immediate code*, and a *body*. When the trigger pattern is matched, an activation record is created and the immediate code is executed. The body is not executed unless the KSAR is later selected by the scheduler. HEARSAY-III provides a default 'base scheduler' which performs the simplest scheduling operations, such as taking the next KSAR off the agenda and executing it. The user is intended to write scheduling KSs which match against changes on either the domain or the scheduling blackboards, and whose actions assign and modify ratings of KSARs.

The main strength of HEARSAY-III was its loosely-knit control regime, which allowed the user great freedom in representing and applying heuristics for the selection of KSARs, and its regularization of blackboard data objects. The main weakness was the lack of a knowledge representation language within the knowledge sources themselves. The intermediate code and the body of a KS were simply arbitrary pieces of LISP code, as in HEARSAY-II. Many of the features of HEARSAY-III were carried over into the ART expert system tool mentioned at the end of Chapter 20. ART's inference engine has a proper production rule language that supports both forward and backward chaining.

22.1.4   Abstraction in AGE and OPM

AGE (Nii and Aiello, 1979) is a collection of tools and partial frameworks for building expert systems. A 'framework' in AGE is a configuration of components, such as the backward-chaining EMYCIN framework or the blackboard framework. A knowledge source in the blackboard framework of AGE was a set of production rules wrapped in a local context that specified a rule evaluation strategy, for example *single-hit* (fire one rule only), or *multiple-hit* (fire as many rules as will fire).

Blackboard objects, and the relationships that hold between them, can be represented in UNITS (Stefik, 1979), while the solution itself is built up in a hierarchical hypothesis structure. Rule actions can post changes, either to UNITS or to the hypothesis structure. These changes can be actual, expected or desired. *Actual changes* are events, to be posted on an event-list on the blackboard after the changes have been made. These drive forward-chaining production rules in an event-driven strategy, generating new events until some termination condition is met. *Expected changes* are expectations derived from some model, and these are posted on the expectation-list. Given a situation where initial data values suggest hypotheses, rules in a model-driven system post expectations whose fulfilment or non-fulfilment would count as evidence for or against a hypothesis. Desired changes are goals, and they are posted on the goal-list. The associated behaviour is that of a backward-chaining goal-driven system like EMYCIN, where production rules perform subgoaling until conditions for concluding hypotheses are satisfied (or not) by data. Aiello (1983) describes and compares three implementations of PUFF using each of these control strategies.

OPM (Hayes-Roth, 1985) is a blackboard control system for multitask planning which integrates domain and control problem solving in a single control loop with no preprogrammed control biases. Actions are chosen by reconciling independent decisions concerning what actions are desirable and what actions are feasible by integrating multiple control heuristics of various grain-size and importance.

OPM's application was errand-planning, and the program used four global data structures:

(1) A *blackboard* split into five panels:

- meta-plan (planning goals);
- plan abstraction (planning decisions);
- knowledge base (cache of observations and computations);
- plan (chosen actions); and
- executive (choosing KSARs to execute the actions).

(2) An event *list* for recording blackboard changes.

(3) A *map* showing the locations of the errands.

(4) An *agenda* for KSARs.

Knowledge sources had both a trigger to determine its relevance to a given node in the blackboard (the 'focus node') and a test which determined whether or not the KSAR was actually applicable at the time of execution. When scheduling, KSARs were preferred which affected the *current focus* (the most recently added or updated node on the blackboard). Such 'focus decisions' drew on the information stored on the executive panel of the blackboard.

Although OPM was intended as a tool for the simulation of human problem solving, it also has clear advantages from a systems engineering point of view. The ability to factor control knowledge into heterogeneous knowledge sources and then reason about their recommendations represents a powerful tool for constructing meta-level architectures. The next section explores the further development of this methodology in the BB* blackboard environment for building knowledge-based systems.

22.2 The blackboard environment BB⋆

Hayes-Roth *et al.* (1987) describes a blackboard environment in which the three levels of applications program, task framework and abstract architecture are sharply differentiated and yet tightly integrated. The emphasis is on intelligent systems which are capable of reasoning about their actions, using knowledge of the events and states that can occur, the actions they can perform, and the relationships that hold among actions, events and states. The authors describe an environment, BB*, which allows the combination of different task- and domain-specific modules under a generic blackboard architecture, BB1.

22.2.1 Architecture, framework and application

It is worth introducing the authors' terminology (briefly mentioned in Chapter 20).

At the most abstract level, an *architecture* comprises a set of basic knowledge structures (representing actions, events, states) and a mechanism for choosing and executing actions. This kind of knowledge is not only domain-free; it is also independent of both task and problem-solving method. The idea is that the architecture should be capable of supporting a wide variety of different tasks in different domains (just as the human cognitive architecture is, whatever it may be). General capabilities, such as reasoning about control, the ability to learn and explain, should also be incorporated at this level.

A *framework* is a set of intermediate knowledge structures representing actions, events, and so on relevant to a particular task, such as diagnosing faults in a system or constructing a system that meets some constraints. These structures contain knowledge which addresses a particular class of problems in a particular way. Such methods should be applicable to more than one domain, just as humans are able to form and execute plans in a variety of different contexts by using only a relatively small number of strategies. The ACCORD knowledge base (see Section 22.2.2) for solving arrangement problems by the method of assembly is an example of such a framework.

At the most specific level, an *application* is a set of knowledge structures that instantiate particular actions, events, and so on to solve a particular class of problems by a particular method in a particular domain. Examples of applications undertaken in the BB* environment include the PROTEAN system for deriving protein structure from constraints (Hayes-Roth *et al.*, 1986) and the SIGHTPLAN system for laying out the facilities of a construction site (Tommelein *et al.*, 1987).

22.2.2 BB1 and ACCORD as architecture and framework

These points will be illustrated with reference to the BB1 architecture, with a particular emphasis on reasoning about control (see Johnson and Hayes-Roth, 1986). The framework under discussion will be the ACCORD knowledge base for solving a class of arrangement problems, and the application will be the PROTEAN system for deriving protein structure.

As in other blackboard systems, BB1 KSs are first triggered by events on their associated input level of the blackboard, creating KSARs. These part-instantiations are not executed immediately, but kept on an agenda pending their selection and the satisfaction of their preconditions, which are typically properties of blackboard objects. However, in addition to domain KSs and a domain blackboard, BB1 also has control KSs and a control blackboard. A scheduler sequences the execution of both domain and control KSARs on an agenda in accordance with a control plan which develops dynamically on the control blackboard. The execution of a KSAR posts changes on its output blackboard level, thereby triggering other KSs.

Thus BB1 executes the following basic cycle:

(1) *Interpret* the action of the next KSAR.

(2) *Update* the agenda with KSARs triggered by that action and rate all KSARs against the current control plan.

(3) *Schedule* the highest-rated KSAR.

ACCORD is a language for representing knowledge underlying the performance of arrangement tasks by the method of assembling components so that they satisfy a set of constraints (as opposed to, say, refining a prototypical arrangement). This method does not entail a particular control regime, but it does require that a number of control decisions be made somehow, such as how to construct and compose partial arrangements. The basic representational device that ACCORD uses is a concept hierarchy of types, individuals and instances; it therefore fulfils roughly the same role as AP3 fulfilled for HEARSAY-III, except that it is more specifically oriented towards arrangement problems.

The types define generic concepts and roles, rather as semantic networks do, by ISA links (see Chapter 9). Individuals exemplify particular concepts without instantiating them. For example, the first element in a sequence of entities of type T exemplifies T but does not instantiate it, since we do not say which particular object is the first in the sequence. Instances instantiate individuals (not concepts) in particular contexts (for example, in a particular sequence), and play particular roles in those contexts (for example, the 'anchor' of a partial arrangement – see below). Concepts can have attributes, and enter into relations with other concepts. These are inheritable along ISA links, although it is also possible to define new inheritance paths.

The framework provides skeletal branches of a hierarchy for the objects to be arranged, the contexts in which they must be arranged, and the constraints that need to be satisfied. For example, ACCORD represents domain-independent arrangement roles, such as arrangement, partial-arrangement and included-object, with an includes relation between them. An important kind of included-object is an anchor – that is, an object that has been assigned a fixed location to define the local context of a partial arrangement – while an anchoree is an included-object that has at least one constraint with an anchor.

22.2.3 PROTEAN: application as framework instantiation

PROTEAN (Hayes-Roth *et al.*, 1986) is a system intended to identify the three-dimensional structure of proteins in solution. The combinatorics of considering all possible conformations prohibit the use of exhaustive search, and so the program employs a number of different techniques to traverse the solution space. In combination, these provide a powerful mechanism for implementing a strategy of successive refinement with an evolving control plan which leaves room for opportunistic focusing.

- PROTEAN combines both local and global constraints on allowable structural hypotheses. Local constraints give some indication of the proximity of constituent atoms in the molecule, and global constraints include such things as the molecule's overall size and shape.

- PROTEAN adopts a 'divide and conquer' approach by defining partial solutions that incorporate different subsets of a protein's structure and different subsets of constraints, instead of trying to apply all the constraints to the whole molecule. Having applied constraints within overlapping partial solutions, it then applies constraints between them.

- PROTEAN reasons bidirectionally across a four-level solution blackboard. The different levels of abstraction are: the molecule level; the solid level of helices, sheets and coils; the superatom level of peptides and side-chains in amino acids; and the atom level about individual atomic constituents. When reasoning top-down, it uses structural hypotheses at one level to focus on positioning structures at a lower level; when reasoning bottom-up, it uses hypotheses at one level to restrict the position of structures at a higher level.

- PROTEAN also factors control knowledge into different levels of abstraction. At the highest level, that of strategy, a particular problem-solving strategy is developed, which involves establishing the longest and most constraining helix as the anchor, and then positioning all other solid level structures relative to it. At the intermediate focus level, PROTEAN records the individual steps necessary to carry out the overall strategy, so that the program always knows where it is in the sequential execution of a strategy. The lowest heuristic level incorporates preferences for rating KSARs; for example, prefer KSARs that operate on long anchors.

Examples of PROTEAN's domain and control knowledge sources can be found in Table 22.1 (after Hayes-Roth *et al.*, 1986).

PROTEAN is interesting because it shows how domain-independent task-related reasoning can be combined with domain-dependent knowledge about constraints in the BB1 architecture. Opportunistic focusing is integrated with hierarchical planning as the control plan unfolds. This occurs when control KSs triggered by partial solution states insert focus decisions which typically serve to restrict the space of possible locations. In other words, when the global strategy of successive refinement fails to narrow the solution space sufficiently, a control KS may cut in and

Table 22.1 Some of PROTEAN's control and domain knowledge sources.

Knowledge source	*Behaviour*
Generic BB1 control knowledge sources	
Initialize-Focus	Identifies the initial focus prescribed by a newly recorded strategy
Terminate-Focus	Changes the status of a focus to inoperative once its goal has been satisfied
Domain-specific control knowledge sources	
Create-Best-Anchor-Space	Records the create-best-anchor-space focus
Prefer-Long-Anchors	Records a heuristic that gives higher ratings to KSARs that operate on long anchors
Domain-specific problem-solving knowledge sources	
Activate-Anchor-Space	Chooses a particular anchor at the solid level to be the anchor of a partial solution
Add-Anchoree-to-Anchor-Space	Chooses a particular solid-anchor to be an anchoree in an existing anchor space

introduce a particular focus with a particular set of constraints. Satisfying the opportunistic focus will then restrict the legal locations at which hierarchical plan foci can be satisfied.

22.2.4 Integrating different reasoning strategies

Johnson and Hayes-Roth (1986) show how goal-directed reasoning can be integrated with both hierarchical planning and opportunistic focusing in the context of PROTEAN. Goal-directed reasoning is required where instrumental action is needed so that other desirable actions may be performed. Thus KSARs that represent desirable actions, but which have unsatisfied preconditions, can give rise to subgoals to perform actions which cause those preconditions to be satisfied (and so on, recursively).

The authors differentiate goal knowledge by distinguishing between the desire to:

(1) *perform an action*, such as executing a KSAR, because it is intrinsically desirable, for example because it satisfies a focus;

(2) *promote a state*, because it enables a desirable KSAR to have its preconditions satisfied, and hence become executable;

(3) *cause an event*, because it will trigger a KSAR which has a desirable action.

Goals of type 1 are simply actions that satisfy foci. Goals of type 2 are relevant when no executable KSAR rates highly against a current focus. In this case, BB1 has a generic control KS called Enable-Priority-Action, which is triggered whenever a desirable KSAR has unsatisfied preconditions. Execution of an Enable-Priority-Action KSAR results in a goal-directed focus being posted for each unsatisfied precondition, which promotes the corresponding state. Goals of type 3 are relevant when no KSAR on the agenda has the potential to perform a desirable action. A control KS for this situation would need to identify KSs capable of performing the desired action and post goal-directed foci to cause the corresponding events.

The authors show how opportunistic focusing and goal-directed reasoning can work together to satisfy hierarchical foci by restricting legal locations and removing obstacles to desirable actions. For example, yoking two helices together in a partial arrangement, using a set of constraints between solids, is a desirable action. However, before yoking can take place, both helices must be anchored in the arrangement (even though yoking actions are preferred to anchoring ones). Posting a goal which promotes the anchoring of an unanchored helix capable of being yoked enables the need for that specific anchoring action to be taken into account when rating KSARs at the next cycle. Goal-directed foci can therefore coexist with opportunistic foci, and interact with them in a well-understood way.

The relationships between the various modules that make up the relevant configuration of the BB* environment are both interesting and instructive. PROTEAN's domain-specific knowledge is layered on the ACCORD framework for solving arrangement problems by the assembly method, that is, PROTEAN instantiates knowledge structures in ACCORD. The ACCORD framework is itself layered on the BB1 architecture, in that its concept network, role vocabulary and type hierarchy become BB1's blackboard representation language.

22.2.5 Summarizing BB*

This environment seems to satisfy many of the desiderata we have discussed so far.

- It separates domain and control knowledge, inasmuch as it is possible to vary the control knowledge sources while holding the task and domain instantiations of the framework constant. Generic control KSs can be held constant over different task and domain instantiations, although domain control KSs are rather more constrained by the domain KSs, since many of them are intended to rate domain KSARs.

- It differentiates between different kinds of both domain and control knowledge. Domain knowledge in ACCORD is factored in terms of knowledge about actions, events and states, as well as knowledge about objects, arrangements and the roles that objects can play in arrangements. Terminological knowledge is also represented in terms of a task-specific network of assembly verbs. Control knowledge is factored into strategies, foci and heuristics, as described above, while foci can be factored further into categories such as hierarchical, opportunistic and goal-directed.

- It provides a basis for explaining system behaviour in terms of control plans. Thus it is possible to explain why PROTEAN prefers one KSAR over another in terms of the current foci and the rating heuristics. Recounting control decisions can be complicated, although BB1's ExAct explanation package uses graphical devices to good effect.

- The use of languages such as ACCORD augments BB1's LISP-based representation facilities with a higher-level programming language which is more concise and uniform. This promotes analysability from the knowledge engineering point of view. The fact that this language is also interpretable renders the knowledge so represented accessible to other modules, such as ExAct.

- Modules are now reusable, in that system builders can select and combine existing modules as a basis for constructing new systems. Thus the SIGHTPLAN configuration of BB* shares modules such as ACCORD and Generic-KS with the PROTEAN configuration. This benefit derives from the uniformity of style and content imposed on modules within a given level.

Building skeletal systems in BB* can be seen as a way of providing some of the structure associated with expert system shells without the attendant inflexibility of such tools. Thus Hayes-Roth *et al.* (1987) suggest that a *shell* level can be interposed between the framework and application levels, by specializing particular frameworks so that they are tailored for particular tasks and/or domains. This would involve augmenting a representation language like ACCORD with prototypical knowledge sources appropriate for subclasses of tasks, such as assembly-arrangement problems of a particular kind. As with earlier Stanford work, the theoretical interest and practical utility of this approach derives from the discovery of useful levels of abstraction from which to view successful applications of AI technology to particular problems.

22.3 Feasibility of the blackboard approach

The power and generality of blackboard systems does not come without price. Explicit reasoning about control and sophisticated scheduling of tasks must incur some computational overhead. Of course, the use of control knowledge sources is intended to focus search, and hence save cycles in the long run. This trade-off has not been well analysed in the literature, but see Reynolds (1988) for some discussion. Neither are performance statistics for blackboard systems freely available.

The question arises as to whether it is possible to exploit the parallelism that appears to be inherent in the underlying architecture, where independent knowledge sources communicate via a global data structure. It is clear that parallelism could be introduced into a blackboard architecture at various levels of granularity, for example:

(1) knowledge source activation;
(2) evaluation of triggers and preconditions within a knowledge source; and
(3) execution of KSAR actions.

However, although 1 seems to be an inherently parallel process, 2 and 3 may contain serializing steps. For example, the preconditions of different rules may share variables, while actions may need to be sequenced in order to achieve the desired effect.

The Advanced Architectures Project at Stanford University has generated two prototype blackboard architectures that exploit parallelism in rather different ways. A brief summary of these systems is attempted below; more details can be found in Nii et al. (1988).

The POLIGON system (Rice, 1986) is designed for distributed-memory, multi-processor hardware, with a large number of processor/memory units enjoying high bandwidth communication. It is intended to run with a high degree of fine-grain parallelism as its default behaviour. Thus knowledge sources are executed as data becomes available (as in data-flow architectures), instead of being polled by a central control module.

The CAGE system (Aiello, 1986) – essentially a concurrent version of AGE blackboard tool described in Section 22.1 – is targeted on a shared memory system with a smaller number of processors. Instead of exhibiting parallel behaviour by default, programming language constructs are introduced to support parallelism at the discretion of the applications programmer. The parallelism is therefore more coarse-grained to avoid performance decrement due to memory contention and bandwidth limitations in the connections between processor and memory.

The main focus of interest in this project is the comparison of these two approaches from the point of view of both programmability and performance. Nii et al. report that performance gains are sensitive to the ways in which applications are formulated and programmed. In other words, one cannot simply take the representation of knowledge from a serial blackboard system, transplant it into the parallel system and expect an increase in performance. This is perhaps not too surprising. Exploiting parallelism in other areas of computer science often requires the use of special algorithms and data structures.

They also point out that concurrent processing of knowledge sources does not lead to gains if control remains centralized (as in CAGE), but decentralizing control (as in POLIGON) decreases programmability. As yet, no actual data have been published from this project. However, it is clear that the task of exploiting parallelism in blackboard architectures is by no means straightforward, and so the computational cost of using blackboard technology is not likely to decrease in the near future.

Bibliographical notes

The review papers by Nii (1986a, 1986b) are recommended as a good starting point. A useful collection of papers on blackboard systems can be found in Englemore and Morgan (1988). Unfortunately, the index is a little thin, so the book is not designed for dipping into. From an expert systems point of view, the following chapters are particularly worth reading. Chapters 5 and 6 cover some early applications not treated here. Chapter 12 gives a good account of AGE, and Chapter 26 briefly describes the implementation of GBB, another generic tool for developing blackboard systems.

Another recent collection of papers can be found in Jagannathan *et al.* (1989). The Advanced Architectures Project of which CAGE and POLIGON form a part is well described in Rice (1989). Its bibliography of project publications will prove useful to any reader wishing to follow up on parallel blackboard systems.

STUDY SUGGESTIONS

22.1 Compare and contrast blackboard architectures with production systems. Under what conditions is the additional complexity of a blackboard system justified?

22.2 Distinguish between the concepts of *architecture*, *framework* and *application* in the context of blackboard systems.

22.3 Read Nii *et al.* (1988) and write a concise summary of CAGE and POLIGON which highlights (a) the important differences between them in terms of the design decisions they incorporate, and (b) the advantages and disadvantages that attach to those decisions.

22.4 Specify a simple blackboard system to solve arrangement problems such as the 'furniture' problem of Study suggestion 18.3. Think of the different knowledge sources you might need, for example, for placing objects, for extending partial arrangements, and for resolving conflicts. Think also about how you would design the blackboard to represent the room and the objects in it in a manner that makes the retrieval and insertion of blackboard objects relatively efficient.

23 Truth Maintenance Systems

Introduction

It has long been felt that a program should not be allowed to perform arbitrary manipulations on its representation of the world. Typically, beliefs influence each other, and there are constraints that any set of beliefs must satisfy. If such influences and constraints are ignored, the representation may become incoherent. Mechanisms for keeping track of dependencies and detecting inconsistency are often referred to as *truth maintenance systems* (TMSs), sometimes called *reason maintenance systems*.

This chapter attempts a review of the computational mechanisms that have been employed to keep track of dependencies between data representing such things as states, actions and assumptions. We shall begin with relatively simple systems and progress towards more complicated ones. Where possible, the mathematical foundations will be neglected in favour of less formal accounts of what these systems do and why they work.

23.1 Keeping track of dependencies

In Chapter 18, we saw that it was convenient for the expert system VT to maintain a *dependency network* to record dependencies between design decisions. In this network, nodes represented the assignment of values to design parameters, while the two main kinds of link between nodes were the *contributes-to* link and the *constrains link*. Node A *contributes-to* node B if the value at A appears in the computation of the value at B, while node A constrains B if the value at A forbids B to take on certain values. In what follows, we shall simplify the discussion by using a little notation, in which upper case letters stand for nodes and lower case letters stand for the values assigned at nodes. Thus the value assigned at node A at any one time will be denoted by *a*.

23.1.1 Relaxation in networks

The main uses of links in a dependency network are

- to propagate values from node to node, and
- to detect contradictions among the values assigned to nodes.

For example, given a network containing nodes A and M, where A holds the value of the acceleration of some particle and M holds the value of its mass, then both A and M would contribute to the node F, which represents the force acting on the particle. Furthermore, given the familiar formula $f = ma$, A and M now constrain F as well as contributing to it, since once a and m are known, f is determined. So if $a = 2$ and $m = 3$, we can set f equal to 6 (given some assumptions about units, friction, and so on). If we already have $f = 7$, we know that the network is in a state of contradiction.

$f = ma$ acts a constraint on the network in the above example. If all the constraints in a network of relations are satisfied, we say that the network is *relaxed*. Thus, in Figure 23.1:

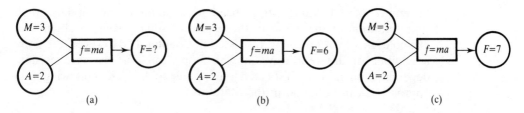

(a) (b) (c)

Figure 23.1 Constraint networks in which circles stand for nodes and rectangles label links connecting them.

- network (a) is not relaxed, because we have not concluded the value for node F;
- network (b) is relaxed; and
- network (c) is inconsistent.

Strictly speaking, the term relaxation applies to networks, not theories. But a network is just a way of representing a theory; thus network (a) can be seen as representing the theory

$$f = ma$$
$$m = 3$$
$$a = 2$$

in which $f = ma$ still functions as a constraint, while network (b) represents the theory

$$f = ma$$
$$m = 3$$
$$a = 2$$
$$f = 6$$

which is 'relaxed' with respect to the $f = ma$ constraint, and network (c) represents the inconsistent theory

$$f = ma$$
$$m = 3$$
$$a = 2$$
$$f = 7$$

We shall switch between talking about networks and talking about theories as appropriate, using the neutral word 'representation' when we do not wish to distinguish the way that facts and constraints are implemented.

23.1.2 Belief revision

Programs of all kinds often need to maintain and update their representation of the world in the course of solving some problem (for example, the STRIPS planner, discussed in Chapter 4). However, there are a number of different ways in which one can perform the revision, depending on how sophisticated one wants to be. The following four approaches can be found in the literature:

(1) *Monotonic revisions*. The simplest case involves assimilating new facts and computing any important consequences, thereby relaxing

the representation. Such a revision is called monotonic because the set of beliefs always increases. Deciding what is 'important' is not always easy, but one can readily see that deriving q from p and $(p \supset q)$ is more likely to be important than deriving $(q \lor p)$ from q.

(2) *Non-monotonic revisions.* Sometimes we also want to retract beliefs, and this may undercut conclusions that we have already drawn. If I see you driving a Mercedes, I may conclude that you own it and therefore that you are rich. But if I subsequently learn that you stole the car, then as well as retracting my belief that you own it, I may also want to retract my belief that you are rich.

(3) *Non-monotonic justifications.* A further complication arises if a program assumes that certain things are true if there is no evidence to the contrary. For example, a program might assume that all students are poor, unless there is specific evidence of wealth. Here it is *absence* of information to the contrary that constitutes a justification for holding a belief, rather than *positive* information that something is the case.

(4) *Hypothetical reasoning.* A program might want to entertain certain assumptions and then see what follows from them, perhaps as a prelude to entertaining some of these assumptions as actual beliefs. This involves reasoning about alternative *possible worlds*: states of the world that may or may not resemble the actual world. Keeping track of multiple theories of this kind, and keeping them distinct from each other, requires a certain amount of organization over and above that required by representations based on a single theory.

Case 1 is fairly trivial; we just add the new information to the theory, plus any additional facts that we derive by relaxing the new theory with respect to the constraints. In the next section, we look at a simple technique for performing truth maintenance that corresponds to case 2, where both kinds of revision are allowed. Sections 23.3 and 23.4 review cases 3 and 4.

23.2 Revising propositional theories

McAllester's (1980) TMS was not the first, but it is perhaps the easiest to explain. The method assumes an assertional database (hereafter DB) in which formulas (the premises) can be designated 'true', 'false' or 'unknown' by the user. Thus the underlying logic is three-valued, unlike the classical two-valued calculus that we studied in Chapter 5.

The system represents assertions by nodes, which hold the appropriate truth values.

The constraints enforced by the TMS on the contents of DB must satisfy are the fundamental axioms of propositional logic. For example,

$$\neg(\psi \wedge \neg\psi)$$

is an axiom which states that no proposition ψ can be both true and false simultaneously. (Note that ψ is a meta-variable that stands for any proposition whatever.) Like most TMSs, McAllester's deals only with formulas that do not contain quantifiers; for example, $DEAD(fred)$ can be in the theory, but not $(\forall X)(DEAD(X))$. This restriction is mainly because it is not always possible to ascertain the consistency of a first-order theory, as pointed out in Chapter 5.

The TMS fulfils four main functions with respect to DB:

(1)   It performs a variety of propositional deduction which McAllester calls *propositional constraint propagation*.

(2)   It generates *justifications* for the assignment of a truth value to a proposition, when that assignment is arrived at via constraint propagation (as opposed to being assigned by the user). Thus, if we conclude that q is true because p and $(p \supset q)$ are true, then p and $(p \supset q)$ form part of the justification for q.

(3)   It *updates* DB whenever propositions are removed. Thus if we conclude that q is true because p and $(p \supset q)$ are true, and we later retract p, then we must dismantle the justification $\{p, (p \supset q)\}$ for q, and we should also retract q, unless it can be rederived from other propositions that remain in DB.

(4)   It is capable of tracking down the premises responsible for contradictions by a method called *dependency-directed back-tracking*. The user is then invited to retract one of the 'guilty' premises, thereby dismantling the justification for the contra-diction.

Given p and $(\neg p \vee q)$ as premises, constraint propagation allows the TMS to derive q. It then builds the support structure shown in Figure 23.2. Each node in the network is a frame (see Chapter 9) with a number of slots, including one that holds the name of the node, one that holds its truth value, and one that holds a pointer to its justification. A justification is another frame that contains a table of supporting propositions and their truth values. Thus, in Figure 23.2, the truth of the node labelled q is justified by the fact that the node representing $(\neg p \vee q)$ is marked as true, as is the node labelled p. Note that nodes

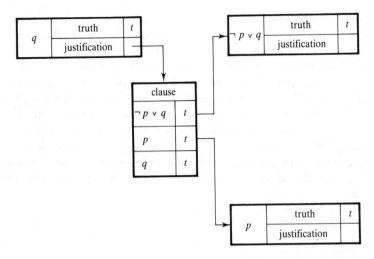

Figure 23.2 The support structure for q as derived from premises p and $(\neg p \vee q)$.

representing premises, such as p, have no pointers to justifications, since they are true by fiat.

If it later turns out that q is inconsistent with other contents of DB, the support structure will track down its justifications. The user is then given the option of retracting either p or $(p \supset q)$. It is important that support structures be *well-founded*; no node must appear in its own justification, otherwise the process of tracing justifications will be circular and fail to terminate.

Propositional constraint propagation is not a complete inference procedure in the sense of Chapter 5, but it is sound, and it does allow a range of useful inferences to be drawn when assertions are added to DB. Note that all assertions are either premises or justified by the presence of another assertion. In the next section, we review a rather more ambitious TMS, which allows the absence of information as a justification for an assertion.

23.3 Non-monotonic justifications

Doyle's (1979) approach to truth maintenance is based on a different inference procedure to McAllester's, and has a rather different philosophical outlook. This approach is intended to model aspects of commonsense reasoning, such as *defaults* (see Chapter 24). Roughly speaking, in addition to holding beliefs because of positive evidence for them, we are also allowed to hold beliefs as *reasoned assumptions*, because we have no evidence against them.

A justification (or *reason*, in Doyle's terminology) for a belief, p, is now an ordered pair of sets of beliefs, which we shall represent by the pair (IN_p, OUT_p). IN_p is a conventional justification of the form used by McAllester; it contains propositions whose truth contributes to the truth of p. OUT_p, on the other hand, is a *non-monotonic justification*; it contains propositions whose presence in the belief set would deny p. Such a justification is non-monotonic because the simple act of accumulating more beliefs could cause us to retract p; this is not the case in McAllester's system.

For example, a reason for p might be

$$(\{\ \}, \{\neg p\})$$

signifying that we are allowed to assume p so long as it is not already believed to be false. A reason for q might be

$$(\{p\}, \{r\})$$

signifying that we are allowed to believe q so long as p is *in* (the current set of beliefs) and r is *out* (not believed). Note that reasons can interact, as in the above example. If $\neg p$ is *out*, then p becomes *in*, so q becomes in too, as long as r is out.

Such reasons as called *SL-justifications* (SL stands for 'support-list'). The general rule for SL-justifications is that a belief p is in the current set of beliefs only if each belief in IN_p is *in* and each belief in OUT_p is *out*. Doyle suggests other kinds of justification in his paper, but we shall not deal with them here.

The dual structure of justifications in Doyle's system can be used to distinguish three different kinds of beliefs with respect to a belief set B:

(1) *Premises* – propositions that are believed without any justification at all. Set-theoretically, the premises are given by

$$\{p \in B \mid IN_p = OUT_p = \emptyset\}$$

(2) *deductions* – propositions which are the conclusions of normal monotonic deductions, given by

$$\{p \in B \mid IN_p \neq \emptyset \text{ and } OUT_p = \emptyset\}$$

(3) *assumptions* – propositions which are held to be true because there is no evidence against them, given by

$$\{p \in B \mid OUT_p \neq \emptyset\}$$

As in McAllester's system, each belief is represented by a node. The TMS can perform the following functions:

- create nodes;
- add or retract justifications from the set of justifications that govern dependencies between nodes; and
- mark a node as a contradiction.

When the TMS makes a contradiction node *in*, dependency-directed backtracking is invoked to identify the assumptions whose retraction would make the contradiction node out.

Unlike McAllester, Doyle's logic is really *four*-valued rather than three-valued. The four truth values are best represented by the sets, { }, {*true*}, {*false*}, {*true, false*}, which denote interdeterminacy, truth, falsity and contradiction respectively. Of course, the truth maintenance process described below is meant to eliminate contradiction from the belief set, so nodes have the valuation {*true, false*} only temporarily.

Doyle uses the following terminology for nodes, which will be useful in outlining the truth maintenance process:

- The *antecedents* of a node are the nodes listed in its *IN* and *OUT* lists.
- The set of *foundations* of a node is just the transitive closure of its antecedents, that is, the node's antecedents, the antecedents' antecedents, and so on.
- The *consequences* of a node are the nodes which mention that node in their *IN* and *OUT* lists.
- The set of *repercussions* of a node is just the transitive closure of its consequences.

The following is a simplified sketch of Doyle's algorithm which uses only SL-justifications. The event that triggers the truth maintenance process is the adding of a justification to a node. If the node is already in, only minor book-keeping is required, otherwise both the node and its repercussions must be updated.

(1) Add the new justification to the node's justification set, and add the node to the set of consequences of each of the nodes mentioned in the justification.

(2) Check the consequences of the node. If there are none, the change the node from out to in, construct its *IN* and *OUT* list, and halt. Otherwise, make a list *L* containing the node and its repercussions, record the *in–out* status of each of these nodes, mark each node with the temporary status of *nil*, and proceed to step 3.

(3)   For each node N in L, try to find a well-founded valid justification that will make it *in*. If none can be found, mark the node as *out*. Either way, propagate any change in N's status to its consequences. (*Comment.* A justification is *valid* if each node in its *IN* list is *in* and each node in its *OUT* list is *out*, and it is *well-founded* if it is not circular. For example, the justifications $(\{\neg p\}, \{\})$ and $(\{\},\ \{p\})$ would both be circular if applied to p. The first states that p is in only if $\neg p$ is in, while the second states that p is in only if p is out. Each justification leads to a contradiction if it is adopted as a reason for p.)

(4)   If any node in L is *in* and marked as a contradiction, then call the dependency-directed backtracking procedure. If truth maintenance (steps 1–3) occurs during backtracking, repeat this step until no contradictions remain to be resolved.

(5)   Compare the current support-status of each node in L with its recorded status, and alert the user to changes in status.

Both Doyle and McAllester's systems can be thought of as representing a more sophisticated approach to the problem of maintaining a coherent world model than we encountered in discussing the STRIPS system (see Chapter 4). Both TMSs perform updates on a world model by propagating the analogues of ADD and DELETE operations through a dependency network. If a contradiction occurs, the user must retract something from the support of the contradiction, so that consistency is restored.

23.4   Maintaining multiple contexts

Each TMS we have met so far concentrates on maintaining a single, consistent world model. However, sometimes it is convenient to perform reasoning in the context of different hypothetical worlds, which may or may not resemble the way the world actually is. For example, in making a diagnosis, it is often worthwhile to assume that a certain fault has occurred and then make predictions on the basis of this assumption and see if they are backed up by evidence. This strategy is particularly useful if there are a large number of hypotheses competing to account for the observations, with the possibility that a composite hypothesis may be required to cover all of them. Another domain of application might be arrangement problems, where the hypothetical worlds represent different ways of arranging objects to satisfy a set of constraints.

In an *assumption-based TMS* (ATMS), the program maintains a number of different contexts, referred to as *environments* (de Kleer,

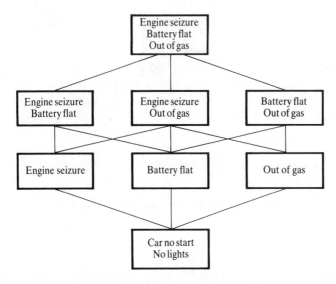

Figure 23.3   An environment lattice.

1986). An environment is best thought of as a view of the world characterized by a set of *assumptions*. Thus the environment characterized by the empty set of assumptions corresponds to the world model of earlier programs. All other environments model hypothetical worlds. These worlds are typically consistent with the world model, but extend it on the basis of various assumptions.

The environments of an ATMS can be arranged in a lattice, since the making of assumptions is an incremental thing. Thus, in Figure 23.3, our world model is such that our car won't start and it has no lights. At the next level up the lattice are hypothetical worlds in which we assume that something is wrong with the car, such as a flat battery. At higher levels, we can combine these assumptions. Note that, as we go up the lattice, hypothetical worlds become more and more specific, in the sense that we know more and more about them.

It will not always be the case that we can pool assumptions arbitrarily. For example, we cannot combine the assumption sets $\{p, q\}$ and $\{\neg p, r\}$ without getting a contradiction. Furthermore, although assumption sets may not be obviously antagonistic, as in the above example, certain combinations may give rise to a contradiction in the presence of other information.

Suppose our world model of faulty cars contains information to the effect that a car cannot be both out of gas and have a flooded carburettor. Then we can deduce that the carburettor is not flooded in the environment in which we assume that we are out of gas, and we can deduce that we are not out of gas in the environment where the carburettor is flooded.

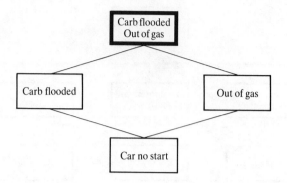

Figure 23.4   Environment lattice with nogood.

Such consequences form what is known as the *context* of an environment: the set of propositions derivable from the assumptions and the facts of the world model. Thus we can have a situation as in Figure 23.4, where the environment formed by the join of two assumption sets is ruled out because its context is inconsistent. Such contexts are called *nogoods*.

This example illustrates the obvious fact that we are allowed to extend our theory of the world only in a manner that respects some body of background knowledge about the way the world is. Put another way, there are dependencies between the individual assumptions that we might make and, as in justification-based truth maintenance, these dependencies must be recorded and enforced.

In ATMS, these dependencies are called *justifications*. This terminology is slightly confusing, because the role of justifications in ATMS is rather different from that in TMS. In TMS, justifications are constructed by the program as a by-product of constraint propagation, and associated with nodes in a dependency network which stand for propositions.

In ATMS, justifications are part of the input to the program. The ATMS then constructs, for each propositional node, a *label* which lists the interesting environments that proposition holds in. We shall see what 'interesting' means shortly, but first let us look at an example.

In Figure 23.4, the proposition that the car is not out of gas holds in the environment where we assume that the carburettor is flooded, given a justification which says something like

If the carburettor is flooded, then the car is not out of gas.

Now this proposition also holds in the nogood, but this environment is not consistent, so *every* proposition holds in it. (Any proposition at all

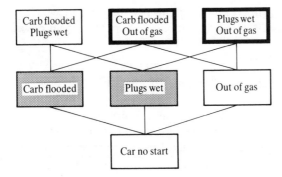

Figure 23.5 Environment lattice showing nogoods (dark border) and labels of
the proposition that the car is not out of gas (stippled boxes).

follows from a contradiction in classical logic.) Such an environment is
not very interesting, so we do not put it in the label.

Suppose we also have a justification that says

If the plugs are wet, then the car is not out of gas.

Then the proposition that the car is not out of gas holds in the environment characterized by the assumption that the plugs are wet, as in
Figure 23.5, so we would also include this environment in the label. The
label of our proposition now contains two environments, each of which is
consistent. These are stippled in Figure 23.5. As before, we ignore nogoods, so this rules out the environment in which the plugs are wet and
the car is out of gas and the environment in which the carburettor is
flooded and out of gas.

Obviously, the proposition also holds in the environment characterized by the join of these two environments, or in any environment that
extends either of the two. However, it is hardly worth recording this fact.
We would rather that the label only contained those environments
characterized by the minimal sets of assumptions needed for the
proposition to hold.

In summary, the basic purpose of an ATMS is to construct a list of
the interesting environments in which a proposition holds. Such a list is
defined as a *sound, complete, consistent and minimal label*. This terminology can be explained as follows.

A label for a propositional node is

- *sound* if the proposition is indeed derivable from each environment
  in its label – that is, if it is *in* the context characterized by each such
  environment;

- *complete* if every consistent environment in which the proposition holds is either in the label or a superset of an environment in the label;
- *consistent* if every environment in the label is consistent; and
- *minimal* if no environment in the label is a superset of any other.

If a propositional node has an empty label, this means that the proposition is not derivable from any consistent set of assumptions. In other words, it is not to be found in the context of any environment that is consistent with the justifications. Thus the node standing for the proposition that the car is out of gas *and* its plugs are wet would have an empty label.

23.5 Summary and comparison of TMSs

The function of a truth maintenance component in the context of a larger problem solving program is:

- to cache inferences made by the problem solver, so that conclusions that have once been derived need never be derived again;
- to allow the problem solver to make useful assumptions and see if useful conclusions can be derived from them; and
- to handle the problem of inconsistency, either by maintaining a single consistent world model, or by managing multiple contexts which are internally consistent but which may be mutually inconsistent.

TMSs such as those of Doyle and McAllester are useful for finding a single solution to a constraint satisfaction problem. For example, the use of a dependency net in the VT expert system described in Chapter 18 is an excellent example of how a simple TMS can be used to good effect. Only one solution to the problem is required; we are not really interested in generating the whole range of alternative designs.

Extra control machinery is required if you want more than one solution, or all solutions. The fact that you are all the time dealing with a single state of the network makes it difficult to compare alternative solutions to the problem, if you really need to do this. For example, in differential diagnosis, it is usually important to compare hypotheses with their competitors to arrive at a composite hypothesis which covers the data and gives the best account of it (as in Chapter 16; see also Chapter 24).

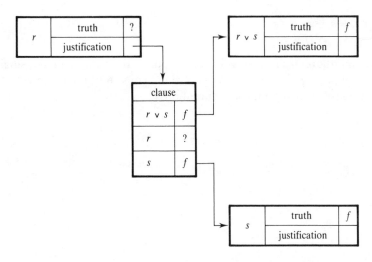

Figure 23.6 A support structure for Study suggestion 23.1.

De Kleer's ATMS is more oriented towards finding all solutions to constraint satisfaction problems – finding all the interesting environments that satisfy the constraints. Extra control machinery is required if you want to find fewer solutions, or a single 'best' solution according to some criteria; such an application of ATMS is described in Chapter 24. However, since you can maintain more than one context, this obviates the need for dependency-directed backtracking in the basic version outlined here.

Bibliographical notes

Dependency networks are well described in Charniak *et al.* (1980, Chapter 16). Unfortunately, the original papers by Doyle (1979) and De Kleer (1986) are not very readable, and do not make good introductions to this area. Readers interested in the theoretical background to truth maintenance may wish to consult papers in Ginsberg (1987).

STUDY SUGGESTIONS

23.1 Fill in the truth value of *r* in the McAllester-style TMS of Figure 23.6.

23.2 Consider the ATMS justifications:

$$p \wedge q \supset r$$
$$\neg p \wedge q \supset s$$

$$p \wedge \neg q \supset t$$
$$\neg p \wedge \neg q \supset u$$

Assume that there are four possible assumptions that can be made, singly or in combination: p, $\neg p$, q, and $\neg q$. What are the consistent environments of this justification set, based on these assumptions?

Part VI

Advanced Topics in Expert Systems

24 Diagnosis from First Principles

Introduction

We have seen that many extant expert systems perform diagnosis by the method of heuristic classification (see Chapters 14 and 15). In this method, diagnostic knowledge is represented mainly in terms of heuristic rules, which perform a mapping between data abstractions (typical symptoms) and solution abstractions (typical disorders). Such a representation of knowledge is sometimes called 'shallow' because it does not contain much information about the causal mechanisms underlying the relationship between symptoms and disorders. The rules typically reflect empirical associations derived from experience, rather than a theory of how the device (or organism) under diagnosis actually works. The latter is sometimes called 'deep' knowledge, because it involves understanding the structure of the device and the way its components function.

It is not that deep knowledge is entirely absent from rule-based expert systems. It is rather that such knowledge is either compiled into the rules in a manner that renders it difficult to differentiate from the shallower stuff, or else hidden in other data structures which serve to control rule-based inference. In any event, it is the shallow knowledge that determines the underlying search space, because this is the knowledge that characterizes the mapping between data and solutions. Empirical knowledge of this sort is largely device dependent, and tends to reside in someone's head, as opposed to being written down or (even less likely) formalized. The only way to gain such knowledge is via the repeated experience of attempting to perform diagnosis on the device in question and then determining the correctness or otherwise of one's hypotheses, or via an extended knowledge elicitation exercise.

Diagnosis from first principles tends to approach the problem from another angle. Rather than assume the existence of an expert experienced in diagnosing the device, we assume the existence of a *system description*: a complete and consistent theory of the correct behaviour of the device. Given a data set supplying evidence of that system's malfunction, the idea is that it should be possible to conjecture one or more minimum perturbations to the system description that would account for the data.

The plan of the chapter is as follows. Section 24.1 delves into the basic assumptions behind the approach, and reviews some early work in the area (Genesereth, 1984; De Kleer and Williams, 1987). Section 24.2 reviews Reiter's (1987) theory of diagnosis, and Section 24.3 presents a critical evaluation of such approaches in the context of diagnostic reasoning based on causal models.

24.1 Basic assumptions of the approach

The apparent advantages of first principles over expert systems approaches are as follows.

- Given a device description, the program designer is able to short-cut the laborious process of eliciting empirical associations from a human expert.

- The reasoning method employed is device independent, so it is not necessary to tailor the inference machinery for different applications.

- Since only knowledge of *correct* device behaviour is required, the method ought to be able to diagnose faults that have never occurred before.

We shall outline additional assumptions relevant to the application of particular approaches as we describe and discuss the corresponding systems.

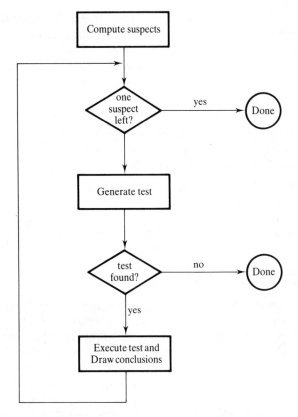

Figure 24.1 Flowchart for the DART program.

24.1.1 Computing suspects in DART

The DART program (Genesereth, 1984) was a prototype for a diagnostic system in the domain of digital circuits. A distinguishing feature of this system was that both the representation language and the inference mechanism were more or less device independent. Genesereth used the predicate calculus to encode design descriptions of devices under diagnosis, and a form of theorem provng (called resolution residue) to generate both sets of suspect components and tests to confirm or refute fault hypotheses.

The basic flowchart for the DART program is reproduced in Figure 24.1 from Genesereth's paper. Although we need not be concerned with the details of DART's implementation, the top-level algorithm is worth studying because it is typical of many other 'first principles' programs. DART was actually implemented in MRS (see Chapter 11). Suspected faults are generated by theorem proving, and then tests are generated to narrow the space of alternatives. Tests embody knowledge of how components work, for example, functions that compute the outputs of a component given its inputs.

DART's problem-solving method relied on a number of simplifying assumptions:

(1) The connections in the device are assumed to be working properly, so we seek faulty *components* to account for symptom data.

(2) Faults are *non-intermittent*, that is, components behave consistently for the duration of the diagnosis.

(3) There is only a *single fault* in the device.

Singh (1987) has since extended DART, by improving the test generation procedure and making the resolution theorem prover more efficient, but has retained the original assumptions.

24.1.2 Computing conflicts in GDE

GDE (De Kleer and Williams, 1987) is a system which retains assumptions 1 and 2 shown above, but concentrates on relaxing 3. (GDE stands for General Diagnostic Engine.) The trouble is that the hypothesis space now grows exponentially with the number of faults, because we now have to consider sets of hypothetical faults. It is therefore important to generate hypotheses in rough order of 'goodness' and then generate tests that will differentiate between competing hypothesis sets in a minimum number of measurements. The inherent complexity of the problem is addressed by a combination of assumption-based truth maintenance and probabilistic inference.

As we saw in Chapter 23, ATMS (De Kleer, 1986) is a method of maintaining a lattice of *environments*: alternative states of the world which are consistent with some theory but in which different *assumptions* hold. In diagnostic applications, this (implicit) theory is the device description, and the alternative states of the world are characterized by the 2^n different ways in which n components can fail. The environments are arranged in a lattice by set inclusion: the least element is the empty set of faulty components, while the greatest element is the set of all components. Each such environment is called a *candidate*: a hypothesis about the way in which a faulty device actually deviates from its description. The environment lattice is called the *candidate space*.

If the device is working perfectly, the least element (representing no faulty components) 'explains' the observation of the correct outputs. Otherwise, faulty outputs are seen as evidence for some component failure in the candidate space. Because the size of this space is exponential in the number of components, we need some way of focusing the search for candidates.

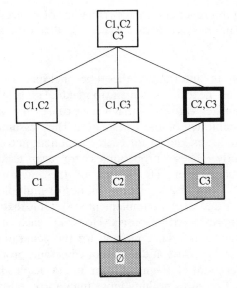

Figure 24.2   An environment lattice of candidates (see text).

The key notion is that of a *conflict set*: a set of components that cannot all be functioning correctly, given the symptom data. The conflict sets are just those assumption sets in the ATMS which generate environments inconsistent with the data. They can be determined by forming the deductive closure of an environment with the data, and then looking for a contradiction. This is obviously a form of constraint propagation (see Chapter 23). The main goal of the truth maintenance system is to identify the complete set of *minimal conflicts*, that is, to detect those conflict sets which subsume all others by set inclusion. From these, one can compute the minimal sets of faulty components that account for all the symptoms.

As a simple example, let C1, C2 and C3 be system components, and let *s* be an observation that is a symptom of system failure (see Figure 24.2). Suppose we know that if *s* occurs then C1 and C2 cannot both be working, and neither can C1 and C3. Thus we can rule out the environments labelled ∅, C2 and C3 (shaded in Figure 24.2), because each has some forbidden conjunction of components working. All other environments are candidate diagnoses. However, the minimal candidates are obviously {C1} and {C2, C3}, shown in heavy outline.

The ATMS uses a number of strategies to control the complexity of the candidate space, for example:

- exploiting a preference for minimal explanations by beginning the search for solutions from the smallest conflict sets;

- recording inferences (such as predictions of device behaviour based on assumption sets) in the ATMS, so that they are never drawn twice.

GDE also uses an information-theoretic measure of uncertainty to determine the best next measurement to make. The best measurement is that which minimizes *entropy* – that which causes the greatest diversity among the probabilities of the candidates. They assume that the prior probability of failure is known for each component and that components fail independently. These probabilities are also used to guide the generation of candidates. The search of the environment lattice is conducted best-first on the joint probabilities of multiple faults.

Both DART and GDE are implemented systems that have exerted an influence over more recent proposals. However, each of these programs relies on a particular inference method for the generation of diagnoses: resolution residue for DART and a kind of constraint propagation in GDE. Reiter's (1987) account of diagnosis from first principles is arguably more general, in that it requires nothing more than a general-purpose theorem prover, at least as far as the formulation of the method is concerned. Implementation is another story, though. The useful notion of a minimal conflict also appears in Reiter's work, and leads to a similar preference for minimal explanations of data.

24.2   Diagnosis from first principles

Reiter's (1987) theory of diagnosis from first principles involves working from a *system description* (SD) featuring a finite set of *system components*, and a set of observations (OBS). Both SD and OBS are finite sets of sentences in first-order predicate logic. (First-order logic includes both functions and identity.)

24.2.1   Computing all diagnoses

A *diagnosis* for (SD, COMPONENTS, OBS) is a minimal set $\triangle \subseteq$ COMPONENTS such that

$$\text{SD} \cup \text{OBS} \cup \{\neg AB(c) \mid c \in \text{COMPONENTS} - \triangle\}$$

is consistent, where AB is the abnormality predicate, such that $AB(c)$ means that component c is abnormal or faulty. The idea is that a diagnosis keeps the set of abnormal components as small as possible. We deem a component to be in the set only if its presence is required by a symptom in OBS.

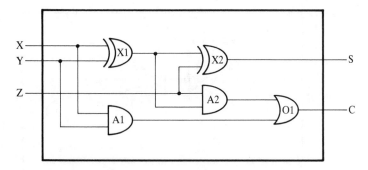

Figure 24.3 Diagram of a full adder. X1 and X2 are exclusive-or-gates, A1 and A2 are and-gates, and O1 is an or-gate.

Of course, there may be more than one way of constructing $\triangle$, leading to multiple diagnoses. Although one could compute these sets by a simple generate and test algorithm, it is more efficient to use de Kleer and Williams' notion of a conflict set: a set of components $\{c_1, \ldots, c_n\}$ such that

$$\text{SD} \cup \text{OBS} \cup \{\neg AB(c_1), \ldots, \neg AB(c_n)\}$$

is inconsistent. Given a theorem prover that will generate conflict sets for (SD, COMPONENTS, OBS), Reiter shows how to compute all diagnoses of (SD, COMPONENTS, OBS). The key idea is that of a *hitting set*: a set formed from the collection of conflict sets C by taking at least one element from each member of C. Minimal hitting sets are defined as follows.

For a set H to be a minimal hitting set of a collection of sets C, we require that

(1) $H \subseteq \cup_{S \in C} S$;
(2) $H \cap S \neq \varnothing$ for each $S \in C$; and
(3) there is no $H' \subset H$ for which both (1) and (2) hold.

In other words, the minimal hitting sets are the smallest sets that 'hit' each set in the collection, and they correspond exactly to diagnoses as defined earlier. Reiter provides an algorithm for computing minimal hitting sets using a data structure called a *hitting set tree* (HS-tree). Heuristics are provided for pruning this tree, which are intended to reduce the cost of obtaining the minimal hitting sets.

These ideas are best illustrated with an example. We shall follow the literature by taking as our device the full adder: a one-bit adder with carry in and carry out. A logic diagram of the device is shown in Figure 24.3.

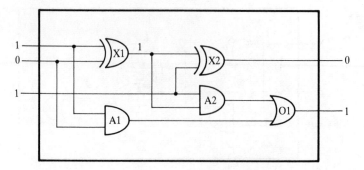

Figure 24.4 Correct outputs for inputs $X = 1$, $Y = 0$, $Z = 1$.

This adder can be represented by the set

COMPONENTS = {A1, A2, O1, X1, X2}

plus a system description that describes the components in terms of their connectivity and their behaviour. We will not reproduce the system description here, but it contains boolean equations, such as

$$XORG(X) \land \neg AB(X) \supset OUT(X) = xor(IN1(X), IN2(X))$$

which states that a normal exclusive-or gate's output is the usual boolean function of its two inputs, together with formulas describing circuit components and their connectivities.

EXAMPLE. Given the inputs $X = 1$, $Y = 0$ and $Z = 1$, we would expect the outputs $S = 0$ and $C = 1$, as shown in Figure 24.4.

Suppose instead that the sum turns out to be 1 and the carry is 0 for the same inputs. One possible cause of these observations is that X1 is faulty. If X1 outputs 0 instead of 1, this would produce the wrong behaviour, as shown in Figure 24.5.

Given that SD contains

$$XORG(X) \land \neg AB(X) \supset OUT(X) = xor(IN1(X), IN2(X))$$

and OBS contains

$$OUT(X2) = 1$$

it is easy to see that

$$SD \cup OBS \cup \{\neg AB(X1), \neg AB(X2)\}$$

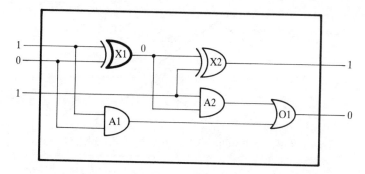

Figure 24.5 A possible diagnosis for the faulty outputs.

is inconsistent, given the inputs. Either X1 passed on the correct outputs to X2, in which case X2 is abnormal, because

$$OUT(X2) \neq xor(IN1(X2), IN2(X2))$$

or X1 computed the wrong outputs and is therefore abnormal, because

$$OUT(X1) \neq xor(IN1(X1), IN2(X1))$$

Thus {X1, X2} is a conflict set for (SD, COMPONENTS, OBS). The other conflict set is {X1, A2, O1}, because one of X1, A2, O1 must be abnormal to explain the wrong carry, $OUT(O1) = 0$. In other words,

$$SD \cup OBS \cup \{\neg AB(X1), \neg AB(A2), \neg AB(O1)\}$$

is inconsistent. The minimal hitting sets of the set of conflict sets

$$C = \{\{X1, X2\}, \{X1, A2, O1\}\}$$

are {X1}, {X2, A2} and {X2, O1}.

Figure 24.6 shows a hitting set tree for this example. The minimal conflicts form the nodes (shown in bold), while a labelled branch B below a given node N corresponds to the selection of component B from the set at node N. The hitting sets are just paths through the tree, and the minimal hitting sets are paths that are not subsumed by any other path. Thus the path X1 subsumes the path X1–X2, so X1–X2 is not minimal. Clearly the minimal paths are X1, X2–A2 and X2–O1.

The reader can easily verify that the minimal hitting sets derived in Figure 24.6 are those sets S with the following properties:

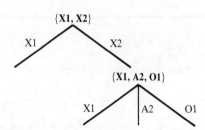

Figure 24.6 A hitting set tree for the full adder example.

(1) the failure of components contained in S would explain the wrong outputs and

(2) there is no subset of S that satisfies 1.

Such sets therefore correspond to the diagnoses of (SD, COMPONENTS, OBS), as defined by Reiter's theory.

Once we have generated alternative diagnoses, we are interested in ruling some of them out. Different diagnoses make different predictions concerning what additional observations we might expect. If we fail to observe phenomena predicted by a diagnosis, we may eliminate that hypothesis from consideration. A diagnosis $\triangle$ *predicts* some first-order sentence P iff

$$SD \cup OBS \cup \{\neg AB(c) \mid c \in COMPONENTS - \triangle\} \models P$$

In other words, P follows as a logical consequence from the facts of the case, SD and OBS, and the assumption that all components not in the diagnosis are working properly.

24.2.2 Applicability of Reiter's approach

Reiter's approach appears to be both elegant and formally correct, but it places three important constraints on the formulation of the diagnostic problem.

- In practice, we can only deal with faulty components. If we try to extend the theory to deal with the connections between components, the number of possible diagnoses becomes much too large. (For non-trivial circuits, the component-based diagnoses are quite numerous enough, and the computational cost of generating them is high.)

- We need a complete system description, not a trivial requirement for an arbitrary system. Determining the completeness and consistency of the system description need not be straightforward yet, if these properties do not hold, the method will not be sound or complete. Such descriptions are seldom available for complex devices, although it is possible that they could be generated as a by-product of computer-aided design.

- The method assumes the availability of a complete theorem prover for the underlying logic. Again, this is no problem for the full adder example, because the theory of Boolean equations is decidable (see Chapter 5). But reasoning about consistency is impossible in the general first-order case in terms of which the theory of diagnosis is formulated, so any automatic diagnostic system using defaults in the full first-order case must have recourse to heuristics.

In many domains, we are interested in doing more than merely identifying faulty components. 'There is something wrong with the patient's heart' is not very illuminating as a medical diagnosis. Therapy and prognosis ultimately depend on having more precise hypotheses. However, in many electronic devices, where components are relatively cheap and easy to replace, identifying sets of components that may be faulty is all we need to effect repair. Often, systematic 'board swapping' replaces the taking of additional measurements; sometimes it replaces the diagnostic process altogether.

24.2.3   Comparison with GDE

To lend concreteness to the discussion, let us redo the diagnosis of the adder in the example, using GDE's approach. Figure 24.7 shows the lower levels of an ATMS environment lattice for this problem. Each node other than ∅ denotes a fault state; for example, the node labelled A1,A2 represents the state of affairs where only the and-gates are faulty.

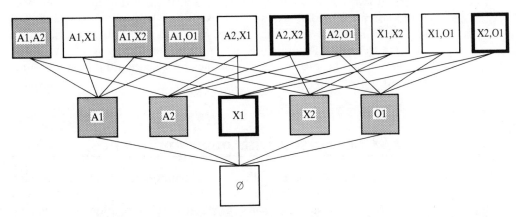

Figure 24.7   GDE's candidate space for the adder example.

As before, the minimal conflicts are {X1, X2} and {X1, A2, O1}. Given the observations, we can say that one of X1 and X2 must be faulty, and that components X1, A2 and O1 cannot all be working correctly. The conflicts allow us to rule out certain nodes, which are shaded in Figure 24.7. Thus, we can rule out the node labelled A1, because both X1 and X2 are deemed to be functioning correctly at this node. The nodes that are left in the lattice fragment are all candidate explanations of the data.

All that remains is to read off the minimal candidates {X1}, {X2, A2}, {X2, O1}: these are clearly the minimal sets of components whose failure is consistent with the observations. Candidates such as {A2, X1} are certainly consistent with the data, but they are subsumed by other candidates, in this case {X1}. The upper levels of the lattice contain no minimal candidates, and are therefore not included in Figure 24.7.

It is relatively easy to see that the diagnoses of the two approaches coincide: Reiter's minimal hitting sets are just GDE's minimal candidates (compare Figures 24.6 and 24.7). Both methods rely on an inference engine to compute the conflict sets; Reiter assumes that a general-purpose theorem prover is available for this. GDE uses the ATMS to calculate the consequences of OBS in each environment, starting with the empty one, and looks for an inconsistency signalling that the environment is a conflict. Needless to say, the general problem of determining these sets is intractable for large numbers of components. However, the search space is normally much sparser than the full lattice, because many joins will contain no consequences not found in their subsets.

The main differences between the two methods are as follows. Firstly, Reiter's algorithm interleaves the generation of conflict sets with the generation of minimal hitting sets, while GDE generates all the minimal conflict sets before computing minimal candidates. Moreover, the algorithm is incremental, in the sense that it generates diagnoses in order of increasing cardinality. Secondly, GDE exploits useful properties of the ATMS, such as the ability to record the drawing of inferences while computing conflicts, as well as using probabilities to guide the search for minimal candidates and cost functions to inform the selection of measurements. Although Reiter proves a number of results about measurements, he provides no guidelines for selecting the next measurement to make.

24.3 Comparison with other approaches

In Section 24.1, we contrasted logic-based approaches to diagnosis using system descriptions with approaches more commonly associated with expert systems technology, such as heuristic classification. In this, the concluding section, we shall dig a little further into the AI literature to effect a slightly deeper (but just as brief) comparison between the utility of non-monotonic approaches to diagnosis and the utility of approaches based on other kinds of causal reasoning. In particular, we shall concentrate on rule-based systems which also use an explicit representation of causal knowledge.

In earlier chapters, we have seen that a number of recent approaches to expert system construction rely on the construction of a *domain model*: some declarative representation of objects in the domain and the (primarily causal) relationships between them. This model is then used as a basis for a further knowledge engineering effort, usually the generation of heuristic rules. These rules are sometimes generated automatically from the model, or else the model is used to supply a knowledge acquisition program with interview strategies for the elicitation of rules from an expert.

MORE (Kahn, 1988) and XPLAIN (Swartout, 1983) are prominent examples of this approach; they are described in Chapters 15 and 19 respectively. These systems are worth mentioning again here because they attempt to combine deeper causal knowledge with the shallower experiential knowledge we associate with the rule-based approach. In particular, we need to consider whether or not this use of domain models takes some of the force out of the arguments for logic-based approaches to diagnosis.

Here a causal model is used not as a replacement for heuristic rules, but as an intermediate stage of representation from which such rules can be derived. Having such an underlying model is intended to make the process of building and debugging rule sets easier. In some systems, such as XPLAIN, it is also used to produce explanations which go beyond rule tracing. (No work appears to have been done so far on the explanation of diagnoses derived from first principles.)

Although systems like MORE are still in their infancy, they demonstrate that the two approaches of causal reasoning from faults to symptoms and heuristic mapping from symptoms to faults can be mutually supportive rather than mutually exclusive strategies. This hybrid approach to diagnosis appears to be more flexible than approaches based solely on a device description, because one does not require a complete domain model in order to generate useful rules. Neither does one need as many simplifying assumptions as seem to be required by logic-based approaches. As Clancey (1985) has pointed out, the deep models required by the latter are hard to construct, even for relatively simple electronic devices. Even Genesereth (1984) acknowledges that 'not all design descriptions are tuned for the task of diagnosis' – although part of the motivation for using design descriptions is surely that (unlike rule sets) they are not supposed to need tuning!

Nevertheless, diagnosis from first principles is intrinsically interesting. Proposals based on device descriptions give us an entirely different perspective on the knowledge engineering problem by shifting some of the responsibility for supplying knowledge from the troubleshooter to the designer. This may facilitate the knowledge acquisition process, if the requisite information is readily available in a form that lends itself to declarative representation in some logical language.

It is possible that diagnosis from first principles, in its purest form, will always be confined to certain domains, namely those governed by a finite (and preferably small) set of laws that are capable of being precisely stated. Thus it is no coincidence that the examples are almost invariably drawn from the domain of electronic circuits. Nevertheless, the link that such work is forging between design and diagnosis may turn out to be an extremely valuable one from the knowledge acquisition point of view.

Bibliographical notes

The material in this chapter is essentially a subset of the review in Jackson (1989), which contains some additional material on other logic-based approaches to diagnosis, such as those of Ginsberg (1986) and Poole (1988). Davis (1984) is an influential paper on electronic troubleshooting from first principles which is well worth reading. His approach is more ambitious than those described here, in that it does not always assume that the connections between components are functioning properly.

STUDY SUGGESTIONS

24.1 What are the simplifying assumptions behind DART's approach to fault diagnosis? How restrictive are these assumptions, if we wish to apply the method to devices other than digital circuits?

24.2 The circuit of Figure 24.8 is called an RS flip-flop. The nodes N1–N4 are all nand gates, so they output 1 so long as it is not the case that both their inputs are equal to 1. (I have used arrows to represent the flow in Figure 24.8 because, unlike the earlier circuit diagrams, the flow is not always from left to right.)

The circuit has three inputs: R (for Reset), S (for Set) and a clock signal. When Clock $= 1$, the Q output will be set to 1 if $S = 1$ and $R = 0$ (as shown in Figure 24.9), or reset to 0 if $S = 0$ and $R = 1$. Q will not change if $S = R = 0$.

When the clock falls, the device *should* behave as in Figure 24.10, with Q still set to 1. But suppose that a fault develops in one or more of the gates just before the clock falls, and that the *actual* outputs are as shown in Figure 24.11.

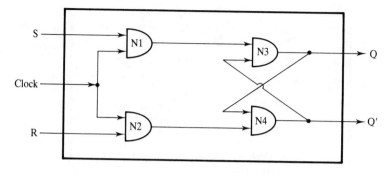

Figure 24.8 An RS flip-flop.

Clearly the value for Q' in Figure 24.11 is wrong. What are the minimal sets of failed components that account for the outputs?

24.3 Suppose that the following letters stand for possible causes of problems with your car:

> c = carburettor flooded
> d = radio disconnected
> f = flat battery
> g = out of gas
> s = light switch faulty

and suppose that the symptoms of your sick vehicle are:

> car will not start
> lights do not work
> radio does not work

Consider the environment lattice of Figure 24.12. Use your knowledge of ATMS and your commonsense knowledge of cars to

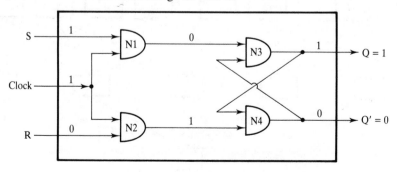

Figure 24.9 The flip-flop correctly setting Q to 1.

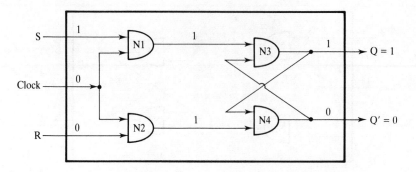

Figure 24.10 Correct behaviour of the flip-flop as the clock falls.

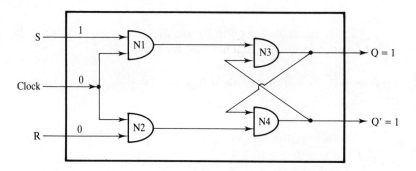

Figure 24.11 Faulty behaviour of the flip-flop as the clock falls.

(a)   identify the nogood environments,

(b)   identify the environments that constitute minimal explanations of the symptoms.

Which explanation 'wins', given the single-fault assumption?

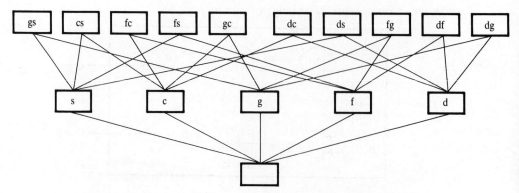

Figure 24.12 An environment lattice for Study suggestion 24.3.

25 Formal Models of Plausible Inference

Introduction

This chapter considers two quantitative methods for reasoning under uncertainty in a structured space of hypotheses. It is arguable that both of them handle belief updating in a more convincing manner than certainty factors do. These methods also represent alternatives to more heuristic methods, such as those described in Chapters 16 and 22, which appear to have very little formal basis.

Gordon and Shortliffe (1985) and Pearl (1986) have each suggested ways in which evidential reasoning in a hierarchical hypothesis space (such as that used by INTERNIST and CENTAUR) can be managed in the context of the Dempster–Shafer theory of evidence and a Bayesian formalism respectively. Each approach involves defining a belief function over a hypothesis set, and then providing mechanisms for updating the current set of beliefs as new evidence is gathered.

The approaches are described in detail, and an attempt is made to compare and contrast them. Finally, we consider a general framework for effecting such comparisons.

25.1   Dempster–Shafer theory

The hypothesis space in Dempster–Shafer theory is called the *frame of discernment*, denoted by Θ. It is assumed that the hypotheses in this space are both exhaustive and mutually exclusive. It is also assumed that we may have means of obtaining evidence not merely for single hypotheses $h_1, \ldots, h_n$ in Θ, but also about one or more subsets $A_1, \ldots, A_k$ of Θ, which are allowed to overlap.

25.1.1   Belief functions

The power set (the set of all possible subsets) of Θ is denoted by 2^Θ, since there are 2^n subsets of a set of n elements, including both the set itself, and the empty set, $\varnothing$. Let us assume a mapping, $\Gamma \colon \Psi \to 2^\Theta$, which associates each element of evidence set Ψ with a subset of Θ. Such a subset is called a *focal element*. Note that the assumption of exhaustiveness means that we do not map any $\psi \in \Psi$ onto the empty set.

The *basic probability assignment* (b.p.a.) of Dempster–Shafer theory, m, is a function from 2^Θ to $[0,1]$ such that

$$m(\varnothing) = 0$$
$$\Sigma_{A_i \in 2^\Theta}(m(A_i)) = 1$$

The total belief, Bel, in any focal element A can be found by summing the b.p.a. values of all subsets of A. Thus Bel is a function from 2^Θ to $[0,1]$ such that

$$\mathrm{Bel}(A) = \Sigma_{B \subset A} m(B)$$

$\mathrm{Bel}(\Theta)$ is always 1, regardless of the value of $m(\Theta)$. This follows from the definition of a b.p.a. $\mathrm{Bel}(\Theta) = 1$ represents the fact that the correct hypothesis is always believed to be in Θ (exhaustiveness again). $m(\Theta)$ reflects the weight of evidence as yet uncommitted to subsets of Θ. Bel and m will be equal for singleton sets.

The probability of a focal element A is bounded below by the belief in A, and above by the plausibility of A, given by $1 - \mathrm{Bel}(A^c)$, where A^c is the complement of A. The plausibility of A, $\mathrm{Pls}(A)$ can also be calculated as follows

$$\mathrm{Pls}(A) = \Sigma_{A \cap B \neq \varnothing} m(B)$$

It represents the degree to which the evidence is consistent with A.

Dempster's rule computes a new belief function, given two belief functions based on two different observations. Let Bel_1 and Bel_2 denote two belief functions with their respective b.p.a. values, m_1 and m_2. The rule computes a new b.p.a., $m_1 \oplus m_2$, and then a new belief function $Bel_1 \oplus Bel_2$ based on the definition of Bel given above.

$m_1 \oplus m_2(A)$, for a given hypothesis A, is given by the sum of all the products of the form $m_1(X)m_2(Y)$, where X and Y range over all subsets of Θ whose intersection is A. When there are empty entries in the intersection table, a normalization is applied which defines $\varkappa$ as the sum of all the non-zero values assigned to $\varnothing$, assigns $m_1 \oplus m_2(\varnothing)$ as zero, and then divides $m_1 \oplus m_2$ for all other hypothesis sets by $1 - \varkappa$.

In summary,

$$m_1 \oplus m_2(A) = \frac{\Sigma_{X \cap Y = A} m_1(X)m_2(Y)}{1 - \Sigma_{X \cap Y = \varnothing} m_1(X)m_2(Y)}$$

but we insist that m_1 and m_2 are induced by independent evidential sources within the same frame of discernment. Note that commutativity of multiplication ensures that Dempster's rule gives the same result regardless of the order in which evidence is combined.

The plausibility of A can be thought of as the extent to which A is capable of improving, given the evidence for competitors of A. It is therefore convenient to think of the information contained in Bel for a given subset as a *belief interval* of the form $[Bel(A), Pls(A)]$. The width of the belief interval can be regarded as the amount of uncertainty with respect to a hypothesis, given the available evidence.

25.1.2 Applying Dempster–Shafer theory to MYCIN

Gordon and Shortliffe advocate the use of Dempster–Shafer theory as an alternative to MYCIN's certainty factors. They note that, when searching for the identity of an organism, MYCIN often narrows the hypothesis set of all possible organisms down to a proper subset, such as the Gram-negative organisms. (This is an example of what Clancey would call the application of structural knowledge.) Moreover, the rules that produce this narrowing typically have nothing to say about the relative likelihoods of organisms in that subset.

A Bayesian approach might assume that each organism in the subset has an equal prior probability, and so distribute the weight of evidence for the subset equally among its elements. But this tends to confound the case of equal evidence for each of the organisms with the case where there is no evidence at all. The Dempster–Shafer b.p.a. does not distinguish prior and posterior probabilities in this way, and so does not sanction such a distribution of probabilities.

Dempster–Shafer belief functions also avoid another counter-intuitive aspect of the Bayesian view. In the latter, a subjective interpretation of probabilities means that a degree of belief in a hypothesis, H, implies that one's remaining belief is committed to its negation, that is, that

$$P(\text{H}) = 1 - P(\neg\text{H})$$

However, one of the desiderata of the confirmation model that gave rise to the use of certainty factors in MYCIN was that evidence partially in favour of a hypothesis should not be construed as evidence partially against the same hypothesis. In Dempster–Shafer, the commitment of belief to a subset A does not force the commitment of the remaining belief to its complement, thus $\text{Bel}(A) + \text{Bel}(A^c) \leq 1$. The amount of belief committed to neither A nor A^c is the degree of ignorance concerning A.

Gordon and Shortliffe go on to show how Dempster–Shafer theory could be applied to evidential reasoning in MYCIN. (object attribute value) triples found in the conclusions of rules represent singleton hypotheses concerning the value of a particular attribute for a particular object. So any set of such triples having the same object and attribute, such as (ORGANISM-1 IDENTITY value), constitutes a frame of discernment in its own right. So long as the parameters are single-valued, the condition concerning mutual exclusivity of hypotheses will be met. The set of values should also exhaust the range.

Rules can therefore be construed as belief functions of a certain sort. If the premises confirm the conclusion of a hypothesis H with degree d, and d is above the threshold set for rule activation, then the CF associated with the H can be regarded as a b.p.a. which assigns d to the singleton set, $\{\text{H}\}$, and $1 - d$ to Θ. If the premises disconfirm a conclusion with degree d, then we assign d to $\{\text{H}\}^c$, and $1 - d$ to Θ, and the CF associated with H is $-d$.

The authors identify three different ways in which evidence could be combined as a consequence of rule triggering in MYCIN, according to the Dempster–Shafer model:

(1) Two rules either both confirm or both disconfirm the same conclusion, $\{\text{H}\}$, with b.p.a. values m_1 and m_2. In this case, some weight of evidence will be transferred between $\{\text{H}\}$ and Θ. The updated belief in these two sets will be $m_1 \oplus m_2(\{\text{H}\})$ and $m_1 \oplus m_2(\Theta)$. There is no need to apply the $\varkappa$ normalization, since $\{\text{H}\} \cap \Theta \neq \varnothing$. It turns out that the original certainty factor model gives the same results as Dempster's rule here.

(2) One rule confirms $\{\text{H}\}$ to degree m_1 and one rule disconfirms $\{\text{H}\}$ to degree m_2, that is confirms $\{\text{H}\}^c$ to degree m_2. In this case, normalization will be necessary, since $\{\text{H}\} \cap \{\text{H}\}^c = \varnothing$. Otherwise b.p.a. values are combined as before to derive $m_1 \oplus m_2(\{\text{H}\})$,

$m_1{\oplus}m_2(\{H\}^c)$ and $m_1{\oplus}m_2(\Theta)$. Here the results will not agree with the CF model. The application of Dempster's rule will result in reduced support for both $\{H\}$ and $\{H\}^c$, with a corresponding gain for Θ. Thus conflicting evidence increases our uncertainty concerning both $\{H\}$ and $\{H\}^c$ by widening their belief intervals. (Each also becomes more plausible as a result of conflicting evidence, since support for its complement is weakened. This may seem less intuitive, if one gives 'plausible' its everyday meaning. However, given the definition of Pls, it is clear why this must be so.) By contrast, MYCIN's combination function (see Chapter 3) tends to come down on the side of the hypothesis with the largest CF.

(3) The rules conclude about competing singleton hypotheses, $\{H_1\}$ and $\{H_2\}$. In this case, normalization will be required if $\{H_1\} \cap \{H_2\} = \varnothing$, and we calculate $m_1{\oplus}m_2(\{H_1\})$, $m_1{\oplus}m_2(\{H_2\})$ and $m_1{\oplus}m_2(\Theta)$. Dempster's rule can be seen to be more general than MYCIN's combination function in that, if a subset relation exists between $\{H_1\}$ and $\{H_2\}$, belief in the subset will be counted in favour of belief in the superset, but not conversely. Thus the pooling of evidence has a wider impact here than it would in the CF model.

Gordon and Shortliffe propose an approximation technique to the Dempster–Shafer method which attempts to minimize computational cost. They also point out that partitioning of the search space, such as that performed by INTERNIST, can help to keep the set of competitors constituting the current frame of discernment sufficiently small. However, the problem remains that systems such as INTERNIST cannot allow a strict mapping such as $\Gamma: \Psi \rightarrow 2^{\Theta}$ between evidential elements and hypothesis sets in the construction of a set of competing hypotheses, given that symptoms may have implications for disjoint hypothesis sets in different parts of the hierarchy.

25.2 Pearl's theory of evidential reasoning in a hierarchy

Pearl's (1986) alternative to Dempster–Shafer theory for evidential reasoning in a hierarchy is based on a Bayesian view of evidence aggregation and updating by propagation. As with Gordon and Shortliffe, it assumes that some subsets of the total hypothesis space are of semantic interest and can be arranged in a hierarchy.

Initially, it is assumed that each singleton hypothesis has a prior degree of belief associated with it. Pearl does not say where the priors come from, but presumably a domain expert provides them.

The expert is also required to determine the set of hypotheses, S, upon which a given piece of evidence, E, bears directly. If E bears directly on S, this can be taken to mean that there is some causal mechanism giving rise to E, and this mechanism is a unique property of the members of S. However, E conveys no information which allows us to prefer one member of S over another, as an explanation of E.

This mapping therefore introduces the notion of conditional independence between evidence and singleton hypotheses, such that

$$p(E|S, h_i) = p(E|S) \quad \text{for all } h_i \in S$$

The degree to which E confirms or disconfirms S can be estimated using the likelihood ratio

$$\lambda_S = \frac{p(E|S)}{p(E|\neg S)}$$

The impact of evidence E on the set S is calculated as follows. Each singleton hypothesis, h_i, in S obtains the weight $W_i = \lambda_S$, while every hypothesis in S^c receives a unity weight, $W_i = 1$. This is the weight distribution phase.

Then updating begins, by computing a new value for the belief function, $Bel'(h_i)$, from $Bel(h_i)$:

$$Bel'(h_i) = p(h_i|E) = \alpha_S W_i Bel(h_i)$$

where α_S is the normalization given by

$$\alpha_S = \frac{1}{\Sigma_i W_i Bel'(h_i)}$$

and $Bel(h_i)$ is just the prior degree of belief.

Thus the belief assigned to a set of hypotheses is distributed among its singleton elements as a function of their prior probabilities, while belief assigned to a non-singleton hypothesis is the sum of the belief in its singleton elements. Updating can proceed recursively, so that posterior beliefs serve as prior beliefs for the next evidence.

The justification for this scheme is that the assumption of conditional independence, together with the symmetrical assumption for the complement of S,

$$p(E|S^c, h_i) = p(E|S^c) \quad \text{for all } h_i \in S^c$$

gives

$$p(E|h_i) = P(E|S) \quad \text{if } h_i \in S \text{ else } p(E|S^c)$$

Put this together with the odds-likelihood form of Bayes rule, and it follows that

$$p(h_i|E) = \alpha_S \lambda_S p(h_i) \quad \text{if } h_i \in S \text{ else } \alpha_S p(h_i)$$

Pearl's 1986 paper does not explicitly compare this formalism with Dempster–Shafer theory, but we can make the following observations:

- The association between evidential elements and hypothesis sets is not unlike the mapping in Dempster–Shafer theory. The principal difference appears to be the assignment of prior degrees of belief to singletons.

- Distributing evidence from subsets to singletons recovers a point probability distribution for the hypothesis space, but at the expense of being more precise about individual hypotheses than the evidence actually warrants. However, Pearl claims that one need not distribute the mass at a subset S to its constituents until further (or all of the) evidence has been received.

- As Yen (1986) points out, one loses the Dempster–Shafer notion of a belief interval within which probability estimates may vary. Belief intervals could be useful for scheduling purposes in the context of expert systems, since they give some indication of the goodness of a hypothesis, its room for improvement, and the degree of uncertainty associated with it.

- Pearl's identification of $Bel(h_i)$ with $p(h_i)$ and $Bel'(h_i)$ with $p(h_i|E)$ gives these functions a firmer foundation in probability theory than Dempster's rule of combination, which has no strong argument associated with it, as Shafer (1976) admits.

- Although Pearl's formalism is Bayesian, partial evidence in favour of a hypothesis can no longer be construed as partially supporting its negation. Evidence for a subset S is never construed as evidence for S^c, while mass assigned to singleton, h, is quite distinct from the mass assigned to its competitors.

- In Pearl's method, normalization can be postponed, until several pieces of evidence have impacted on (possibly different) hypotheses. Thus given evidence $E_1, ..., E_n$ for hypotheses $S_1, ..., S_n$ respectively, the weights are combined multiplicatively by

$$W_i(E_1, ..., E_n) = W_{1,i} W_{2,i} ... W_{n,i}$$

where $W_{k,i} = \lambda_{S_k}$ if $h_i \in S_k$ and 1 otherwise.

- Pearl puts forward an alternative mechanism for updating which avoids the normalization step altogether and involves propagating revisions up and down the hierarchy using message-passing. This appears to be more attractive than Dempster's rule from an implementational point of view.

- Pearl claims a peculiar transparency for his updating by message-passing, since influence flows along pathways that have some semantic justification. Doing away with global normalizations, such as $\varkappa$ and α, makes the intermediate steps easier to understand. This leaves only one numerical parameter, the likelihood ratio, whose significance is easy to understand.

- Both formalisms can be viewed as using the 'mass distribution' metaphor, in that they are concerned with the sharing out of evidence in a structured space of alternatives, and both allow for the computation of belief functions based on simple probability estimates.

It is not easy to make systematic comparisons between alternative quantitative methods of plausible inference. Apart from problems of terminology and notation, comparing two methods is difficult unless they can both be viewed in terms of some common framework. In the next section, we look at just such a framework of comparing different methods which is rooted in probability theory.

25.3   Comparing methods of inexact reasoning

Horvitz *et al.* (1986) propose a general model of belief entailment as a framework for comparing alternative formalisms that sheds further light on the problems of MYCIN. Drawing on the work of Cox (1946), they identify a number of essential properties that a measure of belief should possess. The idea is to provide an intuitive basis for probability theory from which the usual axioms follow.

The properties Horvitz presents can be summarized as follows:

(P1)   *Clarity*. Propositions should be precisely defined, so that their truth conditions can be determined.

(P2)   *Scalar continuity*. The degree of belief in a proposition should be a single real number which varies continuously between certain truth and certain falsehood.

(P3)   *Completeness*. It is possible to ascribe a degree of belief to any well-defined proposition.

(P4)   *Context dependency*. Degree of belief in a proposition may depend on degree of belief in other propositions.

(P5) *Hypothetical conditioning.* There should be a function such that belief in a conjunction of propositions can be calculated from belief in one proposition and belief in the other given that the first is true.

(P6) *Complementarity.* Belief in the negation of a proposition is a monotonically decreasing function of belief in the proposition itself.

(P7) *Consistency.* Propositions with the same truth value will have equal degree of belief.

It can be shown that the axioms of probability theory follow as a logical consequence of these axioms, that is, there exists a continuous monotonic function, Φ, such that

(A1) $0 \le \Phi(Q|e) \le 1$

(A2) $\Phi(\text{TRUE}|e) = 1$

(A3) $\Phi(Q|e) + \Phi(\sim Q|e) = 1$

(A4) $\Phi(QR|e) = \Phi(Q|e)\Phi(R|Qe)$

The semantic properties of belief, P1–P7, can serve as a basis for comparison between formalisms whose axiomatizations are hard to compare. They can also help researchers to identify areas of dissatisfaction with probability theory as a basis for reasoning about degree of belief. Finally, they may help to identify points where various formalisms actually diverge from the axioms of probability theory.

Horvitz uses four categories to classify non-probabilistic approaches to belief entailment:

(C1) *generalization*, where particular properties are weakened or eliminated;

(C2) *specialization*, where existing properties are strengthened or new ones are added;

(C3) *self-inconsistency*, where C2 results in the set of properties becoming inconsistent;

(C4) *substitution*, where properties are changed in a manner other than generalization or specialization.

Horvitz then demonstrates the utility of the framework by using it to compare fuzzy logic (see Zadeh, 1981), Dempster–Shafer theory (Shafer, 1976), and MYCIN certainty factors with probability theory.

- *Fuzzy logics* concerned with vagueness weaken the clarity property (P1), in that ill-defined propositions may still be assigned a degree of belief. They therefore fall into the generalization category (C1) listed above. On the other hand, fuzzy logics concerned with the fuzzification of truth values are inconsistent with the hypothetical conditioning property (P5). This is because degree of belief in a conjunction is given as the minimum of the degree of belief in the conjuncts, in contrast with axiom (A4). So such logics fall into the substitution category (C4).

- The central difference between *Dempster–Shafer theory* and probability theory appears to be a weakening of the completeness property (P3). Dempster–Shafer theory allows one to state that certain prior and conditional probabilities cannot be assessed, and provides the notion of a compatibility relation between beliefs. This difference leads to a violation of both the scalar continuity property (P2) and the complementarity property (P6). Thus Dempster–Shafer theory can be considered as a generalization of probability theory, instead of being in the substitution category.

- The *certainty factor* model used by MYCIN makes stronger assumptions than probabilistic models of belief, and so it could be considered as falling into the specialization category (C2). Yet we have seen that it is also self-inconsistent, and so it really falls into category (C3). Heckerman's (1986) reformulation of certainty factors in terms of the likelihood ratio is a genuine specialization, however.

25.4 Summarizing the state of uncertainty

Horvitz and Heckerman's work is typical of a theoretical approach to uncertainty which is concerned with comparing the semantics of different formal languages for calculating degrees of belief. However, it is worth bearing in mind that standard probability theory may itself admit of more than one semantic interpretation. For example, Shafer and Tversky (1985) note three such ways of vivifying the Bayesian formalism:

(1) the *frequency* semantics, where we ask how often, in evidential situations, a hypothesis would turn out to be true;

(2) the *betting* semantics, where we determine at what odds we would be willing to bet on a hypothesis in the light of evidence;

(3) the *propensity* semantics, where we study a causal model of the situation and ask how well a hypothesis explains the evidence.

Very few expert systems appear to employ a frequency interpretation of measures of belief. Thus Buchanan and Shortliffe (1984, Chapter 11) move away from the notion of relative frequency towards Carnap's notion of degree of confirmation, which is at least consistent with the betting semantics. The betting semantics is also consonant with the view of MYCIN's rules as heuristics which bear a degree of risk. Clearly some of the rules encode causal information; for example, the rules concerning compromised hosts. However, we have already established that such information is compiled into the rules and therefore mixed in with non-causal considerations. Hence it can hardly be said that certainty factors encode the degree to which a hypothesis explains the evidence on the basis of a propensity semantics. The INTERNIST model, where considerations concerning explanatory power and causal factors have the potential to be more explicit, would be a better candidate for a propensity semantics, except that INTERNIST employed rather *ad hoc* scoring methods. To the extent that they are analysable, such methods appear to suffer from the confusion of absolute belief and belief update found in MYCIN (Horvitz and Heckerman, 1986, Section 12) that we mentioned in Chapter 6.

Thus we see a trend towards increasing sophistication in both the theoretical underpinnings of methods for coping with uncertainty and the practical aspects of providing tools for its management. It is possible that such work needs to be integrated with the more differentiated view of knowledge outlined in Part IV for real advances to be made. As expert system applications become more complex, and are involved in the execution of critical tasks, mechanisms for handling uncertainty will require both a more rigorous formal justification and a greater degree of transparency.

Bibliographical notes

Reichenbach (1949) presents a strong case for the use of probability theory in judgemental problems. Papers in Kanal and Lemmer (1986) and Smets *et al.* (1988) provide up-to-date views on the application of formal methods of inexact reasoning to problems in artificial intelligence. Pearl (1988) argues strongly in favour of Bayesian methods, and covers much of the relevant AI background. This book is not a bad place to start, as it is relatively self-contained. It is also structured in such a way that readers can skip highly technical sections and still get the flavour of the debate.

STUDY SUGGESTIONS

25.1   A simple frame of discernment for automotive troubleshooting is given in Figure 25.1. The root node, *car fault*, can be thought of as standing for the set of faults {*fuel fault, electrical fault*}, while *fuel fault* stands for the fault set {*carburettor fault, fuel lead fault*} and *electrical fault* stands for the fault set

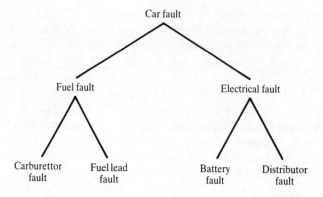

Figure 25.1 A frame of discernment for automotive troubleshooting.

{*battery fault, distributor fault*}. Thus *car fault* can be seen to stand for the whole frame of discernment

$$\Theta = \{fuel\ fault,\ electrical\ fault,\ carburettor\ fault,\ fuel\ lead\ fault\}$$

(a) Suppose that the evidence confirms the diagnosis of *carburettor fault* to degree 0.8. Compute $m(fuel\ lead\ fault)$, $m(electrical\ fault)$, and $m(\Theta)$.

(b) Suppose that the evidence disconfirms *fuel fault* to degree 0.6. Compute $m(electrical\ fault)$.

(c) Suppose that the evidence confirms *carburettor fault* to degree 0.2 and *fuel lead fault* to degree 0.5. Compute $m(fuel\ fault)$.

25.2 With reference to Figure 25.1, suppose that evidence confirms *fuel fault* to degree 0.3 and *battery fault* to degree 0.6. Compute m values for all nodes in the tree, using Dempster's rule.

25.3 Again with reference to Figure 25.1, suppose that the prior probabilities of the singleton hypotheses are as follows:

$p(carburettor\ fault) = 0.4$
$p(fuel\ lead\ fault) = 0.1$
$p(battery\ fault) = 0.3$

Suppose further that we have some evidence, e, such that

$p(e \mid carburettor\ fault) = 0.3$
$p(e \mid \neg carburettor\ fault) = 0.5$
$p(e \mid fuel\ lead\ fault) = 0.2$
$p(e \mid \neg fuel\ lead\ fault) = 0.4$
$p(e \mid battery\ fault) = 0.6$

$p(e \mid \neg battery\ fault) = 0.3$
$p(e \mid distributor\ fault) = 0.7$
$p(e \mid \neg distributor\ fault) = 0.1$

Compute the new belief in each of the singleton hypotheses using Pearl's method of evidential reasoning in a hierarchy.

26 Rule Induction by Machine Learning

Introduction

In Chapter 1, the problem of knowledge acquisition was mentioned, and its relation to machine learning. There appear to be three alternatives to the 'hand-building' of a knowledge base by a combination of domain expert and knowledge engineer:

(1)   Interactive programs which elicit knowledge from the expert during the course of a 'conversation' at the terminal. A range of attempts at this method were discussed in Part IV. We saw that the approach showed great promise, if it were guided by domain knowledge.

(2)   Programs that learn by scanning texts rather as humans read technical books. This method is hampered by the general problem of natural language understanding by machine. Since this is at least as hard as knowledge acquisition, it does not appear to be a promising avenue of research at the moment.

(3)   Programs that learn the concepts of a domain under varying
       degrees of supervision from a human teacher. In one approach, the
       teacher presents the program with a set of examples of a concept,
       and the program's task (roughly speaking) is to identify what
       collection of attributes and values defines the concept. This
       approach has been applied to knowledge acquisition with some
       success, and the basic techniques form the main subject matter of
       this chapter.

The field of machine learning is currently enjoying a period of growth and
progress. Rather than attempt a broad but shallow review of the whole,
this chapter will concentrate on methods that have had direct application
to expert systems technology, namely those which concentrate on:
deriving sets of decision rules from examples; evaluating the importance
of individual rules; and optimizing the performance of sets of rules. There
are other fields of learning research, such as neural networks and
explanation-based generalization, that we shall not touch on at all, because they have yet to make a significant impact on practical expert
systems. (This is not to say that they will not have a significant impact in
the future.) The interested reader is referred to citations in the
Bibliography at the end of the chapter for a broader coverage than can be
attempted here.

26.1   Overview of inductive learning

Precise definitions of learning are hard to find, but most authorities would
agree that it is a characteristic of *adaptive systems* which are capable of
improving their performance on a problem as a function of previous
experience; for example, in solving similar problems (Simon, 1983). Thus
learning is both a capability and an activity. Any learning program must
have the ability to represent and reason about problem-solving experiences, as well as the ability to apply such representations and inferences
to the solution of the current problem.

       Carbonell *et al.* (1983) present a classification of learning programs
in terms of the underlying strategy employed. Roughly speaking, the
strategy used depends on the amount of inference that the program has to
perform on the information available to it. At one extreme, programs
that learn by the direct implanting of new knowledge (by being
reprogrammed, or being supplied with new data) are performing no
inference at all. This is usually referred to as *rote learning*: a reasonable
human analogue would be the learning of multiplication tables. At the
other extreme, there is *unsupervised learning*: a generic term which
covers tasks such as theory formation, which more closely resemble
human efforts at scientific discovery.

In this chapter, the emphasis is on *inductive learning*, which can be regarded as being about half way between the two extremes mentioned above. Michalski (1983, page 83) defines inductive learning as

a heuristic search through a space of symbolic descriptions, generated by the application of various inference rules to the initial observational statements.

The symbolic descriptions usually represent generalizations that could be made about the observations, and these generalizations are a form of inference in that they involve law-like transformations of symbolic descriptions representing observations.

One form of inductive learning is when a learner is provided with a set of data, some of which are examples of a concept and some of which are not (the counter-examples). The learning task is to identify or construct the relevant concept – the concept that includes all of the examples and none of the counterexamples. Examples are sometimes called *positive instances*, and counter-examples are sometimes called *negative instances*. This kind of learning is often called *concept learning*.

Consider the data set

```
{Oldsmobile Cutlass, BMW 320, Thunderbird Roadster,
 Chevrolet Bel Air, Rolls Royce Corniche, VW Cabriolet}
```

Suppose that the positive instances are BMW 320 and VW Cabriolet, and the rest are negative instances. A plausible concept that covers the examples but none of the counter-examples would be German Car. But if the positive instances were Thunderbird Roadster and Chevrolet Bel Air, and Oldsmobile Cutlass is a negative instance, the relevant concept is something like American Dream Machine (in translation: a sporty and stylish American car from the 1950s and 1960s).

Being given both positive and negative examples can be important. In the first learning task considered above, the concept German Car is relatively easy to arrive at. However, without the negative example of the Oldsmobile Cutlass, a learner could be forgiven for arriving at the too general concept American Car in the second task.

Another form of inductive learning has been called *descriptive generalization*. Here one is given a class of objects, representing a concept, and the learning task is to derive a description that specifies the properties of objects belonging to that class. Thus, given the class American Car, with members

```
{Cadillac Seville, Oldsmobile Cutlass, Lincoln Continental}
```

an appropriate descriptive generalization might be:

`big, comfortable, gas-guzzling`

Thus we can distinguish between concept learning and descriptive generalization as follows. In concept learning, one is given a set of positive and negative instances of some concept which belongs to a pre-enumerated set of concepts, and the task is to generate a rule that will 'recognize' unseen instances of the concept. In descriptive generalization, one is given a set of instances which belong to a particular class, and the task is to derive the most parsimonious description which applies to each member of that class.

The next section looks at two learning programs that have been associated with the DENDRAL expert system described in Chapter 3. The initial implementation was complex and does not fit precisely into either of the categories of inductive learning outlined above. The second implementation uses an inductive learning technique called *version spaces*, which more closely resembles the typical concept learning task involving the presentation of positive and negative instances. It is interesting to compare the two approaches, and see how domain-specific knowledge about chemistry can be employed by a domain-free learning algorithm.

Sections 26.3 and 26.4 describe more recent methods of inductive learning, each of which has seen successful application to the generation of rules for expert systems. Section 26.5 describes work on evaluating individual rules and tuning rule sets.

26.2 Early work: META-DENDRAL

META-DENDRAL can be distinguished from DENDRAL in the following way. DENDRAL is a program that uses a set of rules to reason about the domain of mass spectrometry. META-DENDRAL is a program that reasoned about the rules that DENDRAL uses to perform this task. The initial implementation of META-DENDRAL generated rule hypotheses by a process of heuristic search similar to that used by DENDRAL itself (in the generation of structural hypotheses for chemical compounds). In other words, it applied DENDRAL's own search strategy to the problem of deriving DENDRAL rules.

26.2.1 Rule generation and refinement

The role of META-DENDRAL was to help a chemist determine the relationship between molecular fragmentations (spectral processes) and the structural features of compounds. Working together, program and chemist decided which data points were interesting, and then looked for processes which might explain them. Finally, the program tested and modified the derived rules, rather as a chemist would.

The rules of mass spectrometry that chemists use to describe a fragmentation can be expressed symbolically as production rules. Thus the following cleavage rule would be a way of encoding the fact that a particular molecule fragments in a particular way in a mass spectrometer, assuming that '–' stands for a bond and * stands for a break:

$$N - C - C - C \Rightarrow N - C * C - C$$

The left-hand side of such a rule describes a structural feature, while the right-hand side describes a spectral process.

META-DENDRAL's training data was a set of molecules whose three-dimensional structure and mass spectra were known. Thus the input–output pairs which constituted its training instances were respectively a molecular structure, and a point from the histogram of the relative abundances of fragment masses (a spectral peak).

It is important to realize that although the 'vocabulary' for describing atoms in subgraphs is small, and the actual 'grammar' for constructing subgraphs is simple, the number of subgraphs that can be generated is very large. In coping with this potential for combinatorial explosion, META-DENDRAL (like DENDRAL) used a problem-solving strategy of 'plan, generate and test'. Thus META-DENDRAL had a planning phase, involving a program called INTSUM, which stands for the interpretation and summary of data. Its job was to propose simple spectral processes which might have occurred in the training instances. These processes were represented as simple cleavage rules similar to the one shown above, where a whole molecular structure is mapped onto a single broken bond.

The output of INTSUM went to a heuristic search program called RULEGEN. RULEGEN was like DENDRAL's CONGEN, except that its task was to generate more general cleavage rules, such as allowing multiple broken bonds, which would cover the cases covered by INTSUM's output. Once candidate rule had been generated, the last phase of META-DENDRAL, called RULEMOD, tested and modified them.

The division of labour between RULEGEN and RULEMOD was as follows. RULEGEN did a comparatively coarse search of the space of rules that could be constructed from INTSUM's output, generating approximate and possibly redundant rules. RULEMOD performed a finer search to tune the set of rule hypotheses.

The workings of RULEMOD are still interesting today, because the tasks that it performed are typical of rule refinement programs:

(1) *Removing redundancy*. The data may be overdetermined; that is, many rule hypotheses generated by RULEGEN may explain the

same data points. Usually only a subset of the rules is necessary, and there may also be rules that make incorrect predictions.

(2) *Merging rules.* Sometimes a set of rules, taken together, explain a pool of data points that could be accounted for by a single, slightly more general, rule which includes all the positive evidence, but does not introduce any negative evidence. If such a rule can be found, the overlapping rules are deleted and the compact rule retained.

(3) *Making rules more specific.* Often rules are too general, and therefore make incorrect predictions. RULEMOD tries adding feature descriptions to atoms in each rule to try to delete the negative evidence, while retaining the positive evidence of correct predictions.

(4) *Making rules more general.* Given that RULEGEN is reasoning from particular cases, it frequently makes rules that are more specific than they should be. RULEMOD will try to make rules more general, so that they cover the same data points, perhaps including new data, without making any incorrect predictions.

(5) *Selecting the final rules.* It is possible that redundancies may have been introduced by the generalization and specialization operations of RULEMOD. Consequently, the selection procedure of step 1 is applied again to remove them.

The stages of selection, merging, deletion and so on could be applied iteratively by RULEMOD until the user was reasonably satisfied with the rule set. These tasks pretty well exhaust what can be done to a rule set, with the exception of adding weights to rules and then tuning those weights. We shall see examples of this practice later in the chapter.

The quality of rules generated by META-DENDRAL were assessed by testing them on structures not in the training set, by consulting mass spectroscopists, and by comparing them with published rules. The program succeeded in rediscovering known rules of spectrometry that had aleady been published, as well as discovering new rules. Its ability to predict spectra for compounds outside the original set of instances was impressive.

26.2.2 Version spaces

In this section, we review an application of a learning technique known as *version spaces* (Mitchell, 1978, 1982) to the reimplementation of META-DENDRAL. In attempting to derive a general rule of mass spectrometry from a set of examples of how particular molecules fragment, META-DENDRAL is tackling a concept learning problem. Mitchell (1978) defines such problems as follows.

A concept can be conceived of as a pattern which states those properties which are common to instances of the concept. Given (i) a language of patterns for describing concepts, (ii) sets of positive and negative instances of the target concept, and (iii) a way of matching data in the form of training instances against hypothetical descriptions of the concept, the task is to determine concept descriptions in the language that are consistent with the training instances.

In this context, 'consistency' means that the description must match all the positive instances but none of the negative ones.

To reason about the rules for mass spectrometry, META-DENDRAL needs a language for representing concepts and relationships in that domain. The pattern language used by META-DENDRAL is a structured object language (see Chapter 9) in which nodes and links are connected together in a network. The nodes stand for atoms, or configurations of atoms, and the links stand for chemical bonds. A pattern in this language matches some training instance just in case there is a mapping from the nodes and links of the instance to the nodes and links of the pattern that satisfies all the constraints placed on the nodes and links of the pattern. Thus, to match a pattern of nodes and links representing atoms connected by chemical bonds, the components of an instance must not have properties or relationships that violate the stated constraints.

In the context of a concept learning problem, a *version space* is simply a way of representing the space of all concept descriptions consistent with the training instances seen so far. The principal advantage of Mitchell's technique for representing and updating version spaces is that they can be determined instance by instance, without looking back to examine either past training instances or previously rejected concept descriptions.

Mitchell found the key to the problems of efficient representation and update of version spaces by noting that the search space of possible concept descriptions is not without structure – it contains redundancy. In particular, he observed that a partial order can be defined over the patterns generated by any concept description language of the kind described above. Most important is the relation 'more specific than or equal to', which can be defined as follows:

Pattern P1 is more specific than or equal to pattern P2 (written as P1 ≥ P2) if and only if P1 matches a subset off all the instances that P2 matches.

Consider the following simple example from Winston's (1975a) 'blocks world' learning program. In Figure 26.1, the pattern P1 is more specific than pattern P2 because the constraints imposed by P1 are

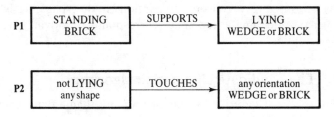

Figure 26.1 Relations between patterns.

satisfied only if the weaker constraints imposed by P2 are satisfied. Another way of looking at this is to say that if P1's constraints· are satisfied, then so are P2's, but not conversely.

Note that, for a program to appreciate an example of partial ordering such as that shown above, it would need to understand a number of concepts and relationships, constituting domain-specific knowledge:

- It would need to know that if B is a brick then B is a shape; that is, it would need to have some criteria for categorizing the kinds of entities in the domain that are represented by nodes in the structural language.

- It would need to know that if A supports B then A touches B in the blocks world; that is, it would need to realize that there is redundancy in the domain relations.

- It would need to understand the logical meaning of terms such as NOT, ANY and OR, in terms of the restrictions or permissions that they imply for the matching process.

The program needs to know these things to satisfy itself that there is a mapping between P1's nodes and links and those of P2 such that each constraint in P1 is in fact more specific than the corresponding constraint in P2. Once it can grasp this relationship of specificity, the way is open for a representation of version spaces in terms of their maximally specific and maximally general patterns. This is because the program can then consider the version space as containing:

- the set of maximally specific patterns;
- the set of maximally general patterns;
- all concept descriptions that occur between these two sets in the partial ordering.

This is called the *boundary sets* representation for version spaces, and it is both compact and easy to update. It is compact because one is not explicitly storing every concept description in the space. It is easy to update because defining a new space corresponds to moving one or both of the boundaries.

26.2.3 The candidate elimination algorithm

A version space, as described so far, is no more than a data structure for representing a set of concept descriptions. However, the term 'version spaces' is often applied to a learning technique which applies a particular algorithm, known as the *candidate elimination* algorithm, to such data structures. This algorithm works by manipulating the boundary sets that represent a given version space.

The algorithm begins by initializing the version space to the set of all concept descriptions consistent with the first positive training instance. In other words, the set of maximally specific patterns (S) is initialized to the most specific concept descriptions that the pattern language is capable of generating, while the set of maximally general patterns (G) is initialized to the most general concept descriptions available in the language. As each subsequent instance is processed, the sets S and G are modified to eliminate from the version space just those concept descriptions which are inconsistent with the current instance.

In the course of learning, the boundaries should move towards each other monotonically, without back and forth movement in which they sometimes move further apart. Moving the S boundary in the direction of greater generality can be considered as a breadth-first search from specific patterns to more general ones. The object of the search is to compute a new boundary set which is just sufficiently general that it does not rule out a newly encountered positive instance. In other words, S moves when the program encounters a new positive instance which does not match all of the patterns in S. Correspondingly, moving the G boundary in the direction of greater specificity can be considered as a breadth-first search from general patterns to more specific ones. The object of this search is to compute a new boundary set which is just specific enough to rule out a newly encountered negative instance. Thus G moves when the program encounters a negative training instance that matches some pattern in G.

This algorithm does not employ heuristic search, because the constraints are exact and they are guaranteed to cause the algorithm to converge on a solution. The restrictions on these searches are the key to controlling the combinatorics of the update problem. As hinted earlier, the version spaces technique has a number of pleasing properties, which are worth listing:

(1) All concept descriptions that are consistent with all of the training instances will be found.

(2) The version space summarizes the alternative interpretations of the observed data.

(3) The results are independent of the order in which training instances are presented.

(4) Each training instance is examined only once.

(5) One never needs to reconsider discarded hypotheses.

The fact that the version space summarizes the data so far means that it can be used as a basis for generating new training instances, that is, instances that might bring the boundaries closer together. The fact that you consider each instance only once means that the program does not need to store past instances. Thus the time required by the algorithm will be proportional to the number of observed instances, rather than some explosive function of this number. The avoidance of backtracking also contributes to the efficiency and simplicity of the algorithm. However, it is well known that the introduction of disjunctive concepts causes severe combinatorial problems, by increasing the branching factor in the partial order of patterns.

26.2.4 Matching instances to patterns in META-DENDRAL

META-DENDRAL uses the same language to describe training instances as it uses to describe patterns, although only a subset of the pattern language is required to do this. Each training instance is a complete molecule with a particular site in the compound, rather than a constrained description of a molecule.

Matching instances to patterns involves defining a connected mapping from pattern nodes to instance nodes. A mapping, X, is connected if the mapping is one-to-one and injective, and if every pair of instance nodes, X(p1) and X(p2), corresponding to pattern nodes p1 and p2 share a common link if and only if p1 and p2 also share a common link. We also require that the feature values of each instance node of the form X(p) satisfy the feature constraints of the corresponding pattern node, p.

It is now possible to give Mitchell's domain-specific definition of partial order for META-DENDRAL, using the definitions given above. Lower case letters stand for pattern nodes, and upper case letters stand for whole patterns. Pattern P1 is more specific than or equal to pattern P2 if and only if there is a connected mapping, X, of nodes in P2 into nodes of P1 such that for each pair of nodes, p2, X(p2), the feature constraints associated with X(p2) are more specific than or equal to the feature constraints associated with p2. In trying to understand this definition, and how it applies to the mass spectrometry domain, it is worth looking back to the blocks world example given earlier. In the world of chemical structure elucidation, the analogue of blocks are the atoms and superatoms, while the analogue of spatial relationships such as 'supports' and 'touches' are chemical bonds.

Knowledge of chemistry can be employed by the candidate elimination algorithm in two ways:

(1) The representation language for chemical substructures allows forms which are syntactically distinct but semantically equivalent patterns; that is, it can generate expressions which are different in form but have the same meaning. Knowledge of the meaning of these patterns can therefore be used to delete redundant patterns from the version space boundaries. This has no effect on the completeness of the version space approach.

(2) Version space boundaries grow quite large for some problems. It is therefore useful to apply various rules of thumb to prune these boundaries. However, if heuristic methods are used, one can no longer be sure that the program will determine all of the concept descriptions that are consistent with the training instances.

Mitchell claimed that the version space approach added the following new capabilities to the original META-DENDRAL program:

- Additional training data can modify existing rules without the original data having to be reconsidered.

- The learning process is properly incremental, in that one can determine to what degree each rule has been learned and reliably employ partially learned rules.

- The new rule formation strategy avoids the expensive 'coarse search' of RULEGEN and focuses on the most 'interesting' training data first.

- The method for considering alternative versions of each rule is more complete than the generalization and specialization operations of RULEMOD.

In summary, the version spaces approach appears to provide an incremental learning methodology that is both principled and efficient. Candidate elimination can be contrasted with depth-first and breadth-first search strategies in that it determines every concept description consistent with the training instances, rather than finding a single acceptable concept description (depth-first search), or all maximally specific such concept descriptions (breadth-first search). As Mitchell points out, the chief manpower cost involved in applying this kind of technology to real problems is the construction of the set of training instances.

26.3 Induction of decision rules in PLANT/DS

In this section, we examine another method of inducing decision rules via a case study: Michalski and Chilausky's (1981) PLANT/DS system for developing rules for diagnosing soybean diseases. This method exemplifies descriptive generalization rather than concept learning; for each class in which we are interested, we seek a rule which can be used to characterize (accurately and economically) all members of that class. The PLANT/DS system is also interesting because it demonstrated that rules derived by machine induction can be at least as effective as rules derived from experts by knowledge-elicitation techniques.

26.3.1 Variable-valued logic

Variable-valued logic (VL) is a calculus developed by Michalski (1974) for representing decision problems involving *many-valued variables* (variables that can take on some range of values). The variable-value notation that Michalski uses is similar to the ⟨object attribute value⟩ triplets that we met in connection with production rules in Chapters 3 and 8. However, the calculus itself is closer in spirit to the formal systems of inference examined in Chapters 5 and 6.

The principal syntactic entity in this representation is called a *selector*, S, and it has the general form

$$[x \# R]$$

where

> x is a variable (or attribute), such as *time-of-year*, *temperature*, *humidity*
> $\#$ is one of the relational operators $=, \neq, \leq, \geq, <, >$
>   R is a *reference*, a list of one or more values that x could take on.

Thus the selector

    [month = (June July August)]

denotes that the month is June, July or August. This condition will be satisfied by an event so long as the instantiated variable takes on (at least) one of the values in the reference. An event is a list of values for an assumed set of variables, for example:

    e = (June, 70°, 50%)

where the assumed variables are *month*, *temperature* and *humidity*. Thus *e* as given above would *satisfy* the selector [month = (June July August)], or the *compound selector*

```
[month = (June July August)]
[temperature = (60° ... 80°)]
[humidity = (40% ... 55%)]
```

which is an implicit conjunction of simple selectors. (References can be specified by numeric ranges.)

More formally, given an event *e*, we define the value of a selector $S = [x \neq R]$ as

$$V(S, e) = 1 \text{ if } x/e \neq R \quad \text{else } 0$$

where *x/e* denotes the value that *x* gets from *e*. Thus

$$V([\text{month} = (\text{June July August})], e) = 1$$

with *e* as given above, but

$$V([\text{month} = (\text{July August September})], e) = 0$$

In specifying rules, Michalski allows a condition to be a *disjunction* of compound selectors. Thus

```
[month = (June July August)]
[temperature = (80° ... 100°)]
[humidity = (50% ... 60%)]
        ∨
[month = (December January February)]
[temperature = (-10° ... 10°)]
[humidity = (30% ... 40%)]
        →
[weather = seasonable]
```

would be a well-formed rule. Disjunctions of compound selectors, such as the condition of the rule shown above, are called *DVL expressions*. We shall shortly see how such expressions form the main representation used by the learning program.

26.3.2 The induction program: AQ11

The soybean study set out to diagnose 15 soybean diseases, such as *diaporthe stem canker* and *frog eye leaf spot*. The variables used were 35 attributes of plants and the environment, plus a decision variable that

---

Environmental descriptors
   Time of occurrence = July
   Temperature = normal
   ...

Plant global descriptors
   Plant height = normal
   Seed germination = less than 80%
   ...

Plant local descriptors
   Condition of leaves = abnormal
     Leafspot size = greater than 1/8 inch
     Leaf mildew growth = absent
     ...
   Condition of stem = abnormal
     Stem cankers = above the second node
     External decay = absent
     ...
   ...

Figure 26.2 An abbreviated questionnaire for the soybean disease *Brown Spot*.

ranged over the possible diagnoses. Thus the environmental variable *Time of Occurrence* (TOC) could take on any value in the list (April, May, June, July, August, September, October), while the plant variable *Condition of Roots* (COR) ranged over the list (Normal, Rotted, Galls-or-Cysts-Present).

Decision rules were generated using a learning program called AQ11 (Michalski and Larson, 1978). The events input to the program were derived from questionnaires filled in by experts on plant pathology, one questionnaire being used for each of the 15 diseases. An abbreviated questionnaire for the disease *Brown Spot* is reproduced in Figure 26.2 from Michalski and Chilausky (1981).

A set of 630 events were then partitioned into a learning set and a testing set. The learning set would be input to AQ11 as data, and the testing set would be used to evaluate the rules derived by AQ11 from those data. However, AQ11 was also supplied with some general knowledge of the problem; for example, if a plant's leaves are healthy, we do not need to consider the variable *Leafspot Size*.

AQ11's top-level algorithm assumes a set of hypotheses, $V = \{v_1,$

..., v_m} and a family of event sets, F = {$f_1, ..., f_n$}. In this case study, the hypotheses are soybean diseases expressed as simple VL selectors of the form

[Diagnosis = d]

for some d in the set of 15 diseases. The event sets are sets of event lists like (June, 70°, 50%) derived from the completed questionnaires.

We assume that each $v_i \in V$ only explains some subset of F. The problem is to generate a set of hypotheses V* which explains all events in some designated event set $f_i \in F$ but does not describe superfluous events from other event sets in F. We shall denote the set of events explained (or *covered*) by a formula v_i by the expression C_i.

The basic idea is to compute a DVL expression which is satisfied by every event in f_j but is not satisfied by any event in f_k such that $j \neq k$ (or by any event in the set difference between f_k and f_j if f_j and f_k overlap). For each f_k, this is called a *cover of f_j against f_k*, written $C(f_j, f_k)$. Of particular importance are the 'negative events' in f_k, that is, those events which we do not want to explain. Explaining the negative events would be tantamount to explaining more than the data, and therefore having a hypothesis that was not parsimonious. The algorithm can be sketched as follows.

Step 1. Isolate the facts which are not consistent with the hypotheses in V. For each hypothesis $v_i \in V$, we compute the set of events f_{i+} that v_i should cover but does not, and the set of events f_{ij-} that v_i does cover but should not. Thus

$$f_{i+} = f_j - C_i \qquad \text{where '}-\text{' denotes set difference}$$

and

$$f_{ik-} = C_i \cap f_k \qquad \text{for } f_k \in F \text{ such that } f_k \neq f_j$$

The events in f_{ik-} are called *exception events*.

Step 2. For each $v_i \in V$, derive a DVL formula X_i which describes all exception events. The set of all exception events is just the union of sets f_{ij-}, for all j such that $1 \leq j \leq m$ and $j \neq i$. This is done by computing, for each i and j, a cover, V_{ij-}, of f_{ij-} against the sets in $C_i \cup f_i$, for i such that $1 \leq i \leq m$. Thus

$$V_{ij-} = C(f_{ij-}, \bigvee_{i = 1 \text{ to } m} (C_i \cup f_i))$$

and then computing the logical union

$$V_{i-} = \bigvee_{j = 1 \text{ to } m \ \& \ j \neq i} V_{ij-}$$

Step 3. New hypotheses are now derived from the v_i by effectively 'subtracting' from each X_i the formula V_{i-} and 'adding' f_{i+} to it. Roughly speaking, we take out the exception events and add the events that v_i leaves out.

Given the soybean data, AQ11 produced a set of 15 decision rules (one for each disease). In parallel, a set of decisions were derived by more conventional knowledge elicitation methods from plant pathologists. The two rule sets differed somewhat in syntax, but the main difference between them was that the expert-derived rules contained weighted selectors, while the weights of the selectors in the inductively derived rules was effectively 1. In other words, experts were able to indicate, by attaching weights to selectors, the relative importance of the various conditions of a rule, and these weights were respected by an evidence combination function.

The performance of these two rule sets was systematically compared on a set of 340 test cases. The details of the experiment do not concern us here; the interested reader is referred to Michalski and Chilausky (1981). However, the AQ11 rule set outperformed the rule set derived directly from the expert, with 100% correct diagnoses as opposed to 96% correct. The conclusion drawn was that induction techniques offer a viable alternative to other knowledge acquisition methods, if the domain is sufficiently simple and well-defined.

26.4   Induction of decision trees in ID3

Rules are not the only way of representing attribute–value information about concepts for the purposes of classification. *Decision trees* are an alternative way of structuring such information, and there are efficient algorithms for constructing such trees from data. These representations are discussed in Section 26.4.1.

The last 20 years have seen the emergence of a family of learning systems that work in this way, such as CLS (Hunt *et al.*, 1966), ID3 (Quinlan, 1979), ACLS (Paterson and Niblett, 1982), and ASSISTANT (Kononenko *et al.*, 1984). ACLS (a generalization of ID3) has given rise to a number of commercial derivatives, such as Expert-Ease and RuleMaster, which have seen successful application in industry. Section 26.4.2 covers the ID3 algorithm in some detail.

26.4.1   The structure of decision trees

The nodes in a decision tree correspond to attributes of the objects to be classified, and the arcs correspond to alternative values for these attributes. Leaves of the tree correspond to sets of objects in the same class. A sample tree is shown in Figure 26.3 (after Quinlan, 1986a).

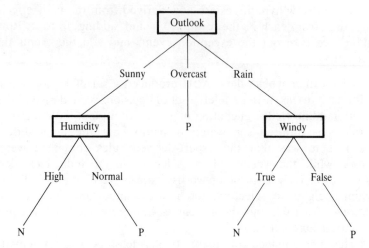

Figure 26.3 A decision tree.

The tree of Figure 26.3 has as its non-terminal nodes the weather attributes outlook, humidity and windy. The leaves are labelled by one of two classes, P or N. One can think of P as the class of positive instances of the concept we are using, and N as the class of negative instances.

Although decision trees are obviously a different form of representation than production rules, one can think of a decision tree as a kind of rule: a classification rule that decides, for any object to which the attributes apply, whether it belongs in P or N. Indeed, it is possible to translate the tree of Figure 26.3 into such a rule (see Figure 26.4). We shall use a subset of the variable–value logic of Section 26.3 to do this.

The reason for using decision trees rather than rules is that there exist comparatively simple algorithms for taking a training set and deriving a decision tree that will correctly classify unseen objects. The training set used to derive the tree in Figure 26.3 is shown in Table 26.1; the reader can check that the tree correctly classifies each of the 14 instances in the set. Note that the temperature attribute does not appear in the tree; it is not needed for classifying the instances.

The ID3 algorithm which performed this task is somewhat simpler than the AQ11 algorithm for deriving classification rules, as we shall see in the next section. It is also computationally efficient, in that the time taken to build such trees increases only linearly with the size of the problem. However, the simple language of attributes and values is more restrictive than variable-value logic; this is yet another example of the trade-off between expressiveness and efficiency that we first encountered in Chapter 4.

```
[outlook = (overcast)]

∨

[outlook = (sunny)]
[humidity = (normal)]

∨

[outlook = (rain)]
[windy = (false)]

→

P
```

Figure 26.4 A classification rule based on the tree in Figure 26.3.

26.4.2 The ID3 algorithm

The ID3 algorithm is iterative. It chooses a subset of the training set (called the *window*) at random, and then forms a decision tree from it. This tree is guaranteed to classify every instance in the window correctly.

All other objects in the training set are then classified using this tree. If every known object is correctly classified by this tree, the algorithm terminates with success. However, on non-trivial training sets, it is more likely that the initial tree will misclassify some of the instances. In this eventuality, a selection of the incorrectly classified objects is added to the window, and the tree is rebuilt. Empirical tests suggest that this

Table 26.1 A small training set (from Quinlan, 1986a).

No.	Outlook	Temperature	Humidity	Windy	Class
1	sunny	hot	high	false	N
2	sunny	hot	high	true	N
3	overcast	hot	high	false	P
4	rain	mild	high	false	P
5	rain	cool	normal	false	P
6	rain	cool	normal	true	N
7	overcast	cool	normal	true	P
8	sunny	mild	high	false	N
9	sunny	cool	normal	false	P
10	rain	mild	normal	false	P
11	sunny	mild	normal	true	P
12	overcast	mild	high	true	P
13	overcast	hot	normal	false	P
14	rain	mild	high	true	N

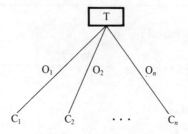

Figure 26.5 A tree structuring of partitioned objects.

iterative method is more efficient than trying to build the tree in a single step using all the data.

The heart of the algorithm is a procedure for building a decision tree for an arbitrary collection of objects, C, where C is not empty and contains objects of more than one class.

Let T be any test on an object x, with $O_1, O_2, ..., O_n$ representing the possible outcomes of $T(x)$. T will therefore produce a partition $\{C_1, C_2, ..., C_n\}$ of C such that

$$C_i = \{x \mid T(x) = O_i\}$$

This partition is shown graphically in Figure 26.5.

If we proceeded recursively to replace each C_i in Figure 26.5 with a decision tree, we would have a decision tree for C. The crucial factor in this problem reduction strategy is the choice of test. For each subtree, we need to find a 'good' attribute for partitioning the objects.

In making this decision, Quinlan employs the notion of *expected information* from communication theory. (Expected information is also called *entropy* and *uncertainty*, but the latter concept is not to be confused with certainty factors.) In communication theory, expected information is a number describing a set of messages, $M = \{m_1, m_2, ..., m_n\}$. Each message m_i in the set has probability $p(m_i)$ and contains an amount of information, $I(m_i)$, defined as

$$I(m_i) = -\log p(m_i)$$

Thus information is an inverse monotonic function of probability.

The expected information or uncertainty of a message set, $U(M)$, is just the sum of the information in the several possible messages multiplied by their probabilities:

$$U(M) = -\Sigma_i \, p(m_i)\log p(m_i) \qquad \text{for } i = 1 \text{ to } n$$

Speaking intuitively, we are uncertain about which message from the set will be sent to the degree to which we expect the message to be informative. Logarithms are generally taken to base 2, so that information and uncertainty are measured in bits.

Quinlan's use of this measure is based on the following assumptions.

- A correct decision tree for C will classify objects in the same proportion as their representation in C. Suppose that p denotes the number of objects of class P in C and n denotes the number of objects in class N in C. Thus an unseen object will belong to class P with probability $p/(p + n)$ and to class N with probability $n/(p + n)$.
- Given an object to classify, a decision tree can be regarded as the source of a message, P or N. The expected information associated with the message set $M = \{P, N\}$ is given by

$$U(M) = - p/(p + n) \log_2 p(p + n) - n/(p + n) \log_2 n/(p + n)$$

It is convenient to write this special 'two-message' case of expected information as a function of the two arguments, p and n:

$$EI(p, n) = - p/(p + n) \log_2 p/(p + n) - n/(p + n) \log_2 n/(p + n)$$

Given a test T with outcomes $O_1, O_2, ..., O_n$ producing a partition $\{C_1, C_2, ..., C_n\}$ as before, suppose that C_i contains p_i objects of class P and n_i objects of class N. The expected information of the subtree is given by $EI(p_i, n_i)$. The expected information of the larger tree with T at its root is then given by the weighted average:

$$E(T) = \Sigma_i \frac{(p_i + n_i)}{(p + n)}. EI(p_i, n_i) \quad \text{for } i = 1 \text{ to } n$$

The ratio $(p_i + n_i)/(p + n)$ corresponds to the weight for the ith branch in a tree such as that shown in Figure 26.5. It represents the proportion of the objects in C that belong to C_i.

The heuristic that ID3 uses in deciding what attribute to branch on next is to *select the test that gains the most information*. The information gained by carrying out a test is given by

$$EI(p, n) - E(T)$$

Such heuristics are sometimes described as 'minimum entropy', because maximizing information gain corresponds to minimizing uncertainty or disorder.

The ID3 algorithm has been successfully applied to large training sets (see Quinlan, 1983). Its computational complexity hinges on the cost of choosing the next test to branch on, which is itself a linear function of the product of the number of objects in the training set and the number of attributes used to describe them. The system has also been adapted to cope with noisy and incomplete data, although we shall not discuss these extensions here (see Quinlan, 1986a, 1986b).

The simplicity and efficiency of Quinlan's algorithm make it a feasible alternative to knowledge elicitation if sufficient data of the right kind are available. However, unlike the version spaces approach to concept learning, this method is not incremental. In other words, you cannot consider additional training data without reconsidering the classification of previous instances.

Also, ID3 is not guaranteed to find the simplest decision tree that characterizes the training instances, because the information-theoretic evaluation function for choosing attributes is only a heuristic. Never-the-less, experience with the algorithm has shown that its decision trees are relatively simple and perform well in classifying unseen objects. Continuing the search for the 'best' solution would increase the complexity of the algorithm; as we noted in Chapters 17 and 18, it is sometimes better to settle for a satisficing solution to a hard problem.

26.5 Recent work on tuning rule sets

Reseachers are also working on the problems of debugging and justifying weighted rules which perform inexact reasoning. Here we shall do no more than consider two recent examples, which will serve to give the reader the flavour of current work and provide pointers to the relevant literature. Despite the theoretical orientation of such work, its practical significance is obvious, in that any reliable tool which helped improve the performance of sets of weighted rules would be welcomed by knowledge engineers.

Given a set of rules, derived by induction or from an expert, we are most interested in

(1)   evaluating the contribution of individual rules, and

(2)   evaluating the performance of the rule set as a whole.

Under 1, our chief concern is the applicability of the rule. How often will it be correctly applied, and how often will it contribute towards error, that is, a wrong decision on the part of the system? Under 2, our main concern is with properties of the rule set, rather than the quality of individual rules. Is the rule set complete – will it handle all the cases that it is likely to encounter? Is it redundant – are there rules that we could

> IF   (1) The therapy under consideration is tetracycline
>   (2) The age (in years) of the patient is less than 8
> THEN There is strongly suggestive evidence (0.8) that
>   tetracycline is not an appropriate therapy for use
>   against the organism.

Figure 26.6 The MYCIN tetracycline heuristic.

delete from the rule set without adversely affecting performance? Bear in mind that such rules may not be 'bad' or 'wrong' in themselves, but their deletion might improve performance because they interact adversely with other rules in the set.

Langlotz *et al.* (1986) present a decision-theoretic method for evaluating individual production rules. Where trade-offs are involved in the specification of a rule (between probability and utility, for example) it is useful to know how robust the recommendations of a system are. In other words, how finely balanced is the judgement to which the rule contributes, and how far would an alteration to the weight of the rule affect the final outcome?

As an illustration, they consider a simplified MYCIN rule (see Figure 26.6) which militates against the prescription of tetracycline to children because, although it is effective against some infections, it causes dental staining. This rule involves a trade-off between curing an infection and risking a negative side-effect. The expected utility of applying this rule is a function of both the utility of the various outcomes and the probability of their occurrence.

In decision theory, the *expected utility* of an action A, with possible outcomes $O_1, O_2, ..., O_n$ having probabilities $p_1, p_2, ..., p_n$ is given by

$$EU(A) = \Sigma_i \, p_i \, u(O_i) \qquad \text{for } i = 1 \text{ to } n$$

where $u(O_i)$ denotes the utility of the outcome O_i. Thus we are interested in how the utility of the action that a rule supports will vary as a function of variations in the parameters p_i and $u(O_i)$. For example, if the infection is resistant to all drugs except tetraycline, and the probability of dental staining is actually quite low, then EU(A) will be high compared to a situation where other drugs are available and the probability of dental staining is high.

The authors describe an application of sensitivity analysis which plots the utility of an outcome against its probability. The point at which alternative therapy recommendations have equal utility represents a probability threshold, thus determining how far the probability assessment in the model must vary before the optimal decision changes. Arguably, the extra effort required to perform the analysis is repaid by the knowledge engineer and domain expert having to be more precise about the rationale behind a rule. In particular, decision analysis makes explicit those variables on which the applicability of a given rule depends. This may help knowledge engineers to identify unwanted interactions between rules in a rule set, including those which result from probabilistic dependencies of the kind discussed in Chapter 6.

Wilkins and Buchanan (1986), on the other hand, concentrate on debugging whole sets of heuristic rules. They argue that the incremental modification of individual rules, using tools such as TEIRESIAS (see Chapter 13) does not guarantee that the knowledge engineer will converge on an optimal rule set. They caution against a strategy of making rules more general or specific, and strengthening or weakening their weights in response to false positive and false negative results. Heuristic rules are inexact and should not be modified simply because they fail; their weights are intended to code for their reliability. In fact, all heuristic rules represent a trade-off between generality and specificity in terms of some overall policy, and it is better to maintain that policy than make arbitrary changes.

The authors define the optimum rule set as that element of the power set of rules in the original set that minimizes error. They assume that individual rules in the rule set all meet some standard of goodness, and then concentrate on deriving the best subset of this original set. The process of deriving such an optimal set is formulated as a bipartite graph minimization problem, based on the mapping between a set of nodes representing the training instances and a set of nodes representing the initial rule set. This problem is shown to be intractable in general, but a heuristic method for solving it is presented. The solution proposed is mainly intended to minimize deleterious interactions between good heuristic rules in rule sets that have been derived by induction methods, such as the META-DENDRAL programs and AQ11 reviewed earlier in this Chapter.

Other work on knowledge refinement includes the Learning Apprentice System (LAS) of Smith *et al.* (1985) and the ODYSSEUS system of Wilkins (1988).

- LAS is an interactive aid for building and improving knowledge bases. It partially automates both the generation of heuristic rules from a domain theory and the debugging of such rules as problems occur during routine use. It uses a kind of dependency network (see Chapter 23) to specify the justification of a rule in terms of the underlying theory, and uses this structure to construct possible explanations for system failures.

- ODYSSEUS is an 'apprenticeship' program, which learns how to improve the knowledge base of an expert system for heuristic classification problems (see Chapters 14 and 15). It observes an expert solving a problem and constructs an explanation for each of the expert's actions (such an asking for the value of some attribute) based on its knowledge of the domain and the underlying problem-solving strategy. When the program fails to construct such an explanation, it initiates a process of knowledge base repair.

The systems mentioned in this section all demonstrate the feasibility of constructing aids that could partially automate the task of improving a knowledge base. Although this work is still at the research stage, it is clear that such progress as has been made derives from more rigorous analyses of the different kinds of knowledge and problem-solving strategy that expert systems use. Theoretical advances such as those described in Part IV are beginning to have practical pay-offs which will result in systems that are easier to design, construct and debug.

In summary, we can see that machine learning research has the potential to make a profound contribution to the theory and practice of expert systems, as well as to other areas of artificial intelligence. Its application to the problem of deriving rule sets from examples is already helping to circumvent the knowledge-acquisition bottleneck discussed in Chapter 13. However, such techniques are also finding application to the problem of evaluating and tuning sets of decision rules, regardless of the manner in which they have been derived.

Bibliographical notes

As noted in the introductory paragraphs of this chapter, there are many areas of machine learning that I have not attempted to cover here. For the reader interested in a more rounded view, the papers in Michalski *et al.* (1983, 1986) make a reasonable starting point, prefaced perhaps by Winston (1984, Chapter 11). These papers cover many different kinds of learning, not all of which are immediately relevant to expert system applications.

Some issues of the journal *Artificial Intelligence* also contain papers, such as Winston (1982) and Lenat (1982), which describe significant pieces of AI research into machine learning. Again, these are somewhat broader in scope than the material covered here. For example, Winston's program creates rules by analogical reasoning, and Lenat's program uses heuristics to discover mathematical concepts in a form of discovery learning.

For a classification of learning programs based on an analysis of basic algorithms, rather than kinds of learning behaviour, see Bundy *et al.* (1985). However, this paper assumes some prior knowledge of the pro-

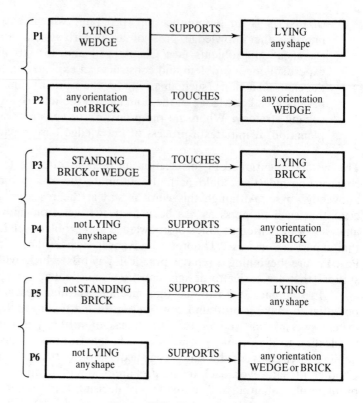

Figure 26.7 Pairs of patterns.

grams being compared, and should therefore be consulted after some of the references cited above. Comparisons of different learning programs are rather thin on the ground. O'Rourke (1982) compares AQ11 with ID3, and Dietterich and Michalski (1983) analyse a number of concept learning programs, including the original META-DENDRAL.

STUDY SUGGESTIONS

26.1 Figure 26.7 shows three pairs of patterns. For each pair, say which, if any, is the more specific of the two.

26.2 List some of the different kinds of learning that humans engage in, and attempt to distinguish clearly between them. For example, learning multiplication tables is rather different from learning to play a musical instrument, because the latter involves motor skills as well as rote memory. Which of these different kinds of learning do you think will be easiest to program, and what are your reasons?

26.3 Look at the training data in Table 26.1. Of the 14 objects, nine are of class P and five are of class N. The expected information of the message set M = {P, N} is therefore given by

$$El(p, n) = -\frac{9}{14} \log_2 \frac{9}{14} - \frac{5}{14} \log_2 \frac{5}{14} = 0.940 \text{ bits}$$

(a) What is the expected information for the attribute outlook?
(b) What is the information gain of branching on outlook?
(c) Repeat this analysis for the attributes humidity and windy.
(d) Which attribute has the highest information gain?

27 Summary and Conclusions

Introduction

This chapter attempts to summarize the topics covered in the previous chapters and provide a few suggestions for further study. It is convenient to organize the summary around the different parts of the book, summarizing the contents in a way that pulls various strands of thought closer together than they might appear in the chapters.

27.1 Part I: Background in artificial intelligence

In building expert systems, why do we need artificial intelligence techniques at all? What is wrong with other kinds of technique, such as mathematical modelling, from other disciplines, such as mainstream Computer Science?

The short answer is that there is nothing wrong with using 'non-AI' techniques, as and when they are appropriate (assuming that one can always make a sharp distinction between a multi-disciplinary research area like AI and 'non-AI'). Thus, DENDRAL's hypothesis generation was founded on an algorithm for enumerating planar graphs, and MYCIN relied on a straightforward statistical approach to therapy based on drug sensitivities. The use of AI architectures, search methods or programming languages does not prevent knowledge engineers from availing themselves of suitable methods from Applied Mathematics, Computer Science, or any other relevant discipline. Knowledge engineers building an application should *always* examine existing methods for solving the problem and take the trouble to analyse their strengths and weaknesses. Some parts of the problem may yield to purely algorithmic or mathematical solutions, in which case it is foolish not to use such methods as long as they are computationally efficient.

What Artificial Intelligence offers is a collection of insights, techniques and architectures for complex problem solving in cases where purely algorithmic or mathematical solutions are either unknown or demonstrably inefficient. Some of the work that has gone on over the last 30 years has involved adapting theoretical and practical results from related areas in mathematics, computer science and the social sciences. However, it usually turns out that translating results from diverse disciplines, such as mathematical logic and the psychology of decision making, in such a way that they can be harnessed for computational purposes is a non-trivial exercise that requires novel approaches.

Research in what I have called the Classical Period of AI showed that axiomatizing a system of logic is one thing, but implementing an efficient theorem prover is quite another. There is still a lot that we do not understand about how to use the power of logicistic systems effectively in problem solving. Interested readers might like to consult Wos *et al.* (1984, 1985) for a more technical introduction and discussion than can be attempted here.

Research in the Romantic Period demonstrated that results from psychological experiments do not obviate the need for research into how computers can be programmed to simulate intelligent behaviour. Few psychological theories are sufficiently precise that they have strong implications for the automation of human cognitive abilities. However, the computational metaphor has provided cognitive scientists with a new way of looking at human information processing and brought AI and psychology closer together (see Pylyshyn, 1978, 1980, 1981).

Research in the Modern Period has shown that AI techniques can be successfully applied to problems of realistic complexity. Increasingly, the prototypes documented in the AI literature are being turned into working systems with commercial value. Each such success is a valuable data point in the empirical enterprise of exploring the mapping between problem-solving architectures and generic tasks, such as classification and construction (Clancey, 1985; Hayes-Roth *et al.*, 1987).

The insights documented in Parts I and II include the realization that:

- all problems, from solving simple puzzles to learning new concepts, can be reduced to *search problems* if we are able to specify them precisely enough;

- search must be *knowledge-based* (guided by knowledge about the problem domain) if it is to address problems which are inherently intractable; that is, problems which are isomorphic with abstract problems (such as maze traversal, optimal tours) which are known to require exponential resources; and

- *knowledge representation* is just as crucial to solving hard problems as inference techniques, because it is the representation of knowledge that determines the underlying search space which inference unfolds.

The techniques documented in Parts III and IV include:

- a range of *high-level languages* for representing knowledge of different kinds, such as empirical associations and conceptual hierarchies;

- a range of *interactive strategies* for eliciting knowledge, compiling it into such representations, and controlling its application to problems of realistic complexity; and

- *design methodologies* for making systems that use such representations transparent to both the end-user and the knowledge engineer.

The architectures documented in Parts V and VI include:

- ways of *combining* different knowledge representation paradigms to trade on their strengths and compensate for their weaknesses;

- ways of *layering* architectures so that domain, task and problem-solving knowledge are cleanly separated yet well integrated; and

- useful tools for *extending* problem solvers which packages that perform tasks such as recording inferences and maintaining the consistency of representations.

We shall return to the subject of techniques and architectures later in this summary. What is important is that we would have had none of these practical benefits without the theoretical insights documented in Part I.

Early systems like MYCIN and DENDRAL, which were surprisingly successful for their time, did not emerge *sui generis* but are recognizable
products of Artificial Intelligence research.

27.2   Part II: Theoretical foundations

In a sense, all computer programs contain knowledge. A 'bubble sort'
program written in BASIC contains the programmer's knowledge about
how to order the elements in an array or list. So what is it that makes
knowledge representation different from ordinary programming?

Computer programs for tasks harder than sorting lists are no-
toriously hard to understand. Certainly they contain the programmer's
knowledge about how to perform the task. But they also contain his or
her knowledge about:

- how to wrestle with constructs in the programming language,
- how to trade clarity for efficiency, and
- how to make important but low-level decisions about data
  manipulation and flow of control.

Knowledge representation languages are high-level languages developed
expressly for the purpose of encoding 'chunks' of human knowledge, such
as rules of thumb and prototypical objects, in a manner that hides the
minutiae of data and control structure from the user as far as possible.
Users can delve into the internals, of course; but the idea is that they do
not have to do this to write programs. Such languages tend to be
extremely economical of code, compared with more conventional programming languages, just because so many of the programming details
are taken care of by the interpreter of the language. Yet most of them
can be shown to have the power of a Turing machine. In other words,
they can compute any function that can be computed using more
conventional programming languages.

However, the news is not all good.

- There is an adverse trade-off between the *expressivity* of a
  knowledge representation language and the *tractability* of its inference procedures, if we wish to retain soundness and completeness. Put another way, the more you can say, the less you can
  prove about what you say in a finite time. (Sometimes, thanks to
  undecidability, you may not be able to prove what you say at all.)
- Much of the knowledge we wish to represent is complicated by
  vagueness and *uncertainty*. Our knowledge is often radically
  incomplete, and therefore contains estimates and assumptions.

Data can be partial, noisy or inherently variable. Furthermore, the concepts that humans use are not crisply defined, and may resist attempts to render them more precise.

The challenge of knowledge representation is that we cannot let ourselves be paralysed by the problems of tractability and uncertainty.

- We are often willing to give up logical completeness in the face of intractability, so long as we can still get all the solutions that we are likely to need. As mentioned in Chapter 18, sometimes we do not need to generate all the logically possible solutions to some problem.

- We are also willing to make some compromises with respect to mathematical correctness when faced with uncertainty. Although many of the inference schemes we use are not quite in accordance with the axioms of probability theory, we typically take some short cuts which simplify the computation of belief measures for practical purposes.

The last paragraphs are not intended to sound complacent, merely realistic. Further research on knowledge representation and inference will ultimately enable us to have a better understanding of these trade-offs, but in the meantime we have methods that suffice for many applications. However, one suspects that the representation of human knowledge will *always* remain a pragmatic enterprise, at least until Psychology becomes an exact science.

Thus knowledge representation is an empirical and experimental research area, and not merely an arena for philosophical debate. The old issues – such as 'Can machines think?' and 'How is knowledge *really* represented in the human brain?' – seem increasingly irrelevant to the Modern Period of AI. The key question is rather 'What can we do with this technology?', and it can only be answered by a concerted programme of theoretical and practical work.

27.3 Part III: Knowledge representation

Artificial Intelligence did not invent rewrite rules or graphs or predicate logic; rather AI researchers have creatively adapted these formalisms to the practical ends of knowledge representation and found efficient implementations for them. The development of modern *production systems*, *object-oriented systems* and *procedural deduction systems* has been driven by AI applications involving classification and construction problems of the kind described in Part IV. Without that impetus, and the empirical enterprise of trying to solve such problems, it is doubtful that many of these innovations would have occurred.

Production systems have turned out to be a surprisingly effective tool for encoding and applying human expertise, particularly where the knowledge is plentiful but relatively unstructured. This style of programming is not particularly easy, and the creation and maintenance of large rule-based programs poses its own problems. Nevertheless, it has provided the basis for a substantial number of successful applications over the last 20 years, such as DENDRAL, R1/XCON and VT. Accounts of these systems are worth reading in the original (Buchanan and Feigenbaum, 1978; McDermott, 1982a; Marcus *et al.*, 1988). For more details about production system architectures, the reader is referred to McDermott and Forgy (1978), Forgy (1982), and Brownston *et al.* (1985).

Systems based on frames and objects have proved particularly useful in applications where a detailed knowledge of domain objects and procedures is essential to performing the task. Thus, in MOLGEN, the use of the UNITS representation language facilitated the encoding of large amounts of knowledge about complex molecules and laboratory procedures. The message-passing style of programming looks particularly promising for applications that involve simulation, although at the time of writing we have yet to see very many systems written in this style (but see the account of COMPASS in Prerau, 1990). For further details on particular object-oriented systems, the reader is referred to Bromley (1986) for FLAVORS and Keene (1989) for the COMMON LISP Object System.

Research on procedural deduction has made substantial advances over the last 10 years, particularly in the field of logic programming. How far this work will impact on practical expert systems applications remains to be seen. The experience with systems such as MRS suggests that knowledge programming requires that the logic programming paradigm be combined with meta-level reasoning to give more flexibility in the specification of control. The next generation of PROLOG systems will undoubtedly provide more options in this respect, as well as providing more access to lower level aspects of storage and access. Relevant literature includes Clark and Tarnlund (1982), Campbell (1984), Maes and Nardi (1988) and Jackson *et al.* (1989).

Although AI has produced a variety of representation languages, they all have certain things in common.

Firstly, they are *declarative*, in the sense that they describe knowledge relevant to solving some task rather than prescribing how the task should be done. The separation between knowledge base and inference engine implicit in most expert systems architectures means that one can experiment with applying the same knowledge under different control regimes; at least, you can if you are crafting the inference engine yourself. Some architectures, such as blackboards, allow you to represent control knowledge declaratively, and reason about it just like any other kind of knowledge.

Secondly, they are highly *modular*. As well as concealing implementation details from the user of the language, modules of knowledge conceal implementation detail from each other, communicating through global data structures (as in production systems and blackboard systems) or via strict protocols (as in object-oriented systems). This feature encourages the piecemeal and incremental encoding of knowledge and supports fast prototyping.

Thirdly, the analogue of procedure invocation in such languages tends to be *pattern-directed*. Thus the firing of rules in production systems, the triggering of knowledge sources in blackboard systems, and the resolution of clauses in deduction systems all rely on a form of pattern matching. This is a very powerful and general mechanism, which aids modularity, although it does not come without computational cost.

Knowledge representation languages of whatever kind are normally implemented as *pattern-directed inference systems* (Waterman and Hayes-Roth, 1978). The resultant programs consist of a number of relatively independent modules (rules, structures or clauses) which are matched against incoming data and which manipulate data structures. There are three essential ingredients to any such system:

(1) a collection of *modules* capable of being activated by incoming data which match their 'trigger' patterns;

(2) one or more *dynamic data structures* that can be examined and modified by an active module;

(3) an *interpreter* that controls the selection and activation of modules on a cyclic basis.

Artificial Intelligence research has concentrated on a number of topics related to pattern-directed inference:

- the *efficient implementation* of such interpreters;
- turning relatively 'pure' formalisms with some mathematical basis into usable *software tools*;
- experimenting with *mixed formalisms* that combine different paradigms.

Arguably, we are still learning to use these languages to maximum effect, both singly and in combination. It has become clear that no single programming paradigm is 'best' for expert systems applications. Today, it seems simply misguided to search for a single universal representation language that is good for all problems.

27.4 Part IV: Practical problem solving

Part IV explored the idea that there are generic tasks which are exemplified again and again in expert systems applications. In particular, we looked at the difference between classification and construction tasks, and saw that in their purest forms they required rather different search strategies for their solution.

- In *classification tasks*, the emphasis is on finding a useful but approximate mapping between data and solutions at some level of abstraction. We have to consider all the evidence, combine it in some way, then refine and rank candidate solutions accordingly. The solution space is usually known in advance, and its categories are capable of being enumerated. Exhaustive search methods that use certainties to order and prune solution paths are adequate for many purposes; for example, if the search space is small or factorable into more or less independent subproblems. Large search spaces which represent interacting subproblems require stronger methods that impose some form of organization on the hypothesis space (for example, hierarchical or causal) and allow for the explicit scheduling of subtasks (for example, subclassification or tracing a causal path).

- In *construction tasks*, we are typically building some complex entity that must satisfy certain constraints, and the solution space may be very large indeed. Consequently, the emphasis is on keeping one's options open, being prepared to guess when a problem is underconstrained, and being able to recover from bad decisions. We will not normally explore all solution paths in search of an optimal solution; rather we are satisfied if we find one that fits the constraints. Constraints may interact, and domain-specific knowledge may be required for the resolution of conflicts. The most general strategy appears to be one of 'propose-and-revise', in which partial solutions are extended until a constraint is violated, and then such violations are 'fixed' by heuristics.

Although it is tempting to think of tasks like diagnosis as being classification tasks and tasks like planning as being construction tasks, the mapping between individual applications and generic tasks is more complicated than that.

- We saw that programs such as INTERNIST can view diagnosis as a construction task: the solution elements are disorders which can be combined into composite hypotheses. It is therefore not practical to enumerate the solution space in advance, given that a patient may be suffering from ten or more disorders. Furthermore, the problem of finding the 'best' explanations of a set of symptoms by the 'cover and differentiate' strategy is intractable without powerful mechanisms for focusing the attention of the program. In this respect, tasks such as differential diagnosis share many of the features of constructive problem solving. To the extent that this is true for a given task, strategies such as 'least commitment' and propose-and-revise become appropriate.

- We also saw that programs such as R1 sometimes have enough knowledge to perform a construction task without recourse to guessing or backtracking. Given an overall strategy of 'top-down refinement', which analyses the computer configuration task into nearly independent subtasks, R1 can afford to reason wholly bottom up. In other words, it can 'propose and extend' without having to revise. In addition, we studied a planner (ONCOCIN) which essentially performs a constructive task by the method of heuristic classification. Thanks to the restricted form of cancer-treatment protocols, the system could merely select skeletal plans from a plan library, and then adapt them to the current situation by a process of plan refinement.

Nevertheless, the theoretical distinction between classification and construction is extremely useful, not least because it aids the process of knowledge acquisition and its automation. We saw that the functionality of a knowledge elicitation tool could be greatly enhanced if it possessed both a declarative model of the domain and some knowledge of how the task would be performed; that is, how domain knowledge would be used by the applications program. Although acquisition systems such as MORE and RIME are still in their infancy, they point the way to powerful methodologies for building knowledge bases. The key insight, that automatic knowledge elicitation should itself be knowledge based, will ultimately lead to effective tools for dealing with the knowledge-acquisition bottleneck. Automatic consistency checking and compilation into an executable form is also facilitated by access to a domain model and a set of problem-solving principles.

Readers interested in delving deeper into the theoretical background, as well as learning more about the experimental systems that embody these ideas, should consult Clancey (1987a,b,c), Chandrasekaran (1983a,b; 1986), Chandrasekaran and Mittal (1985), Hayes-Roth *et al.* (1987), and Marcus (1988a). Also worth consulting is a special issue of the *ACM SIGART Newsletter* (April, 1989) which is devoted to knowledge acquisition. A compendium of knowledge acquisition references also appears in the October 1989 issue.

27.5 Part V: Software tools and architectures

Part V presented a classification of tools for building expert systems that depended largely on different approaches to the trade-off between making representation and control decisions for users and providing them with the tools for implementing their own decisions. We distinguished between:

- *expert system shells* which provide a single representation language and control regime combination which has worked well in the past;
- *high-level programming languages*, such as production rule interpreters and object-oriented systems, which provide basic building blocks for representation and control;
- *mixed paradigm programming environments* which provide a wide range of representational devices and control mechanisms;
- *problem-solving architectures*, such as blackboard systems, where task-oriented frameworks can be instantiated for particular applications;
- *useful packages*, for subtasks such as simulation or truth maintenance, which can be interfaced to the main problem-solving program.

We saw that the first generation of software tools for building expert systems were essentially abstractions over successful applications programs. Many of these attempts at generalization were themselves successful. Thus the EMYCIN shell was applied to problems far from the original domain of blood infections, including structural analysis and troubleshooting electronic circuits. Special-purpose programming languages, such as OPS5 and FLAVORS, also emerged during this period. These eventually made the transition from the research laboratory to more general use, providing the skilled programmer with a viable alternative to shells.

The second generation supported a 'mix and match' style of architecture, which encouraged knowledge engineers to select and combine programming paradigms that features of the problem appeared to demand. Arguably, this was something of a black art, and required a level of experience and sophistication beyond the average consumer. Perhaps the best that can be said about these tools is that they demonstrated the enormous range of possible architectures that could be built around different representations and control regimes.

Hopefully, the next generation of tools will provide a rather more structured approach to the problem of deciding which architecture to use for which problems. At least some current research is focusing on the construction of tools for particular generic tasks, as documented in Part IV. Thus many of Clancey's programs are specifically tailored to the task of heuristic classification, while Hayes-Roth's work on BB* has concentrated on archetypal construction problems, such as arrangement.

As far as usability is concerned, it has sometimes been assumed in the past that giving the programmer 'powerful' tools makes programming easier. However, there is also a trade-off between making decisions for the programmer and allowing him or her more flexibility. To over-simplify, shells sometimes err on the side of constraining the pro-grammer, but mixed programming paradigms give some programmers more options than they can cope with. 'Powerful' progrmming environ-ments are often hard to master, and so the learning curve can be quite steep. Nevertheless, the provision of well-engineered modules, such as truth maintenance systems, which perform essential tasks and which are non-trivial to program efficiently, obviously speeds expert systems development.

Such evidence as there is suggests that knowledge engineering environments need to be more specialized to particular kinds of task. One doubts that these environments will have a gentler learning curve than earlier tools, or that they will help non-programmers build expert systems painlessly. On the other hand, although knowledge engineering may not get easier, good knowledge engineers may be able to get more done.

Artificial Intelligence languages and environments are increasingly reviewed in a variety of journals and magazines, such as *IEEE Software*, *IEEE Expert*, *Communications of the ACM*, and *Byte*. Consulting such publications is the only way to keep really up to date. The Proceedings of the *ACM Conference on Object-Oriented Programming Systems, Languages and Applications* is good source of more technical and theoretical information on new developments, as is the journal *LISP and Symbolic Computation*.

27.6 Part VI: Advanced topics in expert systems

Part VI contains a representative sample of current research problems that impinge on practical aspects of expert systems: *diagnosis from first principles*, *inexact reasoning* and *rule induction*. These topics were chosen because any progress in these areas will have a great impact on the expert systems of the future. In particular, each of these topics has implications for the central problem of knowledge acquisition.

Diagnosis from first principles suggests that it may be possible to side-step the whole business of deriving fault-finding heuristics for some device from a diagnostic expert. Instead, we derive diagnoses of faulty behaviour by reasoning about minimal perturbations to a representation of the device's *correct* behaviour. This approach to diagnosis is sometimes called 'model-based', because it is more firmly based in an explicit model of the domain than most rule-based approaches.

Problems with this approach include the following.

- *Getting a system description in the first place.* In some domains, such as troubleshooting electronic circuits, it is possible that the description could be derived as a by-product of computer-aided design. Certainly this description must be complete and consistent for the method to work properly.

- *Controlling the combinatorial explosion of multiple fault hypotheses.* This problem can be rendered tractable by information-theoretic methods if we make various independence assumptions about component failures. However, in a domain where these assumptions do not hold, or where we also need to consider the failure of connections between components, the combinatorial problems reappear.

Readers interested in this area should supplement Chapter 24 by reading the original papers of Davis (1984), Genesereth (1984), De Kleer and Williams (1987) and Reiter (1987). Some of these papers can be found in Ginsberg (1987).

Research on inexact reasoning is suggesting ways in which belief update can be more closely tied to the structure of the problem. Thus both Dempster–Shafer theory and Bayesian belief updating can be adapted for modelling probabilistic inference in hierarchical hypothesis spaces. The link between Bayesian methods and causal networks suggests another way of tying inexact methods to deeper knowledge of the domain, instead of attaching certainties to more superficial associations between causes and effects. Having a model of hierarchical or causal relationships among data and hypotheses may make the assignment of weights of evidence to hypotheses easier than the assignment of certainties to the conclusions of individual decision rules. For example, having the explicit model to hand may encourage the expert and the knowledge engineer to devise and enforce a coherent policy on the assignment of weights, and help the knowledge engineer to design a knowledge-acquisition program to check that this policy is consistently applied.

The management of uncertainty is now an extremely active and somewhat controversial research area which is far too large and diverse to review in an introductory text. Thus attention has been focused on proposals which can be seen to have seen some direct application to expert systems. The interested reader is invited to consult papers in Kanal *et al.* (1989) for a representative sample of more recent work and Pearl (1988) for a text that combines novel research with insightful review.

Finally, research on rule induction is providing a methodology for deriving, evaluating and tuning sets of decision rules. It seems certain that such methods will be required if we are to build and maintain really large knowledge bases. Also, machine learning is fundamental to the whole area of 'self-improving' systems, which gain in knowledge from their problem-solving experiences.

We saw that the following techniques were of direct relevance to expert systems applications.

- Programs have been built which are capable of learning concepts from examples; that is, of constructing rules which correctly classify a set of positive and negative training instances, and then using these rules to classify unseen data with a high degree of accuracy.

- Work is being done on the application of decision theory to the evaluation of individual heuristic rules and the optimization of sets of such rules, with a view to improving the quality of rule sets in terms of both analysability and performance.

Research on inductive learning has made great progress in the 1980s, and is certain to contribute to future knowledge engineering methodologies. The interested reader is referred to papers in Michalski *et al.* (1983, 1986) for more details than could be supplied in Chapter 26. Meanwhile, research on the evaluation of heuristic rules seeks to demystify the art of encoding expertise in rules by showing to what extent rule weights can be varied before the output of a program is affected. Greater understanding in this area will facilitate knowledge elicitation and lead to more robust systems. Although there are no collections of papers in this area, we can expect further developments to be reported at conferences such as *AAAI* and *IJCAI* (see Bibliography at the end of the chapter).

These and other research efforts in Artificial Intelligence are essential to the further development of expert systems technology. Progress in such core areas as are treated in Part VI is unlikely to be made in the absence of a strong input from the parent discipline. Progress in related areas, such as natural language processing and man–machine interaction, will also shape the systems of the future.

Finally, there are many issues to do with the rights of people affected by this technology that need to be addressed. Professional bodies have an educative role to play in this respect, promoting public awareness and encouraging informed debate in an atmosphere somewhat removed from political pressures and commercial considerations. They also have a role to play in maintaining standards in AI-related products and developing codes of practice for the deployment of AI technology.

27.7 Conclusion

Although Artificial Intelligence has gone in and out of fashion several times over the last 30 years, no-one can seriously doubt that computers present us with a unique tool for emulating and extending human cognitive abilities. Neither can anyone doubt that, in the twenty-first century, human knowledge will be one of the world's most important commodities. At present, it is a scarce (but happily renewable) resource, but there are signs that education may not be able to keep pace with the future global demand for expertise (particularly since no-one seems to want to pay for it).

Expert systems research is developing a methodology for not merely codifying knowledge, but representing it in a form whereby its application to real problems can be wholly or partly automated. Expert systems are capable of amplifying human expertise in a manner that increases productivity on hard problems and enhances our potential to deal with the even harder problems we shall face in the 1990s and beyond. This is rather more than can be said for a number of high-cost, high-risk, high-technology ventures, such as stealth bombers. Although advances in computer architecture and the falling price of memory will facilitate AI applications, none of the techniques described in this book require very special hardware. Most run on personal workstations which are getting cheaper, more powerful and more widespread every year.

As with any difficult enterprise, artificial intelligence has attracted more spectators than players. Scepticism has always been high, just as it was in the early days of aviation. However, the 1980s have seen the beginning of change in this situation, as prototype systems from university laboratories have been developed and subsequently deployed in commercial applications. Not every such venture has been as successful as some of the programs documented here. Perfecting a technology, and making it accessible to all, usually takes longer than doing the original R&D. Thus video was a technical possibility over a decade before it became at all attractive as a commercial proposition. As a result, the world had to wait many years for the wonder of MTV.

Every day, the technology that supports all aspects of modern life, from the medical to the military, becomes more complex and sophisticated, yet our ability to harness this technology to sensible ends does not seem to be enjoying commensurate growth. It is this 'knowledge explosion', rather than the 'information explosion' beloved of technical journalists, which will present the computer and cognitive sciences with their greatest challenge. Artificial intelligence is one of the tools that can help us meet that challenge, as long as it is applied with humanity and common sense.

Bibliographical notes

Business-oriented readers may enjoy Feigenbaum and McCorduck (1983), which offers a controversial but entertaining view of the future of knowledge engineering, followed by the more up-to-date Feigenbaum *et al.* (1988), which catalogues a number of successful applications of expert systems in industry. *AI Magazine* is a good way for the general reader to keep abreast of what is new and interesting in AI research, particularly with regard to novel applications. *Knowledge Engineering Review* is an excellent source of survey and tutorial articles on subjects likely to interest both students and knowledge engineers.

To keep up with a particular area of AI research, it is only necessary to look through the proceedings of conferences such as IJCAI (*International Joint Conference on Artificial Intelligence*), AAAI (The *National Conference on Artificial Intelligence*, sponsored by the American Association for Artificial Intelligence) and ECAI (*European Conference on Artificial Intelligence*), as well as various national conferences.

To keep up with new applications of AI, there are now numerous specialist conferences in areas such as aerospace, defence, design, manufacturing, and so forth. These are normally listed in the Calendars of publications such as *AI Magazine* and *Communications of the Association for Computing Machinery*. The Association for Computing Machinery has a *Special Interest Group on Artificial Intelligence* (SIGART) which publishes a quarterly newsletter.

Bundy and Clutterbuck (1985) raise a number of issues to do with the quality of AI products and professional codes of practice, and Whitby (1988) explores some of the social consequences of AI.

STUDY SUGGESTIONS

27.1 Read Bundy and Clutterbuck (1985). Who should be responsible for the quality of artificial intelligence products?

27.2 In the USA, basic research in expert systems has been funded mostly by the Department of Defense. In the UK, it has been funded on a half-hearted and occasional basis by a variety of government agencies, while on the Continent it has been funded on a multi-national basis by the European Commission. Who do you think should fund expert systems research, and what do you think their priorities should be?

27.3 List five ways in which you think existing expert systems technology could be applied to increase the quality of life on this planet. How likely do you think it is that these applications will receive funding from business or government?

Part VII

Appendices

APPENDIX A

Programming in LISP

This appendix is intended to serve as a compact introduction to LISP programming. It assumes some minimal acquaintance with the concepts of programming, but not fluency in any one language or any practical acquaintance with LISP. It will help if you have read Chapter 7 on Symbolic Computation, and therefore have some background knowledge of functional programming.

A.1   Function definition

In lambda calculus, the square function can be defined as

$$sq(X) = (\lambda X) (X \times X).$$

It is instructive to compare this definition with the following LISP definition of the square function:

```
(defun square (lambda (x) (* x x))).
```

You will see at once the close correspondence between the two expressions. The main differences are the following:

- The $f(a_1,..., a_n)$ of normal mathematical function notation becomes

  ```
  (f a₁ ... aₙ)
  ```

  which is at least as readable and easier to type without the commas.

- There is no mix of prefix notation with infix operators, such as '='
  in the lambda calculus definition. Everything is prefix.
- There is no mix of bracketing conventions between operators, like
  (λX), and matrices, such as (X × X). Thus, if M is a matrix, we
  have (lambda (x) M) and not (λX)M.

There are only two indispensible syntactic classes in LISP: everything is
either an *atom*, like times, x, lambda, 5, and so on, or a *list*, such as (* x x).
One can, of course, have lists of lists such as (lambda (x) (* x x)). LISP
supports data structures other than the list, of course, such as arrays, hash
tables and the like, but we shall not be concerned with them at this point.

Atoms and lists are both symbolic expressions, or *sexprs* for short.
The syntactic definition of an sexpr is given by:

<sexpr> ::= <atom> | (<sexpr> ... <sexpr>)

The semantics is also straightforward. Given a LISP form

(square 2)

the interpreter:

(a) assumes that square is the name of a function and that its argument
     is the atom 2;

(b) substitutes the lambda expression associated with square for square
     in the LISP form to give

     ((lambda (x) (* x x)) 2)

     and

(c) performs lambda conversion to derive

     (* 2 2),

     binding the formal parameter x to the argument 2.

This process repeats until the interpreter arrives at a primitive function,
such as times, which is not defined in terms of any other function. It has
then arrived at the point in which it stops executing LISP and executes a
statement of whatever language LISP is implemented in. The main
exception to this rule is lambda itself. lambda does not denote a function; it
is an operator, just as the universal quantifier of predicate logic is an
operator.

The first argument to lambda is always a list of variables; it should
be plain that:

(lambda (x y) (f x y))

is entirely equivalent to

```
(lambda (x) (lambda (y) (f x y)))
```

or the $(\lambda x)\,(\lambda y)f(x, y)$ of lambda calculus.

Exercise. Code the LISP function cube by analogy with square. (The function '*' takes any number of arguments.)

A.2   Quotation in LISP

In the (square 2) example, the atom 2 is evaluated when the square function is applied to it during lambda conversion. The value of the atom 2 is defined as the fixed point number 2. However, arguments to functions can be symbols or symbol structures of any kind: they need not be numbers. Consider the identity function defined by:

```
(defun identity (x) x).
```

This function simply returns what it is given – for example:

```
(identity 1)
⇒ 1
```

Or does it? Well, not quite. It is not the case that

```
(identity fred)
⇒ fred
```

because the system has no predefined value for fred.

In a real program, we might want to treat the token fred as a handle on whatever bundle of properties fred denotes. How we attach properties to things, and how we use the token fred to find these properties, is the subject of the next section. For the moment, we are only interested in getting our identity function to work. Suppose we have not yet assigned a value to fred, but we want to apply the identity function to fred anyway. The solution is to prevent the interpreter from evaluating fred, using *quotation*.

```
(identity (quote fred))
⇒ fred
```

will do this. So quote is the real identity function in LISP: it always returns exactly what it is given, no more and no less. Thus

```
(quote (a b c))
⇒ (a b c)
```

Like lambda, quote is not a function but a special form. For convenience,

```
'fred
```

is defined to be equivalent to

```
(quote fred)
```

in nearly all implementations of LISP, including COMMON LISP.

In addition to atoms that are numerals, the atoms representing truth and falsity, t and nil, do not need quotation. Thus

```
t
⇒ t
```

and

```
nil
⇒ nil
```

A.3 Associating properties with symbol tokens

Consider the list

```
((name fred) (age 40) (wife freda)).
```

Such as data structure is usually called an *association list*. We can use this particular list to represent a person called Fred, by giving his name, his age in years and the name of his wife. To record this kind of information, and get at it subsequently, we need to be able to process lists, that is, create them, explore them, take them apart, modify them. LISP supplies primitives – functions which are defined by the implementation – to do this.

One of the most fundamental things one might like to do is find the value of a particular property of Fred such as his age. There is a LISP function, assoc, which does this:

```
(assoc 'age fredness)
```

What is fredness, and why isn't it quoted? I am assuming that we have already assigned the list

```
((name fred) (age 40) (wife freda))
```

to be the value of the atom fredness. That is, whenever the LISP interpreter encounters fredness, it will return the right value

```
fredness
⇒ ((name fred) (age 40) (wife freda))
```

How such assignments are achieved is the subject of a later section. For the moment, we simply assume their existence.

The definition of assoc is provided by all LISP implementations. However, assoc is not really a primitive of LISP. For example, it could be defined in terms of more primitive functions.

Suppose that first denotes the first member of a list, such that

```
(first '(a b c))
⇒ a
```

and that rest denotes the rest of the list, such that

```
(rest '(a b c))
⇒ (b c)
```

If COMMON LISP had not provided assoc, one could define it as follows

```
(defun assoc (key alist)
    (if (null alist) nil
        (if (eq (first (first alist)) key) (first alist)
            (assoc key (rest alist)))))
```

There are only three functions here that you haven't met before:

- eq tests that two atoms are the same.
- null returns t if its argument is the empty list nil, and we construe t as meaning truth.
- (if x y z) returns the value of y if x evaluates to truth, otherwise it returns the value of z.

This definition is clearly recursive. The termination condition is when the association list is empty. In this case, we return the empty list nil. Otherwise, we look to see if the head of the head of the list – the head of the first pair – is the key. If so, we return that pair; if not, we call assoc again with the key as before, but passing the tail of the list as the second argument to this new call.

Hence, evaluating

```
(assoc 'age fredness)
⇒ (age 40)
```

succeeds on the second call to the assoc function, because

```
(eq (first (first alist)) key)
```

evaluates to t.

Finding out something about Fred could therefore be accomplished by the following 'Fred function':

```
(defun fredfun (key)
    (first (rest (assoc key fredness)))))
```

so that

```
(fredfun 'age)
⇒ 40
```

Exercises

- Create your own association list of some of the people you know and write some code to retrieve information about them.

- Code the factorial and power functions, such that

```
(factorial x)
```

returns $x!$, and

```
(power m n)
```

returns m^n.

A.4 Control in LISP

if is not the only conditional statement in LISP, there is a more general form, called cond. Using cond, our definition of assoc would look like this:

```
(defun assoc (key assoc_list)
    (cond   ((null assoc_list) nil)
```

```
((equal (first (first assoc_list)) key)
          (first assoc_list))
   (t (assoc key (first assoc_list)))))
```

Each cond form has the following schematic structure:

```
(cond (<condition₁> <action₁>) ...
       (<conditionₙ> <actionₙ>))
```

Cond is not a function, but a special operator, like lambda is. When the interpreter encounters a 'cond' statement, it does the following:

- It takes the first argument to cond and evaluates the first sexpr $<condition_1>$.
- If the value of $<condition_1>$ is non-null, then the sexpr $<action_1>$ is evaluated and its value is returned as the value of the cond.
- If, on the other hand, its value is null, then the interpreter moves on to the next condition-action pair.
- if cond runs out of pairs, then it returns nil.

Note the use of t as the condition in the last clause. This is like saying,

'If all the other clauses higher than me have failed, then do this',

where 'this' is the action of that clause.

You can compose multiple conditions by using the logical operators or and and. These take any number of arguments. For example,

```
(and (numberp 4) (lessp 4 5))
⇒ t

(or (numberp 'fred) (numberp 'freda))
⇒ nil
```

It is a consequence of the way that and and or work that they can also be used to affect the flow of control. For example,

```
(defun abs (number)
    (if (< number 0) (times number −1) number))
```

could be rendered as

```
(defun abs (number)
    (or (and (< number 0) (times number −1)) number))
```

as well as

```
(defun abs (number)
    (cond ((< number 0) (times number -1)) (t number)))
```

< and > are predicates, such that

```
(< 1 2)
⇒ t
```

```
(< 1 1)
⇒ nil
```

```
(> 1 2)
⇒ nil
```

```
(> 2 1)
⇒ t
```

as you might expect. Less obviously,

```
(and nil <errorful_code>)
⇒ nil
```

and

```
(or t <errorful_code>)
⇒ t
```

assuming these forms are to be interpreted and not compiled, since and quits on failure and or quits on success.

A cond clause can have more than one action:

```
(cond ((numberp x) (print x) (square x))
      (t (print "gimme a number") nil))
```

but it should be clear that only the value of the last action will be returned. The intermediate actions may have effects such as printing things out, but their values will be 'thrown away'.

Exercise Rewrite the factorial and power functions using cond instead of if.

A.5   Assignment in LISP

Assignment is something that should be used very sparingly in LISP. The correct way to accomplish assignment is by using let, another special LISP operator.

A let statement has the following form.

```
(let ((<variable₁> <sexpr₁>) ...
      (<variableₙ> <sexprₙ>))
    <form₁> ... <formₙ>)
```

Executing such a statement causes each of the variables to become bound to the value its corresponding sexpr. The LISP forms that follow are then evaluated. On exit from the let, the variable bindings are undone. In fact

```
(let ((x 2) (y 3)) (times x y))
```

is entirely equivalent to

```
((lambda (x y) (times x y) 2 3)
```

and can therefore be dealt with by lambda conversion.

Exercise   What value does the following LISP form return?

```
(let ((x 1) (y 2)) (let ((z (plus x y))) (square z))).
```

Is the following form valid LISP, given the equivalence between lambda and let?

```
(let ((x 1) (y (plus x 1))) (times x y)).
```

A.6   Iteration in LISP

LISP is a recursive language. You can do iteration in LISP, but it's not as natural. Recursion is undoubtedly expensive in interpreted LISP; however, most good LISP compilers perform tail-recursion optimization. LISP programs with a recursive control structure are almost always conceptually clearer than iterative ones. They are also more in keeping with the lambda calculus.

The best construct for doing straight iteration is mapcar. A mapcar statement has the general form

```
(mapcar <function> <list>)
```

The value of this statement is a new list, whose elements are the result of applying the function to each member of the list *in situ*. Thus

```
(mapcar 'square '(1 2 3 4))
⇒ (2 4 9 16)
```

It is interesting to note that <function> can be an 'open lambda' as follows:

```
(mapcar '(lambda (x) (times x x)) '(1 2 3 4))
⇒ (2 4 9 16)
```

However, mapcar is not suitable for iteration which may need to be terminated prematurely. In such cases, one must either use tail recursion or the do construct. do has the general form

```
(do <inits> <test> <form₁> ... <formₙ>)
```

where <*inits*> is a list of triples, each of the form

```
(<variable> <sexpr> <update-fn>).
```

<*variable*> is an atom assigned an initial value which is the value of <*sexpr*>, while <*update-fn*> is the function which applies to <*variable*> to derive a new value for <*variable*>. <*test*> is really a cond clause of the condition-action type. When the condition is true, the actions are performed and the do returns the value of the last action.

The forms are simply LISP expressions which get evaluated in turn at each iterative cycle. This sounds a bit complicated, but the following example should show how simple this really is.

```
(defun print_out (alist)
   (do ((temp alist (rest temp))
        (index 1 (+ index 1)))
       ((or (null temp) (numberp (first temp))) nil)
       (princ index) (princ " ")
       (princ (first temp))
       (princ " ")))


(print_out '(a b c 100 d e f))
1 a 2 b 3 c
⇒ nil
```

There are two things to note about this: forms like princ are evaluated for their side effect, not their value. However, print_out is a function, so it must return a value, even though we are probably not interested in that value.

Exercise. Rewrite the factorial program using the LISP do.

A.7 Backquote: programs as data

We have already met quote. This effectively halts evaluation, such that

```
(quote (a b c))
```

stops the LISP interpreter from taking a as the name of a function and trying to apply it to its 'arguments', b and c. However, there are other useful kinds of quotation, which make it easy to construct LISP forms which we *do* want evaluated eventually, but not straight away. For example, the list

```
(times 2 3)
```

is an evaluable LISP form, as well as being a piece of LISP data. We might want to construct such a form, keep it for a while, and eventually evaluate it. Doing this kind of thing is an essential part of modern LISP programming.

To create this form, one can use two standard LISP list construction predicates, cons and list. These are best demonstrated by example.

```
(list 'times 2 3)
⇒ (times 2 3)

(cons 'times '(2 3))
⇒ (times 2 3)

(cons 'times (cons 2 (cons 3 nil)))
⇒ (times 2 3)

(let ((x 2) (y 3))
    (list 'times x y))
⇒ (times 2 3)
```

list simply turns its arguments into a list, while cons adds a new element to the front of a list.

Another important list constructor is append, which joins two lists together. For example:

```
(append '(a b d) '(d e f))
⇒ (a b c d e f)

(append '(a b c) nil)
⇒ (a b c)
```

It's not hard to see that append could be defined in terms of cond thus:

```
(defun append (list_1 list_2)
    (cond ((null list_1) list_2)
          (t (cons (first list_1)
                   (append (rest list_1) list_2)))))
```

backquote is simply a more convenient way of constructing forms. Again, this is best illustrated with a few examples.

```
`(times 2 3)
⇒ (times 2 3)

(let ((x 2) (y 3)) `(times x y))
⇒ (times x y)

(let ((x 2) (y 3)) `(times ,x ,y))
⇒ (times 2 3)

(let ((list_of_args '(2 3)))  ` (times, @list_of_args))
⇒ (times 2 3)
```

backquote is like quote except that sexprs prefixed by a comma are evaluated *in situ*, while sexprs prefixed by ,@ will be evaluated and spliced *in situ*.

Exercise. What does the following LISP form return?

```
(let ((x 1) (y '(a b c)) (z (square 2)))
    `(x ,@y ,z))
```

A.8 Macros in LISP

I have never liked do very much. I prefer to write my own iteration macros, giving them names like 'while' and 'until' which make their purpose plain. Using backquote and LISP's built-in facilities for defining macros, this is very straightforward to do.

First, let's see how to define really simple macros in LISP, using the special form defmacro. defmacro is like defun, except that it defines macros instead of functions. (Macros can be thought of as functions that write themselves at runtime in an extra round of interpretation.) The only new construct that we shall use is setq. This is the basic LISP assignment function alluded to earlier. Thus

```
(setq x '(a b c))
⇒ (a b c)
```

with the side effect that x is now bound to (a b c).

```
x
⇒ (a b c)
```

It is rarely necessary to use a naked setq in ordinary applications programming; however, it is occasionally useful in systems programming, especially when writing macros.

Here is an example of how to use defmacro, backquote and setq in constructing a useful macro for doing iteration, called incr. incr simply increments an index. Thus, if n is bound to 1, then

```
(incr n)
⇒ 2
```

with the side effect that n is now bound to 2. This is obviously useful for updating local variables used to index iterations.

```
(defmacro incr (index)
   '(setq ,index (plus ,index 1)))
```

Exercise.   Define a macro called pop, such that

```
(let ((alist '(a b c))) (pop alist))
⇒ a
```

with the side effect that alist is now bound to (b c), instead of (a b c).

Now let us look at defining a while macro. A call to while will have the general form

```
(while <test> <form₁> ... <formₙ>)
```

such that while <test> evaluates non-null, the following forms get evaluated.

```
(defmacro while (test &rest body)
 '(cond (,test ,@body (while ,test ,@body))
        (t nil)))
```

The only new feature here is &rest. This a keyword which says: 'Bind the next parameter to the rest of the arguments supplied in the function call'. So, given

```
(defmacro foo (x &rest y) ...)
```

and the call

```
(foo a b c d)
```

x gets lambda bound to a, and y gets bound to (b c d). This is very useful, as you can see, because it means it isn't necessary to specify in advance how many arguments a function will be called with. When these functions are really special constructs which implement control structures, this sort of facility is invaluable.

We can now redo our do example with while.

```
(defun print_out (alist)
  (let ((temp alist) (index 1))
    (while alist
        (princ index)
        (princ " ")
        (princ (first temp))
        (princ " ")
        (setq temp (rest temp))
        (setq index (+ index 1)))))
```

It's not hard to see how you do until, by analogy.

```
(defmacro until (test &rest body)
  `(cond (,test nil)
         (t ,@body (until ,test ,@body))))
```

In fact, you probably wouldn't want to implement these macros recursively in this way. It's worth demonstrating that this is possible, however. To show you what the alternative is, I will have to introduce prog, another LISP construct.

Exercise.   Rewrite the factorial program using while and until.

A.9 Prog: **Please use sparingly**

In its simplest terms, prog creates a context which permits local redirection of control and the introduction of local variables. We can redo our do and while example using prog.

```
(defun print_out (alist)
    (prog (temp index)
        (setq temp alist)
        (setq index 1)
        tag
        (cond ((null alist) (return nil))
              (t (print index)
                 (print " ")
                 (print (pop alist))
                 (incr index)
                 (go tag)))))
```

The first argument to prog is a list of local variables. These are then initialized by setq statements. tag is simply a label for jumping to from the go statement, which is simply LISP's 'go to'. The return statement explicitly states what value will be returned from the prog when the termination condition becomes true. The rest should be self-explanatory, although I think you'll agree that it's not a pretty sight.

There is a time and place for this kind of programming – when you want to create a high-level construct that makes such programming unnecessary in future. prog can be used to implement while as follows.

```
(defmacro while (test &rest body)
    '(prog nil
       whiletag
       (cond (,test ,&body (go whiletag))
             (t (return nil)))))
```

This definition will probably execute more efficiently than the recursive one given earlier, although compilation will undoubtedly narrow the gap, thanks to tail recursion optimization.

Exercise.   Implement until using prog.

A.10 Good LISP style

One excuse often given for prog is the need for local variables. Beginners in LISP always seem to use about three times as many locals as they need. One way to avoid this is by parameterization. A good illustration of this is the reverse function such that

```
(reverse '(a b c))
⇒ (c b a)
```

It might be supposed that you really need a prog and a local variable to do this, along the lines of

```
(defun reverse (alist)
    (prog (temp)
        (setq temp nil)
        tag
        (cond ((null alist)(return temp))
              (t (setq temp (cons (pop alist) temp))
                 (go tag)))))
```

This is, in fact, unnecessary, as well as ugly. Better is

```
(defun reverse (alist)
    (do_reverse alist nil))

(defun do_reverse (alist accum)
    (cond ((null alist) accum)
          (t (do_reverse (rest alist)
                         (cons (first alist) accum)))))
```

You create the accumulator, accum, by calling another function with an initialization value for the new variable. When the flow of control returns from do_reverse, the binding is undone, and accum ceases to be.

The golden rule when writing functions is: Small is beautiful; big is ugly, and hard to debug.

Exercises
Write a suite of recursive LISP functions headed by a function called permute, such that

```
(permute '(a b c))
⇒ ((a b c) (a c b) (b a c) (b c a) (c a b) (c b a))
```

and so on.

Write a LISP program headed by a function called 'powerset', such that

```
(powerset '(a b c))
⇒ ((a b c) (a b) (a c) (b c) (a) (b) (c) nil)
```

and so on.

These are not as easy as they sound. When you have got them right you will understand quite a lot about recursion in LISP.

Write a quicksort program in LISP. Don't try and do it all in one function definition, you need several.

A.11   Sample programs (and answers to selected exercises)

```
;; the old faithful factorial program

(defun factorial (n)
    (if (zerop n) 1 (times n (factorial (difference n 1)))))

;; and the power program

(defun power (m n)
    (if (zerop n) 1 (times m (power m (difference n 1)))))

;; permute generates all the permutations of a list and
;; returns them as a list of lists

(defun permute (alist)
    (cond ((equal (length alist) 2)
           (list alist (reverse alist)))
          (t (mapover (car alist) (permute (cdr alist))))))

(defun mapover (head tail)
    (cond ((null tail) nil)
          (t (append (mapinto head (car tail) nil)
                     (mapover head (cdr tail))))))

(defun mapinto (item tail perm)
    (cond ((null tail) (cons (append perm (list item)) nil))
          (t (cons  (append perm (cons item tail))
                    (mapinto item
                             (cdr tail)
                             (append perm (list
                                           (car tail))))))))

;; powerset generates the power set of a set as a list of
;; lists
```

```
(defun powerset (aset)
  (cond ((equal (length aset) 1) (list aset nil))
        (t (mapset (car aset) (powerset (cdr aset))))))
```

```
(defun mapset (item setofsets)
  (append (mappingof item setofsets) setofsets))
```

```
(defun mappingof (item setofsets)
  (cond ((null setofsets) nil)
        (t (cons  (cons item (car setofsets))
                  (mappingof item (cdr setofsets))))))
```

```
;; The until macro using prog
```

```
(defmacro until (test &rest body)
  `(prog nil
      untiltag
      (and ,test (return nil))
      ,@body
      (go untiltag)))
```

APPENDIX B

Programming in OPS5

OPS5 is a production rule language which has been implemented in both BLISS and LISP. The sample program below runs in the FRANZ LISP version. Running OPS5 in this version involves loading OPS5 into LISP, and then calling it, more often than not, from the top level of the LISP interpreter.

B.1   A simple OPS5 program

Figure B.1 contains a simple OPS5 program the sole function of which is to take bricks from a heap and order them in decreasing size. Such a program does not encode a wealth of human expertise, but it is small enough to be taken in at one glance; a more advanced application of OPS5 is described in detail in Chapter 17. Neither do I claim that this program represents the most elegant solution; rather the code is intended to illustrate a number of subtle points about OPS5 as a programming language.

An OPS5 program is somewhat different in appearance from a program in a more conventional, block-structured language, such as PASCAL. The syntax and semantics are both a good deal simpler than PASCAL, although this simplicity is not always reflected in program behaviour, as we shall see. A walk through the program in Figure B.1 will not take very long.

The first statement, (strategy mea), is a declaration which selects a particular conflict resolution strategy. The two options are mea and lex: each is a mixture of refractoriness, recency and specificity as described in Chapter 8. The basic difference between them is that mea has an extra test which emphasizes the very first condition element in a rule when

Figure B.1 A simple program in OPS5

```
(strategy mea)
(external wm)
(literalize goal task index)
(literalize brick name size place)

(p begin
   (start)
   →
   (make brick ^name A ^size 10 ^place heap)
   (make brick ^name C ^size 30 ^place heap)
   (make brick ^name B ^size 20 ^place heap)
   (remove 1)
   (make goal ^task add ^index 1))

(p pick up
   (goal ^task add)
   (brick ^size <size> ^place heap)
   - (brick ^size { > <size> } ^place heap)
   →
   (modify 2 ^place hand))

(p holding
   (goal ^task add)
   (brick ^place hand)
   →
   (modify 1 ^task put-down))

(p put-down
   (goal ^task put-down ^index <rank>)
   (brick ^place hand)
   →
   (modify 2 ^place <rank>)
   (modify 1 ^task add ^index (compute <rank> + 1)))

(p stop
   (goal ^task add)
   - (brick ^place heap)
   →
   (remove 1)
   (call wm)
   (halt))

(defun rerun nil
   (remove *)
   (make start)
   (run))
```

considering recency. It can be used to factor the ruleset according to the kind of goal statement that they exhibit in their first conditions. Thus, in the sample program, there are rules for getting started (begin), rules for adding bricks (holding, pick-up and stop), and rules for placing bricks (put-down).

(external wm) declares the function wm to be an external function which OPS5 is going to call from LISP. wm is, in fact, a LISP function provided by the OPS system for exhibiting the contents of the working memory. Had wm been a user-defined LISP function, the declaration would have been the same.

The literalize statements declare data structures that will be implemented as LISP vectors. The first declares that a goal has two attributes: a task and an index. The task is just an identifier, like add for 'add a brick to the row' or put-down for 'place a brick in the row'. The index attribute stores a number representing the position in the row that the program is trying to fill at any one time. Thus the attributes are rather like fields in a record, except that they are not strongly typed, as they are in PASCAL, say. In other words, you can have any kind of symbol you like as a value for any attribute. Most programming languages do not allow you to do this, and require that you say in advance what kind of entity the value will be – real number, a character string or a user-defined data type, for example.

Then there are the production rules themselves. As noted in Chapter 8, each rule is of the general form

(p <identifier> <condition>* → <action>*)

where angle brackets denote place-holders for particular identifiers, conditions, and so on and the asterisks indicate that there can be one or more occurrences of conditions and actions.

Finally, there is a little bit of LISP to get things going. Most LISP functions have the general form

(defun <identifier> <argument list> <s-expression>*)

where an S-expression is a list structure in which the first element is usually a function name and the other elements are the arguments supplied for that function call. (See Chapter 7 and Appendix A for more about LISP.)

The LISP code in the above program is trivial and need not daunt the non-LISP user. rerun is a function of no arguments – it needs no input data because it always does the same thing. Let us go through the S-expressions in the function body one at a time.

- (remove *) clears working memory for the current run of the program,

- (make start) adds the token (start) to working memory so that the begin rule can fire,
- (run) simply runs the program.

B.2 The meaning of the rules

Condition elements in the left-hand side of OPS5 rules are templates to be matched against working memory elements (WMEs). The matching conventions in OPS5 are very flexible; thus, a template like (goal ^task add) will match a WME like (goal ^task add ^index 1), since the data in the WME satisfies the pattern of the template, even if the 'index' attribute and its value are left over. However, if pattern and data are swapped over, so that (goal ^task add ^index 1) is a condition and (goal ^task add) is the data, the condition is not satisfied, because there is insufficient data.

Condition elements in more complex programs will typically contain variables, as in the 'put-down' rule. <name> and <rank> are both variables, as denoted by the use of angle brackets. The first condition will match WMEs like (goal ^task put-down ^index 1), while the second will match WMEs like (brick ^name A ^place hand). One can place restrictions on the value assigned to such a variable by using curly brackets, as in the pick-up rule. The restriction placed on the value of the size attribute in the third condition is that it should be larger than the binding for <size> achieved in the matching of the second condition. For example, if the second condition is matched by the WME

(brick ^name B ^size 20 ^place heap)

then only bricks with size greater than 20 can match the third condition.

The third condition of pick-up is further complicated by the fact that it is a negated condition. A condition of the form -C is only satisfied if there is no WME that matches the template specified by C. Thus, the net effect of the conditions of pick-up are to select the biggest brick from the heap.

Action elements are executed to alter working memory, perform incidental computations, or do input/output. The three main actions for altering WM are make, remove and modify. make and remove add and delete WMEs respectively. The result of an action such as

(make brick ^name A ^size 10 ^place heap)

in the begin rule is to add the vector

(brick ^name A ^size 10 ^place heap)

to WM. Thus the head of the list is the command to be carried out, while the tail of the list specifies the contents of the new vector.

remove, on the other hand, is usually given a number as its argument, as in the 'begin' rule. (remove n) means 'remove from working memory the element which matched with the *n*th condition in the current rule'. This obviously saves typing, and allows the system to sort out which condition to delete. However, this convention can be a source of bugs. If you add conditions to a rule at some later stage, and forget to change the number in the remove statement, the wrong WME may subsequently get deleted! The net effect of a modify is the same as a combined make and remove. It is used to alter one or more fields in an existing WME. The general form of modify is

$$(\text{modify } n\ \hat{}\,attr_1\ value_1\ ...\ \hat{}\,attr_m\ value_m)$$

where *n* references the WME that matched the *n*th condition in the current rule, as with remove, and the rest of the list specifies some number of attribute-value pairs. When the modify is executed, the new values are assigned to the attributes, and working memory is adjusted accordingly.

The easiest way to see how it works is to look at the put-down rule, which has two modify statements in its right-hand side.

```
(p put-down
    (goal ^task put-down ^index <rank>)
    (brick ^place hand)
    →
    (modify 2 ^place <rank>)
    (modify 1 ^task add ^index (compute <rank> + 1)))
```

The first modify action changes the place attribute of the vector representing the brick in hand to the current rank in the row, while the second changes the goal task from put-down to add and updates the rank by adding 1 to the index attribute of the current goal vector.

For example, suppose that WM contains the elements

```
(goal ^task put-down ^index 1)
(brick ^name C ^size 30 ^place hand).
```

This will satisfy the left-hand side of the put-down rule, with the variable binding {<rank>/2}. After the right-hand side of the rule has been executed, WM will have changed to

```
(goal ^task add ^index 2)
(brick ^name C ^size 30 ^place 1).
```

The second modify action also exemplifies the use of compute to perform incidental computations in the right-hand side of rules. For an example of an input/output action, the reader is referred to the second action in the stop rule. Just before the program halts, we use call to invoke the system function wm and print out the contents of working memory.

B.3   Synopsis of the program

The program only knows about two kinds of entity, one abstract and one concrete. Firstly, there are goals, which have mnemonic task names like 'add' and 'put-down', and which focus upon particular positions in the row the program is trying to build. Secondly, there are bricks, which have arbitrary distinguishing names, as well as size and place attributes. The value of the size attribute remains constant throughout the program run, but the value for the place attribute changes as the brick is notionally moved about. These are both declared and represented in exactly the same way, as are all attributes. In other words, no distinction is made between abstract or concrete objects, or between attributes whose values are fixed and those that can be altered by program behaviour. Such distinctions exist solely in the mind of the programmer (if they exist at all).

The LISP function rerun is needed to get things started, by clearing WM in case it contains elements from a previous run, entering the start token (start), which doesn't need to be literalized as it is not a vector, and then calling OPS5 with (run).

The make statement in rerun enables the begin rule to fire. The first three actions of begin create three WMEs representing three blocks of different sizes, each of which is located in a place called heap. The remove action deletes (start) from working memory, while the make action initializes the goal statement with the task add and the index 1. WM is now

```
(goal ^task add)
(brick ^name B ^size 20 ^place heap)
(brick ^name C ^size 30 ^place heap)
(brick ^name A ^size 10 ^place heap).
```

This state of working memory enables the pick-up rule to fire with variable binding {<size>/C}. C is the only binding for <size> such that there is no other larger brick on the heap. The modify action 'moves' block C from the heap to the hand. WM is now

```
(goal ^task add)
(brick ^name B ^size 20 ^place heap)
(brick ^name C ^size 30 ^place hand)
(brick ^name A ^size 10 ^place heap).
```

In the first two cycles only one rule was able to fire – the cardinality of the conflict set was one in each case. At the third cycle, both pick-up and holding are able to fire. In other words, the program doesn't realize that it cannot pick up another brick with its notional hand full – after all, there is no reason why it should. The program only possesses as much knowledge as I have given it, and I omitted to encode this fact in any form.

As it happens, conflict resolution will do the right thing. Because the MODIFY action has made

```
(brick ^name ^size 30 ^place hand)
```

the most recent WME, rules which match against it are preferred. Thus holding is preferred to another firing of pick-up. Needless to say, there is something rather serendipitous about this.

Note that refractoriness would not inhibit pick-up because it would be firing on new data. Note also that although pick-up is more specific, in that it has more condition elements than holding, holding still wins because recency criteria are applied before specificity criteria.

As you can see, making such calculations is not exactly trivial, especially with large rule sets. In general, it is best to keep the conflict set small by making the conditions more detailed. Thus, an additional negative condition could be added to pick-up along the lines of

```
- (brick ^place hand)
```

to check that there is no brick currently in hand. Ideally, one ought to be able to add this condition anywhere in the left-hand side of the rule, since it does not depend on variable bindings in any other condition, and creates no variable bindings of its own – such is not the case. If you make it the first condition, OPS5 will complain bitterly, because the first condition in any rule must be a positive one. If you make it the second condition, you had better remember to change the modify in the right-hand side, because the resulting bug may not be instantly obvious when you run the program again. Anywhere else is acceptable, although last would be best. (If you insert this test between the two tests concerning the relative sizes of bricks, it will make the rule harder to read.)

A better solution is probably to scrap the holding rule, and modify pick-up as follows:

```
(p pick-up
  (goal ^task add)
  (brick ^size <size> ^place heap)
  -(brick ^size { > <size> } ^place heap)
  →
  (modify 2 ^place hand)
  (modify 1 ^task put-down))
```

As things stand, the holding rule will fire, changing the task to put-down. This will cause the put-down rule to fire next, not because of the fortuitous agreement in name between the task and the rule, but because WM will satisfy the rule's conditions, and no other rule has put-down as a goal. Putting goal statements first capitalizes on the mea strategy, as described above.

The actions of put-down change the position of the brick from hand to the current row index, reset the task to holding and update the row index. This cycle of pick-up, holding and put-down continues in an entirely predictable way until there are no bricks left on the heap or in the hand. At this point, the stop rule succeeds, removes the now redundant goal statement, prints out the contents of working memory, and then halts. WM is now

```
(brick ^name C ^size 30 ^place 1)
(brick ^name B ^size 20 ^place 2)
(brick ^name A ^size 10 ^place 3)
```

which is the solution to our humble problem.

B.4 The pros and cons of OPS5

Brownston *et al.* (1985, Chapter 1) give a good summary of the potential advantages and disadvantages of using a production system as a model of computation. Advantages cited include expressiveness, simplicity, modularity and modifiability. Let us look at each of these a little more closely from the knowledge representation point of view.

In the seriation program, we noted that there is nothing in the syntax which helps the programmer make and maintain certain semantic distinctions, such as that between 'essential' properties of an object, that cannot change during a program run, and 'accidental' properties that can and will change. Making such distinctions explicit can help program design, debugging and modification, especially in large systems that will be worked on by many people. On the other hand, there will be some overhead in terms of declarations and restrictions which have to be specified.

The last point is relevant to the issue of simplicity. Whatever the shortcomings of OPS5 may be, it is certainly an easy language to learn, and program texts often have a pleasing economy about them. However, we saw that the conflict resolution strategy needs to be considered when writing the rules, and this detracts from the simplicity of program behaviour. There seems to be a trade-off between knowledge-based programs which are easy and quick to write, and those which are easy to understand and debug. In other words, would you rather spend your time typing in extra declarations (some of which might affect the flow of control), or puzzling over the behaviour of the interpreter at run time?

From time to time, I have written fair sized PASCAL programs that have compiled at the first or second attempt and subsequently run without trouble. I have never written an OPS5 program of more than a couple of pages which has run first or even second time. This suggests that the interactive and unrestricted nature of OPS discourages me from sitting down with a pencil and paper, and so I don't plan OPS programs so carefully, while the restrictive and batch-mode nature of Pascal encourages me to take pains over the code I write.

The speed with which one can get OPS code running is therefore a two-edged sword. On the one hand, it facilitates fast prototyping and experimental programming of all kinds. On the other hand, if you want to build a serious program that will be both reliable and easy to extend, you will need to take just as much care as with any other language.

Another point about simplicity is that some conventional constructs, such as bounded loops and recursion are tricky to handle in production systems. The 'pick-up, holding, put-down' loop, in the seriation program is not too hard to follow, but both tighter and looser loops could be hard to engineer and understand. Brownston *et al.* (*op cit*, Chapter 5) show both recursive and iterative programs for computing factorials in OPS5; I find the iterative program the easier to understand, but consider both of them more difficult than more conventional definitions. OPS is simply not designed to deal with nested structures of any kind, either control structures or data structures. The two usually go together, as in LISP, where function application is guided by the recursive structure of data.

A comparison of production systems with other knowledge representation formalisms is attempted at the end of Chapter 12, when other schemes have been considered. For the moment, one can make the following observations about the strengths and weaknesses of rule-based programming.

Firstly, such methodology as presently surrounds rule-based programming has been slow to evolve. There is a good deal more to writing an effective rule-based program than formulating a set of rules which capture the generalizations used by an expert and encoding them in a production rule language. Even in the case where the rules do make true categorical statements about the domain, there is no guarantee that your program will perform in the way that you expect. Unless the rules have been carefully written with the conflict resolution strategy used by the interpreter kept constantly in mind, the first run of your program will almost certainly contain some surprises. It is usually difficult to predict the outcome of competition between the pattern-directed modules for the attention of the interpreter at each recognize-act cycle. As mentioned earlier, this is often a critical consideration when one is adding new rules to the system.

A second criticism that can be levelled at production systems is the fact that representing knowledge as an unordered and unstructured set of rules has certain disadvantages which, taken together, probably outweigh the often stated advantage that one can easily add another rule to the set and let the conflict resolution sort out when it should fire. This convention imposes no discipline whatever upon the programmer, in terms of encouraging him to differentiate between rules or set of rules that perform different functions or address different aspects of the problem. It also fails to take advantage of whatever explicit structure the domain possesses in terms of taxonomic, part-whole or cause-effect relations that hold between objects and between classes of objects.

Finally, although production rules seem well suited to encoding empirical associations between situations and actions of the general form 'if these conditions hold, then do this', they appear to be less effective as a means of expressing more subtle forms of knowledge which can be used to reason about the fundamental nature and causes of interesting phenomena. For example, in the management of chronic illnesses, such as pulmonary dysfunction, the history of the patient is extremely important if the development of the disease is to be understood and an accurate prognosis arrived at.

Production rules in the service of knowledge-based programming can often suffer from the short-sightedness that afflicts evaluation functions in the service of heuristic search. Decisions are made using only a limited amount of local information, with the basic control regime of the interpreter supplying the only global guidelines. In Chapter 17, we examined a rule-based expert system which has been designed with control problems in mind.

Notwithstanding these criticisms, there is little doubt that rule-based programming will remain popular as an implementation vehicle for expert systems for some years to come. The main reasons for this include the fact that many experts find it relatively easy to express their knowledge in this way, and many programmers find it relatively easy to encode in this form. Some of the vices of rule-based programming can be ameliorated by combining rules with other representational devices, as we see in Chapters 16, 19 and 20.

References

Adams, J. B. 1976). A probability model of medical reasoning and the MYCIN model. *Mathematical Biosciences*, **32**, 177–86. See also Buchanan and Shortliffe (1984), Chapter 12

Aiello, N. (1983). A comparative study of control strategies for expert systems: AGE implementation of three variations of PUFF. *Proceedings of the National Conference on Artificial Intelligence*, pp. 1–4

Aiello, N. (1986). *User-Directed Control of Parallelism: The CAGE System*. Technical Report No. KSL-86-31, Knowledge Systems Laboratory, Stanford University

Aikins, J. S. (1983). Prototypical knowledge for expert systems. *Artificial Intelligence*, **20**, 163–210

Aikins, J. S., Kunz, J. C., Shortliffe, E. H. and Fallat, R. J. (1984). PUFF: an expert system for interpretation of pulmonary function data. In Clancey and Shortliffe (1984), Chapter 19

Alexander, J. H., Freilling, M. J., Shulman, S. J., Staley, J. L., Rehfuss, S. and Messick, S. L. (1986). Knowledge level engineering: ontological analysis. *Proceedings of the National Conference on Artificial Intelligence*, pp. 963–8

Allen, J. (1987). *Natural Language Understanding*. Menlo Park CA: Benjamin/Cummings

Alvey, P. (1983). Problems of designing a medical expert system. In *Proceedings of Expert Systems*, **83**, 20–42

Amarel, S. (1968). *On representations of problems of reasoning about actions*. In Michie (1968), pp. 131–71

Anderson, J. R. (1976). *Language, Memory and Thought*. Hillsdale NJ: Lawrence Erlbaum

Andrews, P. B. (1986). *An Introduction to Mathematical Logic and Type Theory: To Truth through Proof*. Orlando FL: Academic Press

Bachant, J. (1988). RIME: preliminary work towards a knowledge acquisition tool. In Marcus (1988a), Chapter 7

Bachant, J. and McDermott, J. (1984). R1 revisited: four years in the trenches. *AI Magazine*, Fall issue, 21–32

Barr, A. and Feigenbaum, E. A., eds. (1981). *The Handbook of Artificial Intelligence* Vol 1. Los Altos CA: Morgan Kaufmann

Barr, A. and Feigenbaum, E. A., eds. (1982). *The Handbook of Artificial Intelligence* Vol 2. Los Altos CA: Morgan Kaufmann

Baumgart, B. (1972). *MICRO-PLANNER Alternative Reference Manual*. Operating Note No. 67, Stanford University

Bennett, J. S., Creary, L., Englemore, R. and Melosh, R. (1978). *SACON: A Knowledge-Based Consultant for Structural Analysis*. Report No. HPP-78-23, Computer Science Department, Stanford University

Bobrow, D. G. and Collins, A., eds. (1975). *Representation and Understanding*. New York: Academic Press

Bobrow, D. G. and Stefik, M. (1983). *The LOOPS manual*. Xerox Corporation

Bobrow, D. G. and Winograd, T. (1977). An overview of KRL, a knowledge representation language. *Cognitive Science*, **1**(1)

Bobrow, D. G. and Winograd, T. (1979). KRL: another perspective. *Cognitive Science*, **3**(1)

Boden, M. (1977). *Artificial Intelligence and Natural Man*. New York: Basic Books

Boose, J. H. (1986). *Expertise Transfer for Expert System Design*. New York: Elsevier

Boose, J. H. and Bradshaw, J. M. (1987). Expertise transfer and complex problems: using AQUINAS as a knowledge-acquisition workbench for knowledge-based systems. *International Journal of Man–Machine Studies*, **26**, 1–28

Boose, J. H. and Gaines, B. (1988). *Knowledge Acquisition Tools for Expert Systems*. New York: Academic Press

Brachman, R. J. (1986). 'I lied about the trees'. *AI Magazine*, **6**(3)

Brachman, R. J. and Levesque, H. J. (1985). *Readings in Knowledge Representation*. Los Altos CA: Morgan Kaufmann

Brachman, R. J. and Schmolze, J. G. (1985). An overview of the KL-ONE knowledge representation system. *Cognitive Science*, **9**, 171–216

Bratko, I. (1986). *PROLOG Programming for Artificial Intelligence*. Wokingham UK: Addison-Wesley

Bromley, H. (1986). *LISP Lore: A Guide to Programming the LISP Machine*. Boston MA: Kluwer Academic

Brown, D. C. and Chandrasekaran, B. (1989). *Design Problem Solving: Knowledge Structures and Control Strategies*. Los Altos CA: Morgan Kaufmann

Brown, J. S., Burton, R. R. and De Kleer, J. (1982). Pedagogical, natural language and knowledge engineering techniques in SOPHIE I, II and III. In Sleeman and Brown, Chapter 11

Brownston, L., Farrell, R., Kant, E. and Martin, N. (1985). *Programming Expert Systems in OPS5*. Reading MA: Addision-Wesley

Buchanan, B. G. and Feigenbaum, E. A. (1978). DENDRAL and META-DENDRAL: their applications dimension. *Artificial Intelligence*, **11**, 5–24

Buchanan, B. G. and Shortliffe, E. H., eds. (1984). *Rule-Based Expert Systems*. Reading MA: Addison-Wesley

Buchanan, B. G., Barstow, D., Bechtel, R., Bennet, J., Clancey, W., Kulikowski, C., Mitchell, T. M. and Waterman, D. A. (1983). Constructing an expert system. In Hayes-Roth *et al.* (1983), Chapter 5

Bundy, A. (1978). Will it reach the top? Prediction in the mechanics world. *Artificial Intelligence*, **10** 129–46

Bundy, A. and Clutterbuck, R. (1985). Raising the standards of AI products. *Proceedings of the 9th International Joint Conference on Artificial Intelligence*, pp. 1289–94

Bundy, A., Byrd, L., Luger, G., Mellish, C. and Palmer, M. (1979). Solving mechanics problems using metalevel inference. In Michie (1979), pp. 50–64

Bundy, A., Silver, B. and Plummer, D. (1985). An analytical comparison of some rule-learning programs. *Artificial Intelligence*, **27**, 137–81

Campbell, J. A. ed. (1984). *Implementations of PROLOG*. Chichester, UK: Ellis Horwood

Cannon, H. I. (1982). FLAVORS: a non-hierarchical approach to object-oriented programming. Unpublished paper

Carbonell, J. G., Michalski, R. and Mitchell, T. (1983). An overview of machine learning. In Michalski *et al.* (1983), Chapter 1

Carnegie Group (1985). *Knowledge Craft 3.0 Reference Manual*. Pittsburgh PA: Carnegie Group

Chandrasekaran, B. (1983a). Towards a taxonomy of problem solving types. *AI Magazine*, Winter/Spring, 9–17

Chandrasekaran, B. (1983b). Expert systems: matching techniques to tasks. In Reitman (1983)

Chandrasekaran, B. (1986). Generic tasks in knowledge-based reasoning: high-level building blocks for expert systems design. *IEEE Expert*, **1**(3), 23–30

Chandrasekaran, B. (1988). Generic tasks as building blocks for knowledge-based systems: the diagnosis and routine design examples. *Knowledge Engineering Review*, **3**(3), 183–210

Chandrasekaran, B. and Mittal, S. (1984). Deep *versus* compiled knowledge approaches to diagnostic problem solving. In Coombs (1984), Chapter 2

Charniak, E. and McDermott, D. (1985). *Introduction to artificial intelligence*. Reading MA: Addison-Wesley

Charniak, E., Reisbeck, C. and McDermott, D. (1980). *Artificial Intelligence Programming*. Hillsdale NJ: Lawrence Erlbaum

Cheeseman, P. (1985). In defense of probability. *Proceedings of the 8th International Joint Conference on Artificial Intelligence*, pp. 1002–9

Cheeseman, P. (1986). Probabilistic *vs.* fuzzy reasoning. In Kanal and Lemmer (1986), pp. 85–102

Church, A. (1941). *The Calculi of Lambda-Conversion*. Annals of Mathematics Studies, Princeton University Press

Clancey, W. J. (1983). The epistemology of a rule-based expert system: a framework for explanation. *Artificial Intelligence*, **20**, 215–51

Clancey, W. J. (1985). Heuristic classification. *Artificial Intelligence*, **27**, 289–350

Clancey, W. J. (1987a). *Knowledge-Based Tutoring: The GUIDON Program*. Cambridge MA: MIT Press

Clancey, W. J. (1987b). *Intelligent Tutoring Systems: A Tutorial Survey*. In van Lamsweerde and Dufour (1987), Chapter 3

Clancey, W. J. (1987c). From GUIDON to NEOMYCIN and HERACLES in twenty short lessons. In van Lamsweerde and Dufour (1987), Chapter 4

Clancey, W. J. and Letsinger, R. (1984). NEOMYCIN: reconfiguring a rule-based expert system for application to teaching. In Clancey and Shortliffe (1984), Chapter 15

Clancey, W. J. and Shortliffe, E. H. eds. (1984). *Readings in Medical Artificial Intelligence*. Reading MA: Addison-Wesley

Clark, K. L. and Tarnlund, S.-A., eds. (1982). *Logic Programming*. London: Academic Press

Clarke, K. L. and McCabe, F. (1982). PROLOG: a language for implementing expert systems. In Hayes *et al.* (1982)

Cohen, P. and Feigenbaum, E. A., eds. (1982). *The Handbook of Artificial Intelligence*, vol 3. Los Altos CA: Morgan Kaufmann

Collins, A. M. and Quillian, M. R. (1969). Retrieval time from semantic memory. *Journal of Verbal Learning and Verbal Behavior*, **8**, 240–7

Coombs, M. J., ed. (1984). *Developments in Expert Systems*. London: Academic Press

Coyne, R. (1988). *Logic Models of Design*. London: Pitman

Cox, R. (1946). Probability frequency and reasonable expectation. *American Journal of Physics*, **14**(1), 1–13

Davis, R. (1980a). Meta-rules: reasoning about control. *Artificial Intelligence*, **15**, 179–222

Davis, R. (1980b). Applications of meta-level knowledge to the construction, maintenance and use of large knowledge bases. In Davis and Lenat (1980), pp. 229–490

Davis, R. (1982). Expert systems: Where are we? And where do we go from here? *AI Magazine*, **3**(2)

Davis, R. (1984). Diagnostic reasoning based on structure and behavior. *Artificial Intelligence*, **24**, 347–410

Davis, R. (1989). Expert systems: how far can they go? Part 2. *AI Magazine*, **10**(2)

Davis, R. and King, J. (1977). An overview of production systems. In Elcock and Michie (1977), pp. 300–32

Davis, R. and Lenat, D. (1980). *Knowledge-Based Systems in Artificial Intelligence*. New York: McGraw-Hill

De Kleer, J. (1986). An assumption-based TMS. *Artificial Intelligence*, **28**, 127–62

De Kleer, J. and Williams, B. C. (1987). Diagnosing multiple faults. *Artificial Intelligence*, **32**, 97–130

Dietterich, T. G. and Mickalski, R. (1983). A comparative review of selected methods for learning from examples. In Michalski *et al.* (1983), Chapter 3

Doyle, J. (1979). A truth maintenance system. *Artificial Intelligence*, **12**, 231–72

Drummond, M., Macintosh, A. and Tate, A. (1987). A framework for technology transfer within AIAI. *Knowledge Engineering Review*, **2**(3), 159–68

Elcock, E. W. and Michie, D., eds. (1977). *Machine Intelligence 8*. New York: John Wiley.

Englemore, R. and Morgan, T., eds. (1988). *Blackboard Systems*. Reading MA: Addison-Wesley

Erman, L., Hayes-Roth, F., Lesser, V. and Reddy, D. (1980). The HEARSAY-II speech understanding system: integrating knowledge to resolve uncertainty. *Computing Surveys*, **12**(2), 213–53

Erman, L. D., London, P. E. and Fickas, S. F. (1983). The design and an example use of HEARSAY-III. *Proceedings of the National Conference on Artificial Intelligence*, pp. 409–15

Erman, L. D., Lark, J. S. and Hayes-Roth, F. (1986). Engineering intelligent systems: progress report on ABE. *Proceedings of Expert Systems Workshop*, Defense Advanced Research Projects Agency

Eshelman, L. (1988). A knowledge acquisition tool for cover-and-differentiate systems. In Marcus (1988a). Chapter 3

Eshelman, L. and McDermott, J. (1986). MOLE: a knowledge acquisition tool that uses its head. *Proceedings of the National Conference on Artificial Intelligence*, pp. 950–5

Eshelman, L., Ehret, D., McDermott, J. and Tan, M. (1987). MOLE: a tenacious knowledge acquisition tool. *International Journal of Man–Machine Studies*, **26**, 41–54

Feigenbaum, E. A. (1977). The art of artificial intelligence: themes and case studies of knowledge engineering. *Proceedings of the 5th International Joint Conference on Artificial Intelligence*, pp. 1014–29

Feigenbaum, E. A. and Feldman, J., eds. (1963). *Computers and Thought*. New York: McGraw-Hill

Feigenbaum, E. A. and McCorduck, P. (1983). *The Fifth Generation*. Reading MA: Addison-Wesley

Feigenbaum, E. A., McCorduck, P. and Nii, H. P. (1988). *The Rise of the Expert Company*. Times Books

Fikes, R. E. and Nilsson, N. J. (1971). STRIPS: a new approach to the application of theorem proving to problem solving. *Artificial Intelligence*, **2**, 189–208

Findler, N. V., ed. (1979). *Associative Networks*. New York: Academic Press

Forgy, C. L. (1982). Rete: a fast algorithm for the many pattern/many object pattern match problem. *Artificial Intelligence*, **19**, 17–37

Gale, W. A. (1986). *Artificial Intelligence and Statistics*. Reading MA: Addison-Wesley

Gale, W. A. (1987). Knowledge-based knowledge acquisition for a statistical consulting system. *International Journal of Man–Machine Studies*, **26**, 54–64

Genesereth, M. W. (1983). An overview of meta-level architecture. *Proceedings of the National Conference on Artificial Intelligence*, 119–23. Los Altos CA: Morgan Kaufmann

Genesereth, M. R. (1984). The use of design descriptions in automated diagnosis. *Artificial Intelligence*, **24**, 411–36

Genesereth, M. R. and Nilsson, N. J. (1987). *Logical foundations of artificial intelligence*. Los Altos CA: Morgan Kaufmann

Ginsberg, M. (1986). Counterfactuals. *Artificial Intelligence*, **30**, 35–30

Ginsberg, M. ed. (1987). *Readings in nonmonotonic reasoning*. Los Altos CA: Morgan Kaufmann

Glaser, H., Hankin, C. and Till, D. (1984). *Functional Programming*. Englewood Cliffs NJ: Prentice-Hall

Goedel, K. (1931). On formally undecidable propositions of *Principia Mathematica* and related systems I. In Van Heijenoort (1967), pp. 1879–931

Goldberg, A. and Robson, D. (1983). *Smalltalk-80: The Language and its Implementation*. Reading MA: Addison-Wesley

Goldman, N. (1978). AP3 *User's Guide*. Information Sciences Institute, University of Southern California

Gordon, J. and Shortliffe, E. H. (1985). A method of managing evidential reasoning in a hierarchical hypothesis space. *Artificial Intelligence*, **26**, 323–57

Green, C. C. (1969). The application of theorem-proving to question-answering systems. *Proceedings of the International Joint Conference on Artificial Intelligence*, pp. 219–37

Hasling, D. W., Clancey, W. J. and Rennels, G. (1984). Strategic explanations for a diagnostic consulting system. *International Journal of Man–Machine Studies*, **20**(1), 3–19

Haugeland, J. ed. (1981). *Mind Design*. Montgomery, VT: Bradford Books

Hayes, J. E. and Michie, D. eds. (1984). *Intelligent Systems – The Unprecedented Opportunity*. Chichester, UK: Ellis Horwood

Hayes, J. E., Michie, D. and Pao Y. H., eds. (1982). *Machine Intelligence 10*. Chichester UK: Ellis Horwood

Hayes, P. J. (1978). The logic of frames. In Metzing (1978), pp. 46–61

Hayes-Roth, B. (1985). Blackboard architecture for control. *Artificial Intelligence*, **26**, 251–321

Hayes-Roth, F., Waterman, D. A. and Lenat, D. (1983). *Building Expert Ssytems*. Reading MA: Addison-Wesley

Hayes-Roth, B., Buchanan, B., Lichtarge, O., Hewett, M., Altman, R., Brinkley, J., Cornelius, C., Duncan, B. and Jardetzky, O. (1986). PROTEAN: deriving protein structure from constraints. *Proceedings of the National Conference on Artificial Intelligence*, pp. 904–9

Hayes-Roth, B., Garvey, A., Johnson, M. V. and Hewett, H. (1987). *A Modular and Layered Environment for Reasoning About Action*. Technical Report No. KSL 86-38, Knowledge Systems Laboratory, Stanford University

Hayes-Roth, B., Johnson, M. V., Garvey, A. and Hewett, H. (1988). Building systems in the BB* environment. In Englemore and Morgan (1988), Chapter 29

Heckerman, D. (1986). Probabilistic interpretation for MYCIN's certainty factors. In Kanal and Lemmer (1986), pp. 167–96

Henderson, P. (1980). *Functional Programming: Application and Implementation*. Englewood Cliffs NJ: Prentice-Hall

Hendrix, G. G. (1979). Encoding knowledge in partitioned networks. In Findler (1979), pp. 51–92

Hewitt, C. (1972). *Description and Theoretical Analysis (Using Schemata) of PLANNER, a Language for Proving Theorems and Manipulating Models in a Robot*. Report No. TR-258, AI Laboratory, Massachusetts Institute of Technology

Hopcroft, J. E. and Ullman, J. D. (1979). *Introduction to Automata Theory, Languages and Computation*. Reading MA: Addison-Wesley

Horty, J. F., Thomason, R. H. and Touretzky, D. S. (1987). A skeptical theory of inheritance in nonmonotonic semantic nets. *Proceedings of the National Conference on Artificial Intelligence*, pp. 358–63

Horvitz, E. and Heckerman, D. (1986). The inconsistent use of measures of certainty in artificial intelligence research. In Kanal and Lemmer (1986) pp. 137–51

Horvitz, E., Heckerman, D. and Langlotz, C. P. (1986). A framework for comparing formalisms for plausible reasoning. *Proceedings of the National Conference on Artificial Intelligence*, pp. 210–14

Hunt, E. B., Marin, J. and Stone, P. T. (1966). *Experiments in Induction*. New York: Academic Press

Intellicorp (1984). *The Knowledge Engineering Environment*. Mountain View CA: Intellicorp

Jackson, P. (1986). *Introduction to expert systems* 1st edn. Wokingham UK: Addison-Wesley

Jackson, P. (1989). Applications of nonmonotonic logic to diagnosis. *Knowledge Engineering Review*, **4**(2)

Jackson, P. and Lefrere, P. (1984). On the application of rule-based techniques to the design of advice giving systems. *International Journal of Man–Machine Studies*, **20**, 63–86

Jackson, P., Reichgelt, H. and van Harmelen, F. eds. (1989). *Logic-Based Knowledge Representation*. Cambridge MA: MIT Press

Jagannathan, V., Dodhiawala, R. and Baum, L. S. eds. (1989). *Blackboard Architectures and Applications*. New York: Academic Press

Johnson, M. V. and Hayes-Roth, B. (1986). *Integrating Diverse Reasoning Methods in the BB1 Blackboard Control Architecture*. Technical Report No. KSL 86-76. Knowledge Systems Laboratory, Stanford University

Kahn, G. (1988). MORE: from observing knowledge engineers to automating knowledge acquisition. In Marcus (1988a), Chapter 2

Kahn, G. and McDermott, J. (1984). The MUD system. *Proceedings of the 1st IEEE Conference on Artificial Intelligence Applications*

Kahn, G., Nowlan, S. and McDermott, J. (1985). MORE: an intelligent knowledge acquisition tool. *Proceedings of the 9th International Joint Conference on Artificial Intelligence*, pp. 581–4

Kahn, G., Kepner, A. and Pepper, J. (1987). TEST: a model-driven application shell. *Proceedings of the National Conference on Artificial Intelligence*, pp. 814–18

Kahneman, D. and Tversky, A. (1972). Subjective probability: a judgement of representativeness. *Cognitive Psychology*, **3**, 430–54

Kahneman, D., Slovic, P. and Tversky, A. eds. (1982). *Judgement under Uncertainty: Heuristics and Biases*. Cambridge: Cambridge University Press.

Kanal, L. N. and Lemmer, J. F. eds. (1986). *Uncertainty in Artificial Intelligence*. Amsterdam: North-Holland

Kanal, L. N., Levitt, T. S. and Lemmer, J. F. eds. (1989). *Uncertainty in Artificial Intelligence 3*. Amsterdam: North-Holland

Keene, S. E. (1989). *Object-Oriented Programming in COMMON LISP*. Reading MA: Addison-Wesley

Klahr, P. and Waterman, D. eds. (1986). *Expert Systems: Techniques, Tools and Applications*. Reading MA: Addison-Wesley

Klahr, P., McArthur, D. and Narain, S. (1982). SWIRL: an object-oriented air battle simulator. *Proceedings of the National Conference on Artificial Intelligence*, pp. 331–4

Kluzniak, F. and Szpakowicz, S. (1984). PROLOG – a panacea? In Campbell (1984), pp. 71–84

Kononenko, I., Bratko, I. and Riskar, E. (1984). *Experiments in Automatic Learning of Medical Diagnostic Rules*. Jozef Stefan Institute, Ljubljana, Yugoslavia

Kowalski, R. A. (1979). *Logic for Problem Solving*. Amsterdam: North-Holland

Kowalski, R. A. (1982). Logic as a computer language. In Clark and Tarnlund (1982) Chapter 1

Kunz, J. C., Fallat, R. J., McClung, D. H., Osborn, J. J., Votteri, R. A., Nii, H. P., Aikins, J. S., Fagan, L. M. and Feigenbaum, E. A. (1978). *A Physiological Rule-Based System for Interpreting Pulmonary Function Test Results*. Report No. HPP-78-19, Heuristic Programming Project, Computer Science Department, Stanford University

Kunz, J. C., Kehler, T. P. and Williams, M. D. (1984). Applications development using a hybrid AI development system. *AI Magazine*, **5**(3)

Lan, M. S., Panos, R. M. and Balban, M. S. (1987). Experience using S.1: an expert system for newspaper printing press configuration. *Knowledge Engineering Review*, **2**(4), 277–85

Langlotz, C. P., Shortliffe, E. H. and Fagan, L. M. (1986). Using decision theory to justify heuristics. *Proceedings of the National Conference on Artificial Intelligence*, pp. 215–19

Laurent, J. P., Ayel, J., Thome, F. and Ziebelin, D. (1986). Comparative evaluation of three expert system development tools: KEE, Knowledge Craft, ART. *Knowledge Engineering Review*, **1**(4), 19–29

Lehnert, W. and Wilks, Y. (1979). A critical perspective on KRL. *Cognitive Science*, **3**, 1–28

Lenat, D. B. (1982). The nature of heuristics. *Artificial Intelligence*, **19**, 189–249

Levesque, H. and Mylopoulos, J. (1979). A procedural semantics for semantic networks. In Findler (1979), pp. 93–120

Lindsay, R., Buchanan, B. G., Feigenbaum, E. A. and Lederberg, R. (1980). DENDRAL. New York: McGraw-Hill

Maes, P. and Nardi, D. (1988). *Meta-level Architectures and Reflection*. Amsterdam: North-Holland

Mamdani, E. H. and Gaines, B. R. (1981). *Fuzzy Reasoning and its Applications*. London: Academic Press

Marcus, S. ed. (1988a). *Automating Knowledge Acquisition for Expert Systems*. Boston: Kluwer Academic

Marcus, S. (1988b). A knowledge acquisition tool for propose-and-revise systems. In Marcus (1988a), Chapter 4

Marcus, S., Stout, J. and McDermott, J. (1988). VT: an expert elevator configurer that uses knowledge-based backtracking. *AI Magazine*, **9**(1), 95–112

McAllester, D. (1980). *An Outlook on Truth Maintenance*. Report No. AIM-551, Artificial Intelligence Laboratory, Massachusetts Institute of Technology

McArthur, D., Klahr, P. and Narain, S. (1986). ROSS: an object-oriented language for constructing simulations. In Klahr and Waterman (1986), Chapter 3

McCarthy, J. (1960). Recursive functions of symbolic expressions and their computation by machine. *Communications of the Association for Computing Machinery*, April, 184–95

McCarthy, J. and Hayes, P. (1969). Some philosophical problems from the standpoint of artificial intelligence. In Meltzer and Michie (1969), pp. 463–502

McCarthy, J., Abrahams, P. W., Edwards, D. J., Hart, T. P. and Levin, M. I. (1965). *LISP 1.5 Programmer's Manual* 2nd edn. Cambridge MA: MIT Press

McDermott, J. (1980). R1: an expert in the computer system domain. *Proceedings of the National Conference on Artificial Intelligence*, 269–71

McDermott, J. (1981). R1's formative years. *AI Magazine*, **2**(2)

McDermott, J. (1982a). R1: a rule-based configurer of computer systems. *Artificial Intelligence*, **19**, 39–88

McDermott, J. (1982b). XSEL: a computer sales person's assistant. In Hayes *et al.* (1982) pp. 325–37

McDermott, J. (1984). Building expert systems. In Reitman (1981)

McDermott, J. (1988). Preliminary steps towards a taxonomy of problem solving methods. In Marcus (1988a), Chapter 8

McDermott, J. and Forgy, C. L. (1978). Production system conflict resolution strategies. In Waterman and Hayes-Roth (1978), pp. 177–99

Meltzer, B. and Michie, D., eds. (1969). *Machine Intelligence 4*. Edinburgh: Edinburgh University Press

Metzing, D. ed. (1978). *Frame Conceptions and Text Understanding*. Berlin: Walter de Gruyter

Michalski, R. S. (1975). Variable-valued logic and its applications to pattern recognition and machine learning. In Rine (1975), pp. 506–34

Michalski, R. S. (1983) A theory and methodology of inductive learning. In Michalski *et al.* (1983), Chapter 4

Michalski, R. S. and Chilausky, R. L. (1981). Knowledge acquisition by encoding expert rules *versus* computer induction from examples: a case study involving soybean pathology. In Mamdani and Gaines (1981), pp. 247–71

Michalski, R. S. and Larson, J. B. (1978). *Selection of Most Representative Training Examples and Incremental Generation of VL1 Hypotheses: The Underlying Methodology and Description of Programs ESEL and AQ11*. Report No. 867, University of Illinois

Michalski, R. S., Carbonell, J. G. and Mitchell, T. M. eds. (1983). *Machine Learning*. Palo Alto CA: Tioga

Michalski, R. S., Carbonell, J. G. and Mitchell, T. M. eds. (1986). *Machine Learning Vol II*. Palto Alto CA: Tioga

Michie, D. ed. (1968). *Machine Intelligence 3*. Edinburgh: Edinburgh University Press

Michie, D. ed. (1979). *Expert Systems in the Micro Electronic Age*. Edinburgh: Edinburgh University Press

Minsky, M. ed. (1968). *Semantic Information Processing*. Cambridge MA: MIT Press

Minsky, M. (1972). *Computation: Finite and Infinite Machines*. London: Prentice-Hall

Minsky, M. (1975). A framework for representing knowledge. In Winston (1975b) pp. 211–77

Mitchell, T. (1978). *Version Spaces: An Approach to Concept Learning*. Report No. STAN-CS-78-711, Computer Science Department, Stanford University

Mitchell, T. (1982). Generalization as search. *Artificial Intelligence*, **18**, 203–26

Moon, D., Stallman, R. M. and Winreb, D. 19893). *LISP machine manual*. Artificial Intelligence Laboratory, Massachusetts Institute of Technology

Moore, R. C. (1975). *Reasoning from Incomplete Knowledge in a Procedural Deduction System*. Report No. TR-347, Artificial Intelligence Laboratory, Massachusetts Institute of Technology

Moser, M. G. (1983). *An Overview of NIKL, the New Implementation of KL-ONE*. Technical Report No. 5421, Cambridge MA: Bolt, Beranek and Newman

Musen, M. A., Fagan, L., Combs, D. M. and Shortliffe, E. H. (1987). Use of a domain model to drive an interactive knowledge-editing tool. *International Journal of Man–Machine Studies*, **26**, 105–21

Myers, C. D., Fox, J., Pegram, S. M. and Greaves, M. F. (1983). Knowledge acquisition for expert systems: experience using EMYCIN for leukaemia diagnosis. *Proceedings of Expert Systems*, **83**, 277–83

Neale, I. M. (1988). First generation expert systems: a review of knowledge acquisition methodologies. *Knowledge Engineering Review*, **3**(2), 105–45

Neches, R., Swartout, W. R. and Moore, J. (1985). Explainable (and maintainable) expert systems. *Proceedings of the 9th International Joint Conference on Artificial Intelligence*, pp. 382–9

Newell, A. (1981). Physical symbol systems. In Norman (1981), Chapter 4

Newell, A. (1982). The knowledge level. *Artificial Intellignece*, **18**, 87–127

Newell, A. and Simon, H. A. (1972). *Human Problem Solving*. Englewood Cliffs NJ: Prentice-Hall

Newell, A. and Simon, H. A. (1976). Computer science as empirical enquiry. *Communications of the Association for Computing Machinery*, **19**(3), 113–26

Nii, H. P. (1986a). Blackboard systems (Part 1). *AI Magazine*, **7**(2), 38–53

Nii, H. P. (1986b). Blackboard systems (Part 2). *AI Magazine*, **7**(3), 82–106

Nii, H. P. and Aiello, N. (1979). AGE (Attempt to GEneralize): a knowledge-based program for building knowledge-based programs. *Proceedings of the 6th International Joint Conference on Artificial Intelligence*, pp. 645–55

Nii, H. P., Aiello, N. and Rice, J. (1988). Frameworks for concurrent problem solving: a report on CAGE and POLIGON. In Englemore and Morgan (1988), Chapter 25

Nilsson, N. J. (1971). *Problem Solving Methods in Artificial Intelligence*. New York: McGraw-Hill

Nilsson, N. J. (1980). *Principles of Artificial Intelligence*. Palo Alto CA: Tioga

Norman, D. A. ed. (1981). *Perspectives on Cognitive Science*. Norwood NJ: Ablex

O'Rourke, P. (1982). *A Comparative Study of Two Inductive Learning Systems AQ11 and ID3 Using a Chess Endgame Test Problem*. Report No. 82-2, Department of Computer Science, University of Illinois

Paterson, A. and Niblett, T. (1982). *ACLS Manual, Version 1*. Glasgow UK: Intelligent Terminals

Pearl, J. (1982). Reverend Bayes on inference engines: a distributed hierarchical approach. *Proceedings of the National Conference on Artificial Intelligence*, pp. 133–6

Pearl, J. (1984). *Heuristics: Intelligent Search Strategies for Computer Problem-Solving*. Reading MA: Addison-Wesley

Pearl, J. (1986). On evidential reasoning in a hierarchy of hypotheses. *Artificial Intelligence*, **28**, 9–15

Pearl, J. (1988). *Probabilistic Reasoning for Intelligent Systems*. Los Altos CA: Morgan Kaufmann

Pepper, J. and Kahn, G. (1987). Repair strategies in a diagnostic expert system. *Proceedings of the 10th International Joint Conference on Artificial Intelligence*, pp. 531–4

Peterson, G. E. ed. (1987). *Object-oriented computing* Vols 1 and 2. Washington DC: The Computer Society Press of the IEEE

Polson, M. C. and Richardson, J. (1988). *Foundations of Intelligent Tutoring Systems*. Hillsdale NJ: Lawrence Erlbaum

Poole, D. (1988). Representing knowledge for logic-based diagnosis. In *Proceedings of the International Conference on Fifth Generation Computer Systems*, pp. 1282–90

Pople, H. E. Jr. (1977). The formation of composite hypotheses in diagnostic problem solving: an exercise in synthetic reasoning. *Proceedings of the 5th International Joint Conference on Artificial Intelligence*, pp. 1030–7

Pople, H. E. Jr. (1982). Heuristic methods for imposing structure on ill-structured problems: the structuring of medical diagnosis. In Szolovits (1982), pp. 119–90

Post, E. L. (1943). Formal reductions of the general combinatorial decision problem. *American Journal of Mathematics*, **65**, 197–268

Poundstone, W. (1988). *Labyrinths of Reason*. New York: Doubleday

Prerau, D. S. (1990). *Developing and Managing Expert Systems*. Reading MA: Addison-Wesley

Pylyshyn, Z. (1978). Computational models and empirical constraints. *Behavioral and Brain Sciences*, **1**, 93–9

Pylyshyn, Z. (1980). Computation and cognition: issues in the foundations of cognitive science. *Behavioral and Brain Sciences*, **3**, 111–32

Pylyshyn, Z. (1981). Complexity and the study of artificial and human intelligence. In Haugeland (1981), Chapter 2

Quillian, M. R. (1968). Semantic memory. In Minsky (1968), pp. 227–70

Quine, W. V. O. (1979). *Methods of Logic*. London: Routledge Kegan Paul

Quinlan, J. R. (1979). Discovering rules from large collections of examples: a case study. In Michie (1979), pp. 168–201

Quinlan, J. R. (1983). Learning efficient classification procedures and their application to chess endgames. In Michalski *et al.* (1983), Chapter 15

Quinlan, J. R. (1986a). Induction of decision trees. *Machine Learning*, **1**, 81–106

Quinlan, J. R. (1986b). The effect of noise on concept learning. In Michalski *et al.* (1986), Chapter 6

Quinlan, J. R. ed. (1987). *Applications of Expert Systems*. Sydney: Addison-Wesley

Raphael, B. (1976). *The Thinking Computer: Mind inside Matter*. San Francisco: W H Freeman

Rawlings, C. and Fox, J. (1983). The UNITS package – a critical appraisal of a frame-based knowledge representation system. *Proceedings of Expert Systems 83*, pp. 15–29

Reichenbach, H. (1949). *Theory of Probability*. Berkeley CA: University of California Press

Reichgelt, H. (1990). *Knowledge Representation: An AI Perspective*. Norwood NJ: Ablex

Reichgelt, H. and van Harmelen, F. (1986). Criteria for choosing representation languages and control regimes for expert systems. *Knowledge Engineering Review*, **1**(4), 2–17

Reiter, R. (1980). A logic for default reasoning. *Artificial Intelligence*, **31**, 81–132

Reiter, R. (1987). A theory of diagnosis from first principles. *Artificial Intelligence*, **32**, 57–95

Reitman, W. ed. (1984). *Artificial Intelligence for Applications for Business*. Norwood NJ: Ablex

Reynolds, D. (1988). MUSE: a toolkit for embedded, real-time, AI. In Englemore and Morgan (1988), Chapter 27

Rice, J. (1986). *POLIGON: A System for Parallel Problem Solving*. Technical Report No. KSL-86-19, Knowledge Systems Laboratory, Stanford University

Rice, J. (1989). The advanced architectures project. *AI Magazine*, **10**(4), 26–39

Rich, E. (1983). *Artificial Intelligence*. New York: McGraw-Hill

Richer, M. H. and Clancey, W. J. (1985). A graphic interface for viewing a knowledge based system. *IEEE Computer Graphics and Applications*, **5**(11), 51–64

Rine, D. C. ed. (1975). *Computer Science and Multiple-Valued Logic Theory and Applications*. Amsterdam: North-Holland

Robinson, J. A. (1965). A machine-oriented logic based on the resolution principle. *Journal of the Associaiton for Computing Machinery*, **12**, 23–41

Robinson, J. A. (1979). *Logic: Form and Function*. Edinburgh: Edinburgh University Press

Robinson, V., Hardy, N. W., Barnes, D. P., Pace, C. J. and Lee, M. H. (1987). Experiences with a knowledge engineering toolkit: an assessment in industrial robotics. *Knowledge Engineering Review*, **2**(1), 43–54

Rosenman, M. A., Coyne, R. D. and Gero, J. S. (1987). Expert systems for design applications. In Quinlan (1987), Chapter 4

Russell, S. (1985). *The Compleat Guide to MRS*. Report No. KSL-85-12, Knowledge Systems Laboratory, Stanford University

Sacerdoti, E. D. (1974). *A Structure for Plans and Behavior*. Amsterdam: Elsevier North-Holland

Sandewall, E. (1986). Nonmonotonic inference rules for multiple inheritance with exceptions. *Proceedings of the IEEE*, **74**, 81–132

Sanford, A. J. (1987). *The Mind of Man: Models of Human Understanding*. Brighton: Harvester Press

Schank, R. C. (1975). *Conceptual Information Processing*. Amsterdam: North-Holland

Schank, R. C. and Abelson, R. (1977). *Scripts, Plans, Goals and Understanding*. Hillsdale NJ: Lawrence Erlbaum

Schubert, L. K. (1976). Extending the expressive power of semantic networks. *Artificial Intelligence*, **7**, 163–98

Self, J. (1974). Student models in CAI. *International Journal of Man–Machine Studies*, **6**, 261–76

Selman, B. and Levesque, H. J. (1989). The tractability of path-based inheritance. *Proceedings of the 11th International Joint Conference on Artificial Intelligence*, pp. 1140–5

Shafer, G. (1976). *A Mathematical Theory of Evidence*. Princeton NJ: Princeton University Press

Shafer, G. and Tversky, A. (1985). Languages and designs for probability judgement. *Cognitive Science*, **9**, 309–39

Shannon, C. E. (1950). Automatic chess player. *Scientific American*, **182**(48)

Shepherdson, J. C. (1984). Negation as failure: a comparison of Clark's completed database and Reiter's closed world assumption. *Journal of Logic Programming*, **1**, 51–81

Shepherdson, J. C. (1985). Negation as failure II. *Journal of Logic Programming*, **3**, 185–202

Shortliffe, E. H. (1976). *Computer-Based Medical Consultations: MYCIN*. New York: Elsevier

Shortliffe, E. H., Scott, A. C., Bischoff, M. B., van Melle, W. and Jacobs, C. D. (1981). ONCOCIN: an expert system for oncology protocol management. *Proceedings of the 7th International Joint Conference on Artificial Intelligence*, pp. 876–81

Sime, M. E. and Coombs, M. J. eds. (1983). *Designing for Human Computer Communication*. London: Academic Press

Simon, H. A. (1976). *The Sciences of the Artificial*. Cambridge MA: MIT Press

Simon, H. A. (1983). Why should machines learn? In Michalski *et al.* (1983), Chapter 2

Singh, N. (1987). *An Artificial Intelligence Approach to Test Generation*. Norwell MA: Kluwer Academic

Sleeman, D. and Brown, J. S., eds. (1982). *Intelligent Tutoring Systems*. London: Academic Press

Smets, P., Mamdani, E. H., Dubois, D. and Prade, H. eds. (1988). *Non-standard Logics for Automated Reasoning*. London: Academic Press

Smith, R. G., Winston, H. A., Mitchell, T. and Buchanan, B. G. (1985). Representation and use of explicit justifications for knowledge base refinement. *Proceedings of the 9th International Joint Conference on Artificial Intelligence*, pp. 673–80

Stefik, M. (1979). An examination of a frame-structured representation system. *Proceedings of the 6th International Joint Conference on Artificial Intelligence*, pp. 845–52

Stefik, M. (1981a). Planning with constraints. *Artificial Intelligence*, **16**, 111–40

Stefik, M. (1981b). Planning and meta-planning. *Artificial Intelligence*, **16**, 141–69

Stefik, M. and Bobrow, D. G. (1986). Object-oriented programming: themes and variations. *AI Magazine*, **6**(4), 40–62

Stefik, M., Aikins, J., Balzer, R., Benoit, J, Birnbaum, L., Hayes-Roth, F. and Sacerdoti, E. (1983). The architecture of expert systems. In Hayes-Roth *et al.* (1983), Chapter 4

Suwa, W., Scott, A. C. and Shortliffe, E. H. (1982). An approach to verifying completeness and consistency in a rule-based expert system. *AI Magazine*, **3**(4), 16–21

Swartout, W. R. (1983). XPLAIN: a system for creating and explaining expert consulting programs. *Artificial Intelligence*, **21**, 285–325

Szolovits, P., ed. (1982). *Artificial Intelligence in Medicine*. Boulder CO: Westview Press

Tate, A. (1977). Generating project networks. *Proceedings of the 5th International Joint Conference on Artificial Intelligence*, pp. 888–93

Teknowledge (1985). *S.1 Reference Manual*. Palo Alto CA: Teknowledge

Tommelein, I. D., Johnson, M. V., Hayes-Roth, B. and Levitt, R. E. (1987). SIGHTPLAN – a blackboard expert system for the layout of temporary facilities on a construction site. *Proceedings of the IFIP WG5.2 Working Conference on Expert Systems in Computer-Aided Design*, Sydney, Australia

Touretzky, D. S. (1986). *The mathematics of inheritance systems*. London: Pitman

Touretzky, D. S., Horty, J. F. and Thomason, R. H. (1987). A clash of intuitions: the current state of nonmonotonic multiple inheritance systems. *Proceedings of the 10th International Joint Conference on Artificial Intelligence*, pp. 476–82

Turing, A. M. (1963). Computing machinery and intelligence. In Feigenbaum and Feldman (1963), pp. 11–35

van Harmelen, F. (1989). A classification of meta-level architectures. In Jackson *et al.* (1989), Chapter 2

van Heijenoort, J., ed. (1967). *From Frege to Goedel: A Source Book in Mathematical Logic*. Cambridge MA: Harvard University Press

van Lamsweerde, A. and Dufour, P., eds (1987). *Current Issues in Expert Systems*. London: Academic Press

van Melle, W. J. (1981). *System Aids in Constructing Consultation Programs*. Ann Arbor MI: UMI Research Press

Ward, R. D. and Sleeman, D. (1987). Learning to use the S.1 knowledge engineering tool. *Knowledge Engineering Review*, **2**(4), 265–76

Waterman, D. A. (1986). *A Guide to Expert Systems*. Reading MA: Addison-Wesley

Waterman, D. A. and Hayes-Roth, F. (1978). *Pattern Directed Inference Systems*. New York: Academic Press

Wellinga, B. J. and Breuker, A. J. (1986). Models of expertise. *Proceedings of 7th European Conference on Artificial Intelligence*, pp. 306–18

Weiss, S. M. and Kulikowski, C. A. (1983). *A Practical Guide to Designing Expert Systems*. London: Chapman & Hall

Weyhrauch R. (1980). Prolegomena to a theory of mechanized formal reasoning. *Artificial Intelligence*, **13**, 133–70

Whitby, B. (1988). *Artificial Intelligence: A Handbook of Professionalism*. Chichester UK: Ellis Horwood

Wilkins, D. C. (1988). Knowledge base refinement using apprenticeship learning techniques. *Proceedings of the National Conference on Artificial Intelligence*, pp. 646–51

Wilkins, D. C. and Buchanan, B. G. (1986). On debugging rule sets when reasoning under certainty. *Proceedings of the National Conference on Artificial Intelligence*, pp. 448–54

Winograd, T. (1972). Understanding natural language. *Cognitive Psychology*, **1**, 1–191

Winograd, T. (1975). Frame representations and the declarative/procedural controversy. In Bobrow and Collins (1975)

Winston, P. H. (1975a). Learning structural descriptions from examples. In Winston (1975b), Chapter 5

Winston, P. H. ed. (1975b). *The Psychology of Computer Vision*. New York: McGraw-Hill

Winston, P. H. (1982). Learning new principles from precedents and examples. *Artificial Intelligence*, **19**, 321–50

Winston, P. H. (1984). *Artificial Intelligence*. Reading MA: Addison-Wesley

Winston, P. H. and Brown, R. H. (1979). *Artificial Intelligence: An MIT Perspective* Vols 1 and 2. Cambridge MA: MIT Press

Winston, P. H. and Horn, K. P. (1981). *LISP*. Reading MA: Addison-Wesley

Winston, P. H. and Horn, K. P. (1984). *LISP* 2nd edn. Reading MA: Addison-Wesley

Wise, B. P. and Henrion, M. (1986). A framework for comparing uncertain inference systems to probability. In Kanal and Lemmer (1986) pp. 69–83

Woods, W. (1975). What's in a link: foundations for semantic networks. In Bobrow and Collins (1975)

Wos, L., Overbeek, R., Lusk, E. and Boyle, J. (1984). *Automated Reasoning: Introduction and Applications*. Englewood Cliffs NJ: Prentice-Hall

Wos, L., Pereira, F., Hong, R., Boyer, R. S., Moore, J. S., Bledsoe, W. W., Henschen, L. J., Buchanan, B. G., Wrightson, G., and Green, C. (1985). An overview of automated reasoning and related fields. *Journal of Automated Reasoning*, **1**(1), 5–48

Wright, J. M. and Fox, M. S. (1983), *SRL/1.5 User Manual*. Robotics Institute, Carnegie-Mellon University

Yen, J. (1986). A reasoning model based on an extended Dempster–Shafer theory. *Proceedings of the National Conference on Artificial Intelligence*, pp. 125–31

Zadeh, L. A. (1965). Fuzzy sets. *Information and Control*, **8**, 338–53

Zadeh, L. A. (1975). Fuzzy logic and approximate reasoning. *Synthese*, **30**, 407–28

Zadeh, L. A. (1978). Fuzzy sets as a basis for a theory of possibility. *Fuzzy Sets and Systems*, **1**, 3–28

Zadeh, L. A. (1981), PUF – a meaning representation language for natural languages. In Mamdani and Gaines (1981), pp. 1–66

Index